In Search of Berlin

'Berlin may well be Europe's most enigmatic city and John Kampfner – curious, sceptical and with an eye for the arresting detail – is the ideal guide.' **Jonathan Freedland**

'No-one is better qualified than John Kampfner to write about Berlin – that living palimpsest of German, and thus European, history. His knowledge is both deep – historical, analytical – and wide, drawn from a large diaspora of knowledgeable contacts. One of Europe's foremost intellectuals, Kampfner is also incapable of writing a dull sentence, which allows this book to succeed as history, travel book, autobiography, treatise and love-letter.' **Andrew Roberts**

'This book will have you hurrying back to one of the most fascinating cities on earth. John Kampfner is a brilliant guide as he excavates layer after layer of Berlin's 800-year history, as it lurches from destruction to decadence, from horror to hope. A gripping, rich read full of personal anecdote seamlessly interwoven with scholarly detail.' **Julie Etchingham**

'A beautifully researched, thoughtful and personal examination of Berlin's history. Sometimes it needs the perspective of an outsider to see a place clearly.' **Annette Dittert**

'A brilliant but vexing love affair with a city that gets under the skin. Kampfner eloquently captures Berlin – a place of perpetual reinvention, lurid dreams, grotesque nightmares and impossible ideas. Rarely is scratching an itch as much fun as it is in Berlin.' **Matt Frei**

'Modern Germany is one of the political wonders of the world and John Kampfner one of its finest interpreters. It is a delight to have the two come together in this fascinating book.' **Daniel Finkelstein**

'John Kampfner is an ideal guide to Berlin, its history and people, in this tour de force.' **Orlando Figes**

Also by John Kampfner

Inside Yeltsin's Russia: Corruption, Conflict, Capitalism

Robin Cook

Blair's Wars

Freedom for Sale: How We Made Money and Lost Our Liberty

The Rich: From Slaves to Super-Yachts: A 2000-Year History

Why the Germans Do it Better: Notes from a Grown-up Country

In Search of Berlin

The Story of a Reinvented City

John Kampfner

Atlantic Books
London

First published in hardback in Great Britain in 2023 by Atlantic Books,
an imprint of Atlantic Books Ltd.

Frond endpaper: Soviet flag flying over the Reichstag, 1945
(ShawStock/Alamy Stock Photo)

Back endpaper: Christopher Street Day, Berlin (ullstein bild Dtl./Getty Images)

2 3 4 5 6 7 8 9

A CIP catalogue record for this book is available from the British Library.

Hardback ISBN: 978 1 83895 481 9
Trade Paperback ISBN: 978 1 83895 482 6
E-book ISBN: 978 1 83895 483 3

Printed in Great Britain by CPI Group (UK) Ltd, Croydon CR0 4YY

Atlantic Books
An Imprint of Atlantic Books Ltd
Ormond House
26–27 Boswell Street
London
WC1N 3JZ

www.atlantic-books.co.uk

*To Eric Ash, and to the many who fled from Berlin
to escape horror, and to the many in recent years
who have fled to Berlin to seek sanctuary*

Contents

PLÖTZENSEE MEMORIAL CENTRE

SEESTRASSE

RATHENOWER STR.

SPANDAU
CITADEL
7 KM

REICHSTAG

NEW SYNAGOGUE

STATUE OF
FREDERICK
THE GREAT

BRANDENBURG
GATE

HUMBOLDT
FORUM

MEMORIAL TO
THE MURDERED
JEWS OF EUROPE

WILHELMSTRASSE

HOUSE

KANTSTRASSE

LINDENSTRASSE

KURFÜRSTENDAMM

SITE OF THE
ELDORADO
NIGHTCLUB

KLEISTSTRASSE

GNEISENAUSTRAS

UHLANDSTRASSE

DAVID BOWIE'S
APARTMENT

MARLENE DIETRICH'S
GRAVE

RHEINSTRASSE

TEMPEL

Cast of Characters

House of Ascania

Albrecht von Ballenstedt, Albert the Bear – first margrave of Brandenburg 1157–70, founder of the Ascanian dynasty

House of Hohenzollern

Friedrich II, Iron Tooth – elector of Brandenburg 1440–70, in power at the time of the *Berliner Unwille*

Georg Wilhelm – Elector of Brandenburg 1619–40, ruled over the Mark (badly) during the Thirty Years War

Friedrich Wilhelm, the Great Elector – Elector of Brandenburg and Duke of Prussia 1640–88

Friedrich I – Elector of Brandenburg 1688–1713 (as Friedrich III) and first King in Prussia 1701–13

Sophie Charlotte – first Queen in Prussia, wife of Friedrich I

Friedrich Wilhelm I, the Soldier King – King in Prussia 1713–40

Friedrich II, the Great – King in Prussia 1740–72 and King of Prussia 1772–86

Friedrich Wilhelm II – King of Prussia 1786–97

Friedrich Wilhelm III – King of Prussia 1797–1840 during the Napoleonic Wars and Elector of Brandenburg until 1806, when the Holy Roman Empire was dissolved

Luise – Queen of Prussia 1797–1810, wife of Friedrich Wilhelm III

Napoleon I – Emperor of the Napoleonic Confederation of the Rhine 1806–13, captured Berlin on 27 October 1806

Friedrich Wilhelm IV – King of Prussia 1840–61

German Empire (1871–1918)

Wilhelm I – King of Prussia 1861–88 and first Emperor of Germany 1871–88 after victory in Franco-Prussian War

Otto von Bismarck – Federal Chancellor of the North German Confederation 1867–71 and Chancellor of the German Empire 1871–90

Friedrich III – King of Prussia and of Germany Emperor of Germany for just ninety-nine days between March and June 1888

Wilhelm II – King of Prussia and Emperor of Germany 1888–1918. His abdication in 1918 marked the end of the German Empire and Hohenzollern rule

Weimar Republic (1919–33)

Friedrich Ebert – Chancellor of Germany 1918–19 and President 1919–25

Paul von Hindenburg – President 1925–34, appointed Hitler as Chancellor in 1933

Third Reich (1933–1945)

Adolf Hitler – Chancellor of Germany 1933–45

German Democratic Republic (1949–90)

Wilhelm Pieck – Joint Chairman of the Socialist Unity Party 1946–50, first president of the German Democratic Republic 1949–60

Walter Ulbricht – First Secretary of the Socialist Unity Party (SED) 1950–71, East German head of state 1960–73

Erich Honecker – General Secretary of the SED 1971–89, East German head of state 1976–89

Egon Krenz – General Secretary of the SED October–December 1989, last communist leader of the GDR

Federal Republic of Germany (1949–present)

Konrad Adenauer – first Chancellor of the Federal Republic of Germany (West Germany) 1949–63

Willy Brandt – Governing Mayor of West Berlin 1957–66 and Chancellor of West Germany 1969–74

Helmut Kohl – Chancellor of West Germany 1982–90 and Chancellor of Germany 1990–98 after reunification on 3 October 1990

Angela Merkel – Chancellor of Germany 2005–21

Frank-Walter Steinmeier – President since 2017

Olaf Scholz – Chancellor of Germany since 2021

Introduction

I cannot get Berlin out of my mind. I have been living in it and coming to it for more than thirty years, first as a young journalist based in the communist East watching the dramatic events of 1989–90 and up to the present day, as the city is confronted by a new version of European conflict.

It is a place where traumas are unleashed. It is also where the traumatized gather.

The city's scars are a source of inspiration and a testament to the power of reinvention. Berlin is a laboratory. Even people who have spent brief periods in the city feel it is part of their lives. I certainly do; that is why I keep coming back.

For much of its existence, Berlin has been dismissed as ugly, uncultured and extreme. After the fall of the Wall, it was expected to become more 'normal'. Start-up entrepreneurs from around the world have been making it their home, providing the first significant economic activity for a long time. Gentrifying Germans from the south have arrived, supposedly bringing with them bourgeois respectability. Yet Berlin is still a mess. It cannot run its own elections properly and often fails to provide basic services. You can't get a death certificate, you can't get a birth certificate, people complain. It is *schmuddelig* (grubby) and often abrupt.

It is a hotchpotch of architecture and a city planning nightmare. It is one of Europe's most sparsely inhabited capitals and yet it suffers one of its most acute housing shortages, a problem it has struggled with for centuries. For decades its standard of living has been below the national average. The city has few natural resources, no manufacturing to speak of and not much wealth.

Berlin has stumbled from enlightenment to militarism, from imperialism to democracy to dictatorship, from village to world city to surrounded island. It has been a trading post, military barracks, a centre of science and learning, industrial powerhouse, a hotbed of self-indulgence and sex – and control centre for the worst experiment in horror known to man. It was at the heart of the Cold War, the front line of communism and hang-out for hippies and draft-dodgers. It has been the site of three failed revolutions and one extraordinarily successful popular uprising.

No other city has fretted so much about its status. No other city has had so many faces, so many disasters and has reinvented itself so many times. No other city is so confused about itself and what it imagines itself to be in the future. Berlin is tortured by its history and yet many buildings look as if they have no history. Each site, almost each paving stone, has lived many lives, each era superimposing itself on the one before. Each plague, each fire, each war, each act of destruction and self-destruction, requires it to start again.

'Berlin is a place you project yourself onto,' says David Chipperfield, the British architect who has left his stamp on the city, with his re-imagining of the Neues Museum and the Neue Nationalgalerie. 'Berlin is not really there. It's an idea. It's been a Prussian idea of a metropolis, a Nazi idea, an Allied idea, an East German communist idea, and more recently a young people's idea. It's not a completed masterpiece, but a canvas on which different generations have painted.'

Its shortfalls are tangible. It is unloved by those who fail to understand it. Its draw is more ephemeral and harder to identify. But when you 'get' Berlin, it seeps into your skin.

When he was made an honorary citizen of Berlin, the German president, Frank-Walter Steinmeier, reminisced about doing his doctoral thesis there in 1989. A decade later, the removal vans brought his family's belongings from Bonn as parliament was transferred. While the new government quarter was still being constructed, he spent the first year and a half in the office of the ousted East German leader, Erich Honecker, 'with a view of the Palace of the Republic and Mongolian goatskin wallpaper in the dark hallway', improvising each day. He, like so many others down the ages, came to Berlin without understanding it. In a speech in October 2021, he ventured to suggest that he now did: 'Berlin has throughout its history been a place of longing for those who have found it too cramped elsewhere, who think more deeply, continue to research, reach higher, who want to change things or live differently,' he said. 'The alien, the different, the new are not rejected or excluded; they are curiously and hungrily embraced and absorbed; this openness characterises Berlin like almost no other city I know.'

That is why Berlin is a magnet for people from around the world. People know they can leave a mark – and, from Slavs to Jews, Huguenots to Dutch, Russians to Turks, and now Afghans to Syrians, they have. Berlin is the destination of choice for people who want to make a new life for themselves. You can always find your niche in Berlin. Everyone, it seems, comes from somewhere else. Everyone, it seems, has a story to tell.

This is an 800-year history, but an unconventional one. It is a dialogue between Berlin's past and present, following a broad chronology, identifying the commonalities between the different eras and linking them to the present day.

For centuries, the world passed it by. Its geography and

topography spell trouble. All around are sweeping plains, exposed to the Siberian winds. The city seemed to have arrived from nowhere, with no connection to the great civilizations. The Romans 'civilized' a number of places in Germania. Not Berlin: they didn't get this far. The city started late and continued late. It is still not complete. It has always been the upstart, the ingenue. It still doesn't quite know when it all began, but in Albrecht (Albert), a twelfth-century conquering count known as 'the Bear', Berlin has found a motif for all time. In an archive in the once-dominant town of Brandenburg, a piece of parchment provides the first evidence of a settlement built on a swamp, dating back to 1237. Historians take that to mark the start of Berlin – they might as well, there is nothing more definitive – and so it became. Thanks to wars and division, however, much archaeological work remains undone. In recent years, Berlin has been catching up fast, excavating across the old centre in a determination better to understand its origins. Barely a month goes past without an announcement of a new find.

It seems as if each building is contested, none more so than the place where in the fifteenth century a palace was built by a prince dubbed 'Iron Tooth'. Local burghers, furious with this outsider taking over, opened the weirs, flooding the foundations. That building has lived many lives, most of them unhappy. It was torn down and rebuilt many times, a palace rarely beloved by kings. After the Second World War it was replaced by a monument to socialism, and then demolished after reunification. The present building, the Humboldt Forum, has been the object of every possible insult to which the German (and English) language can stretch.

History leaves its mark wherever I go. I trace a line between the Thirty Years War and the peace movement of today, yet you have to go an hour out of town to see any memorialization of that terrible conflict. A small museum in the old castle of Wittstock tells the story of three decades of bloodshed that took the lives of more people than either of the two great wars of the twentieth century. Only a few miles away, protesters have spent years trying to stop the present-day army from using the land. Pacifism is now hard-wired.

My account is as much a story of memorialization as a history. How to relate to Friedrich (Frederick) the Great in the eighteenth century, who ushered in the (Jewish) Enlightenment of Moses Mendelssohn, and yet called the Jews 'the most dangerous' of all the 'sects'? How to relate to his father, Friedrich Wilhelm I? The man called the 'Soldier King' executed his son's tutor and lover in front of him, loathed his wife and derived pleasure only from hunting. He turned the city into a garrison and yet never fought a war. Across Berlin statues, like buildings, are erected, damaged, removed, revived. The Soldier King stands in a few spots, often daubed with graffiti. By contrast, a statue of Frederick the Great enjoys a prominent spot in the centre of the city, even if it is surrounded by traffic.

Its electors, kings and kaisers wanted Berlin to become a *Weltstadt* (a world city). Yet only for one period did it manage to match the grandeur of Paris, the economic power of London or the vitality of New York. Even at its peak, Berlin was uncomfortable with itself. The debates around industrialization, rapid growth and inequality are reflected in the fraught politics of housing today. In the Wilhelmine era, from unification in 1871 to the outbreak of war in 1914, Berlin was the scene of conspicuous consumption. Now only the vulgar flaunt their riches, wear flashy clothes or, heaven forbid, talk about property prices. Berliners boast that people are judged, if at all, purely by the power of their ideas.

Berlin exceptionalism: reality, myth, marketing? I look at the role history plays in branding, from Babylon Berlin to Bowie to Berghain. The Weimar era, with which foreigners and Germans are currently obsessed, marked a halcyon moment for science, art and music. The city became a haven for gay people from across Europe and beyond. Berliners like to remind all-comers: the tolerance was confined to a city, not a country. And their memory is selective. The city that likes to call itself 'poor but sexy' reveres the decadence of the 1920s, often playing down the exploitation of that time, the wealthy (often fops from out of town) preying on the impoverished.

Berlin has always been open to outsiders while at once feeling discomfited by them. The *Schnauze*, the gruffness for which original inhabitants are renowned, manifested itself early towards the diligent Dutch, Huguenots, indeed anyone who threatened to outshine them. Present-day *Ur-Berliner*, people who consider themselves natives, grumble that their city is being sanitized; yet it is still rough around the edges. They complain that they are being overrun by outsiders – Germans and foreigners – yet the population remains well below pre-war levels. The old Prussian elite has withered away. One-third of Berlin's present-day inhabitants did not live in the city when the Wall came down in 1989. One-fifth of its population does not have the vote. In some districts, English has taken over as the lingua franca. This begs the question: who can nowadays rightfully claim to speak for the city? Who are the 'real' Berliners?

Of all the many migrant groups, I devote specific chapters to the two that have defined the city. Berlin, as the historian Karl Schlögel suggests, has been a sanctuary, a waiting room and a place of survival for waves of Russians. After the Bolshevik revolution, some 400,000 arrived, taking over entire districts. Communists and monarchists had to share the same space, just as Putin sympathizers, dissidents and Ukrainian refugees do now.

Finally: the Jews. But which Jews? The opening of the grand New Synagogue in 1866 was attended by Bismarck and other members of the Prussian elite, signalling one of the few moments when Jews felt relatively at ease in Berlin. In 1995, it was rebuilt, its resplendent golden dome visible for miles around. The guest of honour at the ceremony, as before, was the chancellor – this time Helmut Kohl. Yet precious few Jews can trace their heritage to pre-war Berlin. By far the biggest number have arrived from the former Soviet Union, often impoverished and with little affinity to the city. An increasing number of Israelis now call Berlin home, though many of them come for the art or music (Israeli restaurants are hyper-fashionable) rather than to confront the demons of the past.

How to remember horror? I have seen so many traces of it, from the gallows of Plötzensee prison, to the Topography of Terror, to the villa in Wannsee where the Final Solution was planned and the railway platform at Grunewald where the transports began. I have been moved to tears by church services. I have stared countless times at the rawness of evil. Berlin cannot stop remembering and yet it still hasn't quite decided how best to do it. Many of its memorials have been argued over and delayed as designers have been asked to think again. The history of the Third Reich is often told in broad brushstrokes, drowning out discussion of so much else, perhaps inevitably so. That may now be changing. Germans and Berliners are less coy when talking about their great, and not-so-great, rulers. The decolonization debate has ignited a new set of difficult questions.

The biggest of Berlin's many tourist attractions is the Wall. In the aftermath of 1989, the prevailing mood was a yearning to move on and to forget. Mercifully, a few important segments remain. I can still trace the line of the Wall, at least in the centre of the city. I think I can still smell it, though I know I am deluding myself. The Wall has been down now longer than it was up. What to do with that memory?

Berlin is no longer the island that its western half was during the Cold War; but it clings to the non-conformism that defined that era. Unification, the building of a new government quarter, globalization and the arrival of tech and other assorted gentrifiers raised rents and challenged the old order (or lack of it). Then came the pandemic; now a new war. Yet the spirit of the city remains unchanged. Four years of walking its streets again has taken me to places where many locals, who boast of rarely leaving their neighbourhood, their *Kiez*, would not have dreamt to tread. I have talked to historians, architects, archaeologists, anthropologists, politicians, city planners, immigration experts and demographers, trying to comprehend it all. Now what of Berlin, this most troubled and beguiling of cities? The question that drew me back to Berlin and impelled me to write its story was this: after nearly 800 years, has it finally reached an equilibrium? Will it ever be normal? And who wants it to be anyway?

ONE

Eight hundred years and one world house

The beginnings of a city

My God, what a boring, hideous city is Berlin.
FYODOR DOSTOYEVSKY (1874)

The story of Berlin begins at a spot now surrounded by a three-lane highway, a four-star hotel and an Amazon engineering hub.

I am standing in the pouring rain next to a huge hole in the ground, at Petriplatz, St Peter's Square, where for seven and a half centuries stood a church. Its pastor, Symeon, is the first person named in the first historical record of the city in 1237. Not that many Berliners used to know or care. It is one of many places long forgotten.

In turn medieval, baroque, then Gothic, St Peter's Church was bombed in the Second World War and then finally demolished by the communists. No illustration or document exists attesting to the original building; there are no physical traces – at least, there weren't until recently. It sat at the heart of Cölln, one of two trading stations that eventually joined and made one city. In the middle of the twentieth century the small street next to the square, Gertraudenstrasse, was concreted over and widened into a highway so that Trabants could splutter at speed. The area is now being rebuilt, again, another giant building site, in order to make it marginally greener, marginally less car-friendly. This, after all, is Germany.

The new Berlin is rediscovering its past, learning more about its horrors, but also its many treasures. The past decade has been an extraordinary boon for archaeologists and historians. Throughout the forty-year life of communist East Germany the authorities had little interest and even less budget to excavate beneath the rubble of war. Much of the heart of East Berlin had more car parks than usable buildings. Some of the most historic parts of Mitte, the centre, ended up close to the Wall. Only those with authorization could get close. Most locals steered clear; the action (such as there was) migrated to districts further east.

Over the thirty years since reunification, much of the centre of the city has been dug up. At one point a huge area of 8,000 square metres was under excavation, ahead of the construction of a new set of stations for the U-Bahn. Planning permission for new buildings has to be preceded by archaeological investigations. Deadlines are repeatedly missed as ancient artefacts are found. So remarkable have some of the discoveries been that the Neues Museum, one of the city's most important, put them on display. Huge crowds came to see them. As recently as January 2022, archaeologists discovered a medieval plank road dating back to the thirteenth century. It was in pristine condition, thanks to a thick peat layer which had kept the wood airtight for more than 800 years.

The first excavations at Petriplatz in 2007 produced evidence that the original church might have been rebuilt five times and that the original Cölln town hall, long lost to history, also occupied an important place on the square. Some of the discoveries can be seen at the adjacent Capri Hotel, which in 2017 created a glass floor in its lobby to display cellar walls, stone floors and a deep well. More than 10,000 people have visited the site – supervised and from a distance. Some 600 tours and lectures have been organized, with interactive maps depicting how the old settlements would have looked.

'Old Cölln has returned to the consciousness of Berlin, and in the very place where it existed,' Claudia Melisch tells me. She is one of the city's most prominent archaeologists, who has spearheaded the project. She is a central figure in this narrative; wherever I go, whatever new site I investigate, such as Hitler's flak towers and wartime bunkers, it seems that she and her small teams of experts and volunteers have something to do with it.

The discoveries at Petriplatz are remarkable. They show that alongside the church and town hall were a cluster of houses, a Latin school and a cemetery. In keeping with the time, it was densely packed with graves (holding between two and eleven skeletons each). The cemetery was closed in 1717 on sanitary grounds – something not uncommon in that era. Of the 3,778 remains Melisch and her team have analysed, a number can be traced back to 1150, eight decades before the city is said to have been founded. Of the first fifty male skeletons, 'not a single one was related to another,' she tells me. 'The population was not as we expected.' Some were from nearby, others from further afield. One man was from Bohemia (present-day Czech Republic), another from the area that is now Cologne (that is, the Cologne on the Rhineland). 'Whoever founded these original settlements is still not known, because of the absence of written testimonies.'

Some of the earliest inhabitants of Cölln are lying in a disused machine-tool plant in the eastern fringes of Berlin. Thousands of skeletal parts dating back to 1150 have been taken there as the city struggles to cope with the amount of human remains that have been discovered during the archaeological digs of the past two decades.

Melisch drives me to the site, to a building called House

Number Four – which she asks me not to locate because of security fears. Across two storeys and in ten rooms she points out row after row of neatly arranged cardboard boxes, 30 by 70 centimetres to be precise. What strikes me first is the wallpaper, faded yellow-and-grey patterned flowers, with matching curtains. And the brown lino floor and the strip lights. East Germany 1970s vintage. 'You can take any of this if you want,' she says. The building will be torn down, but not before the remains find a more appropriate home.

These have all come from St Peter's Square and the other sites in pre-medieval Cölln and Berlin that have been dug up. Some of the remains have been sorted, others have yet to be. Labels on the side of the boxes list either the venue or the body parts: pelvic bone. Spine. Humerus. Femur. Ulna. Claudia tells me not to touch. My DNA has not been processed. She takes some specimens out for me, ever so carefully, including tiny remnants which she says were from a baby boy who died shortly after being born. She wants remains such as these to be given a dignified reburial, not to be put on display to be gawped at. 'How we relate to them all – real people – says much about how we relate to each other now.' She then turns to a theme that I will hear regularly: the need for Berlin to learn more about its history, its ancient history. 'Berliners seem to come and go every ten years or so. The city is constantly renewing itself. But it also needs to feel more grounded in its past.'

Archaeological excavations are part of a wider debate about the relationship with Berlin's origins, a debate that has become deeply political. How do you recreate large parts of the city from scratch? Do you leave parts bare to remember the destruction? How much do you seek to repopulate? Do you try to recreate, or do you go modern?

In the years following unification in 1990, as ideas were sought about the redevelopment of much of the derelict East, the Protestant priest for the area in which St Peter's is located, Gregor

Hohberg, could have applied for the church to be rebuilt. It had been categorized as one of twenty 'lost churches' in the heart of Berlin that were never rebuilt after the destruction of the war. With many church services in Berlin poorly attended, particularly in the parts of the centre that remain sparsely inhabited, Hohberg saw little point. He wanted to try to leave a different mark. He got together with a group of city officials, historians and faith leaders and decided to build something that would appeal to more than one religion, that would challenge many of Berlin's preconceptions. They came up with the idea of the House of One, a multi-faith place of worship for Muslims, Jews and Christians.

The name came from an essay written by Martin Luther King in 1967, three years after he visited Berlin – and one year before his murder. 'This is the great new problem of mankind,' King wrote. 'We have inherited a large house, a great "world house" in which we have to live together – black and white, Easterner and Westerner, Gentile and Jew, Catholic and Protestant, Muslim and Hindu – a family unduly separated in ideas, culture and interest, who, because we can never again live apart, must learn somehow to live with each other in peace.'

In 2012 an architectural competition was launched for the new spaces. The brief ranged widely, from the holy books of the Abrahamic religions to the origins of Berlin, to a denunciation of the demolition of St Peter's in 1964. 'On the orders of the authorities of the East German Democratic Republic, the remaining structures on Petriplatz were demolished using explosives and carted off, erasing the outline and structure of the square to make room for an asphalt parking lot. The birthplace of Berlin was transformed into a non-place and remained that way for almost 50 years.' It concluded: 'At least this symbolic use of Petriplatz provides some glimmer that it is more than an asphalt-covered nowhere.'

The shortlisted models are on display in the House of One's

temporary office around the corner from the site. Many of the submissions, from a galaxy of international architectural practices, were eccentric. In the end they opted for a Berlin practice, Kuehn Malvezzi, whose proposal was, by comparison, relatively safe. The design consists of three separate spaces: the Jewish element is a lozenge, the Islamic element square and the Christian rectangular. Grouped around them will be a 'fourth room', a towering central volume, a collective gathering space which permits 'unity in diversity'.

The ground-breaking ceremony, delayed by the pandemic, took place in 2021 and the building is expected to open in 2026 alongside a new centre for archaeology, at the relatively modest cost of €50 million – although as Berliners know only too well, almost no city project comes in on time or on budget. The process went smoothly at first. Plans were mooted for partnerships in Tbilisi, the Georgian capital, and Haifa in Israel. A House of One was even being planned in the capital of the Central African Republic, Bangui. Then a row broke out, more than one, over the affiliation of a radical Turkish preacher with the Muslim group and of a German rabbi facing allegations of sexual misconduct. Plus donations from Qatar. As is so often the case in Berlin, buildings commemorating the past, or pointing to a different future, come with controversy attached.

Still, it will go ahead, and one of the original spots of old Berlin will return to life, in a new form.

The name Berlin comes either from the word for marshland, *Berl*, from Old Polabian, an extinct West Slav language, or, less exotically, from the German word for bear, *Bär*. Cölln is derived from the Latin word for settlement, *colonia*. There is no single explanation why two separate settlements were founded. The topographer Nicolaus Leuthinger wrote in 1598, in one of the earliest recorded historical accounts, of a 'flat land, wooded and for the most part swamp'. Whenever I drive or take the train out of the city, I am reminded of how empty and how exposed it is. I see unerringly straight lines of farmland, disconcertingly flat, exposed to chill winds from Siberia, with no outlet to the sea, no discernible borders and ripe to be taken by invading forces. What possessed people to make this godforsaken place a major trading post, then the capital of a kingdom, then the capital of a Reich?

It stands at the meeting point of three ancient glaciers, which moved south from Scandinavia during the Ice Age. The first settlers – a vast Germanic tribe known as the Semnones – can be traced back as far as 4000 BC. By the fifth century, the Huns had pushed the Semnones west towards the Rhine and had begun to build up their settlement on the Brandenburg plain. The territory's first known fortifications appeared in the eighth century. The archbishops of Magdeburg (to the west), dukes of Pomerania (to the north and east), margraves of the House of Wettin (to the south) and settlers from across the Slavic lands staked their claim to land that came to be called the Mark ('frontier' or 'march') of Brandenburg. Battles continued to rage until the twelfth century, when the Ascanians arrived. This Germanic dynasty from the Harz mountains, to the west, established fortresses at Spandau in the northwest and Köpenick in the southeast.

The Ascanian settlers were led by Albrecht von Ballenstedt, a count nicknamed 'Albert the Bear', who, typically for a noble of his era, had set out to make his fortune in a heathen land. He put down the indigenous Slav tribes, quashing the claims to sovereignty of the Slavic prince Jacza of Köpenick, and spearheaded the Mark's integration into the German Christian world. Albert was appointed *Markgraf* (margrave) in 1157. In the first years of his reign, he expanded the territory and population of the Mark, introducing settlers from Saxony and Friesland (the first in a line of immigrants), clearing forests and swamps and reviving the bishoprics of Brandenburg and Havelberg. The Mark was situated within the Holy Roman Empire, the vast territory that encompassed large parts of present-day Germany, France, northern Italy and the Netherlands. Emerging in the tenth century, it was considered by the Catholic Church to be the legitimate successor of the Roman Empire. The Emperor appointed a college of electors, each to rule over a region.

For centuries after its founding, Berlin was a mere speck on that grander landscape. Power lay elsewhere; the key defences were provided at Spandau and Köpenick. Meanwhile, Brandenburg an der Havel, the capital of the Mark, had its own bishop and a council of magistrates. Berlin's relationship with the region of Brandenburg which surrounds it, doughnut style, has always been complex. In May 1996, a referendum was held to try to resolve the issue once and for all. Residents were asked whether they should merge. A narrow majority of voters in Berlin were in favour, while a narrow majority in the East and a larger proportion in Brandenburg voted against. The initiative failed; as a result, relations remain as ill-defined as ever. The ring on the outer edge of Berlin – with its neat suburban communities, lakes, canals and green spaces, and convenient trains – is called the *Speckgürtel* (the fat belt). It has become a popular destination for commuters and digital nomads.

The city of Brandenburg, an hour to the west, has been spruced up. I have requested an appointment at the diocesan archive where Berlin's oldest records are kept. Bright and early one April morning, I arrive at a nondescript building close to the cathedral. I am led to a first-floor room, an office like any other, where archivist Konstanze Borowski lays in front of me two white boxes on adjacent tables. I take a breath before opening them. One is the founding document of Cölln from 1237, the one that mentions pastor Symeon: sixty-two lines of ornately written manuscript with wax seals attached, detailing in Latin the rights and responsibilities of the electors of the region. The other document, from seven years later, is the one with the first known reference to 'Berlin'. By this point Symeon has been seemingly promoted to 'provost'. Even though Berlin is not mentioned by name in the earlier document, that is the one that has been used to denote the founding of the city.

These are not the absolute originals, I am told. Those are kept under even stricter lock and key, opened only for VIPs and other state dignitaries (clearly, I haven't made the grade). Yet my disappointment is tempered by the fact that it is still a rare privilege to see the document, with its old German and fine writing, on my own and for as long as I like. Another copy can be found at the Märkisches Museum, Berlin's city museum, but it is behind glass, and you cannot get up close. As I pore over the parchment, I ask Borowski where the original is kept. 'In a safe not far from here,' is all she proffers. These archives in Brandenburg, which were founded in 1821, are a treasure trove of information. To be precise: 6,500 files, 910 documents and 800 maps and pictures. Did many people make the same journey as me, I wonder? 'Not often,' she replies. Some people are studying their family heritage, but for the most part 'people don't care that much about this sort of thing'.

You have to be patient to unearth Berlin's early history because physical evidence is so hard to find. A small remnant of Berlin's first wall, up to two metres thick, which was built in the mid-thirteenth century, was uncovered by accident when the ruins of the bombed houses covering it were cleared away in 1948. The segment is to be found next to a pub called *Zur Letzten Instanz* (As a Last Resort). The first mention of a building on this site came in 1561; sixty years later it was opened as an inn by a stable boy of Georg Wilhelm, one of the town's less impressive ruling princes. It stayed mostly that way throughout the centuries until it was bombed in the Second World War. The East Germans destroyed most of the original facets during post-war reconstruction. Now it boasts celebrity credentials: Napoleon and Beethoven are somewhat speculatively said to have eaten there, Mikhail Gorbachev and Jacques Chirac with more certainty.

Documents attesting to the early years are as hard to come by as physical remains. In August 1380, a fire swept through the city, damaging the records of its first 150 years. The most important of these was the *Stadtbuch* (the city book), a detailed bureaucratic listing of every aspect of life in Berlin and Cölln. A 'notarius' was engaged to salvage what was left and enter it into a proper register; the task took him seven years. Today the extraordinary text can be found in the Landesarchiv Berlin, a brick building in the northwestern district of Reinickendorf that used to house a weapons factory. The archive holds several centuries of city records, including manuscripts, audio files and photos. A project by the state archive to digitize the *Stadtbuch* is underway. The original work contains 168 quarto leaves. The first four books were written on 128 sheets of parchment, the remaining 35 added on sheets of paper in 1398. The first two books stipulate the finances and privileges of the city. Book three sets out relative rights – Jews and women at the bottom of the heap. The remaining books relate to pensions, debt securities and land ownership.

The book dictates what clothing and jewellery could be worn. Dancing on the street was prohibited after the city gates were closed. Beggars were licensed, wearing a patch on their clothes to declare their poverty. The difference between 'lawless' (negligent) and 'unlawful' men (the pedantry of German officialdom started early) was spelled out, as was the mitigation of punishment in cases of pregnancy and 'mental infirmity', and provisions for women who seek to avenge 'lewd acts of the clergy'. The juiciest bit is section four, transgressions. Punishments are meticulously noted. A young man is burned for stealing herring. A young girl is flogged for stealing salt. A woman is buried alive for trespassing. Six people are broken on the wheel for stealing from a church. Floggings and amputations were carried out on Mondays and Saturdays. Executions were performed every second Wednesday at the Oderberg Gate (on the northeast fringe of the city, now roughly Alexanderplatz), using three gallows built in a row. It must be said that the brutality was not out of the ordinary in Europe at the time.

Everything that happened between the years 1272 and 1489 is meticulously registered.

Berlin in the Middle Ages is a cycle of plague, pestilence and provincialism. Compared to other cities in Europe, its development was extremely slow. Settlers in the twelfth and thirteenth centuries included fishing and shipping families, drawn to the area because of its proximity to the water. It was a mercantile trading point, a place to collect customs duty for grain and other wares passing through. Guilds were formed, of tailors, fishermen, bone carvers, butchers, bakers. The most famous were the shoemakers, who by the 1300s had established links across Europe, including to London and Rome. By the end of the thirteenth century, Berlin and Cölln had surpassed the nearby fortress settlements of Köpenick and Spandau in importance; but compared to the city states occupying what came to be the German lands, they were insignificant, overshadowed for centuries by grander towns such as Nuremberg, Frankfurt and Augsburg.

The Ascanian dynasty reigned for a century and a half, and in 1319 the land passed into the hands of margraves from Wittelsbach and Luxembourg, two of the more powerful houses of the Holy Roman Empire. They were primarily interested in extracting customs duty from travelling tradesmen to finance their estates elsewhere. The Mark fell victim to a succession of marauding bandits and armies from Poland, Lithuania and Denmark.

Berlin and Cölln were closely intertwined long before their official union. In 1307, the two towns signed an agreement guaranteeing legal and military cooperation. A new town hall was built for a joint council on the Lange Brücke, the bridge connecting the towns. It wasn't until as late as 1709 that Berlin and Cölln officially came together under a single municipal government, formally enshrining the entity Haupt- und Residenzstadt Berlin (capital and seat of royal power, Berlin).

The population grew slowly. In 1400, the two towns had around 8,000 inhabitants, rising to 14,000 two centuries later. The first known reference to what is now the city's oldest working church, Marienkirche (the Church of St Mary), comes from a letter of indulgence of 1294. At its entrance stands a remarkable fresco. It depicts on one side a hierarchy of church dignitaries – the sexton, chaplain, ecclesiastical judge, the Augustinian, Dominican, the parish priest, canon, abbot, bishop, cardinal, and finally the Pope. They are being led by a skeletal figure in a shroud, representing Death, towards a central figure of the crucified Christ. On the other side of the porch, Death dances with figures representing temporal society – the emperor and empress, king, duke, knight, mayor, usurer, down to the tavern landlady and the fool. Death explains that he comes for everyone regardless of their earthly estate. The figures move calmly towards their fate.

The *Totentanz* (Dance of Death) was painted in 1470 and is more than 20 metres long. It was created after one of Berlin's many attacks of the plague to remind its citizens (as if they needed reminding) of the mortality of man. It was whitewashed over in 1514 as the Reformation took hold, rediscovered in 1860 and restored, then damaged again in the war. Neglected for decades, it was restored (badly) by the GDR in time for the city's 750th anniversary celebrations in 1987. It has been reconditioned again but to preserve what is left it is now behind glass – one of the few precious remnants of early Berlin that still exist.

The first recorded evidence of Jews living in Berlin was at the end of the thirteenth century when a group of families moved, possibly from the Rhineland, into a street that was named Jüdenstrasse (Jew Street) on the edge of the Molkenmarkt. The first time they are mentioned in any city document is an ordinance enacted in 1295, forbidding wool merchants to sell yarn to Jews. Whenever there was trouble, there was always someone to blame. In 1349, the Jews were accused of starting the Black Death that was sweeping through Europe and were expelled – but not before many were killed or had their houses burned down. As soon as a fire started in the city, Jews were deemed responsible. A cycle was established of violence, expulsions, readmission and limited tolerance. Jews were allowed back in 1354 when the margrave guaranteed their protection, only to be kicked out again just under a century later. Between expulsions, they were primarily engaged in moneylending and small trade. Tough restrictions were imposed on them. Jews were not allowed to employ a Christian servant and marriages with Christians were banned. They had to wear a *Judenhut*, a special hat. But they could practise as doctors, as well as lenders and pawnbrokers. They were able to register as citizens but were banned from holding public office.

In February 1510, a coppersmith stole a golden monstrance and two hosts from a church in Knobloch, a small community to the west of Berlin that no longer exists. He was swiftly caught, but instead of confessing, he blamed a Jew from Spandau, who he said had ordered the theft. In the hysteria that followed, fifty-one Jews were rounded up; thirty-eight were sentenced to burn at the stake in the Neuer Markt in front of the Marienkirche. The remaining thirteen died under torture or managed to flee. Sixty years later, rumours circulated that the Jews had poisoned the Elector of Brandenburg and more persecutions took place, culminating in another great expulsion in 1571.

The oldest map of Berlin was drawn by one of its most famous cartographers, Johann Gregor Memhardt, around 1650. It shows six churches within the walls of the two towns. While Petrikirche

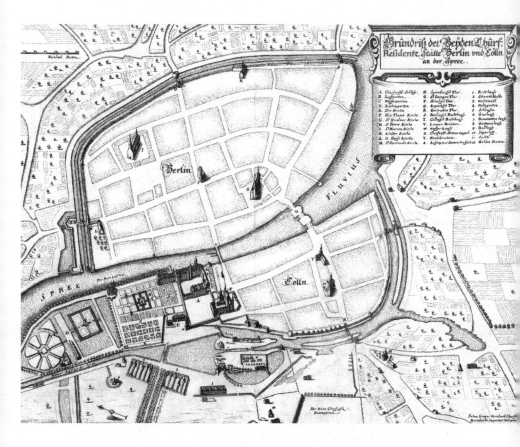

belonged to Cölln, over the water in Berlin the Nikolaikirche
(St Nicholas' Church) was for six and a half centuries the centre of
Christian life, until the construction of a faux Renaissance
cathedral in the late nineteenth century. Founded around 1232, it
has been destroyed twice – in the fire of 1380 and during the
Second World War. This was where the provost had his office,
and it was *the* place to be buried. It was in the church's nave that
Berlin and Cölln first joined forces in 1307.

To understand Berlin's origins, you need to make the trip to its
fringes, now little over half an hour away at the end of the U-Bahn.
The history of Spandau begins in the seventh or eighth century,
when the town was settled by various Slav tribes, such as the
Wends and Sorbs. The first recorded mention of a fortress here

dates back to 1197. Even though it lost its strategic significance many centuries ago, Spandau has long exerted a strange hold on Berlin. What I didn't realize, and I suspect most Berliners also don't, is just how much.

Situated at the confluence of the Havel and Spree rivers, it has always been a strategically important military location. From the seventeenth century, it became a garrison city. Several rulers banished their wives here. Part of the citadel was known as the *Witwensitz*; records bear witness to a lavish lifestyle at the 'widows' residence' in Spandau. For the most part it was an unwelcoming military headquarters. In the nineteenth century, some buildings were used as a centre for weapons technology. During the Third Reich it housed research into the nerve gases Tabun and Sarin.

In the Battle of Berlin in 1945, the Soviets found the citadel tough to storm and instead negotiated the surrender of German troops there. As a result, the building was spared. Under the four-powers agreement the area was designated part of the British Zone, and for the following four decades the word Spandau became synonymous with the detention of one man: Rudolf Hess. When the last of the other six Nazi prisoners completed his time in 1966, Hess was incarcerated on his own for a further two decades. He was guarded by soldiers from all four Allied forces, rotating on the first day of each month. On his death in 1987, the prison on Wilhelmstrasse was demolished, its materials ground to powder to prevent it becoming a shrine for the far right. The spot is now a Kaisers supermarket. There is an intriguing bathos about supermarkets. On Bornholmer Strasse in the north of Berlin stands a Lidl on the spot where the first border gate was opened on 9 November 1989.

Spandau does not seem to know what it is – a town with its own identity, a suburb, or a fully fledged part of Berlin? It also does not realize quite what it has. The citadel is the oldest surviving historic site for miles around, one of the best-preserved Renaissance fortresses in Europe, and yet it is woefully under-appreciated. Walking over a moat and across the first tower, the visitor's first reaction is underwhelming. On my last trip, the only person who approached me asked me if I was coming for a Covid test.

Yet inside it now houses two of the most absorbing exhibitions anywhere in Berlin. The citadel's director, Urte Evert, takes me to the castle's refurbished west wing and what is now called its Archaeological Window. One of the exhibits contains the remains of a Slavic wood and earth wall, and of a later stone castle wall from the Renaissance era. More striking is a series of headstones that were once sited in the nearby *Judenkiewer* (Jewish burial ground). They were removed in medieval times and used as building materials for the citadel. She points me to the oldest, inscribed with the name, 'Jonas, son of Dan, 1244'. Alongside him is 'Libka, daughter of Samson, 1311/12'. This provides further evidence of sophisticated town dwellers earlier than records suggest. 'It was a big surprise. We weren't looking for the graves,' Evert says. What is extraordinary is that they didn't start digging until the 1990s and have only recently stopped.

From the site of the Jewish gravestones, Evert walks me across the courtyard to what was the munitions depot, or the Old Barracks. Of all the exhibitions I have seen in Berlin in all my years, I don't think I have ever been as intrigued and affected as by this. The curators have been hoovering up eight centuries of monuments, resulting in a veritable car boot sale of 120 statues that over time have been damaged, dismantled, dumped or buried. 'Unveiled: Berlin and Its Monuments' opened in 2016 and yet almost no Berliner I have spoken to seems to know about it.

The stories it tells are often uncomfortable to absorb, deliberately so; some of the statues have been made available to the public for the first time. Many had been left for decades in warehouses, even on streets. In these barracks, Berlin is battling its own history. Context is everything: the museum describes not just the story of the artist and location, but also what happened to those statues that were removed. Many were originally on display in and around the Tiergarten: Friedrich Wilhelm III and his wife Queen Luise (the only woman on display); generals such as Gerhard von Scharnhorst and Friedrich Bülow von Dennewitz; thinkers such as Immanuel Kant and botanist Alexander von Humboldt. A touchscreen map shows which monuments would have been on display where, and which have been lost forever – bombed, demolished or hidden in perpetuity.

It is customary in German museums to treat the Nazi era as special, to attach warnings, sealing it off physically or meta-phorically. Here instead visitors are invited to imagine themselves in the Berlin of the 1930s, walking past everyday monuments in everyday squares. I see the memorial to the 'fallen of the movement 1933' in Fehrbelliner Platz, a memorial to policemen who died fighting communists, and the monument to a man called Albert Leo Schlageter, who was hanged by the French in the occupied Ruhr in 1923 on charges of espionage and sabotage. This stone structure was one of around a hundred memorials to 'the first soldier of the Third Reich' around Germany, of which twenty still exist.

One of the more bizarre exhibits entangles the British occupy-ing forces with the Nazi aesthetic. In the run-up to the Olympics in 1936, much-decorated Nazi sculptor Arno Breker was com-missioned to create a life-size nude sculpture, *Decathlete*, the male body in classic triumphal form, all Aryan beauty with more than a hint of homoeroticism. The Brits kept it in the gardens of their Spandau barracks, as they regarded it as a worthy piece of art. Only years later, when the statue had to be moved to enable roadworks, did they realize that it bore a dedication in large, bold letters, later partially covered up, to Hitler himself.

In 2021, Evert invited an Israeli ballerina, accompanied by members of the Deutsches Symphonie-Orchester Berlin, to dance on a memorial stone that was supposed to have commemorated Hitler's assumption of power on 30 January 1933 – adorned with symbols such as the Irminsul (originally Saxon, appropriated by the Nazis) and a swastika, which had been converted into a stylized black sun. At the end of the war, the granite structure was buried close to where it had been installed in the Zehlendorf district and it was recovered only in 2011. 'Many knew where this stone was buried,' Evert says.

Her aim has been to bring these extraordinary relics to life, inviting artists to interact with them. It doesn't always work. In 2019, Rammstein, Germany's most notorious rock band, shot a video here in secret. Over nine gut-wrenching minutes, the song 'Deutschland' shows episodes from 2000 years of history, from the ambush of the Romans by Teutonic 'barbarians' (with some cannibalism thrown in), to witch hunts, the Third Reich, communism, terrorism and much in between. With smoke machines, strobe lighting and close-ups of the statues, members of the band take on different roles, in costume, including concentration camp victims with nooses around their necks. The Central Council of Jews accused the musicians of instrumentalizing and trivializing the Holocaust. They, for sure, do not deploy taste or subtlety in getting the message across: German history, a continuum of terrible violence. The video was a huge hit on its release and has since been viewed 300 million times on YouTube.

The exhibition does not aim for subtlety. Its location, a cavernous set of halls, with grey-brick exteriors, high windows and black dividing walls, adds to a sense of menace. The *pièce de résistance* lies humiliated on his side. In December 1991, the mayor of reunified Berlin decided it was time to take down Vladimir Ilyich Lenin from his massive plinth. Just over two decades earlier, a giant 20-metre-high sculpture had been un-veiled to mark the centenary of the great man's birth. This was Leninplatz, the start of Leninallee, in the heart of the capital of the German Democratic Republic (GDR). The central square had previously been dominated by a statue of Stalin, but he was quickly dismantled in 1961 after being secretly denounced by Nikita Khrushchev. Stalin had lasted a mere ten years on that spot. Lenin did somewhat better and indeed proved resistant to removal.

Demolition workers had to run the gauntlet of protesters. To the embarrassment of the authorities and the contractors, they couldn't get him down. The concrete core was proving to be too tough. They gave up; new contractors were found, and Lenin eventually removed. The square was renamed United Nations Square and in place of the statue came a modest fountain consisting of boulders from all corners of the world. Lenin was chopped into 129 parts and spirited away and buried in a forest in Müggelheim, in the southeasternmost reaches of the city. His 4-tonne head eventually found its way to Evert's exhibition.

Now Lenin lies forlornly on his side on the floor, as if he has rolled off the block on the scaffold, with four huge bolts that were used for the deconstruction still sticking out from his scalp. He is devoid of one ear. Children are invited to clamber on top of him. Everyone is encouraged to touch the statues – 'that is a form of appropriation', Evert says.

Some of the statues have lost their heads; others have had facial details removed. Many were deliberately taken off their pedestals, once-powerful figures forced to meet the visitor at eye level. Traces of their dismantling – fractures, bullet holes and dirt – have not been erased. Yet, I wonder, do they merit being so ostentatiously dishonoured? All the Nazi memorabilia, for sure, Lenin probably, but the others? The unwillingness of some curators to differentiate between the militaristic, who pertained to their time, and the purveyors of more contemporary horrors is baffling to me.

Back to the ancients: Albrecht von Ballenstedt, Albert, the first margrave, the slayer of the Slavs, the pacifier of Berlin, has become the symbol of the contemporary city. The portly figure of a bear stands everywhere a tourist might want to visit. His actual statue, the only one Berlin is aware of, has been shunted from one destination to another. Unveiled as late as 1903 by Kaiser Wilhelm II, he stood first in the Tiergarten, the city's most ornate park, then ended up in Schloss Bellevue, which has become the residence of the German president.

Now Albert is lined up alongside other battered and bruised luminaries in Spandau Citadel, the statue largely forgotten, but the story a marketer's dream. Most of it is a myth. There are few documents, fewer still buildings that can point directly to the past. Yet Berlin is beginning to reclaim its history, to redefine it. It is doing so with its characteristic intensity and bluntness. After all, what other city would dump many of its statues in a warehouse on the edge of town and expect people to find them?

TWO

Nobody's palace

Schloss to Humboldt Forum

Paris is always Paris, and Berlin is never Berlin.
JACK LANG (2001)

'This is one of Berlin's most contaminated sites.' It is a curious remark from a spokesman. After all, it is a beautiful afternoon; dozens of people are sitting drinking, chatting or soaking up the remains of the autumn sunshine.

I am in the courtyard of what is certainly the city's most contested spot, if not necessarily contaminated. Michael Mathis has that 'I can take it; I've heard it all before' look about him. An urbane public relations professional, his previous perch was the Fine Art Museum in Basel, said to house the oldest public art collection in the world, dating back to Hans Holbein. He wouldn't have encountered too many controversies in that job, but in Berlin's cultural circles, it has long been unconscionable to have a good word to say about the Humboldt Forum. A faux baroque, contemporary multi-arts 'meeting space', it was created on the site of what was once Berlin's royal palace thanks to lobbying in the 1990s by a tractor entrepreneur from Hamburg. Everyone has their own reason to dislike it. Some find the building distasteful. The inside is variously described as a Prussian Disneyland and Dubai airport. The contents have been the object of derision for political correctness or fury for a failure fully to show due sensitivity to the decolonization debate. Nobody knows who is in charge. Many regret that it exists at all, insisting that its predecessor building could have been renovated and kept.

The story of this place begins back in 1415, the start of the epic 500-year rule by the Hohenzollern family. The moment came with little fanfare. The Hohenzollerns were a clan of south-German magnates on the make. Friedrich I, a feudal baron from wealthy Nuremberg, purchased the Mark Brandenburg from Sigismund of Luxembourg, who as well as being King of Hungary, King of Bohemia and Holy Roman Emperor, was skint.

Friedrich must have seen some hidden potential because at the time Berlin was a backwater, beset by superstitions and rival clans. He did not dare to live there; for him Spandau Castle was considerably safer. His son, Friedrich II, 'Iron Tooth', had other ideas. He decided he needed a place of his own, both as residence and demonstration of power. He alighted on a patch of land guarding the crossing of the Spree close to the Dominican monastery. Just a year after being sworn in as margrave, Iron Tooth began to disband all the governing bodies of the Mark, including the council and town courts, establishing in their place his own administration. His palace would be the heart of his military and political control. The mercantile class saw rights and privileges that had been accrued over decades wiped away by an arriviste from elsewhere. In 1448, shortly before the completion of his palace, the local burghers opened the weirs, flooding its foundations. Iron Tooth moved in with a force of up to 600 knights to put down the rebellion. He then seized the property of his most uppity citizens and imposed steep taxes to fund his own micro-state. He succeeded in his immediate task, but even so, it would take him several more years to feel secure enough to move into his new schloss.

The legend of the *Berliner Unwille* (the indignation) became popular in the nineteenth century, during the first stirrings of liberalism and German nationalism. Among the many patriotic stories of the time, perhaps the best-known is *Der Roland von Berlin* by the novelist Willibald Alexis. Roland became a mythological hero, a knight protecting civic rights. From the earliest years, statues to Roland, invariably with sword in hand, were popular in many towns. It is said that Iron Tooth chucked Berlin's Roland into the river, just to teach the locals a lesson. There are no memorials to the *Unwille* in the city, which seems strange, given that its legacy continues to this day. Berliners' view of themselves as independent-minded and resistant to power, particularly when it is imposed from outside, emanates from this episode. Much of it is wishful thinking, however. Once the burghers' uprising had been quelled, the townsfolk carried on much as before. A similar cycle of rebellion, subjugation and ultimately adaptation would take place several times more in the city's history.

The Schloss was the first significant fortification in the still quiet and relatively remote trading town. The locals gave it the nickname *Zwingburg* (stronghold). The main role of the palace and its garrison was to assert the authority of the margraves over unruly citizens. New taxes were imposed on those unwilling to give up their privileges, such as the use of marketplaces and the establishment of guilds, to the monarch. The Schloss was the proud seat of many an elector and king, and the object of many a makeover. In the sixteenth century, Margrave Joachim II decided it needed to be rebuilt in a grander Italian Renaissance style. Not satisfied with that, in 1698 Friedrich III commissioned Andreas Schlüter, an architect from Danzig (now Gdansk in Poland). Schlüter created the Prussian baroque version, the design on which the new replica is based.

Embraced by some rulers, shunned by others, the palace has been at the heart of the imperial Reich and the site of several botched revolutions. Its demise coincided with that of the

Hohenzollerns. During the Weimar Republic, the fifteen years of chaotic democracy and decadence from the end of the First World War until the arrival of the Nazis in 1933, it was put to various 'democratic' purposes, as a venue for science and art, even for housing students. Under the Third Reich, it was considered old-fashioned and underwhelming and ignored. Hitler had far more grandiose plans for his city. Then came the Allied bombs.

The communist GDR declared the Stadtschloss a symbol of Prussian militarism and jingoism (conveniently ignoring the liberal Weimar bit). Yet, with so much of the city in ruins, the hulk of the building was initially left as it was. One of the walls still standing was used as a backdrop for the Soviet propaganda war film *The Fall of Berlin*, while another section was patched up to use as a space for an exhibition of socialist realist art. Yet, as the communist regime consolidated, it had plans of its own for Berlin and for the building that had for centuries helped to define it. In 1950, Walter Ulbricht, the East German leader, ordered the palace be pulled down as part of wider plans to rebuild the city. He told the Third Congress of the Socialist Unity Party, the SED, in July of that year: 'The centre of our capital and the area of the palace's ruins must become a grand square for demonstrations, upon which our people's will for struggle and for progress can find expression.'

Demolition began shortly after, the process taking four long months and consuming 19 tonnes of dynamite. Only one aspect of the building was saved, the portal from whose balcony Karl Liebknecht is believed to have declared the German Socialist Republic in 1918. Even in the tightly controlled GDR at a time of heightened Cold War tension, Ulbricht encountered opposition to his decision to tear down the palace. Indeed, a secret Ministry of Construction report, found by a journalist in a hidden file in 2016, calculated that reconstruction of the palace was estimated at 32 million GDR marks, equivalent to almost £90 million today.

For a state on its economic knees that was a considerable sum, but it was a snip compared to what it would later cost.

It took two decades to work out what to do with the site. The original plan was for a government skyscraper. Thanks to a lack of money, this scheme and others came to nothing. So the former palace became what many other vacant lots in East Berlin became – a car park and a parade ground for special events.

Eventually, in 1973, Erich Honecker, Ulbricht's successor, opted to build the Palast der Republik, the Palace of the Republic – a socialist take on the Pompidou Centre, which was being built at the same time. When the skeletal building, with its brightly coloured tubing and exterior escalators, opened in Paris in 1977, it was hailed as a model of modernity, attracting crowds five times larger than had been predicted. The East Germans could not afford starchitects like Renzo Piano and Richard Rogers – nor, probably, would they have given them so much creative freedom. So they did their best with what they had. The Palast, Honecker declared at its opening, was his 'house to the people'. By GDR standards, it was extraordinarily ambitious. The concrete box with reflective windows that shone gold in the sun was the height of glamour. The style came to be known as *DDR Moderne*.

The scale was remarkable. It had enough restaurants to accommodate 15,000 visitors at any one time. A *Jugendtreff* (a basement hall where young people could meet) offered a pinball machine and two dance floors; the older and less energetic were rewarded with a restaurant in which Soviet champagne and Romanian red wines were served by waiters clad in bow ties. A *Bierstube* and a milk and mocha bar served all ages. Everything was affordable, as prices were two-thirds subsidized by the state. At its opening, state television rattled off the statistics: the palace contained sixteen escalators, no less than sixty-eight toilets and 120,000 pieces of cutlery.

With marble floors in the foyer and bright-orange chairs, it was considered socialist 1970s cool. Many people's favourite aspect of the building was the *Stabwerkkugelleuchte*, thousands of giant ball and stick lights whose glowing bulbs reflected light onto the floor of the Palast. They inspired the Palast's new nickname, *Erichs Lampenladen* (Erich's Lamp Shop), and were so popular they were used in other important state buildings.

The most popular venue was the bowling alley. It was booked weeks in advance and communist officials enjoyed taking foreign dignitaries there to show off the building's facilities and avant-garde art and architecture. One of the first exhibitions was called *Are communists allowed to dream?* Sixteen officially sanctioned artists were invited to illustrate on large canvases their vision for the future, as long as they stayed within socialist realist bounds. The paintings have since been rehoused at the German Historical Museum. The centrepiece was a 5,000-seat hexagonal multi-purpose Great Hall. Banks of seats could be electronically moved forwards and backwards (the ultimate in high-tech, so TV reporters told viewers) to accommodate a variety of events. These ranged from classical concerts and waltzes (Strauss was popular), to oom-pah-pah to children's Christmas pantos.

Western artists such as Tangerine Dream, Harry Belafonte and Santana played here. The single most controversial cultural event, and for East Berlin's youth the most exciting, took place in October 1983. This was a time of heightened Cold War tension; with NATO deploying a new range of nuclear weapons, the GDR leadership decided to hold a carefully controlled 'Rock for Peace' festival. One of those invited to perform was a star of West German *Krautrock*, the experimental rock trend that had emerged in West Germany in the late 1960s, Udo Lindenberg. He had been trying since the 1970s to tour the GDR but was repeatedly refused permission. He responded with a song called 'Special Train to Pankow', the district to the northeast of the city which housed the enclave of the communist elite. The lyrics directly mocked Honecker: 'Hey, Honi, I'll sing for little money in the Palace of the Republic.' After all, he 'secretly likes to put on his leather jacket, lock himself up in the loo and listen to West radio'. The song was expressly forbidden, which made it all the cooler to play it at discos and parties in the East. Prone as they were sometimes to yield to popular pressure (when they considered the potential dangers to be minimal), the authorities suddenly told Lindenberg that he could, after all, play at the Palast – but only if he refrained from singing that song. He duly obliged; indeed he pleased the authorities by embarking on a riff about Pershing nuclear missiles, declaring on stage: 'Get rid of your junk weapons, West and East Germany! We don't want to see a single missile anywhere!' Even though he had toed the line, they didn't let Lindenberg come back.

Hidden cameras and listening devices were installed everywhere inside the palace, but it was still regarded as a fun place to hang out. After all, East Berliners didn't have much else in terms of public buildings or late-night offerings, and it was open from 10 a.m. to midnight. In its short life span of less than two decades, some 60 million visits were recorded.

At one end of the building was the Volkskammer, the GDR's 'parliament'. Its plenary hall had 787 seats, of which 541 were in the stalls for deputies and 246 were available in the gallery for observers. Three of the palace's thirteen restaurants were situated above the chamber for the exclusive use of the deputies. However, there were no private offices. The decisions were taken elsewhere, by the heads of the Communist Party, the SED, and the Stasi secret police. It was in the chamber that many of East Germany's most important political events took place. The SED's party congress, with its rubber-stamped decisions and shouts of 'hurrah', was an annual fixture. Celebrations of the 750th anniversary of the founding of Berlin were held (on both sides of the city) in 1987 and, portentously, the fortieth anniversary of the founding of the GDR was marked in the summer of 1989, just as protests were gathering on the street. It was here that Mikhail Gorbachev famously told Honecker of the dangers of standing in the way of change.

The one and only time the Volkskammer came to life as a real legislature was in the eleven months between the fall of the Berlin Wall and reunification, when a hastily assembled generation of democratically elected MPs passed a succession of laws and held passionate debates about what to do with their moribund state and with the economy. One of their final decisions, in September 1990, was to close the palace immediately after publication of an official report stating that 5,000 tonnes of asbestos had been sprayed to fireproof the building when it was constructed.

My most memorable moment in the Palast der Republik took place earlier that year. Amid the hubbub, I had coffee in the foyer with an unassuming adviser to Lothar de Maizière, the first leader of the post-communist GDR. Her name was Angela Merkel. I didn't think much more about it. I was struck by her poise, her restraint, her courtesy, but I had no idea of what she would become. I remember all the excited people rushing around, a building coming to life at the start of what many assumed would be a new political era in the East.

In that period, one of the most fiercely contested issues was what to do with the physical manifestations of communism. Many Berliners, and even more Germans from elsewhere (who were always somewhat sniffy about the divided city), were calling for the remnants of the GDR regime to be torn down as quickly as possible. Statues were seen as fair game. But what to do about the palace? The Bundestag continued to function in Bonn, with the election of additional members from the East, until the issue of the capital could be resolved. Parliament was eventually restored to Berlin in 1999, but to the Reichstag.

Not for the first time this sorry spot on Unter den Linden, in the heart of Berlin, was empty, devoid of purpose.

Cue a man who had made a fortune with his tractor business. Wilhelm von Boddien was born in 1942 in a town called Stargard which is now in northern Poland. He liked to say he was from Pomerania, an imperial region on the Baltic coast stretching all the way to Gdansk, but he made his money in the less exotic city of Hamburg after inheriting his father's company. He first visited East Berlin as a young man in 1961 and was disconcerted by its shabby state. 'The dreariness there blew me away. Before reunification, I already had the palace as a hobby, a very intense hobby,' Boddien said in an interview with another *grand homme* of business, Jörg Woltmann, the owner of the Royal Porcelain Factory. 'At weekends, lunch at our house was served in the kitchen, because the dining table was full of albums and pictures of the palace, and I refused to put them away.'

Thirty years later he spotted an opportunity to restore the city to its former glory, in his mind anyway. Straight after the collapse of the GDR, Boddien and his friends stood on Marx-Engels-Platz, once proudly called Schlossplatz, handing out black-and-white photographs of the old palace to passers-by. His next trick was to lobby the city authorities to allow him to hang a canvas replica painting of the old palace's baroque façade on the front of the Palast. This *trompe-l'oeil* was dramatically reflected in its gold-tinted windows. 'The people rubbed their eyes when the palace was suddenly back. It stayed for two summers and one winter, being illuminated at night,' Boddien wrote in a newspaper article. His plan was to demonstrate the beauty of Schlüter's design and to convince Berliners that Unter den Linden needed a massive building at its end to connect the other monuments around it. The communist Palast was neither grand enough nor big enough, taking up only part of the original site.

Boddien lobbied hard, acquiring friends in high places,

particularly on the right of the political spectrum. Corporates and high net-worth individuals were attracted to the idea of a resurrected grand building. He put in some of his own money and did his own early version of crowdfunding, thanking elderly ladies for giving a small amount from their purses as much as the wealthy for big cheques. 'It was the task of my life,' he told me when I met him in March 2023, invited as part of a small group of besuited and well-heeled folk who came in reverence to a business club to hear him read from his memoirs, *The Berlin Palace and Me: an Unbelievable Story*. I had assumed I wouldn't take to him, but I must admit the man has a considerable old-school charm along with his tenacity. The more people told him he was mad, the more determined he became, he reminisced. 'I needed the patience of an elephant and the bite of a terrier.'

Some East Germans saw the asbestos issue as a ruse, providing the perfect excuse to get rid of the GDR's flagship building, and quickly, before anyone could stand in their way. The palace was probably no more contaminated than any number of 1970s buildings on either side of Berlin and it was not particularly complicated for developers to rid old buildings of the material. The issue, however, was the perfect excuse for advocates of demolition.

In 1995, the 'cleaning up' of the building began. The glass was removed, and after that, many of the steel girders. Much of the steel was melted down and sold to Dubai to build the world's tallest building at the time, the monument to bling that is the Burj Khalifa. Volkswagen also bought some of it for use in engine blocks. Politicians on the left saw the abandonment of the palace as a symbol of a wider jettisoning of everything associated with the GDR. In 1997, the leader of the successor group to the SED, Gregor Gysi, climbed onto the top of the roof of the empty building to unfurl a banner. He was rescued by the fire brigade and threatened with legal action.

Could the Palast der Republik, once cleared of asbestos, have been made to work in the new unified Berlin? Could it not have been reimagined as a curious but fascinating modernist structure in the heart of faux baroque and Gothic Berlin? I couldn't stop asking myself these questions, not least because my landlords had a large black-and-white photograph of the Palast just outside the bathroom of my Berlin apartment. There is no shortage of examples of monuments to socialist planning surviving, even thriving, with or without an architectural makeover. One example close to home is the Kulturpalast in Dresden, opened in 1967 and reopened in 2017 as a concert venue. It and its 'Way of the Red Flag' mural outside may be an incongruous part of the skyline of the rebuilt city, but it works, after a fashion.

As debate continued to rage, the shell of the Palast der Republik was cleared for use as a venue for art installations and a small selection of cultural events. The Terracotta Army models were brought from Xian, China. The popular theatre director Frank Castorf staged a production of Alfred Döblin's epic Weimar-era novel, *Berlin Alexanderplatz*, in 2005. The year before, another art group created a performance called 'The Façade Republic', which involved flooding the building's ground floor with 300,000 litres of water that visitors could drift through in white inflatable boats. Guests were provided with fishing rods that they used to catch floating trays of sushi. One of the final artistic interventions was the placing of giant illuminated white letters, *Zweifel*, on the front. That means 'doubt'.

The Bundestag finally announced in January 2006 it was pulling down the building. The plans were described by the left-wing newspaper *taz* as 'a compromise between Honecker and Hohenzollern'. The project was beset by problems. The building had to be dismantled in individual parts because of the risk to neighbouring buildings. To make matters worse, construction workers kept finding more asbestos. Eventually, more than a year behind schedule and tens of millions of euros over budget, the last remains of the Palast der Republik were taken down at the end of 2008.

For the best part of a decade after that, the entire area from the Schloss and far down Unter den Linden was a building site. The centre of what should have been the bright new city was an eyesore. Plans for the new Humboldt Forum were dogged by disagreement and delay; repeated deadlines were missed. In that respect it was little different to other German infrastructure projects, such as Stuttgart railway station, in which the otherwise wealthy southwestern city had to reckon with a crater for more than two decades, and the extraordinary 'how not to' story of Berlin's BER airport. The final design of the Humboldt Forum, overseen by Franco Stella, an Italian architect who had never built anything comparable, was a mix of neo-baroque and revolving doors. At a cost of €680 million (just to build), you might have thought someone was in charge. The construction part reported to the Federal Housing and Building Ministry; those responsible for some of the galleries would report to the Federal cultural minister, from the conservative Christian Democrats (CDU); other galleries reported to the Berlin state culture minister (who belonged to the party of the far left). Yet others were part of the Stiftung Preussischer Kulturbesitz, the Prussian Culture Heritage Foundation, whose president reported to a board of representatives of all sixteen states which the culture minister chaired but had no casting vote over. Confused? Meanwhile, the people supposedly in charge had no say over the curation, and the curators had no authority over the construction (they couldn't even choose the display cabinets).

Big names were brought in from outside to help navigate the turmoil. One of those was Neil MacGregor, long-time Director of the British Museum and one of a small group of prominent British cultural figures held in great esteem in Germany. He was given the title of Director of the Founding Directorate, but with only an advisory role. He stayed three years and, ever the diplomat, left discreetly in 2018. Another advisor, the French art historian and professor at Berlin's Technical University, Bénédicte Savoy, quit in 2017, claiming that the project had become 'like Chernobyl'; instead of practising 'openness' and 'multiperspectivity', questions about the origins of artworks were to be buried 'like atomic waste', she declared. Not one for understatement, Savoy accused the German government of making common cause with the far right. The advisory board on which she, MacGregor and others sat met only twice after its formation in 2015. It was quietly shelved. David Chipperfield argued that the architecture jury, of which he was a member, had the basic parameters of the building decreed from on high. He describes the Schloss as a 'compromise of the emotional and the political – a lost opportunity'.

Cursed, contaminated, was there ever a chance that the Humboldt Forum would get a sympathetic hearing? Pretty much everything that could go wrong went wrong. Just when it was ready to open, the pandemic struck. In the end, the Humboldt Forum opened its doors in July 2021. The mayor, Michael Müller, and the culture minister, Monika Grütters, were on hand to welcome the first visitors. Two months later, Steinmeier, the president, and the Nigerian author Chimamanda Ngozi Adichie officiated at the official opening.

I struggled to find anyone prepared to defend it. As an instinctive contrarian, I wanted to give it a chance; I went to see the key figures in charge. Why on earth, I asked the spokesman Mathis over our courtyard coffee, did he exchange the quieter climes of the Art Museum in Basel for a role such as this? 'It's an experiment that needs time,' he insisted. 'It's more than a museum, it's an exchange. People are saying, "finally you're listening". We want this to be the place where the world meets, less a museum, more a forum, just like in Roman times. We want people from all over the world to meet here and talk to each other.' The various exhibitions, he added, have been booked out for months, and the museum would hit its previous forecast of three million visitors per year. 'The difference in the reception between ordinary folk and some in the elite is stark.'

Next, the boss: Hartmut Dorgerloh was appointed in 2018 to one of the toughest cultural jobs in the world, having run some of Berlin and Brandenburg's most famous monuments and gardens for nearly two decades, including the Charlottenburg Palace and the stately homes of Potsdam. I ask him why some people were so passionate about the Schloss, on both sides of the ideological and architectural divide? 'It was an indicator of Berlin's unbroken relationship with history,' he says. 'It was an indicator of the triumph of capitalism.' And that leaves many Berliners cold. It is not the kind of statement one would hear from a museum director in New York or London or Paris.

Dorgerloh is conscious of the sensitivities. He reminds me that he was brought up in the GDR, telling the story of the TV Tower that opened in the late 1960s, a building that is now part of Berlin's skyline. 'For me that building was an ideal. I was told that the Americans could fly to the moon, but we had this.' Will the Humboldt Forum eventually be loved?

Every aspect is now dissected, and invariably spat back out: the architecture, the contents, the 'experience'? The battle is a proxy for a wider battle over Berlin's – and Germany's – history and future identity. This is a rare example where *Vergangenheitsbewältigung* (coming to terms with the past) is focused not so much on the crimes of the Nazi era (they are memorialized pretty much everywhere else) but on the decades that preceded it. Germany's relatively short colonial period lasted from the mid-1880s to the confiscation of German colonies with the Treaty of Versailles in 1919. More concerned with the fragile state of equilibrium in Europe than with international expansion,

Bismarck was initially hesitant to plunge Germany into the 'Scramble for Africa' in the 1880s. However, with the support of Britain and goading from his own nationalists and merchants, Bismarck's colonial mission began in the summer of 1884. Within a few months, Germany had seized Southwest Africa (present day Namibia), Cameroon, Togoland (Togo) and German East Africa (today the area encompassing Rwanda, Burundi and Tanzania), as well as parts of New Guinea and the 'Bismarck Archipelago' (today the Solomon Islands). Violence and expropriation of assets were intrinsic to these conquests.

Berlin's fascination with the colonial era began decades before Bismarck and his army began their adventures abroad. In the mid-1840s the Egyptologist Carl Lepsius set up an audience with the formidable Egyptian leader Muhammad Ali and convinced him to exchange a small number of pieces of Prussian porcelain for permission to remove all the treasures he could find. Lepsius returned to Berlin in 1850 a wealthy man, laden with boxes of precious artefacts. Twenty years later, a businessman and amateur archaeologist, Heinrich Schliemann, unearthed the ancient city of Troy, promptly looting it of its treasures and then trying to cut deals with the Turks, Greeks and Russians. In May 2022, an exhibition was staged at Berlin's James Simon Museum to mark the 200th anniversary of Schliemann's birth. The culture minister, Claudia Roth, said Schliemann's legacy was being examined 'against the background of dealing with colonialism and its consequences, which has rightly come into focus today'.

The specific German difficulty with the decolonization debate is that there is always a subsequent crime that dominates. It has rekindled a fierce debate about the *Sonderweg*, the notion of a 'special path' by which Prussian militarism led inexorably to the Third Reich. Can, indeed should, the Holocaust be compared to other horrors in history; should it be considered uniquely evil?

Must it be compared to other genocides for its uniqueness to be fully appreciated?

The Humboldt Forum has become a focal point of the debate, if largely by accident. Having agreed to build, or revive, the palace, those responsible scratched their heads, wondering what to put in it. They decided they might as well move much of the collections of African and Asian works from the rarely visited Ethnological Museum and the Museum for Asian Art in the quiet suburb of Dahlem, an incongruous mix that was then denounced as cultural appropriation. Among the artefacts are some of the Benin Bronzes looted from the royal palace of the Kingdom of Benin, in what is now southern Nigeria, by a British colonial expedition in 1897. The new Ethnological Museum at the forum now contains one of the world's largest collections of historical objects from the kingdom, yet for all its attempts at being 'inclusive' it seems to please nobody. MacGregor describes it to me as 'Germany flagellating its own navel'. He adds: 'It is a collection of amazing African artefacts that tell you little about Africa. Instead, it is all about how bad colonisers the Germans have been.'

As debate raged in former colonies, the ever-meticulous Germans took a little longer than others to respond. The government announced in early 2022 that museums would work on a restitution plan. In December, foreign minister Annalena Baerbock travelled to Abuja for an official handover ceremony. The Culture Ministry pledged its financial support to a new museum in Nigeria which will store and exhibit the repatriated objects. Yet the twenty returned bronzes are just a fraction of the 1,130 stolen artefacts displayed in museums across Germany.

In the meantime, how to display them? When the Humboldt Forum opened, the objects were presented with little curation. A sign on the wall stated that projects aiming to decolonize the collections were 'in progress'. In the meantime, each dimly lit room displays the objects on sober, unlabelled shelves, as if they were in an open storage facility. The same goes for the famous *Lufboot*, for instance, a 16-metre-long, elaborately decorated South Pacific vessel which had to be fork-lifted into the palace before the walls could be closed; it had, according to the historian Götz Aly, been surrendered to German colonizers who had rampaged across Papua New Guinea's New Bismarck Archipelago.

Too many concessions to contemporary sensitivities, or too few? The Humboldt Forum is a patchwork of tastes, seemingly satisfying no one. Africa: second floor. Asia: third floor. They are separated by a giant escalator that would not be out of place in a grandiose airport in China or the UAE.

Undeterred, I am determined to disagree with the *bien pensants* attacking the building and all it stands for. A video panorama telling its story is technically proficient, if superficial in its content. My mood is brightened not by the large spaces but by the artefacts interspersed between, in the quieter spots. A tableau in a corner of the ground floor has a montage of the posters for the shows. Kenny Last's jazz band; the national ballet of Colombia; and the 'construction workers' ball'. Alongside it are other items of communist kitsch, including two ice-cream cups from the milk bar. A small section of a bronze relief created for the foyer of the Volkskammer, entitled *Lob des Kommunismus* (In Praise of Communism) is also on display. A monitor screen from a control centre run by the Stasi bears witness to the surveillance and helps to offset any lingering nostalgia for the quaintness of the GDR.

Then I visit 'Berlin Global' on the first floor, and everything goes wrong. The permanent exhibition is intended as a new way of interpreting the city's history; even though it doesn't quite say so, it is perhaps more a way of compensating for the criticism of the way the colonial art is displayed. Visitors start in a room entitled 'Thinking the World', drawn to a mural containing 'clasped hands, broken chains and doves of peace' alongside symbols of appropriation. I am given a wrist tag, which beeps whenever I make various 'decisions'. The first one is which of two doors to go through into the next room: is it 'I want to help the world', or 'I want to help my community'? The former means you are outward-looking, multicultural, tolerant. Of course, I chose the other, just to see what happened. Nothing, but my sense of annoyance continues to build. Rooms with seven individual themes follow: Revolution, Free Space, Boundaries, Entertainment, War, Fashion and Interconnection.

The room about war displays 'continuities' between the colonial era and the present-day Bundeswehr. One wall lists the two world wars, alongside early-twentieth-century massacres such as the Boxer Rebellion, the Maji Maji War and the Herero and Nama War. The 'colonial division of the world', the exhibition explains, saw German imperial forces annihilate hundreds of thousands in China, German East Africa and German Southwest Africa. The spoils were then divvied up at the 1884–85 Berlin Conference. Further along, the exhibition gives a brief outline of German military missions abroad since 1990, such as Kosovo, Afghanistan and Mali. It is quite something for what is supposed to be Berlin's new showcase museum to indulge in such an absurd attempt at moral equivalence. Instead of focusing on gimmicks, the Humboldt Forum, this most damned of places, could have woven the eight centuries of Berlin's history with more nuance and power.

Locals may complain about the Humboldt Forum, but visitor numbers (mainly out-of-towners and foreigners) are increasing, albeit from a low base. I ask Dorgerloh if the city will ever be at peace with the place. He laughs, shrugs and says, 'I don't know. But it will happen.' Boddien remains proud of his building and thinks that over time it will find its rightful place. He is careful not to be too damning, but he does believe the Humboldt Forum could have gained the stature of the Louvre, the Hermitage or the British Museum. Instead of grandeur they opted instead for didacticism.

Why have I focused so much on this contemporary battle for one building? Because it is part of a continuum. The twenty-first-century version of the *Berliner Unwille* (the indignation) has been less dramatic than its fifteenth-century precursor; protests for sure, but at least no moats were flooded. This single site has been contested for more than six centuries. It may be too much to say it is contaminated but it is a symbol of the continuing struggle to define what the city should look like and represent.

THREE

A very modern conflict

Thirty Years War

*You can drive miles through smoking ruins and see nothing
that is habitable. This city can never be rebuilt.*
AIR CHIEF MARSHAL SIR ARTHUR TEDDER (1945)

A ndreas Gryphius was born in Silesia, in what is now Poland.
His collection of thirty-one sonnets includes 'Tears Of The
Fatherland', 'All Is Vanity', 'Human Misery' and 'Lament of
Devastated Germany'. He wrote it at the height of the Thirty Years
War (1618–48), the most violent of all Europe's wars.

So, now we are destroyed; utterly; more than utterly.
The gang of shameless peoples, the maddening music of war,
The sword fat with blood, the thundering of the guns
Have consumed our sweat and toil, exhausted our reserves.
Towers are on fire, churches turned upside down;
The town hall is in ruins, the strong cut down, destroyed.
Young girls are raped; wherever we turn our gaze,
Fire, plague, and death pierce heart and spirit through.
Here, town and ramparts run with ever-fresh streams of blood.

It was a protracted struggle of extraordinary intensity and futility in which marauding armies laid waste to most of the continent, including the Mark Brandenburg. Its legacy has haunted Germans down the ages. It set the benchmark from which the two world wars of the twentieth century are judged, and it has influenced German thinking on contemporary conflicts, from Afghanistan to Iraq to Libya to Syria, and Vladimir Putin's invasion of Ukraine. Yet even though it reduced the population of Berlin and the surrounding area by half, even though it took more than fifty years for the city to recover, you have to travel some distance out to find the first significant physical memorial to the slaughter.

As with the First World War, the trigger was accidental, but the underlying causes were deep-rooted and prescient for today – religious rivalry, civil strife and land grabs by powerful nation states. After a series of conflicts following the Reformation, a truce had been reached at the Imperial Diet of the Holy Roman Empire. The Peace of Augsburg in 1555 granted tolerances between city states to manage differences, yet they gradually unravelled. The German lands were politically fragmented, with the various princes, bishops, towns and the Holy Roman Emperor himself vying for influence.

The Thirty Years War was triggered in 1617, not in Berlin or the Mark but in Bohemia when two Catholic regents closed Protestant chapels that were being constructed in the small towns of Broumov and Hrob. In doing so, they were violating the guarantees of religious liberty laid down in a Letter of Majesty of the Emperor Rudolf II eight years earlier. In response to the closures, an assembly of Protestants was called at which the officials were tried and found guilty of usurping the authority of the emperor, Ferdinand II. Their punishment was to be thrown out of the top-floor window of the council room of Hradčany (Prague Castle) on 23 May 1618. It was by no means the first time such a penalty was meted out. Nevertheless, that moment marked the signal for the start of a Bohemian revolt. It did not take long for the fighting to spread into all-out war across the continent, pitting Spain and the Austrian Habsburgs on one side against the powerful Swedes and French. What started as a religious war evolved into a more amorphous struggle for power and territory. Others piled in – the Ottomans, the Scots – their war aims changing as they went along. Many recruits were mercenaries; most of them were homeless, outcasts and the poor. Fighting was one of few ways of earning a reliable income, and it didn't matter which side you were on, or whether you switched sides. Catholics ended up working for Protestants and vice versa.

Georg Wilhelm, who became Elector of Brandenburg in 1619, ruled over an expanded and strengthened domain. A diplomatically astute marriage between the daughter of the Duke of Prussia and the son of the prince-elector of Hohenzollern-Brandenburg two decades earlier had united the ruling powers and secured the Hohenzollerns' inheritance of the Prussian duchy upon the death of the Duke, Albrecht Friedrich. As the war reached Brandenburg, Georg Wilhelm tried to maintain a policy of neutrality, or rather flexibility, switching sides three times and hoping that the warring factions wouldn't bother coming this far east. He succeeded in keeping the hordes at bay for several years, only to see his territory eventually and repeatedly plundered by both sides. He was an unheroic figure. Friedrich the Great called it 'a most unfortunate reign', describing him as a 'sovereign incapable of governing'. Georg Wilhelm himself wrote in 1626: 'It pains me greatly that my lands have been wasted in this way and that I have been so disregarded and mocked. The whole world must take me for a cowardly weakling.'

Early territorial gains by the Holy Roman Emperor, Ferdinand II, brought Denmark and Sweden into the war, both to support the Protestants in the northern German lands, and also, for Sweden, for an opportunity to control the Baltic coast. Catholic France supported them in order to break the stranglehold of the

House of Habsburg, which held both the Imperial and the Spanish crowns. Money ran short on all sides; supply lines broke down; mercenaries and regular units frequently were not paid. The soldiers took out their frustration on whichever village they found themselves in, ransacking, raping, killing at will. Only the lucky few managed to flee.

The Swedish army, feared (and admired) across Europe for its ruthless efficiency, razed much of Berlin, just as they had the surrounding villages and towns they had marched through to get there. Even though the king, Gustavus Adolphus, was married to Georg Wilhelm's sister, he did not spare the city in their three years of occupation. By the time they departed there were no young women left in the town; they had been taken away to be raped. The king exercised little control over his troops. One of the occupiers' favoured ploys was to sprinkle gunpowder on children and set them alight in front of their parents. Another was the 'Swedish drink', pouring excrement or sullage down the throats of imprisoned soldiers or civilians by means of a funnel. They then squeezed the victim's distended belly with wooden boards, trampled them underfoot or beat them with sticks.

The warring sides finally sued for peace out of exhaustion. After thirty years of conflict, Berlin was one sixtieth the size of London and one seventy-fifth of Paris, a population that was smaller than when it was founded in the thirteenth century. Across the German lands, the Swedish armies had destroyed 2,000 castles, 18,000 villages and 1,500 towns. Four in ten people died overall. Those who managed to survive were left starving. Scurvy, rickets, meningitis, lung infections and other diseases were rife.

The war has been memorialized in Germany and around the world in literature, art and music. One of the most graphic accounts was believed to have been written in 1638 by a travelling Yorkshireman, Philip Vincent, while the war was still in full flow.

His *Lamentations of Germany* has the alluring subtitle, 'Wherein, as in a glasse, we may behold her miserable condition, and reade the woefull effects of sinne'. Vincent described the mutilations, murder and mayhem in graphic detail, accompanied by illustrations. In a section entitled 'Of torture and torments', he writes, 'They have put and tied burning matches betwixt their fingers, to their noses, tongues, jawes, cheeks, brests, legs, and secret parts.' He continues, for page after page.

Written during the English Civil War, the *Lamentations* was an appeal to avoid the horror that had afflicted the Germans.

In some areas of the Mark no one was left who could remember how things were 'before the Swedes came'. This made testimonials even more important. One of the first significant works in German was written by Hans Jakob Christoffel von Grimmelshausen, who at the age of ten was kidnapped into soldiery. He witnessed the Saxon siege of Magdeburg and the Battle of Wittstock as a stable boy. In 1668, two decades after the end of the war (but when its effects were still being felt), he published his six-part picaresque novel, *Der abenteuerliche Simplicissimus*. Much of it is autobiographical, the protagonist's rustic childhood abruptly terminated when his family's farm is plundered; he is captured while hiding in a forest and taken into army service. Translated into a number of languages, including English in 1912 (just as Germany under Kaiser Wilhelm II was rapidly rearming) as *Simplicius Simplicissimus*, it has come to be seen as one of the great anti-war pleas and a cry of pain against the cruelty of religion – not that one would glean this from its subtitle: 'The account of the life of an odd vagrant named Melchior Sternfels von Fuchshaim: namely where and in what manner he came into this world, what he saw, learned, experienced, and endured therein; also why he again left it of his own free will'.

Another eyewitness account took centuries to be unearthed. In

1988, twelve folded sheets of papers were found by chance in the manuscript store of Berlin State Library. It took a scholar five years to transcribe what he realized was a diary written from the vantage point of a simple mercenary called Peter Hagendorf, who hailed from an area close to Potsdam. The text covers twenty-five years of the war in which he appeared to travel more than 20,000 kilometres, taking part in many of the big battles, such as the Sacking of Magdeburg and the Battle of Nördlingen.

Across a range of artistic forms, depictions of the Thirty Years War have contained messages that are international and transferable to future conflicts elsewhere. In 1633, the artist Jacques Callot completed what came to be known as the 'first anti-war statement' in European art, a remarkable series of eighteen etchings, *The Great Miseries of War*. The pretext was the Thirty Years War, but the artist was also influenced by France's brutal annexation of his native Lorraine under Cardinal Richelieu.

Friedrich Schiller's 1790 *History of the Thirty Years' War in Germany* is one of the first accounts to reflect on the nature of 'total war' and human motivation. He developed the theme further in his trilogy of plays on Albrecht von Wallenstein, one of the towering figures of the conflict. A warlord from lesser nobility, an organizer of armies for the Holy Roman Emperor, Wallenstein is rewarded not with money (the emperor by now is broke) but with territory. Always on the road commanding, he fails to detect plotting against him and a campaign of disinformation – another precursor to the warfare of the present day. Claims swirl that he is about to betray his boss; the emperor discreetly orders his murder.

Each generation has extrapolated its own conclusions. The mid-nineteenth century saw an explosion of plays, literature, poems that used the war legacy to help produce the first stirrings of a German consciousness. Luise Mühlbach's *The Victims of Religious Fanaticism: A Historical Novel of the Thirty Years' War* and Gustav Freytag's *Pictures from the German Past* were among several works that reframed the war as part of the 'tragedy' of the disunited Germans that paved the way for the 'triumph' of the new nation state.

The concept of a 'Second Thirty Years War', referring to the period of violent destabilization from 1914–45, was coined by historians in the mid-twentieth century. Charles de Gaulle and Winston Churchill had cited it in wartime speeches. Throughout the Cold War it was cited as the ultimate example of conflicts escalating out of control. Bertolt Brecht had begun writing *Mother Courage and Her Children* on the day the Nazis occupied Warsaw. Using Grimmelshausen's *Simplicissimus* as his backdrop, he focused on the victims of war: the ordinary soldiers, the peasants, the cooks. The official premiere of the play (it had been first shown in his absence in Zurich in 1941) took place at the Deutsches Theater in East Berlin in January 1949 at a time of extreme Cold War tension. 'A new war threatens,' Brecht wrote. 'Nobody talks about it; everyone knows about it. The majority of people are not for war.'

Soon after the Berlin Wall went up, the government in the West German state of Hessen sent out a survey asking participants to list, in order, the 'seven greatest catastrophes' that Germany had endured in its history. The Black Death, and of course the First World War, the Second World War and the Third Reich were mentioned frequently, but the Thirty Years War topped the list. The seventeenth-century war had killed a greater number of people than any of the others. What seemed to resonate most, however, was that it was not fought on a remote battlefield but in the heart of towns, villages, farms and churches, reaching into every home.

The Thirty Years War is taught in history classes at the start of German secondary school. The basic programme covers its outbreak, the important figures of the time and an overview of the horrors they inflicted – in a way made palatable for twelve-year-old pupils. Most schools spend a few weeks on the topic; some offer pupils the chance to visit local sites. To coincide with the centenaries of both the First World War and the Thirty Years War, the First Channel, ARD, broadcast a five-part docudrama called *Glauben, Leben, Sterben* (Belief, life, death). How different, asked the documentary-maker, Stefan Ludwig, were the soldiers of fortune of the seventeenth century to the warlords of Afghanistan? Around the same time the celebrated author Daniel Kehlmann published his magical realist novel, *Tyll*. Fictionalized it may have been, but his vivid descriptions of the inquisitors' torture and execution of the protagonist's father are historically accurate. Tyll leaves his hometown and becomes a juggler, ventriloquist and trickster, learning to navigate the havoc of bloodshed from street to street. The book topped the bestseller list.

Among some contemporary politicians, a different question has been asked. In a regular meeting with her parliamentary party in April 2018, Angela Merkel didn't focus on any of the usual issues of the day, turning instead to the Augsburg treaty that predated the Thirty Years War. Why, she asked her bemused MPs, did a status quo that had lasted sixty years (not dissimilar in length or ambition to the post-1945 settlement) suddenly fail? What lessons did it have for contemporary geopolitics and the durability of the rule of law? The interchange was revealed by René Pfister, a journalist at *Der Spiegel*. Merkel, he said in his report, had just come back from meeting Donald Trump at a time when Europe and wider Western democracy were being disrupted by populists. 'To Merkel, the Peace of Augsburg is much more than a distant piece of history,' Pfister wrote. 'It is a warning of how thin the varnish covering civilization really is. She compares that to the present day.'

In one of her final interviews before standing down at the end of 2021 Merkel talked of a 'recurring pattern'. She was particularly influenced by two histories that had just been published: one was Christopher Clark's *Sleepwalkers*, on the origins of the First World War, the other an account of the Thirty Years War by the German historian Herfried Münkler. She was struck by his cross-referencing of that conflict with the protracted wars in Syria and across the Middle East in which big and small powers pursue their own interests, sometimes shifting alliances.

What has always struck me is not Germans' reluctance to talk about war, but the template into which such discussions must fit. War equals suffering equals crime and is to be avoided at all costs. I simplify, but not entirely, and I exclude many historians and other experts from such a generalization. Yet so much memorialization is based around the twelve years of Nazi rule that I wonder how easy it is to see other difficult periods of history in their context. Such were my thoughts as I took the train from Berlin to the small town of Wittstock. The journey of just under two hours takes me past the flat and unremarkable Brandenburg plains. For most Berliners, if Wittstock does register, it is as an autobahn interchange that they shoot past on their way to Hamburg and other destinations in the north and west. They are missing one of very few places where the Thirty Years War is remembered. The town, as I discover, is also salient – for an entirely different reason – to the contemporary debate about war and the (wrong) lessons of history.

The Battle of Wittstock is one of the best-known episodes in the Thirty Years War. On 4 October 1636, on the wooded hill of Scharfenberg on the edge of the fortress town, a 22,000-strong Imperial-Saxon army under General Melchior von Hatzfeld and Elector Johann Georg I of Saxony met a 19,000-strong Swedish army under Field Marshal Johan Banér. Despite being outnumbered, the Swedes outmanoeuvred their foe. Having crossed the Elbe with a surprise march, Baner sent half his force on a circuitous route to the enemy's rear, while he led the other half to seize and hold a hill in front of the enemy position. They were on the point of being overrun before being reinforced by an allied force, the Army of the Weser, led by a Scotsman, Alexander Leslie, later the 1st Earl of Leven. They attacked from two sides. The Imperials quickly collapsed and tried to flee in panic. Up to 8,000 men were killed in just three hours of fighting. That victory secured the Swedes' dominance of northern Germany and prolonged the war for more than a decade.

Every other year, the battle is re-enacted in the town square next to a monument of sorts – a towering Swedish poplar tree, replanted in 2005 in place of the original from 1636, and an 80-tonne boulder known as the Swedish Stone, installed in 1997. The performance is called *Die Schweden kommen* (The Swedes are coming). It begins with a rifle salute, before men in traditional bright red military garb process through the town, doffing their caps at bystanders. The confrontation between the people of Wittstock and the Swedes at the castle is performed with gusto by members of the community, complete with horse-drawn carriages, cannons, a huge bonfire and a sword fight. The spectacle ends with a fencing display in the castle grounds.

The seventh and top floor of the Museum of the Thirty Years War affords a perfect view, beyond a communist-era block of flats, of the site of the slaughter a mile or so away. The museum is housed in the Bishop's Castle, which dates to the late Middle Ages and was once the seat of the Catholic bishop of Zechlin. Over the twentieth century, particularly the second half, it fell into disrepair – a familiar story. In GDR times it was turned into a kindergarten. In the 1970s local bosses pondered the idea of building a museum but were more interested in celebrating the peasants' revolt of the sixteenth century. In any case, they didn't get around to it. Then, just before the regime collapsed, the local first secretary, by the name of Manfred Eichelbaum, declared: 'We must do more about the Thirty Years' War.'

They ran out of time, but eight years after unification, their successors eventually got around to it. 'There have always been troops here. This is the right place to have such a museum.' I am being given a tour and told the story by its director, Antje Zeiger. She claims it is the only such museum in the whole of Europe dedicated to the war, though temporary exhibitions take place elsewhere from time to time.

As is often the case with Berlin and its surrounding lands, the process of historical discovery is haphazard and sometimes accidental. In 2007, a team of archaeologists unearthed a mass grave in Wittstock, in a gravel pit. They were investigating the possibility of finding remains which might have been disturbed by clay mining or destroyed during the construction of the industrial park in East German times. What they found, sifting through the grave with plastic spades, spoons, brushes and vacuum cleaners, yielded extraordinary data on how the soldiers of the Thirty Years War lived and how they died. Skeletons of more than a hundred warriors were gathered. They were traced to Scotland, Sweden, Finland, Estonia, Latvia, northern Italy and Spain. And, of course, the German lands. The bodies bore the hallmarks of violent combat: shoulder blades smashed by axes, spines run through with swords, skulls with holes shot through by musket balls. Many of the bones bore shrapnel marks from exploding shells. Many of the men had suffered repeatedly from infections or respiratory diseases. Syphilis could be detected on the lower legs of at least three soldiers.

The museum, which occupies all seven floors of the castle, is strangely understated. Muskets, chain balls, pikes and helmets are displayed. Yet it focuses less on the barbarity, more on folklore and life at the time – the migrations from villages to towns as agriculture was destroyed, and the economy of war (arms sales, horse husbandry and extortion).

Zeiger spends much of her time with me bringing me up to

speed about a more contemporary controversy. Wittstock not only remembers this most senseless of wars, but for nearly twenty years it was also embroiled in a dispute with the Bundeswehr over a huge area of land that was used by Soviet forces for bombing practice and has still not been fully handed back. Activists held more than a hundred demonstrations and initiated thirty court cases to reclaim the land. Ground down by a strong and well-organized public campaign, the military abandoned its plans in 2011.

The story of the Bombodrom begins in 1952. The Soviets identified a vast tract of land around Wittstock, called the Kyritz-Ruppiner Heath, as a suitable site for military training. The surrounding area, Ostprignitz, is one of the least populated parts of Germany and, as with everywhere around Berlin, it is unerringly flat. For forty years, the Russian military used it as an air force training and parachute school, but mostly as a place to practise setting off bombs. Up to 8,000 personnel were stationed there, surrounded by heavily armed patrols and razor wire.

Then the Wall came down and the Russians withdrew. Except they didn't, completely. Cautious estimates put the number of grenades, cluster bombs and duds left behind at 1.5 million. Each bomb dropped on the site contained around 100 steel balls and 100 grams of explosive; munitions dropped from a great height can penetrate deep underground. The occupiers did not give the Germans details of what was dropped where. They did leave behind a model NATO airport in the central area of the site, which they used for bombing simulations. It will take decades to make the area completely safe, if it is possible at all.

Given the futility of the task, and given the need to safeguard Germany's defences, the Bundeswehr decided that they might as well use it, or part of it, themselves. The site was to be turned into a training ground for up to 1,700 missions a year involving low-flying aircraft, with 800 personnel stationed there. This set the military in dispute with the Brandenburg regional government, which in 2001 declared the area a special preserve for flora and fauna. The struggle for Ostprignitz became a *cause célèbre* in a country whose peace movement rarely lacks a reason to protest. A brochure at the museum proudly catalogues the history of the movement and the various staging posts along the way to victory. In 2009 the Higher Administrative Court of Berlin-Brandenburg found definitively against the armed forces and instructed them to drop their plans. A few months later, the Bundeswehr decided not to appeal. Work then began in earnest to return the heathland to the citizenry. Clearance experts were brought in. It is a Sisyphean task; the more they rake and uncover, the more they find. Some areas may remain permanently out of bounds to the public.

Nobody has got what they wanted. 'Restricted military area – no trespassing, risk of death!' signs warn. So far, only one sand path, stretching 13 kilometres on the perimeter of the site, has been opened. From there, grey landscapes stretch into the distance, with bald rows of trees and scorched heather, and a handful of corroded containers and some kerosine tanks that have yet to be taken away. Now the plan is to install solar panels on most of the land. At least that will put it to some good use.

Zeiger has reconfigured part of the ground floor of the museum at Wittstock as an exhibition of the Soviet military presence and of the subsequent peace protests. It conveys the menace of the warning signs in Russian and German of 'shoot on sight' for trespassers. It chronicles the struggle to reclaim the land after half a century of confiscation by two sets of militaries. It was an admirable cause. After all, who wouldn't want the land back? Who would want their children growing up near a no-go zone of cluster bombs and mines? Who would not want to create jobs in sustainable tourism?

Yet the problem across Germany, and particularly around

Berlin, is that nobody wants the military in their back yard. During the GDR era, much of the Brandenburg plains were given over to Soviet and East German armed forces.

My visit to Wittstock took place one month and one day before Putin's attack on Ukraine, which has shaken many Germans' world view to the core. The notion of the just war, of hard power in the service of ethical goals, is something they are now suddenly having to come to terms with. Unification – particularly for East and West Berliners – was supposed to bring a peace dividend, an end to occupation and having to think about spending money on defence or giving up land for soldiers to practise. That supposed dividend is what led to the depletion in Germany's armed forces and its defence budget over the past three decades. It reinforced a deep anxiety about getting involved in war, any war. To help make that case, Germans could always hark back to 1618.

FOUR

Les nouveaux Prussiens

The late seventeenth century and the European influx

From the ruins of the old Germany a new one arises.
WALTER ULBRICHT (1951)

In one of the most beautiful spots in the centre of Berlin, you can while away the time eating merguez, boeuf bourguignon or – in the spirit of bilateral cooperation – coq au Riesling. The square is Gendarmenmarkt and the restaurant is impishly called Hugo et Notte. For four centuries this city has embraced all things French, its language, culture and, inevitably, its food. Yet the origins of the influx were harrowing – the persecution and eventual flight from France of hundreds of thousands of Protestants, the Huguenots.

The hapless Georg Wilhelm died eight years before the end of the Thirty Years War. At the outset of the conflict he sent his son and heir, Friedrich Wilhelm, to be cloistered away in a forest in the fortress of Küstrin, on the east bank of the Oder river, now a couple of miles inside Poland. The crown prince was then, at the age of fourteen, moved to Holland, where his time was divided between the University of Leiden and the court of his future father-in-law, Friedrich Henry of Orange, at the Hague. His four years there left him with a lasting impression. He was strongly influenced by the orderliness of Dutch culture and Calvinism, by the country's architecture, agriculture and commerce, and most by its maritime and military technology.

In 1640, as Friedrich Wilhelm became Elector of Brandenburg and Duke of Prussia, his domain was still under foreign occupation. He divided his time between the eastern stronghold of Königsberg (now the Russian enclave of Kaliningrad) and the comparative calm of Cleves (now Kleve), a Hohenzollern possession near the Dutch border (and the birthplace of Henry VIII's fourth wife, Anne). Friedrich Wilhelm saw in the local population potential entrepreneurs who would help him rebuild his realm. He offered Dutch farmers generous grants of land and tax incentives to revive Brandenburg's ravaged countryside.

Such was his admiration for everything Dutch that by 1646 he had acquired a wife from there, Princess Luise Henriette of Oranien-Nassau. By all accounts she was less enamoured of the arrangement; but duty came first and she abandoned her love for a dashing French nobleman. The Hohenzollerns and the House of Orange were to be united. Two years later, as soon as the war was over, Friedrich Wilhelm moved back to Berlin, a place he had not seen for years. It had a forbidding air; only around 400 families had survived the war and most of its homes were destroyed. It was deemed too gloomy for the queen; as compensation, she was given her own palace out of town.

Friedrich Wilhelm believed *Peuplierung* (repopulation) was central to the revival of his depleted realm. All around him he saw an emaciated, demoralized citizenry. He quickly concluded that he could achieve his aims only by bringing in skilled workers from abroad. He found little of merit in the local populace and went scouting around Europe for talent. His motives were a mix of humanitarianism and savvy business sense. Immigration was central to the remarkable recovery of the devastated Berlin in the

second half of the seventeenth century, under the man who came
to be known as the Great Elector.

He was selective in his choices, preferring peoples he deemed
to be skilled and diligent – from the German lands of East
Friesland (to the west), Holstein and Denmark (to the north), and
from Bohemia and Poland (to the east) to Salzburg (to the south).
In 1671, he issued an edict on the 'Admission of Fifty Families of
Protected Jews; But They Are Not to Have Synagogues'. Their
arrival from Vienna marked the first immigration wave of Jews
since their expulsion exactly a century earlier. They were not
permitted to have public places of worship but could meet in
their own homes to conduct prayers and ceremonies if they
refrained from 'giving offence to Christians'. Still, this was gen-
erosity, of sorts. The new inhabitants became embedded in the
culture. From this point, many Yiddish words entered Berlin
slang, such as *ische* for a young woman, *meschugge* (crazy) and
tacheles, which translates as straight talking.

These immigrants brought economic growth and social tension
in equal measure, a trend that has continued to this day.

Events in France provided the Great Elector with his biggest
opportunity. In October 1685, Louis XIV revoked the Edict of
Nantes, which for nearly a century had guaranteed limited rights
to his country's Protestants. Some 70,000 Huguenots were
massacred; three times that number fled. Those in the west of the
country, from towns such as La Rochelle and Bordeaux, took
refuge in England. Those from Normandy and other places in the
north went to Holland. Others found new homes in Switzerland
and in German principalities and towns such as Frankfurt, the
Palatinate, Stettin and Königsberg. Some even made it further
afield, to (British) America or (Dutch) South Africa.

Eleven days after Louis's assault on the rights of the Huguenots,
the Great Elector issued his own edict inviting them to seek refuge
in Brandenburg. He set up a covert refugee office through his

ambassador in France to process people and establish staging posts to help them reach their destination. They came from Metz, Picardie, Champagne, Provence, Languedoc. Many ended up in the city, but a good number were needed in the countryside. The Uckermark region to the northeast of Berlin became one such enclave. The Edict of Potsdam, written in German and in French and smuggled into France, guaranteed that immigrants would be free to live where they liked in the realm and free to worship in their native language with a priest paid by the prince. He also provided a tax exemption for the first four years, and an option to occupy vacant housing or to build new houses (with more financial support). All of this was offered without a legal requirement to assimilate. The Huguenots enjoyed their own courts of justice, schools and hospitals, while soon becoming key members of the new Berlin establishment. The edict was morally enlightened and economically smart.

The Great Elector had three new districts built beyond the city walls, where farmland once stood. They were the height of modernity, arranged in strict rectangular grids and designed largely to cope with – and appeal to – the new migrants. The first was Friedrichswerder (1662), the second Dorotheenstadt (1674), which he gifted to and named after his second wife, Princess Sophie Dorothea von Schleswig-Holstein-Sonderburg-Glücksburg; in 1688, the year of his death, came Friedrichstadt. He opened a voluntary fund to assist the construction of the three neighbourhoods, but when it received little support from his subjects, he made contributions compulsory. Much of the indigenous population, over half of whom were illiterate, became envious of the influence the wealthier, more entrepreneurial and better-educated immigrants secured. I wonder whether attitudes such as these resonate even today, in the battles over housing and gentrification. Berliners' view of new arrivals seems to follow cycles – they are initially discomfited by them; then they adapt, if grumpily; then they become proud of their city's openness. Those from each influx eventually see themselves as *Ur-Berliner* (true inhabitants), and follow the same pattern.

Within a few years the French made up a quarter of Berlin's population: they were jewellers, tradesmen in felt, silk, leather and other fabrics, and military men. The most senior was Marshal Schomberg, one of Louis XIV's most trusted generals. Friedrich Wilhelm was able to form two companies of musketeers for his guard made up entirely of Huguenot exiles. In total about 600 new officers were appointed. Soon French became as widely spoken as German. The Huguenots brought a new cuisine and new ingredients, such as cauliflowers, mushrooms, artichokes and asparagus (about which Germans now obsess). Two-thirds of the founding members of the Royal Academy of Science and Letters, which opened in 1700, were French. A French-speaking scientific journal was established, which shortly after became the Germanic Library. Berlin's first newspapers were Francophone. Young French ladies were in high demand as tutors to the offspring of the wealthy. As a reaction to the ubiquity of French at court, some German nobles founded their own *Sprachgesellschaften* (language societies) to try to limit the infiltration of foreign tongues.

The French were allowed, even encouraged, to maintain their separate cultural identity for another century to come. Paradoxically, it was the invading Napoleon who abolished their privileges in the early 1800s, by which time, thanks in large part to intermarriage, they were pretty much integrated anyway. Now you would struggle to tell apart anyone with Huguenot heritage. Several Berlin streets bear French names such as Monbijouplatz and Bellevuestrasse. One of my favourites is Savignyplatz in Charlottenburg, which became a refuge of sorts for me during the late 1980s, my regular drinking haunt on the Western side of the Wall with friends from the BBC and

Reuters, which had small offices in the square. It continues to be one of the more serene meeting spots in the city. Throughout the centuries, a number of key figures in all walks of Berlin life, from art to law, medicine to industry, have had French antecedents. Perhaps the best-known is the writer Theodor Fontane. Most recently in politics, Thomas de Maizière was interior minister in Merkel's first administration. His cousin Lothar had been the last and only democratically elected prime minister of the GDR for all of six months in 1990, only later to be outed as a former Stasi informer.

As for the square I mention at the start of the chapter, Gendarmenmarkt, that was originally the stables of the cuirassier cavalry regiment, les Gens d'Armes, until it became a marketplace and later the grand square that it is now, with its cafes, cathedrals and concert halls. The restaurant with the play on French words is situated next to two important buildings. The French Church of Friedrichstadt, opened in 1705 for the new community of Huguenots, was modelled on a church in Charenton, east of Paris, that was built during the brief period of tolerance for Protestantism. It was typically spartan, devoid of all Catholic symbolism and iconography. However, just under a century later, it was decided that the structure needed a tower. And so, a far more impressive structure was created, which came to be known as the French Cathedral. This turned out to be perpetually lost in translation, as the French word dôme refers to a tower or cupola, whereas Dom in German means 'cathedral'.

In 1935, in the run-up to the 250th anniversary of the Revocation of the Edict of Nantes, a parishioner by the name of Alfred Sachse came up with the idea of a museum about Huguenot life in Berlin. It was decided to locate it in the French 'Dom', which wasn't serving any particular function at the time. The first exhibition was housed in a small room, which was opened once a week, after Sunday service. Gradually a collection was assembled. On 24 June

1944, the French Cathedral was badly damaged by Allied bombing. Part of the archive was destroyed, as none of it had been evacuated beforehand. The museum struggled in communist times. It was rebuilt, not to a high standard, and was periodically shut down. In 1976 it was burgled. In 1987, as part of East German efforts to spruce up the city for the 750th anniversary of Berlin, it finally acquired a certain stature.

It is a curious museum, denoting a curious relationship. The curator, Guilhem Zumbaum-Tomasi (no Wilhelm, he), guides me through the story of the Huguenots. Especially poignant is the wall depicting the St Bartholomew's Day Massacre in 1572 during the French Wars of Religion when up to 30,000 Huguenots were hunted down. This genocide lends the Huguenots a historical status in common with other minority populations in history. Yet the curiosity is that no Berliner of French origin (if they even identify themselves as that any more) would consider themselves beleaguered. Such was their assimilation, the privileges and leadership they acquired, particularly in the military, they quickly became synonymous with the very Protestant ethos of Prussia. The museum celebrates the considerable Huguenot contribution to Berlin – through the terrible times and the good – including a recent exhibition of Daniel Chodowiecki's engravings and etchings of the world of French merchants, including everything from tapestries to snuffboxes.

The Dutch influence was equally pronounced. Having been given her hunting lodge to the north of Berlin, in the hamlet of Bötzow (which was first mentioned in documents dating back to Albert the Bear), Luise Henriette set to work remodelling it into something more familiar. She called her palace, and the land around it, Oranienburg, after her family's royal seat. She made her mark by introducing Dutch methods of animal husbandry and brewing. She also assembled a porcelain chamber, Europe's first such collection, brought in by the Dutch East India Company.

The palace and its landscaped garden were soon regarded as one of the most beautiful of all the Prussian residences.

Oranienburg fluctuated between periods of glamour, neglect and horror. Expanded and more lavishly furnished, it came back into fashion briefly in the mid-eighteenth century as the residence of Prince Augustus Wilhelm, one of Friedrich the Great's brothers. In 1802, it was sold to a Berlin pharmacist, Johann Gottfried Hempel; the contract required the owner to operate fifty looms for cotton production, but the war against Napoleon brought production to a standstill in 1807. In 1814, Hempel's son, Georg Friedrich Albrecht Hempel, founded a sulphuric acid factory there. The central building of the palace was heavily damaged in a fire in 1833; another fire nine years later destroyed the south wing, which was subsequently demolished.

A century later, it was turned into a police school by the Nazis, and housed guards watching over the nearby concentration camp at Sachsenhausen. Then it was used for border troops of the GDR. Restoration began again only in the 1990s, after unification, and the palace is now a pleasant if unremarkable destination on the Berlin–Brandenburg tourist trail, particularly if you are interested in porcelain, silver and furniture made of ivory. It must be said that the hundred or so works by Flemish and Dutch artists, including a striking life-sized portrait of England's King Charles I and his wife by Anthony van Dyck, do merit a visit. Sadly, but perhaps inevitably, visits to Oranienburg often combine the baroque beauty of the palace with the concentration camp, built in 1936 on the outskirts of the town. As one travel website describes it: 'A day in a beautiful city combined with dark history.' The day I was there was particularly creepy. I am always struck by how close these camps were built to residential centres. By the time I got to Sachsenhausen, it was dark, the wind was howling, and sleet was teeming down.

Aside from Oranienburg, the other significant landmark is the reimagined 'Dutch Quarter' in the old town of Potsdam, consisting of exactly 134 red, two-storey brick houses arranged on four squares. These gabled *Holländerhäuser* (Dutch houses) were built for immigrant craftsmen between 1734 and 1742, creating the largest single community outside the Netherlands. One of the houses, at Mittelstrasse 8, belonged to Jan Bouman. A master craftsman, together with his brother he accepted an invitation from the king to establish a quarter for his countrymen. He was later responsible for several major building projects in Berlin and Potsdam. The Jan Bouman House fell into neglect during GDR times, as did many of Potsdam's historic buildings and streets. By 1997, as the regeneration of the quarter gained momentum, the small Jan Bouman Museum was opened, telling the story of the Dutch influx, courtesy of some spinning wheels and other folkloric items and an amusingly old-fashioned video that plays on a loop on an old television screen.

Within a decade of the end of the Thirty Years War, Berlin was expanding steadily; the Dutch and the Huguenots had been crucial to its growth. By the end of his rule, the Great Elector had established a bureaucracy of sorts and shored up depleted revenues. He had the first canals built, a vast project with locks linking the Oder and Elbe rivers that significantly boosted trade. By the time he finally chased out the remaining Swedes at the Battle of Fehrbellin of 1675, he had a standing army of 30,000 (compared to a bedraggled 2,000 at the end of the war), along with a small Baltic fleet. He had even procured for himself a modest colony on the west coast of Africa. The Brandenburger Gold Coast was established on the Gulf of Guinea in 1682 by the newly founded Brandenburg Africa Company, Brandenburg's response to the Dutch East India Company. It is estimated that between 17,000 and 30,000 slaves were transported from the colony to the Americas before it was sold to the Dutch in 1721.

*

The period that followed the death of the Great Elector in 1688 saw further rapid change. The new ruler, Friedrich I, looked at Berlin and all around him and was embarrassed by the cultural and architectural shortcomings of his domain. This was the Europe of Michelangelo, Rubens, Van Dyck and Christopher Wren, and Berlin, by contrast, was a minnow. Friedrich was the first ruler to be obsessed with the question of the city's status, but he would by no means be the last. He threw all his efforts at the problem and became known as a great patron of arts and learning, establishing the Academy of Arts in 1696 and the Academy of Sciences four years later. He also had a predilection for vanity and a penchant for spending money – on the city and on himself. It is said that in the first year of his rule, a total of almost 1.4 million thaler, almost £25 million in today's money, went on luxuries at the royal court. That amounted to more than half of all state spending.

In 1701, a dozen years into his reign, Friedrich decided that his title did not afford him the grandeur he deserved. Prussia had emerged as the dominant state of the Holy Roman Empire over the previous century, with the union of Brandenburg and the Duchy of Prussia into one powerful entity, Brandenburg-Prussia, in 1618, and significant military victories in Warsaw (1656) and Fehrbellin (1675). Friedrich saw this as grounds to ask the emperor, Leopold I, for an upgrade. Leopold gave his assent, allowing Friedrich to become Friedrich III, King *in* Prussia (not *of* Prussia, as that would be to court trouble with Leopold's own domain of power), in return for alliance against France in the War of Spanish Succession. Friedrich had himself crowned in an elaborate ceremony at the Palace Church in Königsberg, the coronation city of the Prussian monarchy, and 18 January 1701 was a day of unparalleled excess. Some 30,000 horses transported the soon-to-be king, his family and his luggage. In the Elector's Chamber of the Palace Church, Friedrich sat on a throne built for the occasion,

BRANDENBURG
-PRUSSIA

0   100   200   300
KM

cloaked in scarlet, gold and diamonds. A small gathering of male
family members and senior officials watched him place the crown
on his own head, before proceeding into the next room to crown
his wife, Sophie Charlotte of Hanover, as queen.

The new king, as he would now be called, set about modernizing the city. In 1709, he issued a decree bringing Berlin, Cölln, Dorotheenstadt, Friedrichswerder and Friedrichstadt under a single magistrate, as the Royal Capital and Residence of Berlin, capital of the kingdom of Prussia. To give the city greater gravitas, Friedrich asked Schlüter, the architect responsible for the Royal Palace, to oversee the plans, declaring him court architect, court sculptor and director of the Prussian Academy of Arts.

Aesthetics combined with engineering. New building regulations stipulated that the roads had to be cobbled. Lanterns were installed; pigsties were no longer permitted within the city limits. A modern system of ravelins, moats and bastions, pioneered in France, was used to strengthen the early wooden customs walls. The first outlines of the centre of the city, and its two main arteries, began to emerge. Unter den Linden, the grandest boulevard, with six rows of linden trees, had existed since the sixteenth century as a bridle path to take kings and their entourage from the Royal Palace to their hunting grounds in the Tiergarten. Friedrichstrasse, the other great thoroughfare, was built to connect the existing areas to the new district of Dorotheenstadt. It was more than 3 kilometres in length, large enough for the royal army to use for marching practice.

Friedrich's rule left two great legacies. He established a hospital in 1709 in anticipation of an outbreak of the bubonic plague. The Charité is now Europe's leading teaching hospital and one of the best in the world. More than half of all German Nobel Prize winners, such as Robert Koch, Emil von Behring and Paul Ehrlich, have worked there. His other great gift to the city bears the name of his first wife. As with science, as with the arts, the real power behind the throne was the queen. Sophie Charlotte of Hanover was the younger sister of Georg Ludwig of Hanover, who succeeded to the British throne as George I. Shortly after their elaborate wedding in 1685, Friedrich gave her an estate in the village of Lietzow to the west of the city. It was an ideal location for a summer residence, surrounded by forest and accessible by boat along the Spree river. She immediately set about creating a garden and a palace in her image. She commissioned Siméon Godeau, a pupil of the famous court gardener of Versailles, André Le Nôtre, to lay out the most modern garden in the German-speaking world. From that point she took to travelling by boat from the Berlin Palace to Charlottenburg to the accompaniment of music and fireworks. Or she would take strolls through the manicured gardens with guests such as Gottfried Wilhelm Leibniz, with whom she would discuss mathematics and philosophy.

It took a while for the Lietzenburg Palace to be completed, but it instantly became one of the great courts. Sophie Charlotte played the harpsichord and spoke four languages; she invited poets, musicians and artists to join her at her 'court of the muses'. In 1702 the first opera in the city, Giovanni Bononcini's *Polifemo*, was performed before her and her guests at the palace. Such was Sophie Charlotte's star appeal it is said that a visiting Tsar Peter the Great couldn't muster the strength to speak when granted an audience with her and her mother. Even her husband was allowed to visit her there only by invitation. Her personal ambition was to make Berlin a centre of learning; she had barely begun to fulfil that pledge by the time of her early death from pneumonia in January 1705 at the age of just thirty-six. The king named the palace and the surrounding area Charlottenburg in her honour.

As with the Royal Palace on Unter den Linden, as with Oranienburg to the north of the city and the other estates built by successive kings, the popularity of Charlottenburg waxed and waned over the years. Ignored during much of the nineteenth and twentieth centuries – at times it has served as a theatre, a hospital and a seat of Berlin park management – it was heavily bombed in the Second World War. There then begins a remarkable story. With Berlin in a desperate state, Charlottenburg Palace was slated for demolition, only to be saved by a long-serving state official called Margarete Kühn. She was given the job by the four victorious powers, immediately on the Nazi surrender, of overseeing what was left of Berlin and Brandenburg's cultural estate. She made the case for the preservation of the major palaces. As Cold War tensions intensified, as the Soviets demolished a series of palaces in their sector, Kühn ended up working only for the Western Allies. She immediately halted plans to build a motorway on the site of the Charlottenburg Palace. Even though it was so heavily damaged, she prevailed upon the British, in whose sector it was situated, to preserve it. Restoration took two decades.

The palace, and its sculpted gardens leading on to a lake, forests and riverbank walks, are one of few places in Berlin that are classically beautiful, where you do not have to try hard to imagine past glories. I have walked and jogged many a time down its paths, beguiled by its elegance – and by the rarity of such elegance. The front of the palace, which now borders a main road, has far less to commend it – except for one piece of art. There now stands a commanding equestrian statue of the Great Elector, created by Schlüter in 1708, two months after his death. It was erected in a prime spot on one of the city's most famous bridges, the Lange Brücke, the old link between Berlin and Cölln near the Royal Palace, where it stayed for two and a half centuries.

At the onset of the Second World War, the statue was hidden away in a wharf at Lake Tegel in the north of the city and technically in West Berlin. In 1946 it was taken by a tug with the intention of returning it to its original site (in East Berlin), only for it to capsize and stay stuck in the lake. In 1949, Kühn and her colleagues decided to relocate it to the forecourt of Charlottenburg Palace, firmly back in the West. The communist authorities demanded it be returned; their counterparts in Charlottenburg flatly refused. This was one of the tensest times of the Cold War. Kühn's bravery and determination were recognized in 2005, ten years after her death, when a street in the district was named after her.

In the early 1990s, shortly after unification, the district council of Mitte asked more politely for it to be returned, but their request was once again denied. The Great Elector, the man who rebuilt Berlin after the Thirty Years War, who opened up the city to all-comers and transformed Berlin for the first time into a European city, if not yet a world city, still has pride of place in the Court of Honour of Charlottenburg Palace.

FIVE

The torments of hell

The Soldier King and militarism

Berlin makes the most repugnant impression on me.
It is cold, crude and massive – a real barracks.
ROSA LUXEMBURG (1898)

When he was ten years old, as crown prince, Friedrich Wilhelm (yes, another one) was given a Christmas present by his father; it was not your usual gift, even for a noble, but it was something he would always cherish.

The castle at Königs Wusterhausen was first recorded in 1320 when Jutta von Kranichfeld, abbess of the Quedlinburg convent, gave the moated 'hus to wusterhausen' to the Dukes of Saxony as a fief. It subsequently belonged to a succession of noble families in the Mark Brandenburg. From the late fifteenth century, it was in the hands of the Schenken von Landsbergs. The family ran into financial trouble at the end of the Thirty Years War and were forced to sell to Friedrich von Jena, a university professor and member of the privy council of the Great Elector. The next elector, Friedrich, took it over, had it refurbished and, on 24 December 1698, handed it to his son.

Königs Wusterhausen is now a little-visited attraction in an unremarkable suburb to the southeast of Berlin, just beyond the airport, but it shines a fascinating light on asceticism, militarism and the ideological swings between fathers and sons which defined the Hohenzollern dynasty.

As soon as he came of age, Friedrich Wilhelm developed the castle as a hunting lodge, where he spent every August, September and October, no matter the other calls on his time. For his autumn pleasure, he insisted on killing thousands of birds. He became so obsessed with the pastime that he was known to have fired around 600 shots a day. His real passion, however, was boars – huge ones, some weighing up to 270 kilograms – which he hunted with hounds. In one year alone, 1729, he slaughtered no fewer than 3,600. Inside the palace, the walls were adorned with two artistic themes, military and hunting, including a succession of pictures of foxes being driven into an enclosure and clubbed to death.

When he wasn't butchering animals, Friedrich Wilhelm was preparing for his reign. He had to wait a while, another decade, for his father to die. This was a period which fluctuated wildly between cultural enlightenment and repression, between high spending and austerity. He was the opposite of his father. All around him he saw a realm that was louche – and pretty much broke. From the seclusion of Wusterhausen, he developed new ideas for his future austerity-based administration.

While still crown prince, he commanded his first infantry regiment, Number 6, created just for himself. It was later renamed the Royal Bodyguard Regiment. He had a particular predilection for *Lange Kerle*, the tall guys, and had them recruited from all around Europe, offering large bonuses to his scouts for finding good ones. He took up painting and made sure that three dozen of his pictures of these dashing men would adorn a wall in his palace. They remain there to this day.

On ascending the throne in 1713, he dismantled every facet of his father's court. The jewels, silverware and furniture were sold off; silk bedding was replaced by rough cloth. Extravagant banquets were replaced by functional dinners served on a wooden table. He described the various intellectuals and philosophers who had set up shop at court as 'dog food'. They were summarily banished from the palace. Two-thirds of the servants at court were sacked without notice. The new king's priorities were military and administration reform. He dictated the manual of *Regulations for State Officials*, containing thirty-five sections and 297 paragraphs in which every public servant in Prussia could find his duties precisely set out: a minister or councillor failing to attend a committee meeting, for example, would lose six months' pay.

Friedrich Wilhelm I would come to be known as the 'Soldier King' – even though he would never start a war. He considered them extravagant. Nor would he, unlike his predecessors, build himself or his queen a palace. He was quite happy with the one he had inherited.

The Soldier King turned Berlin into a garrison, developing a standing army of 80,000 and establishing an arms industry that could rival the best in Europe. He decreed that all new houses had to include an attic so that troops could be billeted. The army did much more than prepare for war. They were the police, night watchmen, firemen and street cleaners. They provided the labour force for building projects. Friedrich Wilhelm appeared in public only in uniform and expected men of any reputation to do the same. Spies were deployed to monitor the behaviour of his subjects. Control freak that he was, the king was known to walk the streets disguised as a commoner, and beat up men who looked idle or not smartly dressed. Such was the unrelenting discipline, many soldiers tried to desert by fleeing the city. The king's response? To punish them and to reinforce the fortifications to stop them getting out – just as the GDR would go on to do three hundred years later.

The Soldier King sought to rip up, in some cases literally, many of the refinements of the city. One of those was the Lustgarten. The story of this once-swampy patch of land next to the Royal Palace epitomizes Berlin's lurch from militarism to liberalism, from asceticism to aestheticism and back many times. In the late sixteenth century, Elector Johann Georg – not known for very much except extorting punitive taxes from the peasantry on behalf of the tax-avoiding nobility – had it drained to create room for a fruit and herb garden. The Great Elector was the first to see the potential beauty of the plot. He had it transformed into his personal pleasure garden (it was named the 'Lustgarten' in 1646), decorating it with fountains and sculptures. Fifty years later, the Soldier King wanted it for a different purpose. He uprooted the monuments and dug up the grass, covering it all with sand to turn it into a parade ground. His son Friedrich the Great then made it more beautiful again. Now, as it fronts onto the glorious buildings of the Museum Island, it is where hundreds of people sunbathe in the summer, kick footballs around or play music. As I watched a group taking part in a salsa class one balmy early evening, on the place where soldiers would once parade, I asked myself: where else but Berlin?

The Soldier King wanted his territory demarcated with proper borders. The first ramparts, erected half a century earlier, were now deteriorating and so he ordered that a customs and excise wall be built to encircle the city. He wanted it to be a significant structure, to prevent unauthorized entry and exit, to control the comings and goings of his subjects and also to maximize revenues into the depleted state coffers. Sounds familiar? The Akzisemauer, 15 kilometres long and 3 metres tall, took three years to build and was completed right at the end of his reign. The first wall had fourteen gates, each one closely guarded. Four more would be added in the nineteenth century. Each was named after the city or area to which the road led: Schlesisches Tor, Kottbusser Tor, Hallesches Tor. The gates were opened half an hour before sunrise and closed half an hour before sunset at the sound of a bell. At night, the two narrow entry points on the Spree were blocked with tree trunks covered in metal spikes to prevent smuggling. One of those was the Oberbaumbrücke, Upper Tree Bridge. The red-brick bridge connecting Kreuzberg in the West with Friedrichshain in the East was barred shut again three centuries later in communist times. It is now one of the busiest intersections in the city, with the Mercedes-Benz Arena, the venue for large pop concerts, on one side, and the headquarters of Universal Music on the other.

In much of the centre of Berlin, the walls of these two eras followed the same contours.

The Berlin of the mid-eighteenth century continued to grow; it was home to some 113,000 people, of which 20,000 were soldiers, a high proportion even by the standards of Berlin's more militaristic eras. New streets were built, in the manner of the king. He wanted a grand, but also ascetic and God-fearing city. Through his court architect, Philipp Gerlach, the Soldier King oversaw the construction of nine new churches, all but one of which was destroyed in the Second World War. The one that survived is the Sophienkirche, named after his stepmother, Sophie Luise. I have always found the Sophie Church, with its green spire and copper dome, one of the most evocative in the city, not least because it was from this church's pulpit that Martin Luther King delivered a sermon during communist times.

The Soldier King left his mark on Berlin, though in a far less ostentatious way than most of Prussia's rulers, overseeing the building of town houses and schools, barracks, hospitals and poorhouses. In the early years of his reign, almost 1,000 houses were built in Potsdam in what would later become known as the first baroque city expansion. After his father's death in 1713, he halted plans for the transformation of the east wing of the Königsberg Castle into an elaborate baroque complex. He hardly

**BERLIN
CUSTOMS WALL
1734**
(Modern Berlin roads and districts shown in white)

0   500   1000   1500   2000

Metres

ever used Charlottenburg Palace, choosing instead to live in Potsdam.

Whereas the Great Elector had been urbane and mild-mannered and spoke French and Polish; and Friedrich I, for all his profligacy, had been cultured and urbane, the next in line barely managed to master written German. The Soldier King had a contempt for all things French, sometimes flying into a rage at the mention of that country. He valued some foreigners, but only if they showed humility and worked hard. In 1732, he invited Protestants fleeing the Catholic Archbishopric of Salzburg – hard-working, ascetic folk, he assumed – to settle in Prussia, offering them free land, supplies and a period of tax exemption. He personally greeted the first group of immigrants in Königsberg and sang hymns with them.

A few years later, in 1737, the Soldier King allowed in another group of Protestants, this time cast out from Bohemia by Charles VI of Austria. The first families settled not in the swankier parts of town, Dorotheenstadt or Friedrichstadt, as the Dutch and French had done, but quite some distance away. In the late thirteenth century, the Knights Templar, an elite religious order expelled from the Kingdom of Jerusalem, created a settlement south of Berlin on an unpopulated plain. They called it Tempelhove (the Temple Court). Later they established a second outpost: the first recorded mention of Richardsdorp (one can only assume that one among their number was called Richard) was in 1360. At some point it was taken over by the rival Order of St John.

Initially eighteen colonizer families from Bohemia, most from a single village (as it was then) called Ústí nad Orlicí, to the east of Prague, created a community in Richardsdorp. Nine semi-detached houses were built between Richardstrasse and Kirchgasse, each one housing two families. Each family received two horses, two cows and farming equipment. The existing community resented the new arrivals, not least for the tax exemptions they enjoyed, and for the homesteads, houses and fields they had received gratis from the king. A further twenty houses were built between 1748 and 1751 as Berlin's Bohemian population grew. They became the model industrious immigrants.

Rixdorf, as it came to be known, is one of the precious few parts of Berlin where you can still appreciate the truly old, sandwiched between Karl-Marx-Strasse and Sonnenallee, two of Neukölln's noisiest, party-loving streets. The Bohemian Village, as it is called, still contains a small number of half-timbered houses (others were destroyed by a fire that engulfed the area in 1849 and then by bombing in the Second World War). In the middle of the village stands an old blacksmith's, which dates to 1624 and still produces ironware. Of all Rixdorf's curiosities, my favourite is its museum, housed in a former boarding school for boys whose parents set sail for Africa as Protestant missionaries, which is open every second Sunday for two hours at lunchtime. Susanne Lehmann, one of the volunteers, takes me around its two rooms, pointing out its weaving loom and cabinets of old books, folkloric costumes and musical instruments. Her forebears arrived in the eighteenth century from Bohemia; her husband's family were Huguenots. Yet she doesn't speak Czech, and he has no French. As with all the Protestant migrants from different parts of Europe, the Bohemians gradually assimilated. The last-known Czech speaker in Rixdorf died around 1900, yet, remarkably, despite everything that Berlin endured in the twentieth century, the small community has left a small trace.

One tradition now endangered is the annual Bohemian hay-bale rolling competition, called Popráci. Before 1911, 174 competitions are said to have taken place. The event then disappeared, only to be revived in 2008. In 2022, the festival was cancelled for the third year in a row, initially due to Covid, then to a lack of funding.

So grateful were the Bohemians for the Soldier King's support that in 1912 they erected a statue to him, to mark 175 years since the first Bohemian settlement. On the pedestal, it is written: 'The grateful descendants of the Bohemians taken in here.' It is curious to think of the Soldier King, of all people, still standing in multicultural, modern Neukölln. Pretty much everything about him would, one would think, be considered anathema by contemporary Berlin.

In 1706, he married his first cousin, Sophie Dorothea of Hanover, the younger sister of England's George II. Unsurprisingly theirs was a cold, unhappy relationship. She feared and resented him, both for allowing her no influence or independence at court, and for refusing to pair off her children to their English cousins. His notoriously short temper sometimes led him to hit his servants (and sometimes his own children) with a cane at the slightest perceived provocation. Gout, obesity and crippling stomach pains did not help his mood. Only those who kept on the right side of the king, who were disciplined and frugal, escaped his wrath.

What the queen hated most was being carted off to the hunting lodge at Königs Wusterhausen, the king's realm in microcosm. Unlike the Royal Palace, Charlottenburg or Oranienburg, there was nothing remotely inviting about this place. Austerity and simplicity were its hallmarks: thick walls, painted chalk white with an ochre base and floors covered with square slabs of fired clay. His bedchamber, with a cross vault, was one of the smallest and simplest rooms in the palace. His wife's quarters were bigger, but only slightly.

The two rooms he cared most about were on the top floor. He enjoyed showing visitors the officers' gallery, inviting them to marvel at his portraits of the 'tall guys', all dressed in identical uniform and striking the same pose. His favourite room, next door, was where he convened his *Tabakskollegium* (Tobacco Cabinet). Every evening when the king was in residence, up to a dozen of his councillors gathered to sit around a long rectangular oak table. There they indulged in an interminable smoking marathon and discussion about the politics of the day (Germans retain a curious tolerance towards tobacco). All that remains today is a reproduction of the table and a painting, attributed to a Polish artist, Georg Lisiewski, some chairs, a coin jug and silver statuette. All are derivative. The picture, reproduced in many a history textbook in Germany, shows the Soldier King and three of his four young sons seated among courtiers inhaling from long pipes. The room is dimly lit and barely furnished, save for a few unclear portraits hanging high on the wall. The king's entourage sit on simple wooden benches at a long oak table, each figure homogenous and expressionless. At the end of the table, directly opposite the king, a stiff, phantom-like hare watches over the gathering, presumably one of the king's hunting prizes. The king's oldest surviving son and heir is conspicuously absent.

For his family, sojourns at the hunting lodge were a duty to be submitted to. Wilhelmine, one of six surviving daughters, wrote of life there: 'I had to endure only the pains of purgatory, but in Wusterhausen the torments of hell.' She added:

> My sisters and I, with our suites, were lodged in two rooms which resembled a hospital far more than rooms in a palace. We always dined in a tent, whatever the weather might be. Sometimes, when it rained, we sat up to our ankles in water. The dinner always numbered twenty-four persons, half of whom had to starve, for there were never more than six dishes served, and these were so meagre that one hungry being might easily have eaten them up alone. We had to spend the whole day shut up in the Queen's room, and were not allowed to get any fresh air, even when the weather was fine. It was a wonder we did not get bilious from sitting in-doors all day long, and hearing nothing but disagreeable speeches.

Apart from one man, nobody loved Königs Wusterhausen – neither his family, nor his successors. After his rule, it fell into neglect, to come back into fashion briefly towards the end of the nineteenth century under Kaiser Wilhelm II, the final Hohenzollern king, who was every bit as obsessive about hunting as the Soldier King. At the age of forty-three, he erected a monument to commemorate his 50,000th kill, a white pheasant cockerel; he presided over the final hunt there in 1913. After the fall of the monarchy in 1918, Wusterhausen was run as a museum by the Prussian Palace Department; during the Second World War it served as a military hospital and a storage depot for art from the Hohenzollern Museum at Monbijou Palace. After some basic restoration, it was first used as a local headquarters for the Soviet military authorities and for six years served as a barracks for a signals unit. The baroque garden fell into disrepair, at times filled with building rubbish and landfill.

The hunting lodge therefore followed the pattern of other royal palaces, a cycle of royal occupancy, vacancy, disrepair, use for other purposes and – in some cases – restoration. Wusterhausen has now been meticulously restored, but with modern housing occupying the hunting grounds around it, visitors must work hard to imagine the remoteness of the lodge and the bloodlust of the Soldier King.

The king and his queen had fourteen children in all (four died in infancy). He became consumed by the need to mould his oldest surviving son, Friedrich: to lick his heir into shape, whatever the cost. He had him woken each morning by the firing of a cannon. At the age of seven, young Fritz was given his own miniature arsenal. Whenever he failed to display the required prowess, whenever he fell off his horse, he was beaten. Sophie Dorothea abhorred the cruelty and quietly encouraged her son to show defiance. He did so through a special relationship he had with a man eight years his elder. It is not known when Friedrich met Hans Hermann von Katte, an army lieutenant. They attended mathematics classes together (something the king deemed acceptable); they also shared an interest in poetry and music (subjects the king deemed effete). Friedrich assembled a secret *Wunderkammer*, his own cabinet of curiosities; he read Aristotle and Rabelais. Katte became Friedrich's tutor and, so the assumption goes, his lover. The king was annoyed by the tutor's presence and flew into a rage whenever he saw books stashed away in his son's quarters.

Friedrich made secret plans to escape to England, either for a quieter life or to enlist the help of his uncle, King George II, to topple his own father. Katte initially tried to dissuade him, then, when he realized the young man's mind was made up, agreed to help. On 5 August 1730, Friedrich escaped from his quarters while the royal retinue was near Mannheim. A letter appeared at court and made its way to the king, unmasking Katte as an accomplice. The two fugitives were swiftly found and arrested and sent to the fortress at Küstrin. Katte was sentenced to life imprisonment. Enraged at the leniency, the Soldier King signed a decree insisting on execution. Friedrich, by then eighteen years old, was forced to watch the execution of his friend – beheaded with a sword while kneeling on a heap of sand – from his prison cell. It is said that moments before Katte's execution, Friedrich shouted in French to him, 'Please forgive me, my dear Katte, in God's name, forgive me,' to which Katte is said to have replied, 'There is nothing to forgive, I die for you with joy in my heart.' At which point Friedrich fainted. Katte lies buried in a simple wooden coffin in a church in Wust, a village west of Berlin. It is said that for a few decades after his death, it was not uncommon for a local guide to lift the lid and show visitors the neatly severed bone in Katte's neck.

There are two ways in which this story has been told since; the one that focuses on teenage passion and an abusive father, and the other one somewhat different. Made in the early period of the Weimar Republic, in 1922, the film *Fridericus Rex* glorified the Prussian myth of the strong military man; unsurprisingly, it went on to become a favourite of the Nazis. According to this version, the young man watches the execution of Katte from behind bars, but quickly gets over his grief and finds some inner steel. Three months after his lover's execution, Friedrich is granted a royal pardon and released from his cell, though he remains stripped of his military rank and is forced to remain a while at Küstrin. Son thanks father for instilling discipline in him, bows to his will and devotes the next ten years to his military and government apprenticeship in the War and Estates Department. Just over a year later, he is finally allowed to return to Berlin on condition that he marries the seventeen-year-old Elisabeth Christine of Brunswick-Bevern, a nuptial that cements the links between Prussia and Austria (Friedrich would, despite his wife's origins, declare war on Austria, but that is for later). The original plan, hatched by his mother, was to marry off both Friedrich and his sister to two of the children of England's King George II, but that was deemed to be strategically inopportune. Although he did his best to ignore his new wife (and women in general), Friedrich found one early use for her: her piety endeared her to her father-in-law, thereby consolidating the reconciliation between son and father.

In a review of *Fridericus Rex* at the time of its release, the *New York Times* warned that it would be 'used to stir up passions that were just about to settle down'. It added, presciently, 'The picture remains a dangerous one – dangerous to the internal peace of Germany only, to be sure. For none but a German audience, fed and grown fat on a tradition of militarism and serfdom, could find anything admirable in the life and times of Friedrich Wilhelm.'

The Soldier King died in 1740 at the age of fifty-one. He was buried not in Berlin, not at Wusterhausen, but at the Garrison Church in Potsdam which he had built five years earlier. During the Second World War, to protect it from the Allied advance,

Hitler ordered his coffin to be taken to the Bernterode salt mine where some of the most important monuments and art treasures had been hidden. The Garrison Church was bombed and then demolished by the East Germans. For half a century, the Soldier King's plain coffin was moved around between the states of Hesse and Baden-Württemberg; the original black marble sarcophagus was destroyed in all the upheaval, to be replaced by a simpler copper one. In 1991, he was finally laid to rest in the grounds of Potsdam's Sanssouci Palace, in the mausoleum of the Church of Peace, one of the most remarkable and underappreciated places of worship in all of Brandenburg.

The Soldier King remains an unloved figure. In 1978, the GDR historian Heinz Kathe accused him of contributing personally to 'Brandenburg-Prussia playing the most destructive role of all the German territorial states'. West German journalist Wolfgang Venohr attempted to rehabilitate him in his 1988 biography, praising him as 'the first protector and promoter of human rights in the 18th century', who 'made Prussia the most progressive state in Europe'. That remains a niche view.

Insofar as Berliners know much about him, it is the story of the ascetic, manic hunter that is most told, a comic figure sandwiched between the two more prepossessing monarchs, the Great Elector and Friedrich the Great. Yet he did have an ambition that had its own logic, if inimical (to put it mildly) to contemporary mores.

Aside from Rixdorf, the only other statue of him is a peculiar replica, a small paunchy figure on a raised dais, on Linienstrasse in Mitte, just metres away from the Volksbühne, the proudly radical theatre. It is easy to miss, unless you walk straight past it to go to the doctor's surgery or the sushi restaurant next door. It is a copy of an original bronze work erected in 1796 in the grounds of Monbijou, one of the Hohenzollerns' most beautiful city palaces that was pulled down after Second World War bombing. The replica was made as part of an exhibit called 'Monument for Historical Change – Fragments from the Basement of History' in 2004, involving reproductions of five Berlin monuments from different periods. Alongside the Soldier King stands a reproduction of a monument to the Spanish Civil War and to a Jewish Second World War resistance group.

Linienstrasse is now the epicentre of contemporary hipster Berlin. The Soldier King is surrounded on one side by the Soho House members' club, on another by the offices of the socialist youth newspaper, *Junge Welt*, and on a third by a cafe that advertises its speciality drink, adzuki matcha latte with ice cream. He stands on his own, a graffiti-ridden perspex sign serving as the only guide. One time when I walked past him, I saw that his left nostril was covered in a yellow bird-dropping. When I went back to check a couple of years later, in late 2022, it was still there. Was Berlin sending him a message?

SIX

Sparta and Athens

The era of Friedrich the Great

Berlin, the greatest cultural extravaganza that one could imagine.
DAVID BOWIE (1976)

In the centre of Unter den Linden stands a colossal equestrian statue. Friedrich the Great is astride a trotting horse, resplendent in his military uniform and ermine coat and with his characteristic tricorn hat. He is looking imperiously yet also benignly to his left: the perfectly cultivated image of Prussian valour.

The statue stands nearly six metres tall, mounted on a giant multi-layered plinth that is even higher. Just below him are reliefs of the four cardinal virtues – moderation, justice, courage and prudence. The larger pedestal below them depicts life-size figures of seventy-four famous men of his time. All but fourteen of them are from the military. Among the scientists, authors, poets and diplomats are two philosophers, Immanuel Kant and Gotthold Ephraim Lessing. They are surrounded by further representations of the king in different scenes – seated on a fountain contemplating the changing fate of the war, playing the flute, sitting on an eagle, scenes of his education by Greek gods. The sculpture, by Christian Daniel Rauch, an important classicist sculptor of his time, was unveiled in 1851 during one of the many cyclical upsurges in conservatism. A century later it was removed by the communists, only to be reinstated thirty years later. The historical judgement of Friedrich the Great goes to the heart of what it means to be German, and what it means to be a Berliner.

In 1740, at the age of twenty-eight and exactly a decade after watching his tutor beheaded, Friedrich assumed the throne. He was the opposite of his father – intellectually curious and craving the company of musicians, artists and philosophers. In one respect, though, he emulated him, indeed arguably surpassed him – in his desire to turn Berlin and Prussia into a military great power.

In a reign of almost half a century, and unlike the Soldier King, Friedrich presided over a series of campaigns. Within months of becoming king, he launched an unprovoked invasion of Silesia (then part of the Habsburg empire, now in southwestern Poland). He quickly occupied almost all of it, seizing control of the Oder river to the east. Through a combination of brute force, treaties and alliances, he expanded Prussia's territory and power at Austria's expense. The Empress Maria Theresa had ascended to the Habsburg throne in the same year that Friedrich became King in Prussia (he would later declare himself King *of* Prussia after the First Partition of Poland in 1772). She was young and politically vulnerable, her father, the Holy Roman Emperor Charles VI, having died without a male heir. Friedrich's sustained attacks on Silesia were part of the wider War of the Austrian Succession that preoccupied most of Europe and beyond. Maria Theresa saw Friedrich's actions as a personal attack on her and the Habsburg dynasty, referring to him as 'that evil man'.

Which wasn't how his own people saw him. It is said that after the signing of the Treaty of Dresden in December 1745, which ended the second of Friedrich's three Silesian campaigns, he was welcomed back to Berlin with cries of 'Long live Friedrich the

Great!' The term stuck. After fighting wars with Austria, Russia, Saxony, Poland, France and Bavaria, he expanded Prussian territory by a third. He commanded his forces at sixteen major battles, frequently leading them from the front. He had inherited from his father a strong army and a healthy treasury, but by the end of the campaigns, largely but not invariably successful, his military and financial reserves had both been exhausted. At its lowest points, in 1757 and 1760, Berlin was briefly invaded by the Austrians, Russians and Saxons. They had to be paid off to leave.

His military campaigns were part of a wider strategy to make Prussia a great power, with Berlin at its heart. As Friedrich wrote in his 'Political Testament', written first in 1752 and subsequently revised, 'the power of Prussia is not founded on any intrinsic wealth but uniquely on the efforts of industry.' The document, intended to be confidential and only for his successors, was published in 1920 after the downfall of the Hohenzollerns and the establishment of the Weimar Republic. It provides a compelling insight into notions of the duties of leadership: 'A well-conducted government must have a system as coherent as a system of philosophy; all measures taken must be based on sound reasoning, and finance, policy, and military must collaborate toward one aim, the strengthening of the State and the increase of its power. But a system can be the product of only one brain; it must consequently be that of the sovereign.' The testament shows that his father's disciplinarianism and asceticism had left a mark: 'Idleness, self-indulgence, or weakness are the causes which prevent a Prince from working on the noble task of creating the happiness of his people. Such sovereigns make themselves so contemptible that they become the butts and laughing stocks of their contemporaries, and in history books their names are useful only for the dates.'

Friedrich did not deviate from the long Hohenzollern line of absolutist leaders, albeit in his case an enlightened one. He abolished torture (except for the flogging of soldiers for desertion) and did away with the relentless command and control of all aspects of everyday life that his father had introduced.

Friedrich is remembered perhaps more than anything for his patronage of the arts, leading Voltaire to describe Berlin as 'Sparta in the morning and Athens in the afternoon'. This period came to be called the Berlin Enlightenment, an era of extraordinary cultural blossoming, a confused web of relationships involving a monarch and his self-styled *roi philosophe*, Voltaire. Intellectual societies appeared across the city. Drama groups grew in popularity, culminating in the establishment of the Nationaltheater in 1786. At the heart of this social and intellectual matrix were the philosopher Moses Mendelssohn, and the hostesses of the great salons, Henriette Herz and Rahel Varnhagen. They were Jews (though on marriage Varnhagen converted to Christianity).

The king set about turning Berlin into a great European centre of art, music, science and thought. In 1744, he reopened the Academy of Sciences, which had been shut down by his father, inviting the French mathematician and philosopher Pierre Louis Maupertuis to be its president. He devoured books, but German was a cultural blind spot for him. He denounced the language as 'semi barbarian' in which it was 'physically impossible' for an author of any standing to achieve any form of aesthetic greatness. He considered German culture inferior to French in every way. 'We are emerging from barbarism and are still in our cradles,' he said to his sister Wilhelmine. 'But the French have already gone a long way and are a century ahead of us in every kind of success.'

He didn't think much of Goethe, because he wrote in German. He called one of his first works, *Götz von Berlichingen*, a play based on the memoirs of the eponymous sixteenth-century Swabian imperial knight which had just opened to great plaudits, an 'abominable imitation of those bad English plays'. Goethe, who visited Berlin only once in his life, reciprocated in kind, describing one of Friedrich's military parades in the city as a 'monstrous piece of clockwork'. Friedrich was by no means unique in his Francophilia; much of eighteenth-century Germany looked to France as the model of culture and civilization, with many lesser royals across the wider realm adopting French habits. Young men across the German lands were sent by their fathers to Paris to learn the art of conversation and wit, to stamp out any vestiges of coarse Germanness. It mattered because by now Berlin mattered. The king took music extremely seriously. It is said he played the flute so much that his teeth eventually fell out. His teacher, composer Johann Joachim Quantz, was paid 2,000 thalers a year (about £46,000 in today's money, adjusted for inflation), making him one of the most highly paid state officials.

Historians have long debated the relationship with Voltaire. In 1736, the intellectually curious young prince began corresponding with the French philosopher, eighteen years his senior, asking him to send copies of his works. Several years and countless letters later, and now as king, Friedrich invited Voltaire to take up residence at the royal estate, instructing him to review his own essays and erotic poems. His muse flattered him outrageously, but it was a tumultuous relationship. They had a series of arguments, falling out spectacularly when the king heard that Voltaire had been making fun of his writing behind his back. Friedrich had him arrested for six weeks, before they patched up that particular quarrel.

Voltaire's 1759 *Mémoires*, written after the philosopher had been removed, once and for all, from Friedrich's entourage, described a state of homosexual debauchery in the king's court. After Friedrich's death, his court physician Johann Georg Zimmermann wrote in detail about the king's 'supposed Grecian taste in love'. The level of interest in, and views of, Friedrich the Great's private life has waxed and waned, influenced largely by the mores of the time. The nineteenth-century English writer

Thomas Carlyle dismissed it all as a 'thrice-abominable rumour', whereas during the Weimar Republic, Friedrich was frequently looked to as something of a gay icon.

What is beyond doubt was Friedrich's disdain for women; very few were admitted into his entourage. He reserved a particular scorn for his wife, whom he was forced to marry by his father, the Soldier King. He described Elisabeth Christine as 'this incorrigibly sour subspecies of the female sex'. He dispatched an emissary to find a place where he could banish her. The Palace of Schönhausen was suggested, suitably far away to the north. Just under a century earlier, a countess and scion of a Dutch family acquired the land to build a manor; a few decades later the property was acquired by the Hohenzollerns as a summer residence, only to fall into disrepair. When it was brought to Friedrich's attention, he ordered its immediate refurbishment in order to exile his wife there as quickly as possible. Schönhausen became the home and court for Elisabeth Christine for more than fifty years. It was not used again by royalty after her death. The Nazis would later find a purpose for it, as a place to store more than 1,000 works of art they deemed 'degenerate'. Then, after the war, it became the official residence of the East German head of state for two decades and then a guest house for visiting fraternal dignitaries such as Fidel Castro and Leonid Brezhnev. Now it is a somewhat forgettable exhibition space and multi-purpose government building; since 2004, the Federal Academy for Security Policy has been housed in some of its outbuildings. Its biggest claim to fame is that it was the venue for one round of 'round-table' unification negotiations in 1989–90. The table around which the politicians sat is actually rectangular.

Another sorry tale, but at least the palace survived to become one of several destinations on the Berlin and Brandenburg tourist trail. Not so Monbijou, in the centre of the city, by the river. To go back slightly: after the devastation of the Thirty Years War, the

Great Elector ordered that a rural estate be built on what was then vacant land, partly to alleviate the hunger that was continuing to grip his people. The realm's first ever potatoes were grown in the garden. The property was first used by one of his consorts, later by the long-suffering wife of the Soldier King, Sophie Dorothea. Even though it was relatively spartan, it was a joy compared to the killing fields of Königs Wusterhausen.

Friedrich the Great invited his mother to stay on at the lodge, instructing one of his favourite architects, Georg Wenzeslaus von Knobelsdorff, to improve on it, to construct something more beautiful. Between 1738 and 1742, Knobelsdorff oversaw the expansion of the five-room lodge into a vast, symmetrical palace with grand side wings and small pavilions around it. Sophie Dorothea called it *mon bijou*, my jewel. She spent the summer months there, giving concerts, dinners and masked balls, pleasures previously forbidden during her late husband's reign. The palace had its own jetty, allowing guests to arrive in far greater comfort via boat than by carriage on the rough roads. Beautiful as it was, for nearly two centuries after Sophie Dorothea's death it was seldom used. Almost destroyed in the Second World War, it was converted briefly into a museum of the Hohenzollern dynasty, before the GDR authorities announced it was being pulled down, to the consternation of many. One of the most prominent critics of the decision was the veteran director general of state museums, Ludwig Justi (long-time director of the National Gallery until demoted by the Nazis in 1933). He was assured that the ruins would be preserved, but immediately after his death in 1959, the government went back on its word and demolished it entirely. Now the area is a park, with a football pitch and an open-air theatre which performs Shakespeare. The riverbank alongside is transformed in the summer months to a dance floor for salsa and tango evenings.

One place mattered to the king more than any, and it was not

Berlin. Friedrich the Great inherited his father's love of the serenity of Potsdam, but he wanted to turn it into something far more than a garrison. He had retained his father's court architect, Knobelsdorff, a man who had earned the respect of the Soldier King by resigning his officer's commission and retraining as an architect. The new king disliked the coldness of the Royal Palace of Berlin, as many of his predecessors and successors did. He wanted a summer palace, far enough away to offer sanctuary from the many travails of the big city but close enough to provide him access if he needed it. He called it Sanssouci (French, naturally), which means 'without a care'. It was his 'dream palace', but that didn't stop him firing Knobelsdorff and replacing him mid-project with the Dutchman, Bouman. He was obsessed with getting it right and took personal charge of fitting it out. Friedrich spent as much time as he could in his beloved palace. Such was his desire to create a new life for himself at his retreat, he prohibited his wife from visiting him there.

The more dominant a force Friedrich became across Europe, the more he realized that no matter how endearing it was, this single-storey Potsdam residence of barely ten rooms was below his station. To keep up appearances, he ordered the construction of something considerably grander elsewhere in the grounds. The New Palace had the size and the ornamental design to rival Versailles, but he used it only for functions. It quickly fell into disuse; only Friedrich III used it again – and he lasted just three months as king in 1888. Most of the time, the New Palace has been a museum. As for Sanssouci, after Friedrich's reign it was also little used. Friedrich's great-great-nephew, Friedrich Wilhelm IV, sought to revive its spirit in the late 1840s and early 1850s, if only to escape the whirlwind of revolutionary Berlin.

The king saw expansion of the workforce as key to a thriving economy and public life. He accelerated immigration not just from among the Huguenots and the Dutch, whose diligence and productivity had already been proven, but also from further afield. Colonization agencies opened in Hamburg, Frankfurt, Regensburg, Amsterdam and Geneva. Recruitment drives were launched for wool spinners and skilled labourers in the silk, hat and leather industries. Immigration was built into the growth model.

An early exponent of state corporatism, or public-private partnerships, Friedrich set up a series of administrative bodies complicated even by German standards. More than a tenth of his workforce became bureaucrats in organizations such as the Royal Firewood Administration Office, the Fire Society and the Commission for Royal Buildings, alongside welfare organizations such as the Invalidenhaus for disabled soldiers, the Institute for Poor Widows and the Public Alms Houses. At the same time, Friedrich invested heavily in technologies, from water pumps to new forms of glass-making. He provided tax incentives for industry ranging from textile mills to cannon foundries. In 1751, he granted a wool manufacturer, Wilhelm Caspar Wegely, the royal privilege to set up a porcelain manufactory in Berlin. The company was granted exemptions from import duties for essential materials and was protected against all competition. Despite the help and patronage, the Royal Porcelain Manufactory, or KPM as it is better known, continued to struggle financially. So, in 1763, the king nationalized it, purchasing the factory for 225,000 thalers (around £5 million today) and taking over its staff of 146 workers. KPM was permitted to use the royal sceptre as its symbol. It became a model business (or so the legend goes): no child labour, regular working hours, above-average incomes, secure pensions, a healthcare fund and assistance for widows and orphans. The king called himself its 'best customer', commissioning an entire dinner service for Sanssouci.

Nearly three centuries on, the Manufactory is still going

strong, seeing itself in similar patrician terms, as does much of the *Mittelstand*, the army of successful mid-size German family businesses on which much of the country's post-war wealth was built. KPM's modern Berlin headquarters is part foundry, part museum, teaching tour groups about 'the secrets of producing white gold'. In 2006, the company almost went under and had to be saved by Jörg Woltmann, a banker who put in millions of his own cash to become the sole shareholder. Fifteen years later, in the general election of September 2021, he hosted the closing rally of the Free Democrats (FDP), Germany's only unequivocally free-market party which, though small, is a member of the ruling coalition. The audience was very un-Berlin, or rather they were Berliners of a new minority group: well-groomed women in high heels and well-kempt men in black polo necks and shiny brogues. During a love-in with the party's leader, and now finance minister, Christian Lindner, Woltmann declared that if Friedrich the Great had still been alive, he would have voted for the FDP. I get the impression that the king had somewhat loftier ambitions.

Even though he spent much of his time in his beloved Potsdam, the king oversaw the building of many Berlin landmarks – monuments to rococo and neoclassicism. He used architecture and city planning to project the authority of the state. He attributed much of the city's progress to his grandfather, the Great Elector. '*Celui-ci a fait de grandes choses,*' he said of him.

The new opera house designed by Knobelsdorff was one of the largest in Europe, seating 2,000 people. This was part of an ensemble of public buildings that bordered the Forum Fridericianum (now Bebelplatz). Flanking it would be St Hedwig's, the first Catholic church to be built in the city since the Reformation, to cater for new arrivals from Silesia. The building, also designed by Knobelsdorff, was modelled after the Pantheon in Rome. Construction started in 1747; in time-honoured Berlin fashion, deadlines were repeatedly missed, and it was not opened until 1773. With its classical portico, it is a strikingly simple building, one that served as a monument to religious tolerance. In his evening prayers the night after the pogroms of November 1938, Bernhard Lichtenberg, a canon at the church, prayed publicly for Jews and condemned the Nazis' eugenics programme. He was arrested by the Gestapo and died on the way to Dachau. In 1965 his remains were transferred to the crypt at St Hedwig's. In 1996, during a visit to Berlin, Pope John Paul II beatified Lichtenberg. In 2004, Yad Vashem, Israel's Holocaust Remembrance Centre, honoured him as a 'righteous among the nations', a recognition given to non-Jews.

Knobelsdorff was also instructed by the king to revamp the Tiergarten. In 1742, the fences of the hunting grounds were torn down and the area was transformed into a park that all Berliners could access irrespective of class. Flowerbeds, ornamental ponds and mazes were introduced; a pheasant house was erected inside the park, which would later become the core of the city's zoo. Poor refugees were able to supplement their meagre incomes by selling refreshments at makeshift stalls. For the more refined citizenry, fountains were installed fringed by benches that enabled them to convene mini salons to discuss the burning issues of the day.

Friedrich did not repudiate the militarism of his father; but in all other respects he ushered in a transformation. Berlin was awash with reading societies, lodges and patriotic associations. Everyone who was anyone wanted to be part of a music or literary or philosophical soiree, a learned group in natural science, medicine or foreign languages. The first music shop was opened in 1783 by Johann Carl Friedrich Rellstab, with its own printing press and lending library, selling harpsichords, pianos, violins – and the king's instrument of choice, the flute. In 1769 the philosopher Friedrich Nicolai produced a three-volume *Description of the Royal Court Cities of Berlin and Potsdam*, part guidebook, part gazetteer and encyclopaedia, detailing the cultural and intellectual destinations of note. It was republished three times within twenty years, demonstrating the speed of change.

Each of Berlin's clubs had its own house rules (usually drinking was not allowed) and carefully guarded guest lists. Thirty-six of them are known by name – and there are records of at least sixteen Masonic lodges. Some societies were named after the days of the week when they met. The Monday Club, established in 1783, was perhaps the most radical; not anti-monarchist, not a threat to the status quo as in France, but forthright in its discussions about how government could be improved. That same year a Wednesday Club and a Thursday Circle were founded. One group of writers coalesced around the Berlin Cadet School. The names and areas of 'expertise' of all these clubs became ever more exotic – the Society of Naturalist Friends, the Philomatic Society (for lovers of science), the Pedagogical Society and, not to forget, the Economic Heating Society (which looked at ways of reducing consumption of scarce wood). It was easy for progressive scholars, writers and thinkers to see the state as a partner in their enlightened project because the sovereign championed their values. This was the time of the French Revolution, but these were not revolutionaries. Indeed, one of the most striking characteristics about these networks was their proximity to, and identification with, the state.

Berlin's salons were modelled on those in Paris, held in the private homes of the well-to-do, bringing together intellectuals and impoverished nobles. The best venues mixed *Junkers* (landed noblemen) with scientists, writers and critics, sharing the same sofas and addressing each other with the informal '*du*' – something quite unheard of in polite society – while drinking the finest wines and eating sumptuous canapés. The people everyone wanted to be seen with at the salons were Nicolai, Lessing, the patriotic poet Johann Wilhelm Ludwig Gleim – and a certain Jew, Moses Mendelssohn.

The Jews who had arrived from Vienna in the last wave in the 1670s had been relatively well treated by European standards of the time. They were afforded the status of *Schutzjuden* (protected Jews), who paid for a residence permit allowing them to engage in certain businesses and to worship in their own homes. They were allowed to perform religious ceremonies, such as the *mikveh*, the ritual bath; they were given their own cemetery and a hospital. It would still take nearly half a century, until 1714, for Berlin's first synagogue to be established in a small alleyway called Heidereutergasse.

When Friedrich assumed the throne around 1,000 Jews were registered in Berlin. Many were located in the Scheunenviertel, the Barn District, an area to the north of the city walls that had been developed to store hay for the nearby cattle market in what is now Alexanderplatz. As their numbers grew, Jews were told to settle here in the slum.

Friedrich the Great was torn, unsure how much leeway to give the Jews. One of his most often cited dictums was: '*Jeder soll nach seiner Façon selig werden*' (every man must get to heaven his own way). It applied to some groups, not others. His decree of 1750 – the 'Revised General Privileges and Regulations for the Jews in the Kingdom of Prussia' – restricted all but the richest families from having more than one child. The poorest were prevented from marrying at all. The meticulously detailed regulations set out seven classes of Jews. The top group, the wealthiest, would be provided with a personal privilege (letter of protection) that effectively put them on an equal footing with other citizens. Their legitimate children would also be entitled to settle.

Second-class 'protected Jews' were allowed to stay only in the place assigned to them; the right of residence could be inherited by one child, although two more could be applied for on proof of 1,000 thalers of assets, equivalent to almost £30,000 in today's money. And so on. According to the regulations, 'class number

four' comprised rabbis, while the lowest two categories had
no rights at all and were forbidden to marry. The number of
'protected Jews' was set at 203 ordinary and 63 'extraordinary'
first-class ones. The top three classes were subject to collective
liability. Elders of each community were made co-responsible
for any robbery or any other 'crime', including bankruptcy,
committed by any Jew in the city. Other rules included a ban
on Jews engaging in farming or crafts. Nor could they trade in
leather, wood, furs or any of the other lucrative commodities.
All husbands were required by law to wear a long beard, to
differentiate them from the rest of society. A separate edict
instructed Christians to shave off their beards in order not to be
confused with Jews. (Such physical identifiers were in direct
conflict with the increasing desire, among wealthy Berlin Jews
at least, to assimilate into the general Prussian community.) Ever
more inventive ways were devised to extract money from Jews:
a protection tax, a residence tax and a payment required to
work in certain professions. Worst of all, Jews were subject to a
'body tax' otherwise levied on cattle.

In his 'Political Testament', written two years later in 1752,
Friedrich stated: 'Of all these [religious] sects, the Jews are the
most dangerous, because they do harm to the trade of Christians
and are of no use to the state.' Yet the curiosity of it all is that by
the 1770s, three decades into his rule, the Jewish community was
the wealthiest and most assimilated of all the German states and
across much of Europe. It had more than doubled in size to 2,000.

This era is known as the Jewish Enlightenment, or Haskalah,
from the Hebrew le-haskil, which means 'to enlighten or clarify
with the aid of the intellect'.

The key to the success of Jews, in 'society' as in commerce, was
the close affiliation of the small, assimilated elite to the state and
to the court of the king. The general view was that acculturation
would eventually lead to conversion – or, at the very least, to a

toning down of any religiosity. Some of the most glamorous palaces and town houses of the period were owned by Jews. Well-to-do and 'cultured' Jewish women were central to salons, giving them real influence over the life of the city. The catering became so lavish, the demands so great, that some were driven to the brink of bankruptcy. The two best-known hostesses, Herz and Varnhagen, modelled themselves on Germaine de Staël, vying for the most impressive guest lists. Herz's salon included the academic Wilhelm von Humboldt and the author Heinrich von Kleist. Varnhagen's salon was in Jägerstrasse, one of the city's most prestigious streets. She wrote at the time that she had managed to attract 'as if by magic, all the outstanding young men who were either living in Berlin or else visiting the city'.

Jews excelled as merchants – trading mainly precious metals and stones – and as bankers. On the corner of Poststrasse and Mühlendamm, right at the heart of the city, where the story of Berlin and Cölln began, was the palace of court jeweller and mintmaster Veitel Heine Ephraim. Decorated in the rococo style with columns, pilasters and elegant balconies with gilded railings, the Ephraim-palais is now a museum and one of Berlin's landmarks. Another of the most beautiful private residences dating from that time is no more, and its demise long predated the Second World War. Palais Itzig was owned by one of the most influential men in Berlin, Daniel Itzig, a *Hofjude*. He belonged to the highest category of Jews, Court Jews, who had certain access into the royal household. They were a cut above *Schutzjude*, who had limited protections, including the right to reside. A banker, overseer of the royal finances and supporter of Jewish causes, Itzig belonged to the elite. Seven neighbouring homes were demolished to make room for the palace to accommodate him, his wife Mirjam, and their fifteen children. The manicured gardens, with their own fountain, dominated one bank of the Spree. The house had an art collection, a synagogue for the family and a *mikveh*.

Over a century later, at the height of the Wilhelmine boom, the palace was demolished to make way for the Berlin Stock Exchange, which quickly became one of the three most important in the world – equivalent to New York but lagging a little behind London.

Legend has it that on one October day in 1743 the penniless fourteen-year-old Moses Mendelssohn entered the city via the Rosenthal Gate. That was in the north, the only arrival point that was open to the likes of him, so he had to walk all the way around the city to be let in. Through the gate passed six oxen, seven pigs and a Jew. (Some historians have sought to correct the record since, claiming that his arrival point was the more easily accessible Hallesches Tor in the south, but that would be to detract a little from the drama.)

Mendelssohn was born into a poor family in the town of Dessau, to the south of Berlin. His father struggled to support the family as a *Schulklopfer*, a door-knocker for the local synagogue, whose task was to instruct young children in the Torah and to run from house to house rousing the congregation to prayer in the mornings. At the age of six, Moses began studying with a rabbi and scholar, David Fränkel, who taught him mathematics, physics, Latin, English and French. Eight years later, Fränkel received a position in Berlin as a 'protected Jew'; within months he summoned Mendelssohn to join him. Now a teenager, this extraordinary prodigy moved to the city, to the home of Isaak Bernhard, a tradesman who owned a silk factory on Bischofstrasse and offered him work as a bookkeeper.

Word spread, reaching even into the royal court. Mendelssohn was soon frequenting the salons and coffee houses. He wrote in Hebrew and elegant High German, drawing on themes from John Locke and Gottfried Leibniz. He befriended Nicolai, then Lessing, who would become his lifelong soulmate. The triumvirate met at salons and other gatherings, but also on their own at three locations close to each other: in the garden of Nicolai's home in Brüderstrasse (close to Petriplatz at the start of this tale), a wine cellar called Baumannshöhle a few buildings along, and at an adjacent library-cum-cafe. Spandauer Strasse 68, where Mendelssohn lived for a quarter of a century, is also nearby. In 1887, the building was demolished and rebuilt, only to be destroyed again by bombing raids in 1945. A memorial plaque designed by Israeli artist Micha Ullman was unveiled in 2016 close to where it once stood. The ceremony included Psalm texts sung in Hebrew and a horn ensemble playing compositions by that other famous Mendelssohn, his grandson Felix.

It is said that when Lessing and Mendelssohn met for the first time six years later, they played chess. Lessing had just published his one-act play *Die Juden* (The Jews), whose moral was that a Jew can possess nobility of character, an idea that was outrageous for its time. He also brought Mendelssohn to the public's attention without him knowing: Mendelssohn had written an essay, 'Philosophical Dialogues', criticizing the Germans' neglect of their native philosophers (principally Leibniz) and lent the manuscript to Lessing, who proceeded to have it published without asking him. A few years later, Mendelssohn won the top prize from the Berlin Academy for an essay on metaphysics, beating none other than Kant into second place. The work that brought him perhaps the widest attention was his invocation to faith and the immortality of the soul. Modelled on Plato's dialogue of the same name, it led him to be showered with praise by high society and hailed the 'German Plato', or the 'German Socrates'. Mendelssohn's time in Berlin almost identically spanned that of the king.

As his health deteriorated (he had developed curvature of the spine at a young age), he devoted ever more time to theology and religious rights. In 1783, shortly before his death, Mendelssohn published two works that were remarkable for their time. He produced the first translation of the Torah into German. He expressed the wish to 'dedicate the remains of my strength for the benefit of my children or a goodly portion of my nation', which he did, by bringing the Jews closer to the culture, 'from which my nation, alas! is kept in such a distance, that one might well despair of ever overcoming it'. He then wrote a book entitled *Jerusalem*, in which he joined Prussian officials in exhorting 'a civil improvement of the Jews'. The work was a passionate call for freedom of conscience and the acceptance of a possible plurality of truths: 'Brothers, if you care for true piety, let us not feign agreement, where diversity is evidently the plan and purpose of Providence,' he wrote. 'None of us thinks and feels exactly like his fellow man: why do we wish to deceive each other with delusive words?' Mendelssohn had been moved by a play Lessing had just written called *Nathan the Wise*, imploring the Abrahamic religions to learn to respect and live with each other. Lessing brings two of the protagonists, Nathan (who bears an uncanny resemblance to Mendelssohn) and an enlightened sultan called Saladin together over a game of chess.

Mendelssohn was seen by many as an intermediary between Jewish and German culture. Such was his reputation, he was granted the 'privilege' of 'protected Jew', but his wife and children were not. The Berlin Enlightenment accommodated a small number of acculturated Jews, if they were either very wealthy or intellectually gifted, or preferably both. But they were always demonstrably outsiders, a public differentiation that paved the way for far worse to come. As for the king, he personally rejected Mendelssohn's application to the Academy of Sciences, despite unanimous support from academy members.

Mendelssohn died in 1786, the same year as his king. Of his ten children, six lived to adulthood and only two retained their Jewish faith. His eldest son Joseph established the eponymous bank, soon to be joined by his brother Abraham. Both converted to Christianity, seeing it as the only safe route to success. Abraham would later write to his son, Felix, urging him to drop the Mendelssohn name and use instead the name Bartholdy, which he had taken from one of the properties he owned. 'There can no more be a Christian Mendelssohn than a Jewish Confucius,' he wrote.

For more than a decade and a half, the Mendelssohn family was at the heart of Berlin life. Jägerstrasse, a street just off Gendarmenmarkt in the heart of the city, became synonymous with generations of Mendelssohns. At its high point, the family owned six houses on that single street. The ground floor of number 51, a house which now contains the Irish Embassy and is next to the Belgians, is owned by the Mendelssohn Society, a not-for-profit organization established in 1967 which hosts a small permanent exhibition about the dynasty, and a series of talks and music events. In 2007, some 250 members of the Mendelssohn family diaspora accepted an invitation from the society to visit the city of their ancestors.

Berlin has over many generations venerated all things Mendelssohn, now more than ever. An anniversary edition of his collected writings was published by the Academy for the Study of Judaism and the Society for the Promotion of the Study of Judaism in 1929 to mark his 200th birthday. In 1938 the Gestapo destroyed all but a few copies of the volumes. The project was resumed by the Stuttgart-based academic publisher frommann-holzboog in 1972, with the twenty-fifth and final volume of the collection set to be published shortly.

Alongside the Mendelssohn Society there is the Mendelssohn Centre, an institute now based in Potsdam focusing on Jewish history and culture, and the Mendelssohn Foundation in Charlottenburg which deals with publications. It is run by Julius Schoeps, a seventh-generation descendant of the great man, whose 2009 biography of the family down the ages was a hit. It seems that in any given week, Berliners and visitors can attend a seminar or other event or join a walk commemorating the life of Moses Mendelssohn. Is the brand being pushed a little too far? Or rather, is the Mendelssohn name being used a little too freely as a catch-all to encapsulate the turmoil that is Berlin's relationship with its Jews? Perhaps he is an easy bridge between German and Jewish culture. There is also another reason. The Berlin Enlightenment epitomizes to many Germans what their capital could have been, and what it could yet be. One evening in early 2022 I was invited to a discussion (at the Jewish Association in Charlottenburg) on learning the lessons of the past in the context of the rebuilding of the city.

The debates were impassioned, pitting, as they often do among Berlin planners and architects, so-called modernizers against so-called traditionalists. At stake is the soul of the historical centre; a particularly heated argument is taking place over Spandauer Strasse. It is now one of the ugliest of Berlin's many ugly thoroughfares, with tourist signs seeking to resurrect what is no longer there – the great homes in the 1760s of Nicolai, Lessing and Mendelssohn. Its most recent claim was as the site of the AquaDom, described by Guinness World Records as the world's largest cylindrical aquarium when it opened in 2003 in the lobby of the Radisson Blu hotel. In December 2022, the edifice burst, sending almost a million litres of water into the foyer and killing 1500 fish.

Friedrich the Great died in 1786, childless, alone in an armchair in his study, aged seventy-four. He had made meticulous plans (written in French) for his remembrance: 'I lived as a philosopher and want to be buried as a philosopher, without pomp and luxury, as well as without any ceremony.' His wishes were not fulfilled and for the next two centuries, his memory became a weapon, a motif, in German self-identification. He wanted to be buried next to his eleven greyhounds, Phillis, Superbe, Amouretto, Bigos (or Gigos – the headstone has worn away), Pax, Diana, Thisbe, Hasenfuss, Alcmène, another called Thisbe, and his favourite, Biche, in the terrace of Sanssouci from where he had enjoyed looking out. His nephew and far less accomplished successor, Friedrich Wilhelm II, decreed that this was unbecoming. The king was laid to rest instead next to the father who had guided and tormented him, in Potsdam's Garrison Church, a site that assumed a mythical place in the Prussian-German nationalist cause. The crypt became a shrine for the famous to pay their tributes, from Tsar Alexander I to Napoleon.

The instrumentalization reached its peak during the Third Reich; a straight line was drawn between Friedrich the Great, Bismarck and Hitler. The propagandist Wilhelm Freiherr von Müffling published a brochure, 'Pioneers and Champions for the New Germany', with profiles of the men who had paved the way to Nazi glory. The cover depicts Hitler saluting towards a silhouette of Friedrich in front of his beloved Sanssouci.

In March 1933, immediately following the Reichstag fire, the ailing president Paul von Hindenburg laid a wreath in the crypt where the Soldier King, Friedrich Wilhelm I, and his son Friedrich II are buried. The church was decorated with black-and-white banners of Old Prussia, denoting the symbolic handing over of power from the Prussian monarchy to the new National Socialist government, with emergency powers. After the commemoration, Hitler also laid a garland on Friedrich's coffin. It is said that twelve years later, in April 1945, when Hitler retreated into his bunker, he took with him to his death a portrait of his favourite king by Anton Graff. At the end of the Second World War, as Berlin stood in ruins, the Allies were determined to break that continuum. 'The core of Germany is Prussia,' Winston Churchill had declared to the House of Commons in September 1943. 'There is the source of the recurring pestilence.' On Germany's surrender, de-Prussification became an urgent task. Prussia was officially abolished by the Allies on 25 February 1947.

The remains of Friedrich the Great, like those of his father, were spirited away to safety during the war. Once recovered, his casket was laid in the Elisabeth Church in Marburg, in a simple ceremony in August 1946. Neither the thirteenth-century Gothic church nor the town in the centre of Germany are unimpressive. Nevertheless, those Germans who took a more glorious view of their Prussian past were left devastated. The family itself was not amused. Louis Ferdinand, Prince of Prussia and head of the long-deposed Hohenzollerns, described it as a 'deeply sad, indeed almost macabre ceremony'.

And what of the statue presiding over Unter den Linden? All around was rubble, but it survived the war thanks to a protective sand-filled 'house' constructed to deflect the bombs. The new GDR government, and its Soviet masters, were just as keen as the Western Allies to break the link. In 1950, the East Germans moved the statue to the gardens of Sanssouci.

For its first three decades, the communist regime sought to create a new future, and to curate a new history. As the system began to run out of ideological road, it changed tack. The communist rehabilitation of Friedrich the Great, when it came, was thorough. So desperate was the GDR leadership in the 1980s to find a historic hero for a system that was falling apart, they appropriated and selectively rewrote Prussian history, empha-sizing Friedrich's dedication to the state. They hoped this would provide some form of cultural *Abgrenzung* (differentiation) with decadent West Berlin and West Germany. In 1979 a historian, Ingrid Mittenzwei, was given permission to publish a biography showing Friedrich as a positive figure in the Marxist-Leninist trajectory of history.

Shortly after that, Erich Honecker granted an audience to

Robert Maxwell, the Czech-born British media magnate, former MP, embezzler and suspected spy. The interview was part of a series by Maxwell's publishing house Pergamon Press called *Leaders of the World*, which also featured Leonid Brezhnev, Jimmy Carter and Helmut Schmidt. The mutually fawning conversation was given huge prominence in the party daily, *Neues Deutschland*, displayed over two pages. In their discussion, Honecker praised Mittenzwei's account of King Friedrich, using the moniker 'the Great' – the first time this had been done officially in the GDR. 'It is in line with our world view to grasp history in its objective, actual course, in its entire dialectic,' Honecker told Maxwell.

The historiographical shift was in full swing. The propagandists looked for other famous Prussians. When a new order was created to celebrate officers from the National People's Army for the protection of the GDR, it was named after General Gerhard von Scharnhorst, the first chief of the Prussian general staff at the start of the nineteenth century. A five-part television series on Scharnhorst was made in 1978. Two years later, to mark the 200th anniversary of his birth, the even more illustrious General Carl von Clausewitz was reimagined as a social reformer in a progressive Prussian state. Bach was rediscovered as a musician of the people. Goethe was found to have championed enlightened social change. As for Bismarck, he too was praised as a progressive in a biography by the much-decorated president of the National Committee of East German Historians, Ernst Engelberg. This two-volume work, published in 1985 and 1990, had an impact in both East and West.

Indeed, West Germany had already embarked on a debate of its own about Bismarck, Friedrich the Great and all things Prussian – a more open and heated one. In August 1981 a much-anticipated exhibition, *Prussia – Attempting an Assessment*, had opened in West Berlin's war-damaged Gropius Bau Museum, right next to the Wall. The show attracted an impressive 450,000 visitors, and long queues, in its short three-month run. The idea of such an exhibition was proposed by Dietrich Stobbe, a former mayor of West Berlin, in 1977. Ministers on both sides were wary. The Social Democratic (SPD) chancellor Helmut Schmidt and the CDU president Karl Carstens stayed well away. After all, wasn't Prussia, as Churchill had pointed out, supposed to be synonymous with all that had gone wrong in Germany? Each room was dedicated to a particular period or theme – salon society, trade unions, the Nazi appropriation of 'Prussian' values, Friedrich the Great's army uniform, the history of the potato in Prussia (supposedly one of Friedrich's great contributions to his kingdom). Readings were held of works by Theodore Fontane and Thomas Mann. Musical performances included Friedrich's flute sonatas, Bach's Brandenburg Concertos and Felix Mendelssohn's 'Reformation' symphony, conducted by Herbert von Karajan. The exhibition posed the question of how a society which had largely welcomed Bohemians, Jews and Huguenots could have become a state of persecution. The final room contained two symbolic gravestones – one dedicated to the six million murdered Jews, the other to the fifty million victims of the war.

The exhibition was criticized by the left for what was seen as its ambivalence about the path from Prussia to Nazism. 'It meticulously avoided taking any definite standpoint whatsoever,' said the academic Christine Lattek. *Pravda*, the Soviet Communist Party newspaper, blasted the exhibition as a cunning attempt 'to rehabilitate the Prussian militarism that unleashed two world wars', omitting to mention the rehabilitation that was well underway in the fraternal GDR. Unification in 1990 – and the reappearance of Germany as Europe's dominant state – gave fresh impetus to the discussion about its most famous king. Much of it has been nuanced and balanced; just occasionally, the simple positives or negatives are trotted out.

In 2012, Berlin succumbed to Friedrich-mania for a year of

celebrations in honour of his 300th birthday. The German Historical Museum lent its authority in an attempt to locate Friedrich's place in modern Germany. *Friedrich der Große – verehrt, verklärt, verdammt* (revered, transfigured, condemned) examined his legacy to art, politics and society and opened the conversation about the changing culture of remembrance. Dozens of new biographies were published; commemorative coins were minted. The German toymaker Steiff even brought out a limited-edition teddy bear of the Prussian king in his signature blue coat and tricorn hat. More than a hundred exhibitions were staged. Tillmann Bendikowski, one of the many historians to bring out a new biography that year, took pains to highlight that it was Prussians who had led the 1944 plot to assassinate Hitler. What is more, other historians pointed out, Friedrich was hardly a key influence of German nationalism. He was distinctly Prussian, spoke French as his main language, and was more influential on French Romanticism than its German counterpart. The keynote at the tricentennial festivities was a speech by the German president at the time, Christian Wulff, focusing on Friedrich's worldly tolerance towards immigration.

As for his burial site, finally in 1991 Friedrich had his wishes fulfilled. The initial lobbying for the move had begun a few years earlier, during GDR times. Honecker sent emissaries to Louis Ferdinand, he of the Hohenzollern dynasty, entreating him to return Friedrich's remains to Potsdam. He did, but only after the GDR was no more. Friedrich the Great can now be found under the ground on the terrace of Sanssouci next to his dogs. Well-wishers place potatoes next to his tombstone, in recognition of his contribution to Germany's culinary traditions – and to his fending off of various famines. Whenever I walk through the gardens of Sanssouci to the grave, I am struck by the quaintness, the bathos, the lack of bombast.

Berlin, both West and East, has learned to appreciate Friedrich, to rehabilitate him. But he has not yet been fully restored to hero status. His statue returned to Unter den Linden but, for reasons of traffic flow (not that there were many cars in East Berlin), the monument ended up a few metres further east from its original position. To see him up close and personal, tourists must cross three lines of busy traffic onto a small island in the middle of the road.

SEVEN

Reformers and radicals

From Napoleon to 1848

Imagine Geneva lost in a desert, and you have an idea of Berlin.
It will one of these days become the capital of Germany,
but it will always remain the capital of boredom.
HONORÉ DE BALZAC (1843)

A king of little distinction commissioned the construction of Berlin's most famous landmark. As Friedrich the Great had failed to produce an heir, the throne was handed to his brother's eldest son, Friedrich Wilhelm II. Berlin descended into one of its cyclical moments of anxiety and self-doubt. A reign that lasted barely a decade is remembered for sexual peccadilloes at court, the king's inclination to mysticism and fears arising from the French Revolution. The new king, even before gaining the throne, had fallen in with a faction associated variously with illuminism, Templarism and Rosicrucianism, all cults loosely connected with Freemasonry and various forms of theosophy. He was also addicted to sex, not only having a string of mistresses at court but also entering into at least two successive bigamist marriages.

Yet Friedrich Wilhelm II did make one great contribution – the Brandenburg Gate. In the third year of his rule, 1788, he appointed Carl Gotthard Langhans, a well-known architect from Silesia, to be his first director of the Royal Building

Commission. He immediately tasked him to replace the modest customs houses on the road towards Brandenburg with something more impressive. He planned to call it Friedenstor (Peace Gate). Langhans modelled it on the Propylaea, the ceremonial gateway to the Acropolis of Athens, with which he was familiar from published engravings. Six 15-metre-high Doric half-columns frame five passages, of which the broad central one was reserved for the king. Two flanking outhouses were to provide accommodation for guards and for toll collection. It was to be topped by a bronze statue of the Goddess of Victory driving a four-horse chariot, and cast by another starchitect of his time, Johann Schadow.

Two decades later, the monument became the symbol of humiliation. In October 1806, Napoleon Bonaparte routed the Prussian army at Jena and Auerstedt, to the southwest of Berlin – the most ignominious defeats in Prussian military history. Rather than staying behind to fight, or at least to show solidarity with his people, the Prussian king and his court fled as far away as possible, to Königsberg, on the eastern edge of Prussia. Two weeks later, Napoleon and his forces marched triumphantly through the Brandenburg Gate. The parade formation, the soldiers wearing immaculate uniforms adorned with gleaming medals 'under the finest weather in the world', made quite an impression on a crowd disdainful of its own rulers. The French (Napoleonic propaganda) newspaper *Le Moniteur* reported: 'This evening the entire town was illuminated; the streets were filled with people. To tell the truth, you would have thought you were in France, at a public ceremony.' Napoleon later commissioned Charles Meynier to glorify his arrival in the city, something the artist duly did with a huge 4 by 6 metre painting, which now hangs in Versailles.

With his soldiers safely ensconced in the city, Napoleon stayed for a couple of days before continuing his march to the east. The only purpose he had for Berlin was as a buffer, to protect his growing empire. He did not want to destroy or punish the city, merely to loot it. His commissioner of art compiled a meticulous list of official plunder, comprising 116 paintings, 96 busts and statues, 183 bronzes, 538 gems, 7,262 medals and coins, manuscripts, amber – and the bronze quadriga which had only recently been installed atop the Gate. The emperor thus became known as the 'horse thief of Berlin'. A city that had no cathedral, no parliament building, no Louvre, no Palais du Luxembourg, now had its beloved gate stripped of its majesty. Berlin was left stunted, unadorned. From that moment, the Brandenburg Gate, with its quadriga, became especially significant for the city's self-esteem, as a symbol of Prussian and German resistance – and later of Berlin's division.

Napoleon intended for the quadriga to be placed on top of a new Arc de Triomphe. The goddess and her chariot were dismantled and packed into twelve boxes to be transported to Paris. Damaged during its journey, the booty was sent to the Orangery of the Museum Napoléon (as the Louvre was officially called for ten years in the early 1800s) for extensive restoration. Despite his grand plans, Napoleon then appeared to forget about the quadriga. Berlin's prized possession was left in the Orangery's basement for the next seven years.

Having defeated not just Prussia, but also Austria and Russia, Napoleon was now the pre-eminent figure in Europe. The Holy Roman Empire was dissolved; Emperor Francis II abdicated. A new Confederation of the Rhine took its place, a group of client German kingdoms politically subservient to France. The Napoleonic Confederation was at its largest in 1808, when it included thirty-five states. Tsar Alexander I urged peace talks between himself, Napoleon and the latest Prussian monarch, another Friedrich Wilhelm, this time the Third (Friedrich Wilhelm II had died in 1797) – and another weakling. Alexander instructed his emissary to tell Napoleon that an alliance between

France and Russia 'will ensure the happiness and tranquillity of the world'. Sensing an opportunity to consolidate his position across Europe, and to isolate Britain, Napoleon agreed. In June 1807, peace negotiations started on an ornate raft in the middle of the river near Tilsit, close to Königsberg. Two grand white tents had been erected, one for the French, the other for the Russians; Friedrich Wilhelm III was told to wait on the shore. The outcome was devastating: a humiliated Prussia was made to give up much of its territory for the creation of a new client state, the Grand Duchy of Warsaw (comprising much of present-day Poland), to be run by Napoleon's ally the King of Saxony (who had previously been badly treated by Prussia), and for a Kingdom of Westphalia (a chunk of what is now the centre of Germany) as a gift to Napoleon's youngest brother, Jerome Bonaparte. Prussia was also ordered to cut its army to 40,000 men and pay huge reparations to the French, which they continued to do for half a century – a precursor to the Versailles Treaty of 1919.

Napoleon had contempt for the latest Prussian king. How could he have been so different from his grandfather? During his fleeting visit to Berlin, the French emperor took time out to go to Potsdam, to pay homage at the tomb of Friedrich the Great. He famously remarked to his generals, 'Gentlemen, if this man were still alive, I would not be here.' He would frequently pore over Friedrich the Great's military notes and had a statuette of him placed in his personal cabinet.

Refused an audience with Napoleon, the hapless Friedrich Wilhelm III asked his wife, Queen Luise of Mecklenburg-Strelitz, to plead on his behalf. She was initially reluctant, since she considered the Frenchman 'the monster' who had tried to destroy her reputation by questioning her marital fidelity. Eventually the formidable Luise, who was pregnant at the time, agreed out of duty, 'to save Prussia', so the story goes. 'For God's sake no shameful peace,' she declared. She requested a private interview with Napoleon, whereupon she threw herself at his feet. Napoleon wrote to his wife, Empress Josephine, that Luise 'is really charming and full of coquettishness toward me. But don't be jealous; it would cost me too dearly to play the gallant.'

Luise ultimately failed but, unlike her husband, she was revered as the 'soul of national virtue'. In popular history she came to be known as 'the Queen of Hearts'. Napoleon paid her a somewhat different compliment (he presumably thought it a compliment), describing her as 'the only real man in Prussia'. When she died in 1810, to the horror of her family and subjects, she had not lived to see the liberation of her city. She was only thirty-four years old and had already given birth to ten children. Seventy years later, at the height of the Wilhelmine era, a statue made of Carrara marble was erected to her in a part of the Tiergarten where she liked to walk. Heavily damaged during the Second World War, it was reinstated only in 1987, as part of a wider city 'save the monuments' campaign. Even now, bullet holes can still be seen. The statue overlooks a meticulously landscaped rose garden on the so-called Luiseninsel. On the other side of the garden stands a monument to her husband, Friedrich Wilhelm III. The bas-relief contains the words 'from the grateful citizens of Berlin'. Despite her popularity, such a formal tribute was not afforded to Luise.

Several other monuments to Luise exist in Berlin: a bronze bust in the gardens of Charlottenburg Palace that is still regularly adorned with flowers, an intricate sarcophagus designed by Christian Daniel Rauch depicting the queen – per her husband's wishes – in a state of eternal sleep, and a grand marble statue of her and her sister Frederica, which can be found today in the Alte Nationalgalerie. A life-size plaster copy of this statue is available to buy for just under €24,000 from the Gipsformerei, one of Berlin's state galleries and the largest in the world devoted to replicas. Luise is the closest the wives of Prussian monarchs, often banished to their own palaces, get to public celebrity. In the mid-nineteenth century she was the subject of a series of novels by German historical fiction writer Luise Mühlbach; silent movies as early as 1913 had her as the protagonist. *Napoleon and the Queen of Prussia*, *The Queen of Hearts*; the titles may have varied a little, the genres and the technology changed a huge amount, but the fascination has remained the same.

Napoleon's forces stayed in Berlin barely three years, though much of Prussia remained under occupation for longer. Berliners were ordered by the occupying French to billet many of the soldiers in their own homes. Many were in field camps scattered around strategic points in the city. Their presence was a matter of grave concern for mothers and grandmothers, worried that their young girls would fall prey to these dashing men in uniform. That warning had a mini comeback in the wild West Berlin days of the 1970s and 1980s, as protective Berliners of a certain generation were prone to telling teenage daughters and grand-daughters, before a big Friday or Saturday night out: *Mach mal keine Fisimatenten* (Don't get up to any *Fisimatenten*). This last word may have derived from the French *visiter* but in the vernacular of the time was interpreted more broadly, along the lines of 'Don't get up to any tricks' or 'Don't try to pull the wool over my eyes.'

The looting and strutting of Napoleon's men was the object of fury to some Berliners and fascination to others. The 1789 revolutionary ideals of freedom, equality and fraternity, of the removal of absolute monarchy, as well the introduction of a constitutional state, were galvanizing much of Europe.

Napoleon's reversal of fortune, cataclysmic retreat from Moscow and his subsequent abdication in 1814 led to the return home of the quadriga and other looted treasure. The legacy of the French occupation for Berlin was mixed. The economy suffered under the huge burden of reparations; prices skyrocketed. Yet the city's capture appeared to have woken Prussians from a slumber.

Institutions – military, economic and political – had atrophied. In 1808 wide-ranging reforms were introduced to modernize state administration. On 6 July 1809, Berlin had its first parliament, the Stadtverordnetenversammlung (city chamber of deputies), which met in the Nikolaikirche. Only men with considerable wealth could vote and many areas of decision-making were off limits. Still, it was a start.

The Enlightenment had exited the Prussian stage as quickly as it arrived. Berlin had lost its lustre in the couple of decades that followed the death of Friedrich the Great in 1788 and many leading thinkers left for elsewhere in Europe. The brain drain, however, was short-lived. Newly liberated Berlin became an intellectually vibrant city again. It also became grander. This was the era of Karl Friedrich Schinkel, the architect who has left more of a mark on the present city than any other. After initially studying painting, he left school in 1798 and joined Friedrich Gilly's private school of architecture. Following Napoleon's defeat, Schinkel was tasked by Friedrich Wilhelm III to oversee the Prussian Building Commission. He set about framing the centre of the city as the ancient Greeks might have done. His first assignment was the Neue Wache, a guardhouse for the Royal Palace and the king. Completed in 1818, fronted with a portico of Greek Doric columns, it was by the standards of the time relatively modest. Schinkel's designs became more majestic as he turned his attention to building a theatre in Gendarmenmarkt and the first of the great edifices of Museum Island, the Königliches (Royal) Museum. With its magnificent row of eighteen Ionic columns facing the Lustgarten, the Altes Museum, as it was later called, remains one of Berlin's landmarks. Despite all Berlin's turbulence, the collection of museums on Museum Island has for the best part of two decades displayed one of the great concentrations of ancient and modern art anywhere in the world. In the latter part of his career, Schinkel's ideas became more utopian. He had plans for a residence for the Greek royals on top of the Acropolis, and he proposed a dream palace for the Russian Tsarina, with temples and fountains, overlooking the Black Sea. None of these were built, but in Berlin his legacy survives to this day.

Across the city, reading cafes boomed. Liberals and radicals met at Stehely, conservatives at Café Josty in Potsdamer Platz or at Kranzler. Both schools of thought started to organize politically, exchanging ideas for reviving Prussian self-determination, which developed into the first stirrings of Pan-Germanism.

German Romanticism emerged as an aesthetic revolution led by a movement of unsettled artists and intellectuals against the enlightened rationalism of the eighteenth century, now dismissed as an alien implant. It sought a new way of interpreting life, enriching the present by reviving the mystic wonders of the past. In the early years of Romanticism there was little overlap with the notion of the state. Gradually, the concept of the unique was transferred from the individual to a national community. The envisaged German state, the Romantics began to argue, was the source of all creativity. The progression into nationalism was lauded by intellectuals, politicians and artists alike. The German state became an object of poetry and adoration, a collective uniqueness full of wonder and mystery.

It sometimes manifested itself in curious ways. In a corner of the People's Park Hasenheide in Kreuzberg stands a monument to the body beautiful. The stretch of green had in earlier times been fenced off to indulge the Great Elector in his fondness for hunting. Rabbits and hares were bred for the purpose. Hence the name: 'hare heath'. It later became a park where in 1811 a schoolteacher-cum-gymnastics instructor, Friedrich Ludwig Jahn, opened the first *Turnplatz*, or open-air gymnasium. He, like many, saw the defeat at the hands of Napoleon as a humiliation and he saw the German *Volk* as an intrinsic good to be advanced. After helping establish a volunteer unit in the Prussian army to fight the French force, he was convinced more than ever that the national spirit would be revived by physical strength. Word of his *Turnbewegung* (gymnastics movement) spread quickly; huge crowds gathered in the park to watch not only their exercises, but also jousting tournaments that they laid on for the audience. Sporting the black, red and gold colours of the old order, they re-enacted Romantic stories of medieval knights. The authorities began to see Jahn as a potentially subversive force; such open displays of nationalism, even of the corporeal variety, were deemed dangerous and a threat to the existing order. The clubs were closed in 1820 and he was arrested, banished to castles outside the city and, on his eventual release, forbidden from returning to within 16 kilometres of Berlin. Shortly after his death in 1852, a statue was erected to him in the park. It has survived the vicissitudes of time. More than 130 commemorative plaques from gym clubs around the world decorate the pedestal. The park nowadays still caters for the sporty – but more the modern variant of joggers and rollerbladers. Most recently it entered the headlines during the first lockdown of early 2020, when thousands of people gathered at the weekend for illegal raves.

Reformers regarded education of the masses as key to the moral and physical recovery of their country. Friedrich Wilhelm III accepted the need for change, if only to preserve his shaky hold on power. Amid the humiliation of the Treaties of Tilsit, he stated, 'We have indeed lost territory, and it is true that the state has declined in outward splendour and power, and for that very reason it is my solemn desire that the greatest attention be paid to the education of the people.'

On the north side of Unter den Linden, just a few steps from Friedrich the Great's statue, stand two of the great figures of German education, the brothers Wilhelm and Alexander von Humboldt. The older, more sedate establishment brother Wilhelm joined forces with the younger Alexander, an eccentric botanist and global explorer, to establish Berlin's first university in 1810. Compared to Oxford (founded in 1096), Cambridge (1209), the Sorbonne (1150) and even Heidelberg (1386), the Friedrich Wilhelm University (named in honour of the king, naturally) was a preposterous ingenue. But it quickly acquired prestige, becoming one of Europe's great centres of learning.

The son of a Prussian aristocrat and his wife of French Huguenot descent, and friend of Goethe and Schiller, Wilhelm von Humboldt enjoyed a long period of independent study and travel before entering the diplomatic service. He rose quickly, becoming ambassador to the Vatican, before being recalled to Berlin by the king to lead a directorate on education. Humboldt, who had wanted the higher-ranked position of minister for education, did not reply to Friedrich Wilhelm III for weeks. He eventually accepted, and undertook a series of reforms, introducing a universal system of public instruction with standardized curricula and examinations. By 1830 almost all Germans could read and write, and by the end of the century the illiteracy rate was only 0.05 per cent, among the lowest in Europe.

Academic and vocational education were, from an early stage, given parity of esteem for all, an approach that helped lay the foundations for rapid industrialization and growth in the second half of the nineteenth century and for the *Wirtschaftswunder* (economic miracle) of the second half of the twentieth century. For Humboldt, the 'complete human being' required 'gymnastic, aesthetic, didactic, mathematical, philosophical and historical' capacities. 'The soul of the lowliest labourer must be initially put into harmony with the soul of the most finely cultivated person, if the former is not to fall beneath human dignity and become crude, and if the latter is not to fail in human strength, becoming sentimental, fantasy-ridden, and eccentric.' He concluded: 'In this way, even having learned Greek would be just as useful for the cabinetmaker, as would carpentry for the scholar.'

His brother Alexander befriended Goethe and spent much of his time with him in Jena and Weimar, two towns considered more desirable to a man of letters. He travelled the world to gain knowledge, climbing active volcanoes, crawling into mines and prodding electric eels. When a ship he was on sailed into a hurricane with 12-metre waves, he sat down to calculate the exact angle at which the boat would capsize. Death would be better experienced methodically, he reasoned. The ship stayed afloat. He was equally unsentimental when it came to others: after a thunderstorm killed a farmer and his wife, he obtained their corpses and analysed them in the anatomy tower of Jena University. The historian Andrea Wulf describes him as 'the forgotten father of environmentalism'. During his travels through Venezuela in 1799, he noticed that farmers in the Aragua valley were deforesting the region to grow indigo crops and drying up the nearby lake. Later, in a letter to President Thomas Jefferson dated June 1804, he wrote, 'The wants and restless activity of large communities of men gradually despoil the face of the Earth.' It was one of the first Western observations of human-caused climate change, according to Wulf. Environmentalists and scientists like Charles Darwin, John Muir and Henry David Thoreau were heavily influenced by Alexander's writings. He mixed his writings on ecological degradation with critiques of imperialism and slavery in works such as *Essay on the Kingdom of New Spain* and *Political Essay on the Island of Cuba*. A national park is named after him in Cuba.

Back in Germany, Alexander and Wilhelm travelled across the country on a recruitment drive for professors for their brand-new university. Their results were immediate and impressive. They brought in luminaries such as the philosophers Georg Wilhelm Friedrich Hegel and Friedrich Wilhelm Joseph Schelling, the historian Leopold von Ranke, the Brothers (Wilhelm and Jacob) Grimm and Johann Gottlieb Fichte, who became the first rector and first chair of philosophy. The king donated to the institution one of the palaces on Unter den Linden, belonging to his brother Prince Heinrich, which had been built by the Dutchman Bouman in 1766. This was not just a new university, but a new way of thinking. As the philosopher Friedrich Paulsen would later write, it was 'expressly organised in direct contrast to the higher schools of the military dictator'. Its guiding principle was to be not unity and subordination but freedom and independence. *Bildung und Wissenschaft*: very German concepts of education and knowledge, interpreted in their widest forms. The professors were to be not teaching and examining state officials, but independent scholars. The organizing principles were the 'unity of learning' – the symbiosis of humanism and natural sciences, and the improvement not just of the individual but also of the state. Intellectuals were driven by a sense of frustration that Prussia was being bypassed by the rest of Europe. Use of the German language, so derided by Friedrich the Great, was transformed by the study of *Germanistik*, not just as an academic exercise, but a demonstration of patriotism. It would later be described by the philologist Rudolf Hildebrand as 'not merely a science but a handmaid for the salvation of the nation'.

The ground had already been laid before the founding of the university. In his 'Addresses to the German Nation', delivered in 1807–8, a year into Napoleon's occupation of Berlin, Fichte set out how language and culture would be the vehicles of spiritual development for German nationalism. In his fourteen eagerly devoured lectures, he argued that the true German spirit required the rejection of foreign (particularly French) culture. This school of thought reached its extreme in the writings of Ernst Moritz Arndt, who talked of the French as 'morally depraved', infusing his Francophobia, antisemitism and anti-Slav sentiment with an early and clear ethnocentricity. 'The Germans have not been bastardised by foreign peoples, have not become half-breeds,' he wrote. 'They more than many other peoples have remained in their native state of purity.'

Emboldened by Fichte, Arndt and others, historians began to rewrite the early years of the German lands, airbrushing out the role of Slavs in the founding of Berlin and Brandenburg.

Fichte died in 1814, denied the pleasure of watching Napoleon's retreat from Berlin and the wars of liberation that led to his demise. Even though he was rector of the university for barely four years, Fichte left his mark. His philosopher chair remained vacant for four years until he was succeeded by another enormously influential figure, Hegel. In his 'philosophy of right', Hegel argued that the state enjoyed a quasi-divine purpose. It was not an imposed construct, but the highest expression of the 'objective spirit', he argued, 'the highest form of institutionalised freedom ever reached by man'. His school of thought was intoxicating. For liberals the state was driven by a redemptive social mission. For romantic conservatives, like Ludwig von Gerlach, it was 'the only institution capable of bestowing a sense of purpose and identity upon the masses of the population'.

Hegel sought throughout to reconcile reformist ardour with adherence to the constitutional monarchical order. He was appointed rector of the university in 1830 but died a year later, as cholera swept Berlin. One of Hegel's students was a young man making his name as a poet. Heinrich Heine hailed from a modest Jewish mercantile family in Düsseldorf, then the Duchy of Berg. Having refused to learn a trade, he tried the universities of Bonn and Göttingen, before being captivated by the allure of the more dynamic Berlin.

The Prussia of the mid-nineteenth century fluctuated between bouts of tolerance and authoritarianism. As Heine's poetry became increasingly satirical and radical, he moved to Paris, where he could publish more freely. In 1843, after two fleeting visits back to his homeland, he wrote *Germany: A Winter's Tale*, capturing in verse the oppressiveness of Prussian censors, sniffing through books at borders. As for Wilhelm Humboldt, soon after establishing the university, he ended up in conflict with the king and his ministers, who had become increasingly suspicious of the liberal ideas emanating from there. He resigned from office at the age of fifty-two to retire to his family seat, Tegel Palace, to concentrate on his passion for linguistics.

The list of the university's alumni is august: from Arthur Schopenhauer, Max Planck and Herbert Marcuse to Weimar-era statesmen such as Gustav Streseman and Walter Rathenau. Many of Germany and Russia's communist revolutionaries were educated there, including Mikhail Bakunin, Karl Liebknecht and Friedrich Engels. In 1836, an eighteen-year-old student from a high school in the western city of Trier went to Bonn to study philosophy and literature. His father insisted he read law instead. So, he went to Berlin and to the Friedrich Wilhelm University, where he joined a group of young Hegelians. In March 1953, a sentence from his writings was inscribed in the marble wall of the central building of the university, renamed the Humboldt University in 1949 in honour of its founders. 'Philosophers have hitherto explained the world; it is now time to change it.' That person was Karl Marx.

What is remarkable for a city that lays so much emphasis on political agitation is how many attempted revolts and revolutions have failed.

Two trends occurred in the decades that followed the French occupation: the first moves towards German national self-identity, and the first organized campaigns for economic and social change. When the Congress of Vienna met in 1815, a year after Napoleon's abdication, a major question was what to do with the territory of the Confederation of the Rhine, an artificial construct of the French emperor to replace the Holy Roman Empire. The solution

was to create an even larger German Confederation, a conglom-
eration of thirty-nine states including Austria and Prussia.
Members of the Confederation pledged to come to the aid
of others attacked by a foreign power (a precursor to NATO's
Article 5). However, the Confederation fell short of any economic
or national unity.

The first effort at striking some form of economic unification
came two decades later with the establishment in 1834 of the
Zollverein (customs union), a significant moment marking the
removal of hundreds of trade barriers separating the German
lands since medieval times, and the beginning of a national
economy and putative state. A key question was the role of the
Austrian Empire. Advocates of a 'greater Germany' wanted
Austria in. Proponents of 'smaller' Germany argued that its
inclusion would dilute the essential Germanness of the project, as
it would stretch the borders deep into eastern and southern
Europe.

Also around this time, in 1830, Berlin's first popular uprising
took place when tailors' apprentices took to the streets to protest
at working conditions; they were followed by calico printers. A
prominent scientist and future politician, Rudolf Virchow,
calculated that workers' real wages had dropped by 45 per cent in
three years. With prices at their highest, around 100,000 people
throughout the German lands took part in 200 riots. Between
21 and 22 April 1847, large crowds pulled down sacks of potatoes
and peas at market stalls across Berlin. The object of their ire
was mainly merchants exploiting their monopolies with huge
mark-ups. Although the events are commonly referred to as
the 'potato revolution' (perhaps inspired by the potato revolts
in Russia in the early 1840s), about thirty of the forty-five
documented attacks in Berlin were also directed against bakers
(one of the wealthiest guilds in the city). The crowds also
attacked symbols of wealth: churches, hotels and some non-food

businesses such as watchmakers and porcelain shops. The army was sent in to quell the riots and hundreds of people were arrested. By the standards of the time, the soldiers were relatively benign but, after a brief hiatus, worse violence was to come.

To the southeast of Berlin, rural weavers suddenly found that they could not compete with the new industrialized processes introduced in Britain and copied in Prussia, leaving tens of thousands out of work, penniless and starving. In Schwiebus, a small weaving town near the Silesian border, nearly a quarter of the impoverished population rose up to protest at their worsening conditions, attacking the factories and homes of wealthy middle-men with pitchforks. The army was sent in, and the protests were quickly crushed. The revolt would become one of the totems of future left-wing politics in Berlin. Heine's account of the weavers was published a year later in *Vorwärts* (Forwards), Karl Marx's new Paris-based journal. 'The Silesian Weavers' was subsequently immortalized in theatre, art, heavy metal and punk.

The year of the great, or not-so-great, revolutions of 1848 began in January in Palermo in Sicily with a popular uprising against Bourbon rule. It was the revolution in France the following month that sent shock waves around Europe, producing a chain reaction. On 28 February, the French king Louis Philippe abdicated and fled to England. The sensational events were covered in a special edition of Berlin newspapers, which also reported on popular unrest elsewhere, particularly in Vienna. Berliners went out in search of more information, lingering in the unseasonably mild temperatures to discuss the news. Reading clubs and coffee houses were full to bursting.

Buoyed by successes elsewhere in Europe, Berliners of all ages took to the streets. In their 'address to the king', the better-off focused on issues such as freedom of speech and property rights; much of this was wrapped up in the movement for German nationhood. The poorer had more basic demands: a state that could feed them and house them with decency. The more they were ignored, the more agitated the protesters became. Daily political meetings took place at the houses along In den Zelten, a small street on the edge of the Tiergarten which became a focal point, where speeches were given and petitions were handed around for signing. The 'Marseillaise', which had become the anthem of the protest movement in Berlin, was banned by the authorities but continued to be played in secret.

By now Prussia had a new king, another Friedrich Wilhelm, the Fourth. He had come to the throne in 1840, at a pivotal moment. Influenced by the Romantic movement, he saw opportunities in German nationhood, but one based on *noblesse oblige*. He abhorred 'absolutism', defining it as both excessive militarism and excessive radicalism. His equivocation was about to be put to the ultimate test on the streets of Berlin.

Soldiers and protesters have provided first-hand testimony from those terrible days in March 1848. On 13 March, the king ordered the cavalry to 'clean up' the palace square. The army charged people returning from a meeting in the Tiergarten; they left one person dead and many injured. Five days later, demonstrators regrouped. Two shots were fired unintentionally by an officer on Schlossplatz (Palace Square). Furious Berliners then mounted barricades, using sentry boxes, overturned hackney carriages, a fruit stall, anything they could find. The king's forces opened fire on the crowd, who were armed only with pitchforks, axes and stones. About 200 people were killed before the king ordered his troops to retreat, thirteen hours later.

On 18 March, the army arrested almost 700 people in the houses and streets of Berlin. Bystanders were beaten. Many were locked up overnight in the palace cellars before being taken to Spandau prison. The following day, some thirty relatives of the March Revolution victims laid out their dead in the middle of the palace courtyard and called up to the king, demanding he take his hat off to them. King Friedrich Wilhelm IV ventured towards the barricades and declared to the crowd: 'Germany is in ferment within, and exposed from without, to anger from more than one side. Deliverance from this danger can come only from the most intimate union of the German princes and people under a single leadership.' He made some concessions, including the right to assemble and the withdrawal of troops back to their barracks. The elected national assembly met on 1 May, hundreds of miles away in the St Paul's Church in Frankfurt, but disagreements between factions soon rendered it powerless. By September, the army was back on Berlin's streets; by October the assembly had been dissolved.

How did a revolution that unfolded with such force collapse so comprehensively and so quickly? From that moment on, Berlin's failed 1848 uprising has been intensively researched, each generation interpreting it for its times. Alexis de Tocqueville remarked: 'There are no revolutions in Germany, because the police would not allow it.' Lenin would later be similarly disparaging when commenting on Germany's failed 1918 uprising.

The achievements of the revolutionaries of March 1848 were reversed in all of the German states, and by 1851, the Basic Rights from the Frankfurt Assembly had been abolished. The revolution fizzled out because of the overwhelming military power at the disposal of the king, and his skill at driving a wedge between the various factions. Existing divisions were laid bare. The moderates had wanted to draft a constitution to present to the king, whereas radicals had wanted the assembly unilaterally to grant itself lawmaking powers. The revolution could have been a moment of the great coming together. Instead, it was a defeat not only for liberals but also for advocates of the unification of the German state. They would have to wait two more decades for the efforts of the great arch-conservative, Otto von Bismarck. The radicals, meanwhile, felt betrayed. Some fled, for fear of retribution. The hundreds who died outside the Royal Palace in Berlin, in what has romantically been called 'the people's spring', did so in vain.

Every year on 18 March, a small crowd gathers in a park in Friedrichshain, in the east of the city, to commemorate the March Revolution. The Cemetery of the March Fallen contains the graves of 255 victims, such as bookbinder Theodor Mengel, aged eighteen, Carl Schmidt, a thirty-five-year-old shoemaker and Gustav von Lensky, a Prussian-Polish nobleman, reserve officer and trainee lawyer, who fought on the barricades at Friedrichstrasse.

It is a moving and quiet spot, but as with so much history in Berlin, even this burial site is politically contested. For the past hundred years, Berlin's second failed revolution (or perhaps third, if you add in the uprising of 1448), has also been marked here: the unsuccessful communist revolt of 1919 led by Karl Liebknecht and Rosa Luxemburg. The artist Käthe Kollwitz, a friend of theirs, wrote: 'I used to visit the cemetery of the March Fallen every year. A slow procession of workers marched in long lines past the graves from morning to night.' During the Third Reich such processions were banned. In March 1946, 10,000 people marched to the cemetery for the first time since the Nazi era. Yet, as the city divided, both sides argued over how to mark 1848 – or how to interpret it historically.

The one hundredth anniversary in 1948 led to a definitive schism. Delegations from the Communist Party (the SED) and the West Berlin Social Democrats laid wreaths separately, claiming the revolution for themselves. The SPD saw the Weimar democracy as realizing significant goals that emanated from 1848; the SED saw both as betrayals of the working class, which had only finally prevailed after the war. As the GDR took over the site, individual gravestones were replaced by larger sarcophagus plates. One tombstone has a line from Liebknecht: 'To firmly establish working-class rule, be resolute against anyone who resists.' The site has been sensitively redeveloped in recent years and graves have been restored. A new exhibition area, housed in a refurbished sea container, holds exhibitions related to these two failed revolutions.

It may be a strange habit, but I have made a point of visiting as many of Berlin's cemeteries as possible. Each tells its own story, or multiplicity of stories, in turns chilling and uplifting. On 18 March 2021, Steinmeier became the first head of state of reunified Germany to visit the Cemetery of the March Fallen. He did so with little fanfare. As he laid a wreath, he told a small gaggle of journalists and dignitaries that the events of 1848 were a milestone on the road to modern democracy.

EIGHT

Finally, very rich

The new German state, money and power

*Berlin is the newest city I have come across. The main mass of the
city looks as if it had been built last week. Even Chicago would
appear old and grey in comparison.*
MARK TWAIN (1891)

Leipziger Strasse must rank as one of the ugliest streets in
Berlin. That is some accolade in a city with what might seem
a somewhat idiosyncratic view of aesthetics.

This street was at the heart of the ideological rivalry of the Cold
War. The moment the Soviets began to close off their sector, West
Germany's most powerful press magnate and arch-conservative,
Axel Springer, decided to relocate his media empire right on the
border. The foundation stone was laid in 1959 on the site where
the ancient Jerusalem Church once stood. Inscribed on it were the
words, 'With confidence in the future of Germany'. Two years
later the East Germans put up the wall and the newspaper group
defiantly found itself 50 metres away from the front line of the
Cold War. 'My name is Axel Springer. I am a German. My city,
Berlin, is divided by a wall. My country is divided by barbed wire,'
declared the entrepreneur and scourge of the left who dominated
German media and politics for more than a generation. The
Springer HQ, nineteen storeys of glass and metal, was completed

in 1966. The Wall was not tall enough to obscure the view, so the East Berlin authorities decided to build a '*Springerdecker*', a line of twenty-five-storey 'Springer concealer' buildings to hide the offensive monument to capitalism. Construction began in 1969 with the demolition of all the remaining pre-war buildings in the neighbourhood. The high-rise complex on both sides of Leipziger Strasse was considered a model socialist living quarter, with 2,000 apartments, plus shops, a cultural centre and a medical centre. All with grey concrete and a wide, bare pavement separated by a six-lane highway. So proud were the authorities of the design that they put it on a stamp in 1979.

I lived on Leipziger Strasse in 1988 when I was working as a correspondent, just as the regime was starting to crumble. By then state surveillance was such that only citizens deemed reliable – or foreigners – were allowed to live so close to the Wall. For me, as a citizen of an Allied power, the proximity of Checkpoint Charlie was helpful. I could walk or drive over whenever I wanted, not something I would boast about to my East German friends. In the block itself, I sometimes found myself in the cranky old lift alongside a middle-aged man in an ill-fitting jacket and wearing grey plastic shoes. He was a Stasi cardboard cut-out, so vividly rendered in the film *The Lives of Others*. He was heading for the sealed-off top floor to listen in to the building's residents, and I enjoyed extracting an awkward 'good morning' from him as he went on his way.

Thirty years on, the Wall may be a distant memory, but Leipziger Strasse remains just as hideous as ever. The supermarkets have gone a little more upmarket. One or two commercial art galleries have moved into vacant lots. My old flat is now over a shop selling wedding dresses. It is neither shabby nor chic.

How different it used to be. In the late nineteenth century Leipziger Strasse and its adjoining Leipziger Platz were the epitome of glamour. The upper classes would be driven here in their hackney carriages from their villas in Charlottenburg or further away in Grunewald for glittering afternoons of shopping. This was home to one of the great temples of consumption, Germany's first department store. Georg Wertheim, the son of a haberdasher, came up with the idea of a single shop selling multiple items; customers would be lured not only by the variety and scale of what was on offer, but by the experience. His first Wertheim store was not just a place to buy, but a place to be seen. When it opened in 1898 it was the most lavish in Europe, with 100,000 lights illuminating the glass-roofed atrium, ornate staircases, elevators, fountains and palm trees. It had the city's most expensive restaurants and sought-after tables, a summer garden, winter garden and a roof garden. Just in case its wealthy customers ran out of money it had its own bank, with a strongroom and security guards. Extended several times over the next four decades, it eventually had a floor area double that of the Reichstag.

Not to be outdone, another entrepreneur, Hermann Tietz, opened another sumptuous outlet nearby. His stores would be, he declared, 'a model and guide for achieving an elevated life-style'. Competition became increasingly intense. Each new shop that opened sought to outdo the others for luxury. The grand stores were just one of the manifestations of the boom of the late nineteenth century, a period variously known as the *Gründerzeit* (foundation years) or *Kaiserzeit*, when Berlin finally turned into a metropolis.

Longer term, though, there was a problem. Both the men who founded these emporia were Jews. Tietz died in 1907, leaving the company to his nephew. Within months of the start of the Third Reich, both family firms were forced to hand over their assets. The Tietz firm was bought by the non-Jewish businessman Georg Karg, who renamed the stores 'Hertie' (an abbreviation of the original founder's name). The stores were 'Aryanized'; members of both families fled, most to the US, and after the war were embroiled in protracted restitution claims. The Hertie name is now associated with one of the largest charitable institutions in Germany; after being accused of glossing over parts of its history, in 2020 the foundation commissioned a review of the company's assets.

The last decades of the nineteenth century were a time of high living, of making money and spending it. The aristocratic German-born English writer Sybille Bedford described Berlin as 'the parvenu capital of Europe'. It was loud and pushy, with 'big money, big enterprise and big buildings, a city of Wagnerian flourishes'. It had all happened at breakneck speed. Not so long before, in his wanderings through Berlin and outlying Brandenburg, Theodor Fontane had written of a 'desert panorama, crisscrossed with asparagus beds'. It was still possible to cross the city from one end to the other by foot. It did not take long to get to the woods and fields. Now, suddenly, that bucolic world was gone.

For the first time, Berlin was firmly at the centre of European politics, industry, science and culture – and military prowess.

'Prussia's borders according to the Vienna treaties are not favourable for a healthy, vital state; it is not by speeches and majority resolutions that the great questions of the time are decided – that was the big mistake of 1848 and 1849 – but by iron and blood.' Bismarck delivered these ominous lines, referring to a poem by Max von Schenkendorf written during the Napoleonic wars, in a speech to the budget commission of the Prussian parliament in September 1862.

This was a year and a half into the reign of a new king of Prussia, Wilhelm I. Friedrich Wilhelm IV had died childless, leaving his younger brother, by now aged sixty-four, to take the throne. A staunch military man, Wilhelm had fought against Napoleon and had also played an important role in putting down the 1848 revolution in Berlin. He had already been in charge de facto for four years, as regent, after his brother suffered a stroke from which he didn't recover. During that time the increasingly assertive Prussian parliament, the Landtag, had repeatedly refused to sanction an increase in military spending. Wilhelm considered abdicating but instead was persuaded by his aides to appoint Bismarck as his prime minister and foreign minister, with a mandate to impose order.

Originally a sceptic of unification, Bismarck's experience of German politics and of international affairs (he had been ambassador to Moscow and Paris as well as a member of the Landtag) had convinced him of the need for a strong single state, with an army to be reckoned with. In the two great military figures of the day – Helmuth von Moltke and Albrecht von Roon – he found comrades in arms.

In less than a decade, between 1864 and 1871, Prussia fought three short wars, first against Denmark (the Danes were forced to cede control of the duchies of Schleswig, Holstein and Lauenburg) and then Austria and France. Victory in the 1866 Austro-Prussian War enabled Prussia to annex more territory, creating a North German Confederation under Prussian hegemony. This served as the prototype of the state that was about to emerge. The third and final act of German unification was the Franco-Prussian War of 1870–71, orchestrated by Bismarck to draw German states further to the west into allying with his Confederation.

These victories were portrayed as transcending individual rulers. Statues were erected across Berlin that emphasized a divine, mythical greatness. As early as 1865, after Prussia had seen off the Danes, construction began on a Victoria Column, the Siegessäule. It was situated at Königsplatz (now Platz der Republik, the square where the Reichstag was later built). The project took eight years to complete, by which point Berlin's place in the world had dramatically changed and the design was changed to reflect that. The base, made of polished red granite, features four bronze reliefs depicting scenes from the three victories and measures nearly 19 metres high. On the top stands the bronze sculpture of Victoria, the Roman goddess of victory. Sixty years later, the column was moved by the Nazis to its current location in the Tiergarten. That statue still stands. In spite of its grandiosity and military symbolism, Berliners regard it with equanimity, indeed even a modicum of affection, rewarding it with a nickname, 'Gold Else'.

Another allegorical figure of Berlin has not survived. In 1871, the king presented to the city an 11-metre-tall statue of Berolina, the female personification of the city, at Belle-Alliance-Platz, now called Mehringplatz, in Kreuzberg. It was inaugurated before a crowd of 500,000 to greet troops returning from the Franco-Prussian war. Its existence was fleeting; the festive decoration was

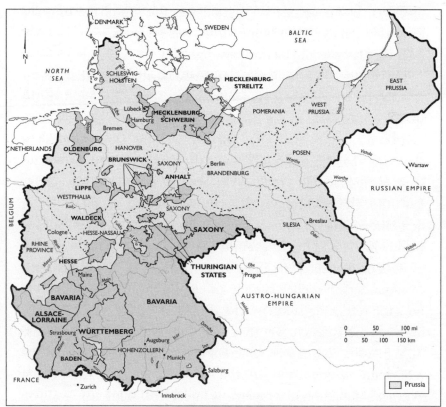

Unification of Germany, 1871

removed soon after the victory parade. A second Berolina was later unveiled in Alexanderplatz in 1895. That too didn't last long. It was dismantled in 1942 and is thought to have been melted down to build munitions.

On 18 January 1871, the new Germany was born. Wilhelm I was crowned Kaiser, no longer merely King of Prussia but the first emperor of a new German Reich, in the Hall of Mirrors at the Palace of Versailles, with his Iron Chancellor alongside. For several months, Versailles had been besieged by Prussian troops and was the seat of the headquarters of the German armies. Six hundred officers and all the German princes attended the ceremony, except for Ludwig II of Bavaria, who detested all things Prussian and was mourning the loss of Bavaria's independence. The French saw the use of Versailles as the site of the Imperial Proclamation as a great humiliation. The Treaty of Versailles half a century later would be their revenge.

On 16 June, on a brilliantly clear Sunday, 40,000 soldiers, some wearing laurel wreaths, paraded from the Tempelhof Field via the Brandenburg Gate to the Royal Palace. All wore iron crosses on their tunics, and many had victory wreaths slung over their shoulders. Lasting five hours, it was the largest military parade yet seen. More than half a million visitors are said to have travelled to Berlin for the celebrations. The city was bathed in colour. Unter den Linden, the *via triumphalis*, was lined with flagpoles adorned with banners and bright garlands; on the façade of the Academy of Arts on Pariser Platz hung giant pictures of victorious army commanders. A golden canopy and amphitheatre were put up to host the returning soldiers. The people of Berlin were handed a hefty tax increase to cover the costs of the elaborate celebrations.

While the Kaiser was reluctant to humiliate the defeated (he reportedly disapproved of the German painter Anton von Werner's depiction of Emperor Napoleon III lying helplessly on the ground in his allegorical depiction of the Battle of Sedan), the public were bloodthirsty, eager to rewrite the legacy of the French dynasty who had marched victoriously through the same city gates sixty-five years before. At the end of the five-hour-long parade, captured French flags were laid down in front of the (still unfinished) equestrian statue of King Friedrich Wilhelm III at the Lustgarten.

Berlin was approved as the capital of the new Germany, but the decision was not taken lightly. Many Germans saw Berlin as a relic of the old Prussia, militaristic and bombastic. Important cities such as Munich, Cologne and Hamburg feared that they would be overshadowed. Other options had been considered, from the smaller Kassel, Aachen and Erfurt to the most likely contender, Frankfurt, site of the ill-fated assembly after 1848. (A similarly fraught debate would be had more than a century later, in the early 1990s after reunification. The Bundestag then voted to restore the capital to Berlin, but only by a narrow majority. Four and a half decades of bourgeois calm in Bonn had been much to the liking of many in the political class. Berlin was, in the late twentieth as in the late nineteenth century, considered by many Germans as a little too uppity and unpredictable.)

It would have been hard to do anything else, however. By the 1870s Berlin had become the pre-eminent economic and financial force in Germany and increasingly across Europe.

This was the era of Borsig and Siemens, of rapid industrialization, and of the development of the railway that would give Berlin easy access across Europe. In 1836 a carpenter turned industrialist by the name of August Borsig bought a plot of land in a sparsely populated and poor part of the city called Moabit (named after the land where the Israelites had to wait before being allowed to enter the promised land of Canaan). He started an iron foundry in the district of Tegel; within a few years he had become the largest locomotive maker in Europe. As rivalry intensified with Britain, he invented a model that proved faster than Stephenson's *Rocket*. He was one of the first patricians of the era, building himself a sumptuous villa near his factory 'to bring beauty and harmony' to the workforce. To mark the completion of his 1000th locomotive, he invited 30,000 workers and local people to his grounds to drink and dance and to watch a Greek drama adapted for the emerging industrial class in which the gods celebrated the virtues of steam and a strong Germany.

Borsig died relatively young, but his company grew and in 1925 would build one of the city's monuments to industrial glamour: an Expressionist gem, the Borsig Tower. What remains of it now is the outline of a shopping centre.

Berliners watched as the railway forged a shapeless Prussia into a state so powerful that it could subjugate all of Germany and beyond. Thousands of factories were built in Berlin's industrial revolution, expanding into new districts. In 1884 a young artillery officer by the name of Werner Siemens decommissioned from the army. He had taken over charge of his three younger brothers following his parents' early deaths. He needed to try something different to make ends meet, so he took a room in Schöneberg to see what he could do with his nascent skills in telegraphy. After a five-month wait, he received the patent he had been waiting for to build a new kind of electric pointer telegraph for the railway.

'The German Empire was founded when the first railway was built,' wrote the novelist Wilhelm Raabe. The concept of *Kleinstaaterei* (small states doing their own thing) was dwindling as they began to be connected at speed. Train stations were built, monuments not just to a new technology, but also to a new aesthetic and sense of national self-confidence. The Potsdamer Bahnhof was the first, built in 1838 on Potsdamer Platz to link the two great cities. In quick succession came Lehrter station, which went to Hanover and the west (and is now Berlin's gleaming multi-storey central station), and Hamburg station, which was quickly subsumed by its bigger neighbour and has for the last thirty years been a museum of contemporary art.

The astonishing financial returns of the railways led to rapid expansion. Hundreds of kilometres of track were laid over the Prussian plain. A bewildering array of stations were built at the entrance points to the city. The Frankfurter station went east, all the way to Moscow. That was renamed the Ostbahnhof, and during the GDR era, because other routes had been closed off, it became East Berlin's main terminus. The area around the Frankfurter station, Friedrichshain, grew rapidly once the station opened. First came a waterworks at Stralauer Tor, then a large machine factory, then a sprawling slaughterhouse, and finally a factory owned by Julius Pintsch. His company produced a new form of compressed gas, Pintsch gas, that became the standard for illuminating railway carriages across Europe. The area where these industrial behemoths were located is now occupied by clubs and bars, most famously Berghain.

Getting across Berlin was becoming ever more arduous as the population and traffic grew. In March 1865 a licence was granted for the first horse-drawn railway between Charlottenburg and Kupfergraben. Two years later, city planners began an infrastructure project that would transform Berlin. They demolished the city's centuries-old fortifications, creating a path for an elevated beltway. Initially horse-drawn, the circle line, or Ringbahn, was powered soon after by steam engines. Its windows afforded views onto two entirely different worlds. On the outer side was the squalor of the new housing blocks springing up on the agricultural land over which Fontane had once strolled. Looking towards the city were the new factories, heralding a new age.

The pace of modernization increased further. In 1879, Siemens presented the world's first electric streetcar at the Berlin Industrial Exhibition. An overground train line going east to west was inaugurated shortly after. It is still debated whether the 'S' stands for *Schnellbahn* (fast train) or *Stadtbahn* (city train). North–South connections were somehow not deemed as important, and it would take more than half a century – indeed for the Nazis – to open such an S-Bahn track. In 1902, the first underground railway was opened (although part of it was elevated), running from Stralauer Tor in the southeast of the city to the Zoo in the centre. Berlin, with its Unterpflasterbahn, or U-Bahn, was the fifth European city to have an underground system, following London, Budapest, Glasgow and Paris. It did at least come in two years ahead of New York. The elegant stations and carriages were fitted out with red leather and mahogany. The price of tickets ensured that travellers were, initially, of an exclusive class. A new urban aesthetic was being created.

In 1892, the first private car was registered. Germany's obsession with the motor vehicle began. Originally the preserve of the super-wealthy, cars gradually became more affordable to the middle classes. Much of the action congregated around Potsdamer Platz, which had both the advantage and disadvantage of originally being outside the city wall. This new district of Friedrichstadt was first populated by immigrants – Austrians, Jews and Huguenots – in the late seventeenth century. It was not subject to the same regulations as those areas inside, and so was developed haphazardly. Moneymaking opportunities were grasped; vendors set up cheap food and drink stalls for passersby. At the other end of the scale, luxurious department stores, cafes and restaurants opened their doors, giving Potsdamer Platz the buzz of Times Square or Piccadilly Circus. Everything was about scale and glamour. One of the draws was Haus Piccadilly, with a 35-metre-high cupola dominating the skyline. It was opened in 1912 and contained the world's largest restaurant serving dishes from around the world, that could accommodate 2,500 people; its own theatre seated a mere 1,200. Up to eight orchestras and dance bands could perform in different parts of the building. Two years later, three weeks after the start of the war it was given the more patriotic name of Haus Vaterland. Opposite was the elegant belle époque Hotel Esplanade, with its neo-rococo Kaisersaal where Kaiser Wilhelm II invited friends for 'gentlemen's evenings' of card games and political chats. Charlie Chaplin and Greta Garbo were among its many celebrity guests.

Germany's first electric streetlights, courtesy of Siemens, had been installed in 1882. By the turn of the century the traffic was getting out of control, with more than 170,000 cars crossing the intersection per hour and just a few police officers trying vainly to instil some order. The city authorities looked abroad for a solution and found it in New York's Fifth Avenue. Europe's first traffic light arrived, mounted on a tower. A solitary policeman sat in a small cabin on the top, switching the lights around manually, until a way to automate them was found two years later.

With the car came the German obsession with speed. In 1913, the Automobil-, Verkehrs- and Übungsstrassen GmbH (roughly translated as the car, traffic and practice track limited company) built a racetrack through the Grünewald forest – the site of centuries of royal hunts and strolls. This 19-kilometre stretch, known as the AVUS, quickly became the world's first motorway, ferrying cars at speed into and out of the city, as it does now. The only thing that has changed is that it is no longer used for competitions. On one side stands an empty spectator tribune. The road was the brainchild of an architect, Hermann Jansen. He was awarded first place in the 1910 Greater Berlin Competition for his entry proposing radial roads for cars so that they could 'put the pedal to the metal'. It was also part of a wider scheme of orbital routes and green belts. This was the first concerted attempt to bring some planning to a city that had grown out of control.

The economic boom was fuelled by three factors: the removal

of internal tariffs; the liberalization of rules governing banks and joint-stock companies; and war reparations from France. From the mid-nineteenth century until the outbreak of the First World War, Berlin was rebuilt – not as a result of bombardment, but a thirst for progress. Buildings considered old or down-at-heel were primed for demolition. It took a considerable amount of lobbying to stop the bulldozer in its tracks, as the philosopher Walter Benjamin would later write: 'Destruction revitalises because it eliminates the traces of our own age.'

This was the one and only time when Berlin achieved the status many had long wished for, a *Weltstadt* (a world city). The arriviste had surpassed Paris and London in industrial output. It was the only time when it functioned like other major capitals – bringing business, finance, politics, media and art together in one metropolis, a centripetal force in a country of proud but ultimately provincial city states.

People of all classes dressed up just to stroll down streets such as Friedrichstrasse, where they would stop to admire the first electrical interior lighting at Café Bauer, installed in 1884. (The system malfunctioned a few days after opening and the whole place burnt down and had to be rebuilt.) Ordinary homes were converted into marble palaces for a new banking quarter established on Behrenstrasse and Französische Strasse, projecting an unshakeable faith in wealth and in Germany's role in creating it. Fashion established itself in Spittelmarkt. Newspapers set up shop in Zimmerstrasse and Kochstrasse. New hotels were also built. The Kaiserhof, which had so impressed the king when it first opened, was soon considered out of date, as was the Bristol. Neither was up to the standards of the Ritz in Paris or the Savoy in London. A former carpenter's apprentice, Lorenz Adlon, who had made a bit of a name for himself in the restaurant trade, came up with an idea. He persuaded a man about town, a Prussian colonel, privy councillor and music impresario called Count

Friedrich Wilhelm von Redern, to sell his palace in order to build a hotel. That wasn't a hard task: Redern had gambling debts and desperately needed the money.

The problem was that his palace was classed as a historical monument, and it needed the intervention of the king to agree to its demolition. Located in the heart of Pariser Platz by the Brandenburg Gate and designed by Schinkel in the 1830s, it was one of the centres of Berlin social and cultural life. The house contained an impressive collection of old master paintings from Dürer to Rubens. Another of the draws was the opulent garden designed by landscape architect Peter Joseph Lenné. Adlon also managed to persuade the British government, whose embassy was next door, to sell part of their garden. When it opened, the Adlon (why not call it after yourself?) was dubbed 'half museum, half living room'. It personified style and wealth. The vast central hall featured a bust of the Kaiser. It was the place to be seen, particularly for English tea at 5 p.m. Since reopening in 1997 it has brought back many of the features such as the fountain in the centre of the foyer, ensuring that it is once again a place to be seen (by some) for an overpriced beer or cappuccino. It has also retained the tag as hotel of choice for some celebrities – Michael Jackson infamously dangled his baby over one of its fourth-floor balconies in 2002.

The Kaiser became obsessed with the English, with their colonies, their wealth and their grand buildings. He wanted something to outshine the Palace of Westminster in London, which had just been rebuilt in grand style after a fire. It would take a quarter of a century to realize these plans, by which time neither the king nor his chancellor would still be in charge. In the meantime, the Landtag would be housed in Leipziger Strasse at the headquarters of the Royal Porcelain Manufactory – the corporate favourite of Friedrich the Great – which had been told to find new premises.

A location for a new parliament was finally found. Once again, a nobleman and art collector, this time a Polish one, was called upon to do the decent thing. Atanazy Raczynski had moved to Berlin in 1834, choosing a property at 21 Unter den Linden to house his collection of old masters. A decade later, as his collection expanded, he acquired some prime real estate on Königsplatz to construct a palace. The king allowed him to have the site as long as the gallery was open to the public. On the count's death in 1874, his descendants were instructed to sell it to the government. The building was subsequently demolished.

That was just the start of the trouble. The Frankfurt architect Paul Wallot soon despaired of the difficulty of the task, complaining of the absence of any form of national identity or parliamentarism to work from. 'We are building a national edifice without having a national style,' he said. It took until 1894 for the new Reichstag to be opened, by which point Berlin and Germany had undergone a series of political shocks. In March 1888, Wilhelm I died, just short of his ninety-first birthday. Three days before his death, his only son, Friedrich III, was diagnosed with cancer. His reign lasted three months, resulting in that year being dubbed the 'year of the three Kaisers'.

The new Kaiser, Wilhelm II, was disdainful of the current crop of politicians, and even more contemptuous of the building that was to house them, calling it 'the imperial monkey house'. He entered it only twice in the course of his thirty-year reign. He also vetoed the inscription that Wallot planned for the entrance portal – *Dem Deutschen Volke* (To the German people) – regarding it as pretentious. It was finally added in 1916, as a way of garnering popular support for the failing war effort. The monkey house endured decades of upheaval – the fire of 1933, the hoisting of the Soviet flag in 1945 and decades of division and dereliction. It is now quite simply one of the world's great parliamentary buildings, its combination of old and new architecture a manifestation of democratic transformation. In 1993, three years after unification, a global competition for its renovation was won by British-based starchitects Foster and Partners; the aspect for which it is best known, its glass dome, was agreed two years later. In 1995, just before the renovation began, the edifice was wrapped in a million square feet of aluminium-coated fabric by French artist duo Christo and Jeanne-Claude, who have created sensations by covering many public buildings around the world, including the Arc de Triomphe in Paris. Huge crowds came to see the installation, which was described by the artists as a rite of passage into a new era.

On 19 April 1999, Norman Foster presented a symbolic key to the new building to Bundestag president Wolfgang Thierse. Visitors marvel when taking the circular walk up the cupola, gazing down below them at the hemicycle chamber. Equally impressive are the areas where the members of parliament work and meet in committees: bright, modern but ever mindful of the burdens of the past. The main hallways are studded with art installations such as the acrylic panels hanging from the ceiling, the work of Carlfriedrich Claus, a GDR artist influenced by kabbalah and Marxism, and Gerhard Richter's haunting cycle of paintings, *Birkenau*, depicting the Auschwitz-Birkenau concentration camp. Only in Berlin.

Back to Wilhelm II: the Kaiser also rejected the plan for a World Fair in the manner of Paris, London or Philadelphia, on the grounds that Berlin was not yet grand enough. The city had to make do with a lesser title. Still, the Great Industrial Exhibition in the new Treptow Park was impressive. On display were Borsig engines, cranes from Julius Pintsch, gadgets from Siemens and AEG. Luxury consumer products ranged from Bechstein pianos to electric ovens. There was even a 'hall of appetite', a monument to gluttony. Despite recording five million visitors, the fair was a financial disaster, an example of hubris and over-stretch.

Yet in other ways the new Kaiser was just as prone as his predecessors to grandiloquence. He had long been frustrated by the lack of a cathedral for the capital city, anything to compare with Notre Dame or St Paul's. Most of all, he wanted a Protestant counterpoint to St Peter's in Rome. He considered the original Schinkel-designed church, on the site opposite the Royal Palace and bordering the Lustgarten, to be too modest. It was demolished in 1893. Architect Julius Carl Raschdorff was commissioned for the new church but had to present three designs before Wilhelm II was satisfied. It took ten years for the more pompous, neo-baroque new cathedral to be built, dominated by an ornate dome that was crowned by a lantern with a golden cross. This was to be a celebration of the Hohenzollern dynasty, with ninety sarcophagi in the family crypt.

The cathedral was heavily damaged by war bombing. Ulbricht had intended to tear it down, partly due to lack of money, but other buildings were higher on his list for demolition. In the end, the West German Protestant church picked up most of the bill for renovation. The church partially reopened in 1983, but even at the time of reunification it was still being rebuilt. The original style was described as 'Wilhelminismus' or 'Historismus'. Kaiser Wilhelm II ushered in a programme for public buildings marking a return to traditional religious values, as a counterweight to growing radical tendencies.

Across the city, in the heart of Charlottenburg, the foundation stone was laid in March 1891 for a new church to be named after his grandfather. The Kaiser Wilhelm Memorial Church was consecrated in September 1895, another monument to bombast. Intricate mosaics inside the church depicted scenes from the life and work of Wilhelm I. Between the wars this was the church of choice for society weddings. On the night of 23 November

1943, the church was destroyed in an RAF air raid. The city government, the Senate, wanted to remove what was left of it and construct something afresh. The initial design included the demolition of the spire of the old church but following pressure from the public, it was decided to incorporate it into the new design. The stump of the west tower became the centre of a five-piece ensemble. The square in which it stands was renamed in 1947 to Breitscheidplatz after Rudolf Breitscheid, a Social Democrat murdered at Buchenwald. The Gedächtniskirche, as it has come to be known, or 'the chipped tooth flanked by a lipstick tube', as it is also called, is nothing if not striking.

This building personifies perhaps more than any other the struggles between modernity, history and destruction, all concertina-ing into an eyesore of which the city is curiously proud. Throughout the period of division from 1945 to 1989 the church found itself demarcating the centre of the unofficial city of 'West Berlin'. It marked the apex of the grand Kurfürstendamm. A few hundred metres beyond was KaDeWe. The Department Store of the West was originally built in 1907 at the peak of Wilhelmine hubris. Bombed, as were all the surrounding buildings, it was given a grand reopening in 1950. This was the place where you could buy everything; the West was mocking the communist East.

By the turn of the twentieth century, three faces of the city vied for influence – politics, economics and military. The tensions were evident throughout. Berlin was home to more than a hundred military institutions and barracks. Wilhelm II built up his army and developed his navy, sending Germany into ever more distant imperial skirmishes. The Kaiser, who loved to parade down Unter den Linden in his golden helmet with its ornate plumes, famously declared in 1901 his intention to extend his imperial domain, to seek for Germany 'a place in the sun'.

Less discussed is another line in the speech. 'For when the German has once learned to direct his glance upon what is distant and great, the pettiness which surrounds him in daily life on all sides will disappear.'

For all the advances, Berlin was not at ease with itself. Many Berliners themselves shared a disdain for a city that had grown out of all proportion. It had finally made it as a *Weltstadt*, but, they asked, what did it stand for? Whose interests did it serve?

'The most beautiful city in the world', was the ironic title of an essay written in 1899 by the industrialist Walter Rathenau. He loved Berlin, he contended, 'more than all the other big cities in the world put together'. It might not match its rivals for history or culture, but 'as a factory city' it excelled. Baedeker's guide of 1903 showed similar disdain: 'Three quarters of its buildings are quite new; [Berlin] suffers from a certain lack of historical interest.'

A study published in 1904 found that 372 monuments had been erected to Wilhelm I. The most hubristic of them all is the Siegesallee, a monumental boulevard created in 1901, with a chain of more than thirty-two marble monumental statues of Hohenzollern and pre-Hohenzollern heroes stretching for 750 metres along each side of the road, from Albert the Bear to (inevitably) Kaiser Wilhelm I. Only one of the statues is of a woman: Elisabeth of Bavaria, *Schöne Else*, or Beautiful Beth, praying on her knees before her husband.

The king loved his grand highway. Foreign dignitaries were required to be driven down the Siegesallee if they were arriving from either the Potsdam or Anhalter railway stations to the Royal Palace. It was also the most direct route to the Reichstag for members of parliament, who were reminded of the supremacy and grandeur of the monarchy. Straddling the Tiergarten, the Avenue of Victory was a popular place for Berliners to walk. It was also a popular place to mock. A famous advertisement for a brand of toothpaste in 1903 featured the street lined with gigantic bottles of Odol. Locals dubbed it 'Puppenallee' (the Avenue of the Dolls).

In 1918, after Germany's defeat and the abdication of the king, demands grew to have the statues destroyed. The soldiers' and workers' council voted instead to keep them. One supporter of that decision was the Jewish left-wing journalist and author, Kurt Tucholsky. A satirist who spared no one in his denunciations of philistinism, nationalism and militarism, he pleaded to leave the 'dolls' as documents of a 'great age' – and to smile.

Ironically, it was Hitler who wanted to do away with them, as they got in the way of his plans for the new city, Germania. Many of the statues were damaged in the war, some were destroyed. In a 1948 film called *The Berliner*, the lead character, Otto Normalverbraucher, aka Ordinary Otto, is a soldier struggling to return to civilian life. In one scene, he gives an ironic salute to the Kaiser's dolls. Back in real life, the Brits, who were in charge of the district, wanted to remove what was left of the statues; a curator intervened and persuaded them to allow him to bury a number of them in the grounds of the nearby Schloss Bellevue. In 1979 they were rediscovered and relocated to a museum called the Lapidarium, on the site of Berlin's first sewage-pumping station. In 2006, that closed; they would subsequently be put on display in Spandau Citadel.

Vain, petty, unaesthetic and spiritually barren: just some of the depictions of late Wilhelmine Berlin. The playwright Frank Wedekind wrote that dark forces were at large and had been given the keys of the kingdom by the bourgeoisie out of greed or cowardice or lack of wit. And then there was the smut. The artist George Grosz describes Berlin on the eve of war. The rich were diverted by shopping trips to Wertheim by day and masked balls by night. And everyone availed themselves of the prostitutes. 'Because we had read Flaubert and Maupassant, we endowed this form of night life with lyrical qualities. Many younger poets wrote odes to girls of easy virtue, to pimps, and to free love in general.'

One book encapsulates the case against Berlin, the vulgar, debauched faux capital city. In *Berlin – ein Stadtschicksal*, published in 1910 and translated either as 'A city's fate' or 'Psychogram of a city', the cultural critic Karl Scheffler describes women 'trying to be cultured' by using too much make-up, powder and expensive hats. They look nothing better than servant girls: 'sentimental, profane, affected, demanding and frightfully uneducated'. As for the men, these jumped-up subalterns, 'you don't know where to begin'. The modern Berliner, he suggests, 'has not a drop of a born gentleman'. Berlin had been baptized late, the 'most easterly periphery of the zone of German culture'. In short it could never be compared to great imperial cities such as Athens or Rome, London or Paris.

Scheffler's hatred of the city was, if nothing else, mistimed. The parvenu label no longer applied. Finally, after all these years, this was Berlin's moment. Its population had increased, it had enjoyed years of growth; it was the sophisticated *Weltstadt* everyone envied, and some feared. If it was not at ease with itself now, then when would it ever be? His work ends with this polemic: 'Berlin does not want love from its inhabitants. If the spirit of the city is not deeply national, it is not sentimental either.' He concludes with a phrase that Berliners all seem to remember by heart, that has become synonymous with their anxiety about their place in the world and in history. The hidden tragedy of its existence, he writes, condemns Berlin 'forever to become, never to be'. The even greater tragedy is that Scheffler would not have to wait long to be proven right. Thanks to the Nazis, the expulsion and murder of Berlin's Jews, the war and division, his dictum would come true again after all.

NINE

Sleeping in shifts

The nineteenth-century industrialized poor

Berlin is a skeleton which aches in the cold.
CHRISTOPHER ISHERWOOD (1945)

The history of great cities is often confined to the grand boulevards and the grand monuments. But one very ordinary street encapsulates the vicissitudes of Berlin's past two centuries and more.

In the mid-eighteenth century, during the time of Friedrich the Great, Berlin had grown to capacity inside its customs gates; farming lands beyond were identified for construction. Thirty new homes were to be created to the north, between the Hamburg and Rosenthal gates, to house sixty families. The streets were laid out in parallel lines and designated numerically. It was originally called the *Dritte Reihe* (the third row), but later came to be known as Ackerstrasse, Field Street. As the area grew, further houses were built, all with symmetrical designs and identical land parcels for small gardens. By the middle of the nineteenth century, the population was booming as new factories demanded an influx of workers. Soon over half of the city's inhabitants would be migrants from within Germany and further afield. With housing in desperately short supply, the chief of police turned to a surveyor, a qualified civil engineer for just one year, to come up with a plan for a city of up to two million people. The *Bebauungsplan der Umgebungen Berlins* (Building Land Use Plan for the Environs of Berlin) produced by James Hobrecht, a thirty-six-year-old official at the Baupolizei (the Prussian Building Police) has formed the foundation of the city ever since.

While Schinkel and other architects before had inspired many of the great landmarks, this was a charge of a different order. Hobrecht travelled across Europe to learn from other cities seeking to cope with rapid urban expansion. In Hamburg and London he was particularly interested in the development of sewerage systems and other infrastructure. He admired the precision and scale of Baron Haussmann's grand project for Paris, the first stage of which was already underway. The plan Hobrecht produced in 1862 was nothing short of revolutionary. This was social engineering on an epic scale. The idea was to mix people of all classes in large, self-contained blocks usually five storeys high and extending six courtyards back. The wealthy would be at the front with direct access to the street, shops and services. The next step down would be in the first courtyard and so on, with the poorest at the very back, out of sight, where nowadays the recycling bins are put. Buildings such as these were called *Mietskaserne* (rental barracks).

Regulations required that the courtyards had to be wide enough, precisely 5.34 metres by 5.34 metres, to allow for a fire engine to turn. A policeman was stationed to keep order. In response to daily fires across the network of tenement buildings, the fire brigade was provided with special axes with small heads and curved picks to break into doors. The largest of these rental barracks was called Meyers Hof, named after a textile factory owner and one of the major local employers. The address was Ackerstrasse 132; at its peak 2000 people were crammed into 300 flats across six courtyards. It was in Wedding, a district that has a special place in working-class folklore.

When you walk past the building now, a drab post-war grey concrete residential block, you would have no idea that this was the site of one of the great housing experiments of the nineteenth century. You would also struggle to appreciate the later importance of the street. A century later, when the Berlin Wall was erected along the perpendicular street, Bernauer Strasse, Ackerstrasse was divided in two.

As ever in the city, one trauma is superimposed on another on the same site.

The first records of a village called Weddingcke date back to 1384 and over the centuries it was avoided by neighbours for its Satanic associations. During Berlin's last witch trial in 1728, a miller's daughter from the village called Miss D. Steffin confessed to having had sex with the Devil. By the mid-nineteenth century, an abundance of cheap, unused land made Wedding popular with the first wave of industrialists to build factories. The problem was the shortage of accommodation that was barely habitable for people on slender or middle incomes. Even public officials struggled. The city's mayor, Arthur Hobrecht (the older brother of James), had to scour far and wide to find an apartment in his own city that he could afford on a bureaucrat's salary. The gap between the rich and the new army of industrial poor was as high as anywhere in Europe. In Tiergarten and other comfortable areas stretching to the west and southwest, the infant mortality rate was 52 per 1,000 births, an impressively low figure for its time. By contrast, in Wedding and similar working-class districts, the rate was ten times higher. Just under half of children born would die before they reached their first birthday. Red Wedding, as it came to be known, became a hotbed of political radicalism.

A distinctive feature of apartment blocks of the time was the *Berliner Zimmer*, a *Gelenkraum* (hinge room) connecting the wealthier front tenements to the side wings at each corner of the rental barracks. Although these rooms were large, they provided very little light, with just one corner window looking out onto the courtyard. Some families used the room as a narrow dining room or library, others as a passageway. Engels saw the *Zimmer* as the epitome of working-class misery, bemoaning in an 1893 letter 'this hostel of darkness, of stuffy air, and of the Berlin philistinism that feels comfortable in it, impossible in all the rest of the world'. They are now marketed as something 'distinctly Berlin'.

Almost immediately, the concept of the *Mietskaserne* became highly politicized; it continues to be hotly debated by contemporary architects, city planners and social historians today, as they engage in a furious political battle over housing in Berlin. James Hobrecht's notion of mixed-use housing is not dissimilar to that of many planners in the late twentieth and into the twenty-first century, even if the language he used was of his era. In his plan, he spoke of 'the children from the basement flats going along the same corridors to the free school as the children from the upper classes go to the grammar school'. He went on, 'In between the extremes of the social classes the poor will be nurtured by the cultured life of the civil servants, artists, professors and teachers.' It seems he did not anticipate his housing blocks would provide rich pickings for speculative landlords, driving many in the newly industrialized working class into even greater penury.

The case against the rental barracks goes like this: these quarters were squalid, poorly lit and disease-ridden. The industrialists who built them were interested only in cheap labour and maximizing profit. In the poorest parts of the city, life expectancy for men was as low as thirty; for women working in the sewing sweatshops of Berlin it was twenty-six. Contaminated drinking water led to typhus and cholera epidemics. Tuberculosis was rife. Most residents relied on public pumps for drinking water. A smallpox epidemic in 1871 swept through the city with such force that the

Berlin garrison made provisions for hospital tents to be set up on their parade ground at Tempelhof. It took another three years for the first municipal hospital to open, in Friedrichshain.

Desperate to make a few extra coppers, people rented out their beds during the day to strangers. Many slept in shifts. It was estimated that even by the end of the century fewer than one in ten dwellings in Berlin had a toilet. (By contrast, most households in London had at least an outdoor privy.)

For much of the nineteenth century, before and after the advent of the rental barracks, conditions in Berlin spawned a canon of literature and art focusing on inequality, poverty and anomie. One of the earliest accounts of this genre was written by Ernst Dronke, a young radical and later in life a friend of Karl Marx. Dronke spent time in the capital conducting on-the-ground reportage of extraordinary detail. His two-volume book, *Berlin*, published in 1846, landed him two years in jail for insulting the dignity of His Majesty, for misuse of office and defamation. It was reprinted only in modern times. He found everything about Berlin and its environs alien to human dignity. His first impressions of the Brandenburg countryside, as he approached the city, were of 'flat, barren plains with their burning dust'. He fulminated about Berlin's decadence, inequality and a sense of impermanence. It was the plight of the very poor that stirred him to the greatest fury. Children, he noted, were

> sent to the factories as soon as they are the least bit strong enough. They work here from 5 a.m. to 9 p.m. They suffer not only physically, for example through coughing, deformed posture and crooked legs, but also morally and psychologically. They are totally ruined in the bleach factories where they inhale poisonous fumes the whole day. Even grown men can hardly survive a few years in these factories. And yet mothers still send their children here even though they know this means a sure

death for their little ones. Maybe they do it for this very reason. The children are a burden to them, and misery robs them of every sense of being human. From time to time, parents get rid of their children through blatant crime; they have no food for the young ones and perhaps only a few bare bones to nibble on themselves, so what should they do with their children? Berlin newspapers frequently report on small, unidentified corpses being found in sewers.

Sarcasm was also used as a tool by writers drawing attention to the poverty and squalor of mid-nineteenth century Berlin. In a one-act vaudeville performed in 1866 entitled *Domestic Bliss – or, Berlin becomes a World City*, a servant says: 'Yet another building has collapsed, three people have disappeared without a trace and the bodies of six new-born babies have been found on the Orphans' Bridge. London and Paris can no longer compete with us.' Berlin 'did not emerge from a state of barbarism and into civilisation until after 1870', declared one of Germany's first socialist politicians, August Bebel, using a phrase almost identical to one used by Friedrich the Great. Bebel was exercised initially by the lack of sanitation.

Visitors, especially women, often became desperate when nature called. In the public buildings, the sanitary facilities were un-believably primitive. One evening I went with my wife to the Royal Theatre. I was revolted when, between acts, I visited the room designated for the relief of men's bodily needs. In the middle of the room stood a giant tub, and along the sides were chamber pots which each user had to empty himself into the communal pot.

Hobrecht's boss, Carl Ludwig Friedrich von Hinckeldey, was another remarkable individual. The conservative general director of police for Prussia believed that the only way to keep in check the revolutionary ardour that had been unleashed in 1848 was for the state to oversee the provision of basic services for the working class. Not for the first time, the roots of social reform could be found in the state's desire for control. Berlin's Waterworks Company began operating in 1856, a professional fire brigade not long after. Hinckeldey did not see the fruits of Hobrecht's endeavours. When he tried to shut down an illegal gambling session at the exclusive Hotel du Nord club, he was insulted by a nobleman taking part. The story goes that Hinckeldey challenged the man to a duel, assuming that the king would intervene, which he didn't.

Writers of the time and after focused on a variety of aspects of the social stratification of the Wilhelmine period. In his 1896 novel, *Die Poggenpuhls*, Theodor Fontane wrote of industrialization eroding the tranquillity of rural Brandenburg. Werner Hegemann, in his 1930 book, *Das Steinerne Berlin* (Berlin of stone), described the city as the largest tenement in the world. He drew a straight line between city planning, impoverishment and susceptibility to dictatorship. Unsurprisingly, his books were publicly burned by the Nazis in 1933.

How did Berlin's industrialism and poverty compare with others? In March 1839, Prussia passed a law controlling the practice of child labour in its industrial regions. It prohibited the employment of children in factories under the age of nine and limited those under sixteen to ten hours a day. These regulations were, in nineteenth-century terms, fairly progressive, and the first of their kind on the European continent. France's first major child labour law was not passed until two years later. Britain had already passed the first Factory Act (outlining regulations for children under fourteen) six years before, but Prussia's law was more extensive.

Towards the end of the century the quality of housing started to improve. The Berliner Spar- und Bauverein (Berlin Savings and Building Society) was the first institution to finance construction of better-quality blocks for working people, allowing the circulation of fresh air, adequate sanitation and access to green space. The consensus among contemporary historians is that these welfare reforms were motivated by the state's desire to dictate the terms of social provision, thereby neutralizing the threat of socialism or other moves towards the politicization of the workforce. The sociologist George Steinmetz points out that national health insurance, industrial accident insurance and old-age pensions, all introduced by Bismarck in the 1880s, were an effective way of lulling the working classes into complacency.

Given the nature of Berlin's politics, often a left-liberal echo chamber, it comes as a relief occasionally to hear a counterview. Dieter Hoffmann-Axthelm has written a series of books on the history of housing and city planning in Berlin, from the high-rise to the town house. He has written entire tomes on individual buildings and streets. In one of his most impressive works, *Prussians at Schlesisches Tor: The Story of Köpenicker Strasse 1589–1989*, he examines 'from below' how the rapid development of the timber trade, the textile industry, the emergence of a civic self-government and social liberalism, as well as residential growth, played out on the stage of one street in the centre of the city.

We are discussing the historiography of urban poverty while sipping artisanal apple and wild berry juice at tables outside a wine bar in Prenzlauer Berg. Estate agents now refer to this micro-district as NOTO, north of Torstrasse, the road that used to form the customs wall. We are not far from Ackerstrasse and the site of the most notorious rental barracks. Hoffmann-Axthelm insists that much of the denunciation of the Berlin of the mid-to-late nineteenth century is a construct that is used by the contemporary left in their arguments – and laments – about the present-day housing shortages. He refrains from using the catch-all term of reproach, woke (as beloved by the German right as any other), but he does rail at what he calls 'the historical ignorance and nonchalance of today'. While zealous developers, aided by weak regulators, tried to maximize profit and exacerbated hardship, working-class Berliners were not, he says, treated worse than their equivalents in London or Paris. He invites me instead to focus on the extraordinary ambition of the time.

In 1800, Berlin's population stood at 915,000. By 1890 it had doubled to two million. Within barely two decades, by the start of the First World War, it had doubled again to almost four million, making it the largest city in Europe. By 1900, more than 60 per cent of Berliners had come from elsewhere. One statistic, highlighted in a tableau at the Märkisches Museum, is remarkable. It shows that population density in Berlin in 1900 (30,000 people per square kilometre) was double that of Tokyo in 2017. Yet Hoffmann-Axthelm also says that inhabitants of the rental barracks were provided with an average of 34 square metres of living space per person – the same amount they had in their homes outside the city.

On one point, conservative and liberal historians largely agree: the internal courtyards of these buildings should also be seen in the context of social reform. They formed self-sustaining, often proud, communities where children played, women hung laundry, grocers tended their produce and independent craftsmen plied their trades. These *Hinterhöfe* (back yards) have a similar function now, with mini playgrounds, bike racks and recycling bins.

A third of all the buildings currently standing in Berlin were built in just twenty years, 1890–1910. Contemporary estate agents seize with alacrity on properties from the Wilhelmine era, with their wrought-iron front doors, wide staircases and high ceilings. A few have remained largely untouched, most have been restored and spruced up; other buildings are being 'reinterpreted', ersatz designs built from scratch. Whenever one of these *Altbauten* (old buildings) goes on the market for rental or purchase, they can attract hundreds of interested customers, with queues for viewing stretching around the block.

Throughout this period, infrastructure was growing apace – public transport, sewerage, bathhouses, medical care. One development became intrinsic to life in Berlin, for rich and poor, and profits – the brewery. They were popping up across the city, but they were concentrated in one area above all. In the early nineteenth century, Prenzlauer Berg was still part of the rural Feldmark region beyond the city walls. Farms harvested grain and the landscape was known as Windmühlenberg (Windmill Hill). The first beer garden, Prater, sprang up in 1837 on what is now Kastanienallee, one of the most prominent streets. It became a meeting place for families needing fresh countryside air away from the cramped rental barracks. It also became a centre for political agitation. It still stands, serving beer and sausages in the same large courtyard. The difference is that Kastanienallee (Chestnut Alley) is now mocked as 'Casting Alley', a place where wannabe creatives pose, surrounded by some of the most expensive real estate in the city. By 1900 there were fourteen breweries in Prenzlauer Berg alone. One of the largest, Schultheiss, is now a multi-space arts centre called KulturBrauerei. Not only was the brewery a huge source of local jobs, but it was also admirably active in the social reforms of the late nineteenth century, providing subsidized hot meals, bathhouses, free coal deliveries and loans for workers, even insurance policies for workplace accidents. *Kneipen* (pubs) were by now springing up everywhere and you didn't have to go far to find one. Wedding, for example, had 1,307 taverns, one for every 345 inhabitants; in Kreuzberg the proportion was one in 230.

The first stirrings of socialism came in 1863 with the founding of the German Workers' Association, the precursor to the SPD, on the Prater's stage. Even though the party's original demands were relatively mild – an expansion of factory inspections along with minor reforms in military service – Bismarck immediately smelt danger. A series of anti-socialist laws were passed; constituencies were gerrymandered to ensure minimal representation in the Reichstag. In 1878 he had the party banned for twelve years, which served only to increase its support and radicalize its demands. In the federal election of 1890, the party secured the highest share of the vote, but fewer than 10 per cent of the seats. Both trends continued and it took another two decades before the SPD became the largest bloc. All the while Berlin was its hotbed.

Bismarck stayed away from the city as much as possible, preferring the sanctuary of his country estates at Varzin in eastern Pomerania, now Warcino in Poland, and Friedrichsruh, just outside Hamburg. For more traditional Germans, Berliners were too liberal, too subversive, with a press too outspoken and politicians prone to socialist intrigue. One conservative newspaper article, marking the twentieth anniversary of the declaration of the Reich, concluded: 'There is no place as unloved in all Germany as the capital Berlin.' Even as early as the 1860s, Berlin had an astonishing fifty-eight weekly and thirty-two daily papers. Many called it the city of newspapers, *Zeitungsstadt*, reflecting its thirst for knowledge and involvement in politics of all persuasions. The traditional seat of learning and books, Leipzig, was being challenged. On every street, newspaper kiosks and bookshops did a flourishing trade. To capitalize on the trend, a printer by the name of Ernst Litfass pitched the idea of installing advertising pillars on street corners. The chief of police agreed, giving Litfass a monopoly on the hundreds of columns made from iron plates. The *Litfasssäulen*, which stand to this day, were intended for the growing consumer culture. They became a place where people posted political calls to action. They also became a place where the state could easily monitor agitation. Those requesting space for political material were noted on police files.

The last two decades of the nineteenth century were also a time of huge cultural expansion. Some seventy-five theatres were established in short order thanks to private finance. This was about profit, not philanthropy. Investors were convinced that such was the enthusiasm, and such was the disposable income, of Berlin's nouveaux riches, that they could make money. And they did. Artists followed and fuelled the political agitation. Salons dating back to the eighteenth century continued to be popular among mainstream society, but in 1892 a group of artists decided to set up something new, the Berlin Secession. The catalyst was a decision by the officially recognized Association of Berlin Artists to close down an exhibition by the Norwegian artist Edvard Munch (he of the *The Scream*), denouncing his work as 'repugnant, ugly and mean'. The Secession, which held its first exhibition in an outhouse of the Theater des Westens in Charlottenburg, became the home of the Expressionist move-ment around the turn of the century, bringing into its fold the likes of Emil Nolde, Max Beckmann, Heinrich Zille and Wassily Kandinsky. It was led by Max Liebermann. The son of a wealthy cotton manufacturer, Liebermann was prevented on the Kaiser's personal orders from exhibiting in public, though he got away with it by holding private shows.

The king took to intervening personally on artistic matters, seeing himself as the ultimate determiner of taste and decency of the Reich. He denounced realist portrayals of workers and farmers and other unseemly depictions as *Rinnsteinkunst* (gutter art). This served only to make Wilhelm an object of ridicule among a bourgeoisie increasingly drawn to the new cultural offerings. Another artist to earn the scorn of Wilhelm II was Käthe Kollwitz. In 1898 a jury at the Great Berlin Art Exhibition, on which Liebermann sat, recommended that a gold medal be awarded to Kollwitz for her etching cycle depicting the failed Silesian weavers' revolt half a century earlier. Kollwitz had been drawn to the subject after watching a banned, and therefore private, performance of a naturalist drama called *The Weavers* by Gerhart Hauptmann. Liebermann and Hauptmann would stay lifelong friends of hers. The king was furious at the award. 'Please, gentlemen, a medal for a woman, that is really going too far,' he declared. 'That would amount to a debasement of every high distinction.' The scandal brought Kollwitz to fame. She would later become the first woman elected as a member of the Prussian Academy of Arts.

Born in 1867 in Königsberg, Käthe Schmidt was the fifth child of radical parents. They recognized her talent early on in childhood, putting her under the tutelage of a series of prominent artists. At sixteen, she was already involved in the School for Women Artists, making drawings of working people, sailors and peasants she saw in her father's office. While studying in Munich (very much the centre of German art) she met a medical student called Karl Kollwitz. They married and in 1891 moved to Berlin, to a square called Wörther Platz in Prenzlauer Berg, where he tended to the poor. Their house, Weissenburger Strasse 25, was later bombed, and the rubble removed. The reconstructed building where she lived, now named Kollwitzstrasse 56a, is situated in one of the areas with the highest property values in Berlin. But not then. Her husband's medical practice in that building allowed him to study closely the link between unemployment, illness, child hunger and lack of basic rights.

'All middle-class life seemed pedantic to me. On the other hand, I felt the proletariat had guts,' she later wrote. 'Compassion and commiseration were at first of very little importance in attracting me to the representation of proletarian life; what mattered was simply that I found it beautiful.' Such self-deprecation was perhaps required of a woman at the time, but it did not tell the full story of an artist driven by political conviction. A few years after completing *The Weavers' Revolt*, Kollwitz embarked on her second cycle, the *Peasants' War*. In the 1520s in southern Germany, peasants took up arms against feudal lords and the church. The title of each work in the cycle, 'Ploughing', 'Raped', 'Sharpening the Scythe', 'Arming in the Vault', 'Outbreak', 'The Prisoners' and 'After the Battle', depicts the violence baldly but also passionately. She produced posters of emaciated proletarian women to draw attention to exploitation in the garment industry, where 60,000 women in Berlin alone worked in terrible conditions.

Tragedy defined the rest of her life. Weeks after the outbreak of war in 1914 the younger of her two sons, Peter, volunteered to serve. Aged eighteen, he needed his parents' consent. They initially refused, but a combination of his insistence and the fervour sweeping the country led them to change their minds. He became a musketeer in the 207th Reserve Infantry Regiment; ten days after bidding his parents farewell and with almost no training, he fell in the trenches of Flanders, at Diksmuide, in one of the first battles of the war.

Kollwitz never recovered from her loss and from an aching sense of regret. She became an ardent pacifist, and in 1923 produced another cycle, called *War*. She wanted to show the horrors to combat the jingoistic sentiment gripping Germany again. A decade later she and her husband were among a small group of artists and scientists who signed an appeal against National Socialism in June 1932, before the party had taken over, and again in February 1933, weeks after they had. She was immediately thrown out of the Academy of Arts, rejecting friends' lobbying to have her membership reinstated. 'The souls of countless workers burn for me; they would cease to do so if I were to be respectfully honoured once again,' she said. 'I will and must remain among the censured.'

In 1986, an art collector called Hans Pels-Leusden donated his entire collection of Kollwitz's drawings and prints. The Käthe

Kollwitz Museum combined her art with her political activism. It was housed in a building next to the Literaturhaus on Fasanenstrasse, one of Charlottenburg's most elegant buildings on one of its most elegant streets; both opened at roughly the same time and share a similar history. For the past thirty-five years, the Literature House has held poetry readings, workshops and symposia, together with one of the district's most refined cafes and courtyards. Neither of these buildings might have stood. Both had been sold and resold by different wealthy owners, falling into disrepair and used at different times as a military hospital, soup kitchen, brothel, nightclub and processing centre for East German refugees. On two occasions – straight after both world wars – they were slated for demolition. On the first occasion Wertheim wanted to build a department store, taking up the entire street. Later, city planners had the bright idea of building a motorway underpass. Mercifully, they now enjoy heritage protection.

In 2022, the museum moved a few kilometres to the west, to one of the buildings of Charlottenburg Palace. On the other side of town, in the square where Kollwitz lived for so long, stands a statue of her. In 1947 the East German authorities gave the square her name, and in 1958 Gustav Seitz created the larger-than-life bronze monument of the sitting artist in the middle of the small park in Kollwitzplatz. Her serious expression is familiar from her many self-portraits. Although Seitz placed a sketchbook and a charcoal pencil in her hand, Kollwitz appears deep in thought, motionless. A heaviness hangs over the block-like figure – as if the focus of her life and work weighs on her.

One of the most remarkable things about it is that it exists at all. Berlin has few monuments to famous women. One is Gold Else, the winged goddess on top of the Victory Monument; another is Queen Luise, the one who tried to coax Napoleon, in the Tiergarten. Then there is the revolutionary Rosa Luxemburg who is memorialized, discreetly, on the banks of the canal where her body was found, and more ornately in a square that bears her name. In Hasenheide Park stands a monument to the Rubble Women who rebuilt the city after the Second World War. One recent addition is a memorial to Korean comfort women in Moabit which has enraged the South Korean and Japanese governments. All very random, but given that this is Berlin, perhaps that is as it should be.

Käthe Kollwitz is memorialized repeatedly in Berlin, not unlike Moses Mendelssohn. Two schools are named after her in the city and many more across the country. Three museums are dedicated to her in Germany alone, including one in the town of Moritzburg, near Dresden, where she spent her final year. Exhibitions abound around the world.

Kollwitz's art describes a continuum between the extreme inequality of nineteenth-century rapidly industrializing Berlin and the horrors that followed in the twentieth. Her most visible contribution to the city stands in one of its most militarized buildings. After the end of the Hohenzollern dynasty in 1918, the Neue Wache guardhouse was turned into a memorial to the victims of the First World War and under the Nazis it served as the centrepiece for their grandiose annual Heroes' Commemoration Day. Under the East German communists, it was rededicated as the Memorial to the Victims of Fascism and Militarism, with a goose-stepping honour guard standing watch at its entrance.

What to do on reunification? After endless soul-searching, in 1993 the government of Helmut Kohl rededicated the site as a 'Central Memorial to the Victims of War and Tyranny'. Controversy raged over whether this implied equality of victims. Most of the guardhouse was reverted to the original design – except for one addition. In 1937, even though banned by the Nazis from producing work, Kollwitz secretly made one of her last major pieces, only 40 centimetres high. It is a sculpture of the draped figure of a mother, sharing a silhouette while cradling her grown son. This was twenty-three years after Peter's death. 'It has now become something of a pietà,' Kollwitz wrote in her diary. 'It is no longer pain, but reflection.' More than half a century of even greater cruelty and suffering later, a new version of the sculpture was made, four times its size, specifically to become the centrepiece of the Neue Wache. At its unveiling in 1990, Kohl declared it to embody 'indestructible humanity' and hope. He was attacked by some for political opportunism. Yet on this highly charged site, I can think of few more appropriate memorials than this very personal reflection on grief.

TEN

At the edge of my days

The marketing of Weimar Berlin

Berlin is a psychologically and morally cursed nest.
ARTHUR SCHOPENHAUER (1831)

A s you walk past, you would have no clue about what used to go on inside. The basement window looks into a storage room for the organic supermarket next door, on a nondescript street called Kalckreuthstrasse, near Nollendorfplatz. This building used to house Eldorado, the variety club memorialized in folklore by Christopher Isherwood. The dark room I'm peering into was a much smaller club called La Garçon (note the definite article) and the individual story to tell is that of Anita Berber, actor, poet and stripper, famous for wearing a monocle, ankle-length sable coat and nothing underneath. Anita Berber was the personification of Weimar Berlin, in its most extreme form.

But much of this era was extreme, and exotic, and exciting, or at least that is how history prefers to remember it.

Berber married three times, had several lesbian relationships and imbibed copious amounts of alcohol and cocaine. Whatever she did, she scandalized, which was some feat in a city that had long lost the capacity for shock. The final straw for her promoters was when, during an after-midnight show, she hit an audience member over the head with a champagne bottle and then urinated on his head while he was bleeding. His crime or misdemeanour was not to have been paying due attention to her routine on stage.

Born in Leipzig into a middle-class family, she moved as a teenager to Berlin to study traditional ballet. The country was in chaos; her life turned upside down. Censorship – so tight under Wilhelm II – all but disappeared. The art world embraced Expressionism and the cabaret scene exploded. By the age of twenty, Berber was performing nude. The film industry embraced the new wave with alacrity, especially the young women prepared to do anything. Berber made more than a dozen appearances, including a role in the 1919 silent movie *Different From the Others*. It is often considered the first sympathetic portrayal of homosexuality on screen.

Now a minor celebrity, her private life blended seamlessly with her public appearances. Berber's bisexuality and her overall defiance of traditional gender norms were the subject of the tabloid news-sheets. It was said – and rumours were as powerful as facts – that she had a brief liaison with a young Marlene Dietrich. Aged only twenty, she married a wealthy screenwriter, Eberhard von Nathusius, a man about whom the world knew little, and she knew seemingly even less. They divorced almost immediately after she fell in love with Susi Wanowski, the manager of La Garçon who also became her manager. The affair did not work out too well, so it wasn't long before she married a dancer called Sebastian Droste. The pair created a book of poetry and photography entitled *Dances of Vice, Horror and Ecstasy*, along with a show that they performed in various nightclubs. Only 1,000 copies were published and, even though much of the subject matter was harrowing, owning a copy rendered a certain cachet. This was one of their poems:

Cocaine
Outcry
Animals
Blood
Alcohol
Pains
Many pains
And the eyes

As for the look, Berber made her late-night entrances clad only in very high heels, an heirloom silver brooch containing the white substance, a fur coat and sometimes a pet monkey hanging from her neck. It was said that she suffocated one of the monkeys inside her coat. Her risqué androgynous look was quickly commercialized. Young women with chic bobbed haircuts and shaved, pencilled-in eyebrows, wearing French male fashions, were soon catered for with their own magazine, *Garçonne*. Its motto: 'For Friendship, Love, and Sexual Enlightenment'.

In addition to her addiction to cocaine, opium and morphine, one of Berber's favourite forms of inebriation was chloroform and ether mixed in a bowl. This would be stirred with a white rose, the petals of which she would then eat – on stage. Berber and Droste's performances continued to outrage. She was sent to jail for a few weeks after calling the visiting King of Yugoslavia a peasant. As a result, they were both banned from performing in a number of European cities.

Berber was called everything at the time: demonic, a cult figure, a diva. The clichés continue to be deployed. A recent documentary about her by the radio station SWR2 was labelled 'The Femme Fatale of the Golden Twenties'. At her peak, she was a commodity highly in demand. The writer Klaus Mann, who knew a thing or two about living on the brink, came to Berlin to imbibe the atmosphere. He became fascinated by Berber, writing this of her in his autobiography, *The Turning Point*: 'Depraved bourgeois girls copied Berber, and every slightly more ambitious cocotte wanted to look exactly like her. Postwar-erotic, cocaine, Salomé, ultimate perversity: such terms formed the sparkling crown of her glory.' Somewhat implausibly, he saw a link between her excitable stage performances and 'the dance' – by that he meant the wild fluctuations – of the stock market.

By the mid-1920s, as the post-war economy recovered and rampant inflation came under control, thanks to American intervention, Berber's career went into decline. Nightclub owners and film-makers no longer found her interesting. They had seen it all before. After Droste was arrested for drug-dealing and several other criminal enterprises and deported to Hungary, Berber married American dancer Henri Châtin Hofmann. They had met only two weeks earlier. His career progressed; hers did not. Blacklisted back home, she collapsed while performing in Beirut, aged only twenty-nine, a drug addict, alcoholic, and broke. A few months later she died in a Berlin hospital from tuberculosis.

Given the outlandish life she led, it is surprising what a small role Anita Berber plays in Weimar memory. For decades, if she was mentioned at all, it was invariably in a negative context: the decadent drug-taker. More recently she's been seen in a new light, in part as an early feminist and LGBTQ+ idol. One bar and music club in Pankstrasse, Wedding, is named after her but most of those who go there have little idea who she was. One travel/ nightlife website says the club is named 'in honour of a 1920s Berlin cocaine addict dancer'. Another passing reference is a short film made in 2012 called *Frida & Anita*, intersecting the lives of Frida Kahlo and Anita Berber, imagining that they meet one night in 1924 at La Garçon.

The only piece of iconography that has lasted is a 1925 painting, *The Portrait of the Dancer Anita Berber*, by Otto Dix. He knew her personally and was a regular guest at her performances. Although his work usually engaged with social issues of the post-war era, Dix was an enthusiastic consumer of all distractions, from cinema to cabaret, fairgrounds to dance halls. He enjoyed the role of *flâneur*, and took a particular interest in the grotesque.

Although Berber posed for him in the nude, Dix decided to depict her on a red background, wearing a long red dress. She strikes a vamp-like pose, with her right hand in front and her left hand resting on her hip. Her hair is red too, while she wears very thick white make-up, which gives her face a mask-like appearance: the enigma and the Everywoman. The painting, now housed at the Art Museum of Stuttgart, was rendered on two stamps by Deutsche Post in 1991 to commemorate the centennial of Dix's birth.

Just as with their views of Berber, it seems that everyone interested in the Weimar story, whether in Germany or elsewhere, has over the years projected whatever they wanted onto it. The Golden Twenties, reinforced by Isherwood, Liza Minnelli and, more recently, the hit German TV series *Babylon Berlin*, is glorified more than ever now. The sense of devil-may-care abandonment is artfully promoted and given a modern twist for the present-day Berlin brand. But the glamour and decadence of the 1920s was based on chronic instability; it was covering over a void. It was the manifestation of the centuries-old cycle of Berlin – growth, learning, then militarism leading to disaster – this time compressed into just a few years.

In order to understand the decade, it is important to appreciate the starting point. Germany was defeated and humiliated. Starvation and disease were rife. The five-century-long Hohenzollern dynasty was no more. In this power vacuum, Soviet communism saw its opportunity. In only four years of war, Berlin had gone from a *Weltstadt*, a military and economic world city, to destitution. The jubilation at the outbreak of hostilities in 1914, the pride of parents in sending their sons to fight for the Reich, quickly dissipated. Only months into the war, bread rationing had been introduced. Deprivation was already evident throughout the city, though the wealthier classes were able to obtain most items as the black market flourished.

Chaos and grinding poverty followed surrender. *Hamsterzüge* (hamster trains) would leave Berlin for the countryside, where city folk could exchange their Meissen porcelain or paintings for eggs or potatoes from villagers. They had to conceal their booty on the journey back to avoid being mugged or having their bags confiscated by train guards (who would give the food to their own families). The word *Hamsterkauf* is made up of *hamstern* (to hoard) and *kaufen* (to buy). The link to the rodent is because it stores food in its cheeks. These words came back into fashion in the early weeks of the Covid pandemic, when Germans, like others around the world, panic-bought.

Freezing and malnourished, Berliners then perished in their thousands in the Spanish flu epidemic of 1918–19. On the worst single day, over 1,700 died, their bodies piling up in the city morgues. Stray cats and even rats were killed for food. If a horse died in harness, it was unlikely to make it to the knacker's. The lack of coal, horses and other transport led to elephants being taken from the zoo and pressed into service. In order to hang onto meagre ration allowances, dead relatives were not declared as deceased, their bodies hidden instead.

The futility of the war, the arrogance and deception that had led to it, was captured by many writers and artists. 'People have said that I don't know the way a German can die; I know it well enough. But I also know how a German woman can weep – and I know how she weeps today, now that she slowly, excruciatingly slowly, realises what her man has died for,' wrote Kurt Tucholsky in 'White Spots', one of a collection of essays in his book *Berlin! Berlin!* 'I should like to burn the celestial fire into wounds.

I should like to cry out to the mourners: He died for nothing, for a madness, for nothing, nothing, nothing!'

Even before revolutionary fervour had engulfed Berlin in late 1918, the Kaiser had fled, setting up a headquarters in Spa in Belgium. He tried to cling on, but within weeks, on 9 November, announced his abdication. Reports circulated that at least sixty railway wagons were needed to carry his furniture, art, porcelain and silver from Germany to exile in the small Dutch town of Doorn.

This was the time of 'Red Berlin', a post-imperial government cobbled together by the Social Democrats and trying to hold the line as everything around it collapsed. Two days before the armistice, workers and soldiers marched to the Reichstag. Inside, in the restaurant, the SPD chancellor, Friedrich Ebert, was quietly eating his potato soup with his colleague, state secretary Phillip Scheidemann. A crowd of MPs barged into the room demanding action. Workers outside were heard chanting slogans – 'Down with the Kaiser! Down with the war!'

Ebert ignored the entreaties and continued to eat his soup. It was left to Scheidemann, who marched down the corridor towards the balcony and took it upon himself to address the crowd. He pondered, as he walked, what to say: 'The cursed war is at an end,' he declared. 'The Emperor has abdicated (he hadn't, though he would, within hours). The people have won! Long live the Republic!' Then he returned to his soup.

Around two hours later, a mile down the road, Karl Liebknecht made a speech of his own. Originally an SPD member of parliament, he had on May Day 1916 led an anti-war protest and was sentenced to four years' jail for treason. Under an amnesty in October 1918, designed to cool tensions in fevered Berlin, he was released. Sensing the chaos, Liebknecht seized his moment. From the balcony of the Royal Palace, he declared a rival Free Socialist Republic of Germany.

Ebert might initially have been slow to understand the danger, but he quickly decided to ally himself with what was left of the military command to ward off the socialist threat. One of his first actions as chancellor was to take a phone call from First Quartermaster General Wilhelm Groener on a secure phone line he had previously not known existed. The deal they struck was this: the armed forces would continue to enjoy relative autonomy, a state within a state, operating outside of civilian control. In return they would pledge loyalty to the first post-imperial government – and both would work together to restore order. They would speak in secret on what Groener would later describe in his memoirs as 'the necessary measures'.

A parallel administration was operating elsewhere in the city, led by Liebknecht and his co-revolutionary Rosa Luxemburg and their Spartacus League, which had been founded in 1914 in protest at the Social Democrats' support for the war. One of the early resolutions of the National Workers' and Soldiers' Council was to claim control of food, raw materials, money and law and order for itself. The revolutionaries seized vacant properties, turning them into emergency accommodation for the poor. Soldiers returning from war were guaranteed medical treatment and care, housed and given money.

The artist George Grosz recalls this moment of chaos in his autobiography: 'The cauldron was growing hotter. Speakers stood on every street corner; songs of hate rose up everywhere: against Jews, capitalists, Junkers, Communists, the Army, homeowners, workers, the unemployed, the department stores and again against the Jews. It added up to an orgy of execration.' Yet most Berliners went about their business as normally as they could. Theatres and cinemas continued to operate. Grosz described it as rehearsing for a Wagnerian cataclysm. 'Beneath all the glittering frivolity lay a swamp of fratricidal hatred and internal dissension, and the troops were even then lining up for the final battle.'

The man Ebert turned to was Gustav Noske. A master butcher by trade, he worked his way up in the trade union movement and the SPD, becoming a member of the Reichstag in 1906. He had strongly supported the war. On his appointment as defence minister in early 1919, he declared: 'someone must be the bloodhound'. The 'bloody week' began on 10 January. In an empty girls' school in Dahlem (where the Americans would base themselves during the Cold War), the *Freikorps* were lying in wait. It was Friedrich the Great who first deployed volunteer, irregular units when he was fighting successively the Austrians and the French. They were used again against Napoleon and later than that – generally considered less accountable and therefore sometimes more useful than regular troops. It had not been hard to summon units of *Freikorps* after the capitulation of German imperial forces a couple of months earlier. Many officers and soldiers had struggled to adjust to civilian life; they were angry and wanted to restore order – if not the old order, then some order. Businessmen alarmed by the prospect of communism were happy to fund them.

At the head of 3,000 men, Noske marched from Dahlem, receiving cheers in middle-class Charlottenburg as he made his way towards the city hall; in one single attack, his men opened fire, killing or injuring 1,500 Spartacists. A cartoon by Grosz depicts a street littered with bloodstained bodies, one of them disembowelled. The caption reads, 'Cheers Noske! The proletariat is disarmed!' Käthe Kollwitz recorded the scene at the central morgue: 'A dense crowd of people filing by the glass windows, behind which the naked bodies lie. Each has its clothing in a bundle lying upon the abdomen. On top is the number. I read up to number 244.'

The two leaders of the Spartacist insurrection, Luxemburg and Liebknecht, were taken to the Hotel Eden, on the corner of the Ku'damm, for interrogation. They were led out, supposedly to be taken into custody. A soldier was waiting by a side door of the hotel (which had become a makeshift headquarters of the Guards Cavalry Rifle Division) and clubbed them over the head with a rifle. Liebknecht was bundled to the Tiergarten where he was shot 'trying to escape'. Luxemburg was finished off in the car by a shot to the head and thrown into the Landwehr Canal. Four months later her barely recognizable body was recovered from the river. On the banks of the canal, below the bridge from where her body was discarded, now stands an unobtrusive monument to her, a metallic structure protruding from the ground spelling out her name in capital letters. On any given day a few bunches of roses can be found here, sometimes wilting. Liebknecht has a more prominent monument. It stands close to one of the main paths in the Tiergarten, the Grosser Weg. In the summer, families picnic and hang out next to a brick pillar with the words, 'In the fight against oppression, militarism and war the convinced socialist Karl Liebknecht died as the victim of treacherous political murder.'

The best place to fully understand Berlin's socialist and communist narrative of the past century and a half is on the other side of the city. Close to the former Stasi headquarters and to Karl-Marx-Allee, the triumphal thoroughfare of the GDR, in the district of Lichtenberg, is the Friedrichsfelde Central Cemetery. It was opened in May 1881 because all the other main cemeteries had reached capacity, as a place of rest for all confessions and all social strata. The cost of headstones was paid by the city. The cemetery first became famous when one of the founders of the SPD, Liebknecht's father, Wilhelm, was buried here. Ever since then it has been the burial place of choice for prominent figures of the German left.

One area has been sectioned off, a pantheon to past heroes of the cause. The monument was originally designed by Ludwig Mies van der Rohe, one of the architectural greats of the first half of the twentieth century and the last director of the Bauhaus school. It was to this spot that Liebknecht and Luxemburg were brought after their murder – except that it has long been questioned whether Luxemburg's body is actually there.

Mies van der Rohe's Monument to the Revolution lasted only nine years before it was pulled down by the Nazis in 1935. In 1951, the GDR government built a replacement, the Memorial to the Socialists. In its central site lie ten graves. My stomach begins to churn when, next to Luxemburg and Liebknecht, I see Walter Ulbricht, the first leader of the GDR and the man who ordered the Wall to be built, alongside other notables of East German dictatorship, former president Wilhelm Pieck and former prime minister Otto Grotewohl. Not far away is the grave of Konrad Wolf, a pro-regime film director, and his brother, the GDR's most famous foreign agent, Markus Wolf.

I have been several times to Friedrichsfelde because I never know quite what to make of it, and of contemporary Berlin's unwillingness to differentiate between the major figures of its socialist history. A cemetery that memorializes Käthe Kollwitz can also blithely pay tribute to those who oversaw the GDR police state. At least the cemetery authorities had the good sense to bury the head of the Stasi, Erich Mielke, in a more out-of-the-way part of the grounds. The monument's central obelisk bears the inscription: *Die Toten mahnen uns.* (The dead remind us.) Indeed they do, but possibly not in the way they intended. Nevertheless, every January thousands of Berliners come to Friedrichsfelde to lay red carnations here.

Ebert and Noske won their test of strength. The Social Democrat government prevailed, thanks to the violent intervention of army units. But the left split and stayed irrevocably split. Even with Hitler standing at the gates a decade later, they could not reunite. These scores are still being settled even now.

*

As more fighting raged in Berlin throughout 1919, the putative state took refuge in a small city in Thuringia 300 kilometres to the south that had been the home or inspiration to many of the great figures of German culture – including Goethe, Schiller, Franz Liszt. A constituent assembly was formed to come up with a new republican political system. Over eight months, what became known as the Weimar constitution was pieced together. The term 'Weimar Republic' would come into common parlance only later under the Nazis, who used it derogatorily, and has stuck. In the first National Assembly elections in February 1919, women had the vote and 80 per cent of the seats were won by democratic parties. Weimar may have been a brief interlude of excitement and freedom, but from its foundation onwards it was never stable. It endured seventeen changes of government in less than fifteen years, alongside repeated attempted right-wing putsches and workers' uprisings.

Königsallee is a rare example of conspicuous privilege in Berlin. The 4-kilometre-long winding road, named after the banker Felix Koenigs, is at the heart of what is known as Grunewald's villa colony – from where, by horse and carriage, later by car, the great and the good embarked on a trip 'in the city'. Now, as before, it is home to the rich and powerful, with ambassadors' residences alongside oligarchs' new-builds, flanked by forest, lakes and tennis clubs. But even in this most bucolic of settings, darkness is to be found. 'The health of a people comes only from its inner life – from the life of its soul and its spirit.' So reads a dark metal plaque outside a yellow stucco villa at number 65, near where the road meets the city.

The Liberal Democratic Party of Germany
To the memory of Walther Rathenau
Foreign Minister of the German Republic
He fell at this spot at the hands of murderers on 24 June 1922

This was home to Walter Rathenau, businessman, sardonic author, politician – and Jew.

His father, Emil, had established the General Electricity Company, Allgemeine Elektrizitäts-Gesellschaft, known by its initials AEG. Yet although he took over as chairman on his father's death in 1915 and was on the board of numerous other companies, he flitted between careers. The writer Stefan Zweig described him as an 'amphibious being, somewhere between a businessman and an artist, a man of action and a thinker'. Nephew of the painter Max Liebermann, he collected works by Edvard Munch and Max Pechstein. He counted as friends the radical playwrights and directors Frank Wedekind, Gerhart Hauptmann and Max Reinhardt. His politics fluctuated between socialism, liberalism and conservatism. He became a staunch supporter of the First World War, and then found himself in government, first as minister for reconstruction and then as foreign minister, trying to implement the Versailles reparations that were immediately denounced as a stab in the back. From that moment his card was marked. He was called a national traitor, a godforsaken Jewish pig.

On a beautiful summer's morning on 24 June 1922, Rathenau was collected by his chauffeur from his home. As the open-top sedan turned onto the road, two assassins on motorbikes pulled up alongside and sprayed him with automatic pistol fire, then threw in a grenade, just to make sure. Up to a million people turned out to view his body as it lay in state in the Reichstag. To many Berliners, this event, above all others, reflected the new reality. The Weimar Republic was built on sand. The abiding symbol of the era, particularly the hyperinflationary early years, is the wheelbarrow carting wodges of useless money. In 1919, a loaf of bread cost one mark; by 1923, the same loaf cost 100 billion marks. Figures produced by the German Trade Union Federation, comparing the purchasing power of a Berlin carpenter's wages in

1914 and 1922, showed that he would later have to work three times as many hours just to buy the same amount of beef or eggs for his family.

Many Berliners sought refuge through hedonism. After all, when one dollar is worth 4.2 trillion marks, what else were they supposed to do?

The supposed halcyon era, the 'Golden Era', only took off, however, after the intervention of an American civil servant. The plan drawn up in 1924 by a committee led by Charles Dawes produced a formula that would stagger the huge payments decreed at Versailles over a much longer period. It bought Germany time and instilled a semblance of confidence.

Much of the plan was based on loans from Wall Street, and when the US banks defaulted in October 1929, the edifice collapsed. But for five years, 1924–29, Berlin was once again transformed. Industrial production grew by 50 per cent, albeit from a low base. Picture the scene, Unter den Linden, 1925: there were nineteen travel agents, six banks, eighteen car dealers, seventeen jewellers, fifteen fashion stores, thirteen tobacconists, five cafes, four restaurants – plus a shop selling safes. The city was packed with bars, dance halls and cabaret theatres. The standard view of that time relies on terms such as decadent (positive) or debauched (usually negative). Both tend to be simultaneously correct, but in any case, they applied only to a small slice of the population.

Weimar was also a fertile time for serious art, literature and media. At its peak some 5,000 daily and weekly newspapers and magazines were being published; such was the appetite for news that some were printed three times a day, providing morning, lunchtime and evening editions on sale at kiosks and also available to read on the *Litfasssäulen*, the advertising pillars on every street corner.

Then there were the self-styled debating chambers. Of all the venues in Charlottenburg, the place to be seen, from the moment it opened in 1916 until it was bombed in 1943, was the Romanisches Café. The place was dubbed 'the waiting room for talent', and it was a mark of success (not dissimilar to Berghain in contemporary times) to get past the man at the door. Herr Nietz was a man to be feared. Emil Nolde, Walter Gropius, Bertolt Brecht and Kurt Weill had their own tables. The withering essayist, Tucholsky, and the withering man of art, Grosz, were regulars. A revolving door gave access to two rooms and a gallery. The smaller room on the left called the swimming pool was reserved for generous tippers, big-name writers and well-known prostitutes, while the larger room on the right, called the wading basin, housed aspiring artists.

This was not the only cafe with cachet. In 1922 the theatre director Viktor Schwannecke opened a wine bar in his name, close to the Ku'damm, which was patronized by the likes of the satirist Erich Kästner and artist Otto Dix. Other celebrity hangouts came and went. These cafes, and others like them, are long gone. On the site of the Romanisches Café stands the Europa Centre, a twenty-two-storey glass slab with its revolving Mercedes star on the roof – one of West Berlin's many architectural eyesores that were supposed to express modernity and progress when it was built in 1965.

Some of the most enduring representations of the era are captured by Franz Hessel. When not translating Proust with his friend Walter Benjamin, Hessel spent his time observing his native city at close quarters. Taking their cues from Edgar Allan Poe and Charles Baudelaire, Hessel and Benjamin also spent time in Paris, adapting the nineteenth-century concept of the *flâneur* for their depictions of the early-twentieth-century German capital. Nearly all of the essays in his classic *Walking in Berlin* take the form of a walk or outing, focusing on either a theme or a part of the city, and many end at a theatre, cinema, or club. Like Scheffler, like so many before him, Hessel cannot resist a dig at his fellow city-dwellers. 'In his zeal for pleasure, the Berliner . . . still lapses into the dangers of accumulation, quantity, excess. His coffee houses are establishments of pretentious refinement. Nowhere to be found are the cosy, unremarkable leather sofas, the quiet corners, so loved by the Parisians and the Viennese.' Just why do they have to be so uncouth, he asks? Why can't they be like others?

Scientific research was thriving. Max Planck had just won the Nobel Prize for physics, his work laying the ground for quantum theory. Albert Einstein moved to Berlin in 1914, establishing the Kaiser Wilhelm Institute for Physics the year before the king's abdication. Although he spent much of the 1920s travelling to the United States and elsewhere and was finally hounded out of Germany for good by the Nazis in 1933, he is regarded as one of Berlin's chosen sons.

This was the era of the heedless optimism of the first Zeppelin flights, of Walter Gropius and the Bauhaus architecture movement, the atonal music of Arnold Schoenberg. In the richness and variety of its accomplishments, Weimar has few rivals in German history: in just four years, forty-one new operas premiered in the three great houses, each with their own renowned director – the State Opera (Eric Kleiber), the Municipal (Bruno Walter), and Otto Klemperer's Kroll Opera – that building achieving later ignominy after being taken over by the Nazis for their sham parliament after the destruction of the Reichstag in 1933.

A key motivation of many artists and their backers was to provoke. When the First International Dada Fair opened on 1 July 1920, the organizers marketed it as a 'monster' event. It was hosted by a private gallerist, Otto Burchard, in his small and unassuming building on a stretch of the Landwehr Canal just south of the Tiergarten.

With some 180 exhibits and 31 participants, the Dada Fair was the biggest show of its kind. The installations – photomontage, paintings and posters – were angry responses to the war and imperial 'bourgeois' values. Suspended from the ceiling was the Prussian Archangel, a mannequin of a military officer with a pig's head instead of a face. On the wall below, guests were confronted with Otto Dix's print *War Cripples* (*45% Fit for Work!*), which showed disfigured veterans begging for loose change. Their broken bodies, grotesquely distorted to disturbing effect but decked out in uniform, lined up in an absurd military parade. The most talked-about ticket was a 'trial' in which the charges were 'insulting the Reichswehr' and incitement to class hatred. It brought fines from the state – and the desired publicity.

At the time, the area was packed with galleries, displaying some of the most radical and innovative art – Picasso, Kandinsky and Braque at Alfred Flechteim's gallery, Expressionists and Bauhaus artists at Ferdinand Möller's. Alongside Dada came the New Objectivity, *Neue Sachlichkeit*, a movement that also saw its mission as exposing the injustices and hypocrisies of its time. Artists were told to abandon the 'bourgeois studio' for the factory. But while New Objectivity aimed to capture reality, Dada questioned the very meaning of reality, employing chaotic methods of depiction to turn the very idea of art on its head. Despite their different approaches, both movements were unified in their rejection of war. Like the Dadaists, the artists of the New Objectivity movement such as George Grosz and Max Beckmann spoke to their times, with their focus on the grotesque – the porcine profiteers and the mutilated beggars. One of Grosz's most famous illustrations is of a disillusioned soldier in a steel helmet who goes to relax by the riverside only to find a bloated corpse there. Its title is *Feierabend*, a traditional greeting to a work colleague clocking off at the end of the day. Another, *Dedication to Oskar Panizza*, depicts Berlin as a bedlam of flag-waving patriots, strutting generals and priests, along with three grotesque figures representing alcoholism, syphilis and plague.

Although Grosz's art is widely shown, it was only in May 2022 that a museum dedicated to him was opened, in a former petrol station next to an overground railway line in Schöneberg. Its first exhibition traces his life, before and after he took the decision to leave for the US in 1933 (he had already evaded Nazi death squads on more than one occasion), returning only shortly before his death in 1959 to a city he couldn't abide. In 1916, in the middle of the war, he renounced his birth name, Georg Ehrenfried Gross, to show his contempt for his country; he declared how proud he was to live in a place that smelt so thoroughly of shit: 'My drawings expressed my despair, hate and disillusionment, I drew drunkards; puking men; men with clenched fists cursing at the moon.'

Most Berliners did not want their misery lobbed back at them; they wanted escapism and entertainment. Two years before the outbreak of war, Germany had produced its first silent movie, called *The Dance of Death*, with a suitably dark plot involving infatuation, duty and murder. It was produced at Babelsberg in Potsdam, the second-oldest studio in the world, which to this day is the centre of German film-making. Babelsberg was a city within a city, spawning a conveyor belt of blockbusters by the likes of Alfred Hitchcock and Billy Wilder and stars such as Fritzi Massary and a certain Marlene Dietrich.

As with the rest of Berlin, over the decades the studio lurched between anything-goes creativity and state diktat. In 1917 the war government sought to develop the propaganda possibilities of the newly emerging film industry. Universum Film AG (UFA) was created to make films rallying around the war effort and the flag. The first Weimar government sold its interest in UFA and abolished all censorship. Movie-going boomed overnight. In 1919, the UFA cinema opened near the Zoo. Max Reinhardt's new dream palace for the masses had a capacity of more than 1,000 and a dome resembling a grotto of stalactites, with a full-sized symphony orchestra of seventy musicians providing live musical accompaniment to the silent films, many of which were from America. Within a few years Germany had more than 4,000 cinemas.

Of all the many remarkable films of the Weimar era, Fritz Lang's *Metropolis* imagines a dystopian city of super-rich industrialists peering down from colossal skyscrapers, while workers living underground toil to operate the great machines that power it. Denounced and praised in equal measure when it was released in 1927, the film excited both communists and fascists. Goebbels is said later to have appreciated Lang's technical abilities, urging him to work for the Nazi cause. In *Berlin, Symphony of a City*, made the same year, the director Walter Ruttmann takes his audience through a single day, not in science fiction but in five acts of real life. The camera roams the city with its shutter open, recording hawkers, women bashing dust off carpets, men arguing on the streets, people begging, others eating oysters.

Berliners could not get enough, particularly of the great American movies of the time, dressing up whenever they went to the palaces built to show them. The most stylish of the lot was the Gloria-Palast, a neo-baroque cinema inside Kurfürstendamm's grand Romanisches Haus designed by Franz Schwechten, the same architect who had been responsible for the Kaiser Wilhelm church. It was fitted out to include seven staircases, three lifts, a mirror-lined winter garden, crystal chandeliers, marble steps and silk wallpaper. It was here, in 1930, that the first German talkie debuted, *The Blue Angel*, a story of desire, glamour, risk and low-life, aka Berlin, starring Marlene Dietrich.

This great era of film-making was soon to come to a thudding halt. In its place, around 1,000 films were churned out under the Nazis, the most famous of which was Leni Riefenstahl's openly propagandistic *Triumph of the Will* in 1935. Few of the palaces of the 1920s remain today, thanks largely but not always to Allied bombing. Some were torn down, others turned into multiplexes; one is an indoor market, another houses a Zara clothes store. Berlin garlands its great names of the 1920s – the artists, the scientists, the political martyrs – with statues and memorials. In its keenness to draw attention to the risk-takers, the 'great men' (and the odd woman), it has largely forgotten those who held the city together at a time of perpetual upheaval, who modernized it without fanfare.

In amongst the post-war mayhem, on 27 April 1920, the Prussian regional assembly passed the Law on the Formation of the New Municipality of Greater Berlin. This was the culmination of work that had begun a decade earlier but had been interrupted by war. Under the new plans, the outlying region of Brandenburg – which for centuries had been the dominant political and geographical force – was to be significantly reduced in size. The new municipality was divided into twenty boroughs, bringing in areas previously outside the city's jurisdiction, such as Charlottenburg. The landmass of the city suddenly increased more than tenfold. This is the Berlin of today. The achievement was largely the work of the mayor, a man by the name of Gustav Böss, who managed to keep his job for the entirety of the 1920s but is little remembered now. Similarly forgotten are his two predecessors, who helped to give the city a unified status and greater political heft – Martin Kirschner and Adolf Wermuth. A city that doles out memorials to so many has yet to give due weight to them.

The assembly's decision went almost unreported in the newspapers; perhaps that was not surprising, given that barely a month earlier, parts of the army had tried to carry out a coup. The Kapp putsch collapsed, but only just. Administrative reform, no matter how radical, was hardly going to compete for people's attention. Municipal stability did not equate to social stability.

*

People from around Europe and further afield flocked to Berlin to savour freedoms often denied back home. That scene had been around for a long time, although invariably hidden away. In 1782 one guidebook devoted a short section to where to find 'warm brothers'. As a garrison city, Berlin had been known for its male prostitution since at least the eighteenth century, if not earlier. In the mid-to-late nineteenth century, it was exceptional in Europe for tolerating – or at least turning a blind eye to – homosexuality. Clubs and meeting places abounded. One of the most popular was Seeger's, a small bar on Jägerstrasse, the street of the Mendelssohn dynasty and the salons of the Enlightenment. The police would regularly raid the bar, but their actions seemed part of the ritual, the excitement. Another venue was the Pariser Keller, a club inside the French embassy complex.

One of the first public pioneers of gay life in Berlin was Karl Heinrich Ulrichs, a lawyer who worked for the Kingdom of Hanover and who in 1862 confided in his friends about his homosexuality. He wrote a series of essays entitled *Studies on the Riddle of Male–Male Love* and travelled the country trying to raise awareness of the issue; his mission landed him in jail from time to time. His courage led to the launch of a *schwul* (gay) movement in 1897. Compared with Britain, where the Oscar Wilde trial had taken place two years before, Germany was markedly liberal. For much of the twentieth century, Ulrichs was a largely forgotten figure. It was only in 2013 that Berlin honoured him (after all, he came from Hanover), naming a street after him. The choice was poetic justice; the street had previously been dedicated to Karl von Einem, an ultra-conservative minister of war under Kaiser Wilhelm II, who had called for the persecution of homosexuals.

More than any other manifestation of the Weimar era, Berlin markets its gay scene, and its gay history. A third of all tourism to the city is now related to a club scene with as much emphasis on sexual hedonism and experimentation as on music. That is also packaged up in the daytime on family-friendly walking tours.

Brendan Nash, an Irishman living in Berlin, is a novelist and guide. His fascinating tour of the Berlin of Christopher Isherwood begins on Nollendorfplatz, 'Nolli', the centre of the gay scene. Outside the U-Bahn station, a large pink marble triangle serves as a memorial to the thousands of homosexuals who died under the Nazis. Nearby is a plaque in memory of Isherwood.

At its peak, Berlin offered 160 gay bars. The city's embrace in the 1920s of its estimated 85,000 lesbians was also remarkable for its time. It offered two ice-skating leagues, a women-only nudist retreat, and a guidebook, *Berlin's Lesbische Frauen*, written in 1928 by Ruth Margarete Roellig to help locals and visitors navigate the fifty or so lesbian clubs. But the lesbian scene, Nash notes, has received far less attention than the male gay scene. When it is featured, it tends to be reduced to titillation.

When Isherwood arrived in Berlin in 1929 aged twenty-five, he moved into a room at Nollendorfstrasse 17. He describes it thus in the opening lines of his book *Goodbye to Berlin*: 'From my window, the deep solemn massive street. Cellar-shops where the lamps burn all day, under the shadow of top-heavy balconied façades, dirty plaster frontages embossed with scroll-work and heraldic devices.' He lived off coffee, horsemeat and lung soup (which was made from the bones of any dead animal, a smattering of flour and, if you could get hold of it, a spoonful of semolina). His friend, Stephen Spender, described the neighbourhood as 'an eyrie of concrete eagles, with verandas like breasts shedding stony flakes of whatever glory they once had into the grime of soot which caked the walls of this part of Berlin'.

Nash recites lines such as these by heart. 'Nolli' is one of few places in the city where you don't have to try hard to reimagine how life was before. It may not be quite what it was, neither in outrage nor in glamour, but it tries. Across the street, visitors can choose between a sushi bar (it used to be a kabbalah centre) and a speakeasy-style cocktail bar called Stagger Lee, with a brass doorbell to enter. Other clubs nearby include Sally Bowles, the Green Door, Romeo and Romeo, and Tom's Hotel. The venue that all tourists look for, immortalized on the silver screen in *Cabaret*, is Eldorado, on the corner of Motzstrasse and Kalckreuthstrasse.

Isherwood was a regular patron of this particular *Tanzlokal für Herren* (men's dancing club), as it playfully called itself. Its owner was Ludwig Konjetschni, a Jew from a small town in Austrian Silesia (now part of the Czech Republic). After arriving in Berlin at the end of the war, Konjetschni set himself up as a restaurateur and nightlife entrepreneur; he owned another club, also named Eldorado, in Kreuzberg. In 1928 he and his wife, Edith Elsa, leased a larger premises, the Grand Café Luitpold on Motzstrasse. He saw himself as merely serving the market, a clientele that included the rich, the famous, the gay, the straight, the liberal and the Nazi. Within weeks, it had become the most sought-after night spot in the city. A banner over the door proclaimed, 'HIER IST'S RICHTIG!' That translates as 'Here it's all right!' But it meant more than that – here you can leave your worries at the door. Next door, Konjetschni also ran a soup kitchen, catering for the huge lines of poor and homeless.

By late 1932, even before the Nazis had gained power, the tide was turning. Gay bars and other venues deemed decadent were being shut down or pressured to limit their hours. Konjetschni had a glimpse of what was to come when his two applications for German citizenship were turned down. He was forced to close the Eldorado. It was taken over by the local Nazi militia, the *Sturmabteilung* – a decision not as bizarre as it might appear. Senior members of the SA had been regular customers, among them its (gay) leader Ernst Röhm, whom Hitler had murdered in July 1934. The SA turned the Eldorado into their new local headquarters, which it remained until the end of the war. Ever since, it has been a humdrum spot. For the past few years this is what has confronted visitors: *Speisekammer im Eldorado. Bio Market.* An organic supermarket.

Nash says most of his groups laugh at the bathos of it, but not so long ago he received a more solemn response from one man, who quietly explained that he was Konjetschni's grandson, a theatre producer who had come over from Australia to join the tour and see the place for himself. As for his grandfather, he fled first to Czechoslovakia in 1934, getting out four years later, before Hitler's invasion, and moving briefly to France. In 1939 he made it to Sydney, where he and Edith opened a sandwich bar. At the start of the 1950s, Louis Conney (as he had renamed himself) filed a claim for compensation with the Berlin authorities. He died in 1968.

Nollendorfstrasse was bombed during the war, and now the stately pre-war buildings, including the one where Isherwood lived, with its pale-yellow façade mounted with concrete lion heads, are interspersed with 1950s concrete constructions. This mix of beauty and ugliness is typical for the city. Not all of it was the result of the war; the Nazis subsidized residents to remove the stucco reliefs from their homes. After the war the defacement continued, as many Berliners removed ornate decorations to save money on restoration.

As for Isherwood, he fled Berlin in May 1933, three days after the burning of the books on Opera Square. For several years he travelled across Europe with his German boyfriend to try to get him a new citizenship, eventually seeking refuge in the US. He returned to Berlin and to his neighbourhood only once, in 1952, to file a feature for the *Observer* newspaper. He found 'smashed buildings along that familiar street', and house fronts 'pitted by bomb fragments and eaten by decay'.

*

In September 2017, a memorial was unveiled to a remarkable movement and a remarkable individual. It comprises six 4-metre-high statues of calla lilies in bright rainbow colours and it stands on the banks of the Spree opposite the Federal Chancellery. Students from the University of the Arts had been invited to submit their designs to a competition to remember the work of Magnus Hirschfeld and, as it is officially called, the First Homosexual Emancipation Movement.

Hirschfeld had opened his Institut für Sexualwissenschaft (Institute of Sexual Research) almost exactly a century earlier, located not far away, in a villa at the northern edge of the Tiergarten. After finishing his medical degree, he travelled to Chicago where he was struck by what he deemed the similarity of the gay subculture there with that in Berlin. His research led him to probe the link between high suicide rates and gay men at the turn of the century. He campaigned for gay rights, for the legalization of abortion and he supported women's rights through the Bund für Mutterschutz (League for the Protection of Mothers). Repeated attempts to repeal Paragraph 175 of the imperial constitution, which outlawed homosexuality, had ended in failure. But the local authorities in the new era in Berlin decided not to enforce it. This was a tacit and shaky compromise.

In 1919, the same year as he opened his institute, Hirschfeld brought out a film, *Anders als die Andern* (Different from the Others), one of the first films to have an openly gay leading role. The film was shunned; the censor's office banned public screenings, though it did leave the door open for private audiences. The only venue where the film was allowed to be shown was at the institute, and even then, only at special events. The film, which co-starred and was co-written by Hirschfeld, was based on his notion of 'sexual intermediacy', a precursor to gender fluidity. Scenes included some of the earliest footage of gay men and lesbians dancing intimately. Hirschfeld, himself gay and Jewish, was badly beaten up and repeatedly threatened by brownshirts. His institute, which sported portraits of famous homosexuals, including Friedrich the Great, became a haven for sexual minorities, and carried out what are thought to be the first sexual reassignment operations. The first patient is believed to have been Dora Richter, the eldest of six children born to a poor farming family in Karlsbad, now Karlovy Vary in the Czech Republic. Having fled the army after two weeks and failed to find secure employment, Richter ended up working as a domestic servant at the institute, one of the few places where a trans woman could be employed, and where she was affectionately known as Dorchen. It is assumed that she was killed by the Nazis, though one unlikely witness reported spotting someone resembling her as the owner of a small cafe in her hometown in 1955.

As the atmosphere turned, Hirschfeld started looking for a place where he could continue his work. He made it to France within months of the Nazi takeover and tried unsuccessfully to open a new institute in Nice. Many of his colleagues back in Germany did not have such foresight and were murdered. The institute was ransacked by the brownshirts. Its entire library was burnt. All copies of his film were destroyed, except for one. It was cut up into pieces and smuggled to America, where the fragments were stitched together. Some sections went missing forever.

The Nazis may have persecuted the gay community and publicly called for a return to traditional 'family values' – *Kinder, Kirche, Küche* (children, church, kitchen) – but behind the scenes the higher echelons of the party were not averse to their own version of sexual decadence, particularly if it produced other hidden benefits.

All the way through the Third Reich, Salon Kitty did a roaring trade. Katharina Zammit was born in 1882, one of six children of a butcher. She moved to England and worked as a governess and piano teacher but left for Berlin having been told of the money that could be made in sex work. She opened her brothel at Giese-brechtstrasse, number 11 – turn right off the Ku'damm, as taxi drivers were told. It originally bore the unerotic name of Pension Schmidt (she had taken to calling herself Kitty Schmidt by this point) and was advertised as a boarding house for actors. Visitors were greeted by a young woman in a maid's uniform. In the reception room – with heavy carpet, sofas, chandelier, gramophone and a grand piano – two or three young women in cocktail dresses (whatever the time of day) made polite conversation.

Schmidt changed the name of her establishment to Salon Kitty, and its operating model as well. She had been caught red-handed sending some of her earnings to British banks to pay for newly arrived refugees. She was threatened with arrest unless she cooperated. One version of the story has it that she struck a deal with SS security chief Reinhard Heydrich, and from that point, the brothel was stuffed with bugs to listen in on conversations and the sex involving industrialists, diplomats and others of potential interest. One was said to be Mussolini's son-in-law. During renovation of the building in the 1960s builders found wires hidden under the plaster, leading to the cellar. Speculation continues to this day (Schmidt took her secrets to her grave in 1954) over whether she was a victim, a collaborator or an opportunist somewhere in the middle. The story has spawned several books and a notorious 1976 film, available for the undiscerning on Netflix.

More than 100,000 German men were charged under Para-graph 175 during the Third Reich. An estimated 15,000 perished in prisons and concentration camps. It would take decades for their suffering to be officially recognized. Indeed, while limited reforms were introduced, it was not until 1994 that the offending article was removed from the statute book; the Catholic Church had steadfastly stood in the way. It took more than another fourteen years after that for an official monument to be built. At the northern end of the Tiergarten stands a large dark grey slab of stone, the Memorial to Homosexuals Persecuted under Nazism. In the middle and to the left, a glass window shows on a loop a short film celebrating gay culture, in which two men hug and kiss endlessly. The memorial is not to everyone's taste. Some consider it drab, a wasted opportunity. Some have lamented the failure to mark the suffering of lesbians and other targeted minorities. Some Jewish groups complained that it was too close to the Holocaust Memorial on the other side of the road. Some would rather it was not there at all, regularly daubing the monument with paint. What the memorial does not say (and this was not part of its remit) is that between 1945 and 1969, democratic West Germany convicted about 50,000 men for homosexuality-related 'offences' – the same number as the Nazis had convicted during their twelve-year rule.

The Weimar era was the epitome of excitement – for some. It was extremely cheap for anyone with dollars or any other foreign currency. But it was also a dark and unforgiving era for many, the epicentre of prostitution, violence and drugs. One in ten hospital admissions involved cocaine abuse. In a dispatch for the *Toronto Star Weekly* in December 1923, headlined 'European Nightlife: A Disease', Ernest Hemingway wrote: 'If champagne is the *deus ex machina* of the after-hours existence of Paris, cocaine takes its place in the German capital. Cocaine peddlers get short shrift from the Paris police. But in Berlin they sell their wares openly all over the city. In some cafés cocaine is served at the tables by the waiters.' Grosz described the city as 'dark, cold and full of rumours. The streets were wild ravines haunted by murderers and cocaine peddlers.'

The hyperinflation of the early part of the decade and then the stock market crash of 1929 drove many to crime, often falling under the influence of *Ringvereine* (organized gangs). By 1930 Berlin registered a record 280,000 tourists in one year, drawn by the 'anything goes' reputation of the city. Sexual exploitation came as part of the package. The centre of prostitution was the *Geile Meile* on Oranienburger Strasse; nearby Chausseestrasse was the place for pre-teen girls. 'Along the entire Kurfürstendamm powdered and rouged young men sauntered and they were not all professionals,' observed Stefan Zweig. 'Every high school boy wanted to earn some money and in the dimly lit bars one might see government officials and men of the world of finance tenderly courting drunken sailors without any shame.'

If one piece of work epitomized the city's underworld at this time, it was Alfred Döblin's 1929 Expressionist masterpiece, *Berlin Alexanderplatz*. The novel's protagonist, Franz Biberkopf, is a war veteran, pimp and thief, freshly released from Tegel prison, where he served time for killing his girlfriend. On his release, he tries again and again to set himself on the right path, never to succeed, as he succumbs to an underworld dominated by seediness, social breakdown and violence that a few years later would deliver Germany into the hands of Hitler. Over the course of the story, Franz is run over and loses an arm, and one of his girlfriends is murdered and buried in a suitcase. He is sent to a mental hospital, never resisting, always accepting his fate.

Berlin Alexanderplatz was a triumph. It has been adapted many times, most famously in 1980 with Rainer Werner Fassbinder's fifteen-hour TV epic. In 2020, a new version was premiered: the German-Afghan director Burhan Qurbani sets the story among illegal African immigrants to Berlin and we watch the protagonist's struggle to break out of a cycle of drugs and violence and to find a foothold in mainstream society. It is stark and realistic; hard drugs are openly sold in a number of Berlin parks, to the apparent disinterest of the authorities. Yet despite the many woes that befall the protagonist, the film strikes a more upbeat tone than its predecessors, seeing some positivity in contemporary multicultural Berlin.

Many of the cultural greats of the Weimar era fled Berlin at the outset of the Third Reich, some never to return. Döblin left Berlin the day after the Reichstag fire on 27 February 1933, settling first in Zurich, eventually California. In 1947 he risked a brief trip back to Berlin, to deliver a lecture to an audience in Charlottenburg Palace. He entered wearing his French uniform. The crowd were aghast, but he did so partly to honour his son. A prodigious mathematician, whom Döblin had to leave in France when he fled to America, twenty-five-year-old Wolfgang had died two years earlier in his own French uniform. Döblin saw in post-war West Germany the restoration of another conservative order. He also shunned Brecht's invitations to join him in the communist East, quitting Germany for good. Two years later, he was buried next to his son in France. Yet he had never quite shaken off Berlin. He wrote in 1930, 'I grew up in this big, sober, austere Berlin; this sea of stones is the mother soil of all my thoughts.'

In a quiet spot in a quiet cemetery, a black headstone bears the inscription: *Hier steh ich an den Marken meiner Tage* (Here I stand at the edge of my days). This is the third line of the first stanza of a beautiful sonnet, 'Farewell to Life'. It was written in 1813 by Theodor Körner, a soldier and poet, as he lay in a wood and prepared to die after he was attacked by Napoleonic forces. The line is engraved in gold above a single word, 'Marlene'. The cemetery in Stubenrauchstrasse was created back in 1881 when Friedenau was still a rural community. As with so many of Berlin's burial sites, it tells many stories. The photographer Helmut Newton, who died in 2004, is also laid to rest here. The most famous spot is that of Marie Magdalene Dietrich, but it comes with no pomp.

In 1930, immediately after the premiere of *The Blue Angel*, with a six-film deal with Paramount freshly signed, Dietrich set off for Hollywood. During that ten-day journey – a train from

Berlin to Hamburg, a ship from there to New York and onwards towards the west coast – she became a sensation. She would enjoy a decade of uninterrupted success. Dietrich was one of the earliest cultural figures to denounce the Nazis. In 1939 she publicly renounced her German citizenship and became an American, refusing a series of blandishments by Hitler to return home. She became a darling of Allied servicemen, appearing more than 500 times for the United Service Organizations to entertain the troops. She was one of the first public figures to sell war bonds. Throughout, she retained deeply mixed emotions about her city and her people. On one occasion, she said, 'When I die, I would like to be buried in Paris. I would leave my heart to England, and to Germany nothing.' On another, she stated, 'America took me into her bosom when I no longer had a native country worthy of the name, but in my heart I am German – German in my soul.' She most evocatively expressed her homesickness in a 1950s song:

> *I still have a suitcase in Berlin*
> *That's why I have to go back there next time*
> *The bliss of bygone times*
> *They're all still in that little suitcase*
> *Inside*

When she returned briefly to Germany in 1960, she played to packed-out auditoria at the Titania theatre in Steglitz. She was also booed and had stink bombs thrown at her. 'MARLENE, GO HOME' was a popular banner. The press response was vicious in places. One paper denounced her for 'traitorously wearing the uniform of the enemy'. Her dark green army jumpsuit is now on display at the Military History Museum Dresden, though curiously it isn't particularly prominently displayed.

It took Berlin a long time to make peace with Dietrich, both in death and in life.

On her death aged ninety-one, Dietrich was accorded a lavish funeral by the French authorities. Her service on 16 May 1992 was attended by 1500 mourners, including ambassadors of all the major European states, and of course the United States. Her closed coffin, draped in the French flag, was adorned with a presidential bouquet. France's Legion of Honour and the US Medal of Freedom were displayed at the foot of the coffin. Ten days later the coffin was flown to Berlin, in accordance with her final wishes. She had changed her mind and wanted to be buried close to her mother, Josefine, and near to her family home.

Berlin did not cover itself in glory. A *New York Times* report that day states, 'City officials are under heavy criticism for the way they have handled the funeral. At first, they announced that a gala tribute to Miss Dietrich's life and work would be held at the Deutsche Theater, where she began her career. But after a day and a half of confusion, they cancelled the tribute, saying prominent invitees like James Stewart and Billy Wilder were unable to attend.' That was one excuse. Then the authorities said they had to limit the number of mourners, for fear of neo-Nazi demonstrations.

In response, hundreds of Berliners lined the route, throwing flowers on the Cadillac hearse. The service, shown live on national TV, was conducted in German, although many of the family members who had come from the United States didn't speak it. In later years, in the mix of inefficiency and bureaucracy that is the city's hallmark, the cemetery threatened to remove her mother's grave because the rights to use the site had expired. It took a decade after her death for Berlin to begin to atone for its treatment of Marlene Dietrich. On what would have been her hundredth birthday, on 27 December 2001, the city formally apologized. Five months later she was posthumously made an honorary citizen.

The legalese was no match for the tribute written by fellow actor Hanna Schygulla to the symbol of Weimar and the symbol of post-Weimar resistance: 'We, the ones born afterward, the postwar generation, are proud that there were people like you, people who during the Hitler period took the side of the enemy and did it out of love for a better Germany.'

ELEVEN

The city that cannot stop remembering

Berlin and the Third Reich

In good and in evil, Berlin is the trustee of German history,
which has left its scars here as nowhere else.
RICHARD VON WEIZSÄCKER (1983)

I t is dusk, mid-December. I am the only person around.

I have been walking down a nondescript street not far from the old Tegel airport on the northwest edges of the city. I walk past a logistics warehouse, a housing estate and a colony of allotment gardens. On the other side of the road is a youth justice centre with a banner at its entrance that reads: 'YOUNG PEOPLE ARE OUR FUTURE. WE'RE WITH YOU.' On the far side of this building from the adjacent street is Plötzensee, a prison with a particular history.

In total, more than 2,800 prisoners from twenty countries were beheaded or hanged here between 1933 and 1945. What makes this place curious is that the inmates were not Jews, but foreigners (and the odd German) deemed dangerous to the Third Reich. The most famous victims were the so-called 20 July conspirators (the men whose assassination attempt on the Führer failed). They were hanged in autumn 1944 with piano wire; the performance was filmed so that Hitler could watch their last twitches. Opened in

1879, Plötzensee housed 1,200 inmates, most of whom served short sentences. When the National Socialists took it over, it was immediately identified as a convenient and relatively out-of-the-way place to dispose of political enemies.

The speed of executions was relatively low in the first few years. As war loomed, an increasingly exasperated Hitler decreed that the pace be stepped up. The pretend judicial processes were drastically shortened. Prisoners sentenced to death by the 'People's Court' could in theory petition for clemency. Their pleas were invariably rejected, to enable summary executions. The condemned were held in a large cell block, adjacent to the execution shed, and spent their last hours shackled in special cells on the ground floor. They could ask to be visited by a clergyman if they wished, but the request was not always granted. Their last walk took them across a small courtyard. The executioner, aided by two or three assistants, carried out the beheading or hanging in a matter of seconds. The numbers rose quickly, as required, from a few dozen to sixty-one by 1939. From then the rate increased exponentially: 192 in 1940, 542 in 1942, 1,158 in 1943. In September of that year, immediately after one of the RAF's fiercest air raids on Berlin, the Führer ordered a mass slaughter. Between 7 and 10 September, the *Blutnächte* (Bloody Nights), 250 prisoners were murdered, 186 of them on the first night alone.

Such was the speed demanded that pretty much everyone sent to Plötzensee ended up dead, no matter how large or small their 'crimes'. One of the most poignant stories is that of a Dutchman called Albert Tamboer who began working in Berlin as a coachman in 1942. On 30 October 1944 he stole two tins of fish from the basement of a bomb-damaged building. He ate one of them immediately and concealed the other on his person. The Berlin Special Court IV sentenced him to death for this offence on 24 November 1944; he was beheaded sixteen days later.

The Nazis relied on a mix of engineering, bureaucracy and

incentives to increase productivity. At the end of 1942, a steel beam was installed in the execution room, with eight meat hooks attached. One can still see the whitewashed stone execution chamber, the hooks suspended from the ceiling. Executioners were paid an annual wage of 3,000 Reichsmarks (just over £11,000 today, taking inflation into account), plus 60 Reichsmarks per execution. The public prosecution department then invoiced the relatives of the dead for 'costs incurred': 1.50 Reichsmarks for each day's imprisonment (£5.70), 300 for the execution (£1,147) – plus 12 pfennigs (just under a pound) postage for a receipt. Corpses were delivered to Berlin University's anatomical institute for research.

I was recounting to a friend, Boris Ruge, how Plötzensee had affected me at least as much as any of the many sites of Nazi horror I have visited over the years (and not just in Berlin, but across Germany and Europe). He smiled wanly and told me his family story. His grandfather, Fritz-Dietlof von der Schulenburg, was a Nazi civil servant from a prominent Prussian family. He was part of a conspiracy to depose Hitler as early as 1938, and later joined the Stauffenberg plotters against Hitler (he was to be interior minister if they had succeeded). After the failure of the plot on 20 July 1944, he was arrested at Bendlerblock and hanged – from one of the meat hooks – at Plötzensee after a show trial. Although there were official ceremonies from 1954 onwards to commemorate 20 July and the plotters, it took decades for his family's history to be properly acknowledged by the broader public. Ruge, who is a German diplomat, was on the Plötzensee memorial committee for several years and attends the annual Remembrance Day there. In 2022, the Belarussian opposition leader, Svetlana Tskikhanovskaya, was a speaker and guest of honour.

Plötzensee was liberated by Red Army soldiers on 25 April 1945. Seven years later a memorial was inaugurated on the site, a place of remembrance and silent commemoration, dedicated to all victims of National Socialism – the first such monument to be erected. Why start any assessment of Nazi crimes here? Why not at, say, the concentration camp of Sachsenhausen, to the north of the city next to Oranienburg? Or the Topography of Terror? The Holocaust Memorial? The villa at Wannsee, where the Final Solution was planned, or platform 17 at Grunewald station where the first consignments of Jews were taken away to be killed?

There is something about the rawness of Plötzensee. Enough of the original site still exists for visitors to put themselves in the shoes of the condemned. Many of Berlin's historical moments are monumentalized, either emotionalized or sanitized. They invariably have to be imagined. This place, like some of the concentration camps dotted around Germany and beyond, can be felt, smelt. Yet very few Berliners I know have ever been here. It might be a little off the beaten track, but it is not far from the centre of the city. In the old days of Tegel airport, it would have been just a five-minute detour. In all the times I had flown in and out, I too had never bothered to go. It is not on the tourist trail.

But in researching this book, I became somewhat of an obsessive, constantly on the lookout for places of commemoration, or sites that have slipped away or victims who have been forgotten. I have visited more cemeteries than I would ever have done in any other city in the world, stopping to ponder the names of people unknown.

Berlin likes to think of itself as the city that cannot stop remembering. That is true, but it wasn't always so. It has become axiomatic to praise Germans for their yearning to remember and atone for their parents' and grandparents' crimes. An entire phraseology has built up around it: *Vergangenheitsbewältigung* (coming to terms with history), *Vergangenheitsaufarbeitung* (working on history), *Erinnerungskultur* (a culture of remembrance). Most of that work began in earnest only after the 1968 protest movement, which raged against the Vietnam War, and America and capitalism in general; it was also personal. The movement was laced with anger towards an elite that, to many of those coming of age, had, in their rush to create the economic miracle of the 1950s, not even begun to address the past. Everywhere you looked, someone in a high position was hiding something.

You could spend an entire month in Berlin visiting its many monuments to shame – the famous ones, the quieter ones (often more powerful) and the ones that arouse passions, either because they do not commemorate the right people, or because the tone is not quite right. More often than not, memorials and the architectural competitions surrounding them have led to furious rows and protracted delays. That is because, to this day, some of the history is still argued over.

The Memorial to the Murdered Jews of Europe sits close to the Brandenburg Gate and the Reichstag in the heart of Berlin. Containing 2,711 rectangular concrete slabs, each resembling a coffin, it was inaugurated in 2005. An adjacent exhibition space called the Place of Remembrance, *Ort der Erinnerung*, provides the historical context.

School groups descend on it from all parts of the country, and visitors from across the world. This is now the most famous site of remembrance to the Holocaust within Germany, but it is only one of many.

The memorial was first mooted as an idea back in 1988 – by a television talk-show host. As ever with Berlin's history, and its memorialization, the idea led to an argument. Or rather, many arguments spanning many years. What type of monument should it be? And should it exclusively represent murdered Jews or other victims too? The first design competition was launched in 1995, attracting more than 500 entries, among them a Ferris wheel equipped with freight cars resembling the transports, and another featuring a giant oven, burning around the clock. In 1997 the government commissioned a second contest, by invitation only. The jury chose a design of a giant labyrinth of 4,000 concrete pillars on an undulating concrete field. The idea was to pull visitors into a maze. Chancellor Helmut Kohl intervened and requested that it be reworked, at which point one of the artists, Richard Serra, pulled out. Kohl's successor, Gerhard Schröder, appeared ready to jettison the whole project but, stung by criticism, he approved a further design by the American architect Peter Eisenman, the one that came to be.

Some historians and architects have criticized it as cold. It isn't that, but perhaps it is too abstract, so much so that some people profess not to know what it is. That I experienced for myself one winter's night. I was walking past the monument and, instead of sticking to the road, I descended one of its many passageways, engulfed by darkness and a sense of claustrophobia. Suddenly two teenage boys rushed either side of me in adjacent strips on their e-scooters, sending me into a panic. Did they not know what this place meant? It wasn't supposed to be a racetrack. But I didn't detect any malice, let alone any worse motive. After all, the site is open 24/7 with almost no signage.

At another spot nearby, greater efforts are made to prevent any sense of normality. 'You don't want people to feel a sense of well-being. You don't want them to lie on the grass and eat their sandwiches on a nice day.' Kay-Uwe von Damaros is showing me around the Topography of Terror, a documentation centre, and its grounds – a bleak, flat landscape of grey stones, with no trees, nowhere to sit. 'All the crimes of the Nazi era were encapsulated here,' he tells me. Here on Prinz-Albrecht-Strasse the most important institutions of Nazi terror operated. This was the headquarters of the Gestapo. The neighbouring Hotel Prinz Albrecht was taken over in 1934 by the intelligence service, the Sicherheitsdienst (SD) under Reinhard Heydrich, one of the

architects of the Final Solution. In 1939, Heinrich Himmler and
other SS leaders moved their offices onto the top floor. In adjacent
rooms, prisoners were brought up for what was called 'intensified
interrogation'.

Heavily damaged or destroyed in the war, this cluster of
buildings ended up just inside the Western sector while most of
what had been the centre of Nazi power ended up in the East.
Many of the buildings were patched up and turned into GDR
government offices. The most forbidding of these was the Luftwaffe
Ministry of Hermann Göring, which became the East German
House of Ministries – government headquarters.

When the Wall was built, the area immediately on the Western
side was left to rot. It became a wasteland for two decades, used as
a rubbish tip and open territory for joyriders. By the late 1970s,
the first signs of life stirred again. Reconstruction began on the
Martin-Gropius-Bau, a neo-Renaissance art gallery that dated
back to the 1880s and occupied the building next door to the old
Gestapo HQ. Neither the federal government in Bonn nor the
West Berlin city authorities seemed to have any interest in any
further investigation into what happened in Prinz-Albrecht-
Strasse.

Nothing further would have happened had it not been for a
group of civil society activists. As the fiftieth anniversary of the
Nazi seizure of power loomed in January 1983, they founded a
historical society, the 'Active Museum of Fascism and Resistance
in Berlin', and organized a series of events to mark the moment.
Their first action was to mount a plaque in three languages,
German, English and French: 'You are entering the grounds of
the former torture chamber of the Gestapo.' They then held a
public debate about what to do with the site. The fact that it was
next to the Wall was a side issue; the various plans that were
debated all assumed that it would remain. The group stepped up
their work, with a series of demonstrations calling for a memorial

site on the grounds. They eventually succeeded in persuading the city government to give them jurisdiction over the land. Excavation works began, quickly uncovering the foundations of several prison cells.

The Topography of Terror opened with little fanfare in 1987. It would take a further twenty-three years for a modern documentation centre to be built, a giant rectangular box, devoid of dramatic flourishes. Adjacent to it is a trench with an exhibition called Between Propaganda and Terror, at the bottom of the longest remaining continuous piece of the Wall. To establish the centre, researchers pored over tens of thousands of documents in archives from across Germany. The end product is essentially a series of photographs and papers in glass boxes, with a minimum of explanation. It takes steel to go round it. More than a million visitors a year do. Many of the photographs were official (the Nazis were proud of their handiwork) or taken by the perpetrators for posterity. One montage shows people being shot, one by one, their bodies falling into a pit of fresh corpses. Next to it is a picture of partisans hanging from ropes on trees, alongside members of the *Einsatzkommando*, paramilitary death squads, enjoying picnics with local women.

Downfall and aftermath also feature. One photograph depicts Himmler's corpse immediately after his suicide in prison, as he eluded the reckoning for his crimes at the Nuremberg trials. Another shows citizens being forced to walk past mass graves of prisoners murdered by the Gestapo, and to watch the exhumation of victims of concentration camps. Under the caption 'Continuities', the story is told of German officials who were prosecuted, spared and then reintegrated into public life. Several worked in intelligence, working for the Allies straight after the war. For the Allies, the immediate post-war situation required pragmatism. Two processes were set in motion: economic assistance for Germany through emergency aid and then the

Marshall Plan and a decision to focus more on the dangers of communism than the crimes of fascism. That meant turning many blind eyes.

Perhaps the most remarkable of these stories is that of Paul Dickopf, a young officer in the SS and SD. He ended up as president of Germany's equivalent of the FBI, the Federal Criminal Investigation Office, or BKA, from 1965 to 1971. For four of these years, he was also president of Interpol, even though his history was known to all. He was praised for his work by Hans-Dietrich Genscher, interior minister and then long-time foreign minister, as a 'role model for the German police'. After his death in 1973, it transpired that Dickopf had funnelled a number of senior Nazis into the intelligence services. And to cap it all, documents in the National Archives in Washington released in 2007 showed that throughout this period he had been a paid informant to the CIA.

It is no coincidence therefore that education is at the heart of the work of the curators. The basement is given over to a library of some 27,000 volumes of National Socialist documentation. It also has an auditorium and classrooms for seminars. Soldiers and police are brought here as part of their training.

The Topography of Terror works because it does not try too hard. Similarly low-key, and powerful, is platform 17 at Grunewald. From this quiet suburban railway station in the west of the city, which traditionally served some of its wealthiest inhabitants, more than 10,000 Jews were deported to the camps. The first sealed train left on 18 October 1941, taking 1,013 Jews to Litzmannstadt (now Lodz in Poland) and to their death. The final train left for Sachsenhausen on 5 January 1945.

In 1933, Berlin had 160,000 registered Jews, a third of the total Jewish population in Germany. By 1939, almost 100,000 of those had emigrated. Of the remaining 66,000, around 55,000 were taken away in so-called 'East Transports'. Grunewald was an important starting point of this meticulously organized mass murder. Yet for nearly half a century after the war there was no remembrance of what had happened under the noses of the good burghers. Platform 17 became overgrown, but the rest of the station was restored, as if nothing had happened. Since 1987 a succession of artistic interventions and memorials have been created, firstly a bronze plaque placed on the former signalman's house by members of the Grunewald Protestant community in memory of the 'victims of extermination'. In 1991, the Polish artist Karol Broniatowski constructed a concrete wall to the right of the station entrance with hollow imprints of human bodies. Seven years later, Deutsche Bahn unveiled another memorial on the platform itself. The Gleis 17 Mahnmal displays 186 cast-iron plates embedded in the railway tracks recording the date of each transport, the number of people they carried and their destinations in chronological order.

As late as 2021, the state railway company – which for decades had refused to acknowledge its role in the mass murder – laid a wreath at the site, together with representatives of Borussia Dortmund football club, Daimler and Volkswagen; the organizations published a joint statement against antisemitism together with Yad Vashem. Eliding two political principles into one, the CEO of Deutsche Bahn, Richard Lutz, declared, 'As Deutsche Bahn, we bring people together, overcome distances and contribute to European integration. We are acutely aware of our historical responsibility and are resolutely committed to a society and a future without hate and extremism.' Plans are afoot for a documentary centre tracing the history of the deportations and for a student residence named after Else Ury, a German-Jewish novelist sent to Auschwitz in 1943. Platform 17 is no longer overgrown, but many, in and outside the Jewish community, are underwhelmed by the latest plans. As ever, memorialization brings its own complexities.

On the southwestern reaches of the city, on the road to

Potsdam, stands its largest and one of its most popular lakes, Wannsee. Artists, entrepreneurs and politicians built their summer residences here. There could have been no more relaxing surroundings in which to plan genocide. An elegant villa provided the setting for a meeting between a select group of Hitler's confidants. It was here in January 1942 that Reinhard Heydrich, Adolf Eichmann and others engineered the Final Solution. From a large bay window, they could watch sailing and rowing boats glide along the lake – a bucolic view then as now – as they documented in minute detail the extermination of the Jews.

After the war, the building was used first by the Soviets, then the Americans. From 1952 to 1988 it was used as a recreation centre for schoolchildren. For decades the city refused requests to turn it over to a house of remembrance, even declining an offer by the World Jewish Congress to finance such a project. Eventually it relented and the Memorial and Educational Site, House of the Wannsee Conference, opened in January 1992 on the fiftieth anniversary of the meeting.

The exhibition shows the invitation to a select group to attend a meeting at the villa's address, am Grossen Wannsee 56–58, 'with breakfast to follow'. It displays the minutes of that meeting, the only one of thirty copies to survive. The most chilling of the items on display is the simplest: a denunciation of one neighbour by another. Dated August 1943 and addressed 'to the Gestapo', the typewritten letter says that 'the Jew (Lotte) Blumenfeld' is being hidden away by Mrs Weichers at number 38 front house, third floor. This Jew has always behaved in an impudent and arrogant manner. The snitch, called Else, suggests that officers should get there quickly – she suggests 7 a.m. – to 'take this woman away quickly'. She signs off 'Heil Hitler'.

The memorial in Bebelplatz (formerly Opera Square), marking the spot where on one day 20,000 books were set ablaze on a pyre, is one of those where the aesthetic ends up obscuring the purpose.

Designed in 1995 by Micha Ullman, the Israeli artist responsible also for the Mendelssohn memorial on Spandauer Strasse, the underground *Empty Library* in the middle of the square is a white room lined with shelves that are completely empty, but that would fit the exact number of books that were destroyed. Curious tourists strain to work out what they are looking for, as much of the time the glass around it is smudged.

Similarly opaque is a site outside the Philharmonic. The villa at Tiergartenstrasse 4 had been requisitioned from the Liebermann family by the Nazis and slated to be demolished to make way for Hitler's grand project, Germania. When war broke out it was used instead as headquarters of the Nazis' euthanasia programme. Inside the house, code-named T4, dozens of doctors, nurses and porters worked ever so efficiently, filling out forms and having them properly stamped, as they consigned hundreds of thousands of psychiatric patients, or those deemed otherwise undesirable, to the gas chambers. In 1988 the city bought a Richard Serra sculpture, called *Berlin Junction*, consisting of two almost vertical free-standing curved steel plates; the sculpture forms a narrow, threatening passageway that visitors walk through. Whatever its artistic quality, it does not speak to the subject. It took until 2014, after decades of further argument, for a more appropriate tableau to be erected.

Schöneberg had been a village since the thirteenth century. At the end of the nineteenth century, it suddenly boomed, and its agricultural land was sold off. A new district came into being, the Bavarian Quarter. Between 1900 and 1914, Georg Haberland created a community of residential streets lined with grand buildings decorated with stucco and marble. Haberland was not just one of the most prominent developers of his time, he was also an author and a political player. Alongside the great industrialization and moneymaking of that era, he wanted to create communities in Berlin that would attract respectable middle-class professionals. The main square outside the S-Bahn was landscaped in 1908, with a green area, benches and a fountain. Prestigious shops were opened, alongside cafes, banks and doctors' surgeries. Lawyers, doctors and businessmen flocked to the new quarter, as did scientists, writers and intellectuals such as Hannah Arendt, Albert Einstein, Walter Benjamin and Billy Wilder. It became known as the Jewish Switzerland.

Then came 1933. Haberland died that year, and his firm was 'Aryanized' step by step. His son Kurt was ousted from the board of directors, imprisoned in 1941 and murdered in the Mauthausen Concentration Camp the year after. In the year of the Nazi ascent to power, there had been over 16,000 Jews in the area. By the end of February 1943, Schöneberg was declared *judenfrei* (free of Jews). More than 6,000 Jewish inhabitants of the Bavarian Quarter were deported to extermination camps, often as their neighbours looked on. In the final years of the war, three-quarters of the buildings in the district were destroyed by Allied bombing.

Nearly half a century later, in 1987, a local film-maker and civil servant, Andreas Wilcke, embarked on a project to record all the names of the Quarter's former Jewish inhabitants. In 2005, in the Schöneberg City Hall, the place where Kennedy uttered his famous '*Ich bin ein Berliner*' words, an exhibition was opened entitled *We Were Neighbours*. Inside the room were over 170 biographical albums set out on reading tables documenting what was known of the residents, from the famous like Einstein and Wilder to the unknown. Wilcke's small, handwritten reference cards, listed under street and time and place of murder, were pinned to the walls. Having done so little to mark the area's sad history, the local council went into overdrive in the 2000s. The Bayerischer Platz U-Bahn station has a permanent wall display of local Jewish heritage. Café just above it opened a small exhibition in 2014, with artefacts and film and audio material. It provides a who's who of residents, pointing out where Einstein lived, at 5

Haberlandstrasse, between 1917 and 1932. The Nazis changed the name of the street in 1938; it was eventually restored in 1996.

The most remarkable of the local memorials to the Holocaust are both obtrusive and unobtrusive. Passers-by can be forgiven for initially not noticing the artworks. Yet when they were erected in early 1993, after a competition run by the local council, some people were so taken aback they called the police to report that neo-Nazis had covered the neighbourhood with antisemitic slogans. *Places of Remembrance*, created by Berlin-based artists Renata Stih and Frieder Schnock, is a collection of eighty white boards hanging 3 metres high from streetlamps. On one side is an illustration; on the other, in black writing, are rules introduced under the Third Reich between 1938 and 1940 determining what should be done with the Jews. They manage to be bureaucratic, petty and very sinister.

> 'Aryan and non-Aryan children are forbidden to play together.'
> 'Jewish members of the Greater German Chess Association are expelled.'
> 'Only respectable national comrades of German or congeneric blood may become allotment plot holders.'
> 'Postmen who marry Jews will be made to retire.'
> 'Jews in Berlin are allowed to buy groceries only between 4 and 5 in the afternoon.'

Stih has produced several subsequent displays with Schnock. This one, she notes, continues to have the capacity to alarm. 'People were not used to this kind of truth,' she says.

Why is my chapter on the Third Reich based around memorials? Because that is the way Berliners, and those who visit the city, relate to their history and their horror. It helps to tell the story of the successes and the failures in remembering, but in most places people have to imagine what is being described to them. As each decade passes, the task becomes harder. Historians, artists, museum curators feel under ever more pressure to innovate to get the message across. The simplest approach, however, is usually the most powerful.

In 1992, the artist Gunter Demnig came up with the idea of *Stolpersteine*. Three decades on, there are more than 80,000 of these 'stumbling stones' in twenty languages in 120 cities across Europe. The first one in Berlin appeared in Kreuzberg in 1996. Now there are nearly 10,000. They are located outside the last-known homes of the victims, mainly but not exclusively Jews. Some are Roma, others are homosexuals or disabled people. The inscription on each stone begins, 'Here lived', followed by the victim's name, date of birth, deportation date and death date (if known). It is easy to tread on them. They are, after all, paving stones. It is instructive to people-watch, to see if there is any pattern to discern between those who stop and reflect and those who do not.

Equally moving are the memorials to the small number of Jews who went to extraordinary lengths to survive. One of the 1,700 Jews who lived in hiding and escaped with their lives was Inge Deutschkron. Her autobiography, *I Wore the Yellow Star*, was a big hit when it was published in 1978 and ten years later was adapted for the Berlin stage. She, like dozens of Jews, had one person to thank for her survival. The story of Otto Weidt and his heroism is now told in his workshop that became a museum, down a shabby-chic alleyway right across from the Apple Store on Rosenthaler Strasse. The son of an impoverished upholsterer from Rostock, Weidt had ear problems and eventually went almost blind. He tried to establish himself in Berlin as a decorator but turned instead to brush-making. He opened a workshop in 1936. By the start of the war, he was employing thirty-five people, mainly blind and deaf Jews, to produce brooms and brushes.

Every time the Gestapo came round for inspections, an internal bell system sounded, and the workers were hurriedly hidden in a recess under the stairs in a false room. On one occasion in 1942, the alarm malfunctioned. The blind and deaf Jewish employees were rounded up and taken to the nearby deportation assembly point at Grosse Hamburger Strasse 26, the site of the original Jewish cemetery. Remarkably, Weidt rushed after them, pointing out to the officers that they were part of the war effort, while handing out discreet bribes, to get them released. At other times, falsified papers did the trick; Deutschkron was able to pass undetected through spot-checks for two years with a factory identity card. A year later, however, Weidt's efforts failed and several of his employees were taken away to their deaths. After the war, Weidt established an orphanage for survivors of the camps, only to die of heart failure in 1947. On 7 September 1971, Yad Vashem recognized Weidt as a 'righteous man among the nations' (the honour given to non-Jews). The East German authorities were somewhat less respectful of his work. Despite his wife, Else's, determination to keep the workshop open, it was dissolved in 1952. Only after unification, in 1991, was a museum opened on the site.

As for Deutschkron, she went straight to London in 1946, joining the Socialist International. She came back to Germany, to Bonn, as a journalist and was hired by the Israeli newspaper *Maariv* to cover the Frankfurt Auschwitz trials in 1963.

In 1914, a complex of buildings just off the Tiergarten was opened to serve as the Ministry of the Reichswehr. During the Third Reich it became the High Command of the army. Since 1993, it has been the Berlin headquarters of the Defence Ministry, though the Ministry continues to retain its primary presence at its post-war site just outside Bonn. It chose the Bendlerblock partly for its size and convenience, but mainly because of its history. It was here that Operation Valkyrie, the plan to assassinate

Hitler in 1944, was hatched – and narrowly failed; it was here that Colonel Claus von Stauffenberg and several of his co-conspirators were summarily executed. The courtyard stands as the Memorial to the German Resistance.

Over three floors of one of the buildings, the Silent Heroes Memorial Centre tells the story of those Germans (the few) who helped Jews survive the war, spiriting them over the border, hiding them in the cellars of their homes, providing them with false IDs – both the known (Weidt and, of course, Otto Schindler) and the less known. It is still a work in progress, with reports, photographs, documents, video and audio continuing to be collected. The resistance exhibition also tells the story of how a group of military officers planned to kill Hitler and change the course of the war. In October 1943, Colonel Claus von Stauffenberg was transferred to German army HQ as chief of staff. From his office in Bendlerblock, he used the existing 'Valkyrie' plans (intended to deal with uprisings in the Reich) to organize a *coup d'état* following the planned assassination of Hitler. Stauffenberg was to be the assassin (having access to briefings with Hitler) as well as the de facto leader and driving force of the coup in Berlin. On 20 July 1944, Stauffenberg deposited a bomb in the briefing room at the Wolf's Lair in East Prussia, but a thick wooden tabletop protected Hitler from the blast. By the time Stauffenberg arrived back in Berlin, too much time had been wasted and the conspirators were unable to take control of Germany. Stauffenberg and three of his co-conspirators were shot in the courtyard, while a fifth was allowed to shoot himself. Others were taken elsewhere (for example to Plotzensee) to be disposed of. Some of their wives were imprisoned; their children were sent to new homes and given new identities.

Discussion of Germans as heroes remains as contentious as any notion of victims. The issue is further complicated by discussion around Berlin and Germanness. The city clings to the idea that, like, say, New York, it doesn't represent the wider country. This self-identification as a hub of dissent or difference reached its peak in the Western half of the city during the Cold War, the place where West Germans could go to avoid military service, the place that was so rebellious and un-German. But how accurate is this portrait really?

The exceptionalists' case, in brief: Berlin may have been mission control but it was not where the Führer wanted to be. He spent as much time as he could at his Austrian or Bavarian hideouts, such as Berchtesgaden. He viewed Berlin as modern, decadent and un-German. Wilhelm Stapel, editor of the antisemitic monthly *Deutsche Volkstum*, referred to the city as the 'cesspool of the Republic, the spoiler of all noble and healthy life'. American and other 'cosmopolitan' influences, such as jazz music, were blamed for the decay. Munich, the Bavarian capital more in keeping with cultural norms, was chosen as the location for the Degenerate Art exhibition in 1937. Its intention was to 'reveal the philosophical, political, racial and moral goals and intentions behind this collection, and the driving forces of corruption which follow them'.

Goebbels was said to have called Berlin 'the reddest city in Europe besides Moscow'. Some districts, like Friedrichshain and Wedding, were proudly red all the way through. In the 1925 municipal elections, for example, the combined vote for the SPD and the Communist Party (KPD) was over 52 per cent in the city overall. Even as Hitler was knocking on the gates of power, Berlin consistently voted differently. In the November 1932 general election, it recorded 26 per cent for the NSDAP (the Nazi Party), against 31 per cent for the communists. The national share was 33 per cent and 17 per cent in Berlin. In the May 1928 election, the Nazis had received just 39,000 votes (1.6 per cent of the votes cast); in September 1930, that figure had risen to 396,000 (14.6 per cent), by March 1933 it had reached 34.6 per cent of the vote.

That may have been a fraction lower than elsewhere, but still it constituted a lot of Nazis. Yes, Berlin voted less for the Nazis than the rest of Germany – but nonetheless more than Berliners themselves would like to admit. The support was deep and genuine, long before Berliners felt any pressure to provide it. Cast back to the SA violence against Jews in Prenzlauer Berg and the Scheunenviertel even in the late 1920s; that was almost never challenged. The SA's domination of Berlin's streets was not just through acts of violence. Their physical presence was visible throughout the city in 'storm bars', requisitioned local buildings where brownshirts gathered to relax, drink and sing military anthems. By 1931, there were 107 such hostelries in the city.

As early as in September 1930 more than 100,000 people turned up outside the Sportpalast to gain entry to a rally attended by Hitler; that number doubled to catch a glimpse of him on Unter den Linden in April 1932. He was still months away from taking power; Berliners were not forced to attend against their will. In February 1933, the Sportpalast was filled to overflowing as he delivered his first speech as Führer. Watch the newsreels of the *Fackelzug*, his triumphal march through the Brandenburg Gate in March 1933, and the unbridled enthusiasm of the crowds. There are many more examples to cite: the Berlin of the 1936 Olympics was a roaring success. Undesirables were spirited out of the way, buildings were spruced up, new lime trees were planted. The quadriga atop the Brandenburg Gate was re-gilded. Tolerance was back in fashion, briefly. Notices forbidding Jewish access to public buildings were removed. Local women were allowed to wear hemlines 5 centimetres higher than had been previously permitted. A certain number of gay bars were reopened. Hitler and his henchmen strained to be on their best behaviour. And how the world was taken in.

The issue may therefore be less the attitude of Berliners to the Third Reich, and more the Third Reich's attitude to Berlin. The year after the Olympics, the city was preparing to celebrate its 700th anniversary. Yet Hitler did not bother to attend, choosing a few days in Bayreuth instead. Göring went on holiday. Goebbels was tasked to lead the festivities, but his heart was not in it. The monuments were not monumental enough. The Royal Palace, largely ignored since the demise of the Hohenzollerns two decades earlier, was underwhelming to Nazi taste. Unter den Linden had its merits, as did the Brandenburg Gate, but even they did not quite evoke the grandeur the Führer was looking for. Most of all, he struggled to erase Berlin's recent history. He saw decadence and disobedience wherever he looked. The fourteen years of Weimar were, he said, *ein Trümmerfeld*, a field of debris.

Why not therefore bulldoze the whole thing and build a city much more spectacular?

Hitler's dream was to raze swathes of Berlin and turn it into the capital of the Thousand Year Reich, 'comparable only to ancient Egypt, Babylon or Rome'. Its foundations were laid in 1938. The plan was for it to be fully completed by 1950, not long after the 'final victory' had been achieved. Albert Speer, an aspiring architect of no great distinction, applied for his National Socialist party card in March 1931. Two years after he started volunteering for the cause, the eager young man was introduced to Goebbels. His rise was meteoric. The organizers of the 1933 Nuremberg Rally asked him to submit designs for the event, bringing him into contact with Hitler for the first time. His work won him his first national post, as 'Commissioner for the Artistic and Technical Presentation of Party Rallies and Demonstrations'.

Speer's breakthrough came when he was appointed as supervisor of the plans to renovate the Chancellery, to satisfy Hitler's grand ambitions. He was soon briefing the Führer personally, and was, to his surprise and delight, invited for lunch. His place in the inner circle was assured. It was partly his personality and his desire to please, and partly his ability to anticipate his boss's wishes. Most of all, it was his understanding of Hitler's obsession with architecture and the need for it to serve as an expression of monumentality and power (a theme set out in *Mein Kampf*). Nuremberg was the place of Hitler's dreams. The development of 11 square kilometres in the south of the city as an ideal Nazi parade centre was in many ways a prototype of what would be planned for Berlin. The Zeppelin Field stadium, designed to hold 200,000 people and one of only three sites completed, was used for rallies and is at the heart of Leni Riefenstahl's propaganda film *Triumph of the Will*. The scale of the nearby German Stadium, whose foundations were laid, was to have been even greater. Never completed, it is salutary to visit Nuremberg now to see what is left of the superstructure, empty for the past eighty years, alongside a well-curated documentation centre.

Speer's position was formalized in 1937 when he was appointed general building inspector (GBI) for the Reich capital; he was tasked with drawing up a 'comprehensive construction plan'. 'Berlin is a big city, but not a real metropolis,' Hitler told him. 'Look at Paris, the most beautiful city in the world. Or even Vienna. Those are cities with grand style. Berlin is nothing but an unregulated accumulation of buildings.' Speer was given untrammelled power. The new GBI acquired for himself a palatial building at the heart of Pariser Platz 4, next to the Brandenburg Gate. The existing tenant, the Academy of Arts, was shipped off to a lesser building. (The Academy returned to its rightful post-reunification home in 1993.) Under the Nazis, an entirely new urban development system was created. The formal framework for the expanded capital was to be a system of main roads made up of axes and ring roads.

The first plan submitted by Speer included a large new university and medical quarter, a new airport outside the centre, and the conversion of Tempelhof into an amusement park, similar

The Nazi plan for the new Berlin, 'Germania'

to the Tivoli in Copenhagen. Hitler was unenthusiastic. He
wanted something far more grandiose. Speer quickly concluded
that he would need to demolish entire districts of the city, seizing
buildings and deploying forced labour. The Nuremberg Race

Laws were used to force out some 75,000 Jews, almost all of whom were directly shipped off to concentration camps, in part to free up housing for 'proper Germans' whose homes would be demolished as part of the Germania plan.

One of the first districts to be razed by Speer is now the heart of German power, between the chancellor's office (nicknamed the 'washing machine') and the glass buildings housing members of parliament. This was called the Alsenviertel in the second half of the nineteenth century – not that many remember that any more. What was left was bombed in the war, and then the area was chopped in half by the Berlin Wall. After 1990, the new government district, the *Spreebogen* (Spree Arc), was created, deliberately at an angle to Speer's plans, a decision that its architects described as 'historical decontamination'. It represents one of the more uplifting examples of modern Berlin architecture. Few other capitals provide an urban beach on the banks of the river in the heart of their government district.

Those who are particularly interested in Speer, Hitler and architecture should visit an exhibition called *Germania Myth*. It is not easy to find; it is housed just off the entrance hall of the U8 U-Bahn line at Gesundbrunnen. It is hard to believe that this area was once desirable. First mentioned as a mineral spa in 1748, it became a popular destination for workers escaping the dirt of the city. Now it is a giant railway interchange and shopping centre.

Germania Myth is open only once a week, on a Saturday; it is staffed by volunteers and has virtually no budget. Yet it is a hidden gem. Inside its three rooms, models reconstruct the project in meticulous detail, a new city along a north–south axis. It starts with a north station, via the Naval High Command, to the Great Hall of the People that would seat 180,000, the Führer's Palace, the Reichsmarschall's office, culminating in a triumphal arch (larger, naturally, than the Arc de Triomphe) large enough to carry the names of all 1.8 million German soldiers killed in the

First World War. Some of the buildings were modelled on existing monumental classicist buildings in Europe, such as the former German embassy in St Petersburg and the University of London's Senate House, on which George Orwell based his Ministry of Truth in *1984*. The axis would end with a south station. All of it would be built in Greek, Roman or Mussolini-style classicism. The Brandenburg Gate would have been spared, but such was the staggering scale, it would have resembled a hut by comparison to everything around it. Among the many buildings that would have been pulled down or moved was the renowned Charité hospital, which stood in the way of the Great Hall. So proud was Speer of his plans that, even in the middle of war, he ensured the *New German Art of Building* architectural show went on tour across Europe, from Copenhagen to Barcelona to Istanbul.

Hitler's madcap project has earned the name Germania. In fact, he used the word in only one speech, in June 1942 when declaring that his dream city should stand among the great civilizations of the ancient world. Mercifully, war intervened. Some streets were torn down, but very little was actually built. Today's Strasse des 17 Juni would have been the east–west axis. It remains the city's widest street. Almost entirely hidden in the pavement opposite the Soviet war memorial, two kerbs seem to have been sunk into the pavement, disappearing into the park. These would have marked the north–south axis. The Siegessäule, the old Prussian Victory Column, was moved to its present home in 1939 and the plinth was raised by more than 6 metres.

There is one place it is both easy to miss and impossible to miss. 'Information Centre Heavy Load-Bearing Body' is not the most enticing-sounding name for a tourist attraction. It sounds even better in German: *Informationsort Schwerbelastungskörper*. It is a site of striking ugliness, but also of reflection. From atop a viewing platform, the visitor can see the extraordinary lengths that Speer and Hitler were prepared to go to fulfil their Nazi urban fantasy. The dimensions of this concrete cylinder are staggering: 21 metres tall, weighing 13,000 tonnes. Its one and only job was to test whether Berlin's sandy, marshy ground could support buildings of the magnitude that were being planned for Germania, particularly the triumphal arch.

In Project Number 15, as it was code-named, 13,000 tonnes of concrete were poured into the ground between April and November 1941. Speer and his engineers planned to measure the depth that the *Schwerbelastungskörper* sank into the ground. In 1941, after dozens of buildings had been demolished and thousands of forced labourers brought in, they finally constructed it. The weight-bearing load sank by 20 centimetres in the first two years; they were hoping for a maximum of two. At least it did not collapse. But it never served its purpose. It just stayed there. It still does, not because anyone knows what to do with it, but because it was deemed too dangerous and too expensive to try to remove it. Researchers continued engineering tests on it after the war (they might as well), finally abandoning it in 1983. It fell into disrepair and was revived a dozen years later when it was given heritage status and turned into a monument. Residents in and around the intersection of Dudenstrasse and General-Pape-Strasse in Schöneberg have grown, if not to appreciate it, then to accept it. The structure is nicknamed *Naziklotz*, the 'Nazi lump'.

Forced to put his grand plans on hold, Hitler then ordered a series of equally large structures but for defensive purposes. In 1940, as the Allies mounted their first air raids on the German capital, three giant towers were constructed. One was in the eastern district of Friedrichshain, the second was in the centre, at the Zoo. The third was in the north, in a giant landscaped garden called Humboldthain opened in 1870 to commemorate the centenary of the birth of Alexander von Humboldt. Much of it was destroyed and paved over to make room for the structure, which was built at extraordinary speed.

The result was three hulking structures up to 50 metres high, with reinforced concrete walls 2.5 metres thick, window slits sheathed in steel, and towers bristling with 128-mm anti-aircraft gun turrets and 27-mm cannons for cutting down low-flying aircraft. Three hundred bombing raids were launched on the area, which was one of the most concentrated military-industrial complexes in the region, with companies such as AEG and Bayer churning out munitions. In total, thirty-two Allied planes were shot down. The towers had a dual purpose. They also served as air-raid shelters and during the war accommodated 30,000 people. They had their own water supplies, air-conditioning systems, generating plants, dining hall, cinema, even a hospital ward. Each stored enough food to last its occupants for a year. Children were born there. Marriages were made and broken there. Goebbels organized orchestras and chanteuses to entertain the troops and civilians. Hitler believed these towers would stave off the enemy and then become one of the architectural delights of Germania, celebrating the survival of the super-race and the start of the 1,000-year Reich. He ordered decorative façades to display his ambition, much to the consternation of his generals who wanted to keep the towers as functional as possible, with a minimum number of windows and access points.

In 1945, with all around reduced to rubble, the Humboldthain flak tower – full name *Flugabwehrkanone* (aircraft defence cannon) – was among a small number of structures to survive the Battle of Berlin. The Red Army simply could not penetrate it, so it decided to sit it out, depriving those still inside of food and water. Some soldiers continued fighting long after they were surrounded; others tried to slink away disguised as civilians. The French, who commanded the northwest of the city, blew up part of Humboldthain but then stopped halfway through, fearing that the debris on the north side would hurtle across the railway tracks and into the Soviet sector, potentially causing a military incident.

What was left remained a useless hulk, a favourite place for children to explore. In 2004, the flak tower was taken over by a volunteer group called *Berliner Unterwelten* (Berlin Underworld) – the same volunteers who run the *Germania Myth* exhibition around the corner at the station. The group has done an extraordinary job in clearing up and providing access to several of the city's bunkers. Humboldthain has now been cleared of much of the rubble and is open for tours, but only for part of the year. Between October and April, it is reserved for bats and has become one of the city's most important colonies. In the summer, visitors can book hard-hat visits – only three of the seven floors are open – where guides explain the history of the site.

These tours help subsidize the wider work the group is doing uncovering ever more underground sites and buried artefacts. Once in a while that work reveals something remarkable. In April 2022, Claudia Melisch (the archaeologist who had shown me around the House of One and who is the leading light of Berlin Underworld) discovered a marble bull. After a tip-off, and with the permission of the local council, she and her team began a dig next to the rose garden, just below the flak tower. They found one of the park's lost treasures. When it was originally unveiled on a wall in the park in 1901, the larger-than-life *weisse Stier* (white bull) had pride of place. It was the work of Ernst Moritz Geyger, who became one of Hitler's favourite sculptors. It is assumed that it was removed from its perch and buried 1.5 metres down – quite a feat – just before the French bombing of the flak tower in 1948. Melisch told me shortly before the announcement of both her excitement and the task ahead. It is badly damaged, with bullet holes. After repairs she hopes it will find a home in the Church of the Ascension on the edge of the park.

Buildings that still stand from the Nazi era produce complicated emotions among Berliners. Some are ignored. Others are memorialized; some are just plain weird. Some attempt to banish the past by showing a modern face.

At the end of the U-Bahn line in Mariendorf stands the Martin Luther Church. There is evidence of a place of worship of some sort here dating back to the thirteenth century, but it was only after the First World War, as Berlin was expanding into its suburbs, that the congregation decided to build a church of their own. The money eventually came in during the mid-1930s and they were able to enlist one of Brandenburg's foremost church architects.

Curt Carl Ernst Steinberg, a Nazi Party member, set about his task with relish, combining fealty to God with fealty to the man he presumably considered his representative on earth. He inserted some dramatic flourishes. The carved-oak baptismal font features a Nazi SA officer, cap in hand; the wooden pulpit depicts Christ flanked by a member of the Hitler Youth and a uniformed Wehrmacht soldier; the entrance is illuminated by a chandelier in the form of an Iron Cross, and the 800 terracotta plaques adorning the 'triumphal arch' include busts of helmeted soldiers and martial eagles. The sumptuously decorated organ had made its debut at a 1935 Nazi Party conference in Nuremberg, while even the golden figure of Christ above the altar has a certain Aryan erotic glamour – a muscular, taut hero looking straight ahead and showing no signs of suffering.

The church was bombed during the war, but the damage was slight. It was used for several years by the US Army as one of its places of worship, but no attempt was made to force the authorities to remove the Nazi emblems (the swastikas on a small number of terracotta plaques were subsequently chiselled out because their depiction is against the law). In 1953, Steinberg was awarded the Federal Cross of Merit for services to architecture by the president, Theodor Heuss. An outrage? At the time, Germany still had a long way to go in addressing its crimes.

Over 900 churches were built or remodelled during Hitler's

rule, but this one is commonly referred to in the guidebooks as 'the Nazi church'. I assumed I was inured to Nazi horror; after all, I thought I had seen everything. But as I entered the Martin Luther Church for the first time on 9 November 2022, the eighty-fourth anniversary of Kristallnacht, I became over-whelmed with emotion.

On the altar front, they had just opened an exhibition dedicated to Jochen Klepper. A journalist, writer and musician, he is known for composing some of Germany's best-loved hymns. As the exhibition pointed out, he is also known for a desperate suicide pact. The son of a Protestant pastor from Silesia, Klepper moved to Berlin in 1931, where he became a member of the congregation. In 1933 he joined a radio station only to be thrown out months later after it was discovered he had married a Jew, Johanna Stein. His eldest stepdaughter, Brigitte, fled to England just before the war, but when Klepper then personally pleaded with Adolf Eichmann to let his younger stepdaughter, Renata, follow her, he was refused. Shortly after, knowing they would be deported to the camps, husband, wife and stepdaughter took their own lives. 'Tonight, we die together,' Klepper wrote in his journal. 'Over us stands in the last moments the image of the blessed Christ who surrounds us.' His sister Hildegard gave the diary to Allied prosecutors at the Nuremberg trials where it was used against Eichmann.

For ninety minutes, in this dark and cavernous space, prayers and lessons were interspersed by cello and piano music written by Jewish composers. Two members of the congregation read out extracts of a diary kept by an eight-year-old Jewish boy in Hamburg, as he watched his world destroyed around him. The service, entitled 'As the synagogues burned', ended with a blessing and the singing of the Kaddish, the climax of the traditional mourning ritual and one of the most important prayers in the Jewish liturgy.

I have heard many *mea culpas* in my time in Germany, many attempts by people, young and old, not to try to explain or even to pretend to understand, but to come to terms with what was done by their forefathers. Few were as raw as this, the sermon given by a young clergyman, Benedikt Zimmermann. It is far too long to reproduce, but I was struck by the historical linkages he drew. 'I'm not embarrassed to say I feel ashamed that this is my country, and this is my city,' he began. He talked about continued antisemitism across Germany and Europe, about the fact that Jews in Berlin are still wary of wearing the kippah in public and about 'a Russian leader who attacks another country and calls its Jewish president a Nazi', and how many in Germany and elsewhere still don't want to know. He had no answers, he said, to what happened eighty-four years ago on that night. 'I am ashamed. I am furious. I am insulted. I shouldn't use such language in a church, but I have to say it makes me want to throw up.'

With so many places in Berlin stained by the association, how do Berliners cope in their daily lives? Can over-memorialization dull the senses? Should each venue used in some way by the Nazis be defined by that in perpetuity? Krumme Lanke is one of my favourite lakes, popular too with joggers, wild swimmers, barbecuers and nude sunbathers (you can't escape them any-where). A village close to the spot called Crumense was first recorded in the thirteenth century. The Cistercian Abbey of Lehnin bought it from the Ascanian margraves Johann I and Otto III, who ruled the area together. As the village is not regi-stered in the land book of Charles IV of 1375, it is likely that it was abandoned soon after the purchase. It has since been a place of repose for Berliners, on the southern edge of the Grunewald forest, for centuries the preserve of the wealthy on their horses, but from the late nineteenth century accessible by public transport.

Then in 1937 Himmler had an idea. He loved Krumme Lanke,

both the lake and the forest surrounding it. This would be a perfect location for a closed community for SS officers. It would be called Camaraderie Colony, evoking time-honoured rustic charm. Work was completed two years later, producing rows of near-identical small houses with neat wooden shutters and gabled roofs. (Flat roofs were considered a Jewish-Bolshevik aberration.)

The colony would, Himmler declared, provide 'satisfactory and healthy housing particularly suited to the raising of (SS) families'. Officers and their families were allocated houses according to their rank and number of children. A competition was held to find suitable names for the new streets, with winners including Führerplatz, Siegstrasse (Victory Street) and Dienstweg (Duty Way). One street, called Im Kinderland (In the land of children) was suggested by the wife of an SS officer, on the grounds that 'the men, who represent the racial elite of the German people, pass on their high-quality genetic material to a large number of genetically wealthy offspring'. The old SS colony is intact; the small houses have become desirable property. Whenever I visit Krumme Lanke's pleasant shore or sit on the terrace of the restaurant at the adjacent Schlachtensee, I cannot help thinking about SS families frolicking here.

To end my horror tour, I return to the centre of Berlin, to Wilhelmstrasse, the street that was once at the heart of Nazi power. This unprepossessing street does at least have a good coffee shop, the Steel Vintage Bikes Café, where I've had some discreet flat whites with folk from the nearby British Embassy.

On Good Friday 2022 I meet historian Benedikt Goebel around the corner. He has rented the top-floor apartment on Gertrud-Kolmar-Strasse, a boxlike structure of late-1980s GDR vintage. This was supposed to be luxury. Only reliable and privileged citizens, mainly Stasi, were allowed to live here as it was so close to the Wall. The corridors resemble prisons, but the flat is functional, and it offers great views. Benedikt is here for a reason.

He has decided to spend part of the weekend away from his family (they live in Charlottenburg) in order better to understand what happens in a part of a city where nobody feels at home.

The street is named after a Jewish poet from Berlin who was murdered in Auschwitz in 1943. To our left is a handball court that belongs to a local school. Alongside is another dumpy block of flats and a hotel. Ahead of us, a few hundred metres away, is the Holocaust Memorial. To the right is a car park, with an information board put up for the 2006 World Cup, and a Chinese restaurant just behind. This is the site of Hitler's bunker.

Hitler officially opened his new-look Chancellery on 12 January 1939 with his annual New Year's reception for the diplomatic corps. He was already planning something far grander, courtesy of Speer, but for the moment this would do. With its brutalist exterior and cavernous interior, it was designed less to impress, more to intimidate. Visitors arriving for an audience were driven through the main entrance into a 'court of honour', ringed with heroic statuary. From there they ascended a staircase leading to a reception room. Passing through huge double doors, they entered a long hall clad in mosaic. Another flight of steps took them into a round room with a domed ceiling. They finally made it to a central gallery, twice as long as the Hall of Mirrors at Versailles – another German leader obsessed with that palace and with the grandiosity of French royalty.

By January 1945, with the war effort collapsing and the Allies advancing, Hitler moved his office and his close entourage into his bunker below the Chancellery's garden. Originally an air-raid shelter, it had been successively expanded and reinforced. The Vorbunker (the upper bunker), was located 1.5 metres below the cellar of a reception hall in the old building. The Führerbunker, reinforced by concrete almost 3 metres thick, was beneath that, and contained thirty rooms. Some of his best furniture and paintings were brought underground for him, including his beloved large portrait of Friedrich the Great, in what turned out to be his final days.

Immediately after capitulation and in the ensuing chaos, the destroyed complex was relatively easy to visit. The first photographs of the interior of the bunker were taken in July 1945 by American writer James P. O'Donnell, who bribed a Russian soldier with a packet of cigarettes to let him in. A few days later, Winston Churchill visited the site. As Cold War tensions increased, the Soviets restricted movement between the zones, and tried to seal off the site. They tried repeatedly in the late 1940s and 1950s to blow it up, even resorting to flooding it. Even after filling the bunker with sand, they were only able to destroy the interior of the heavily fortified structure. They finally concluded that the best solution would be to construct a car park on top (much of Mitte was given over to car parks, in spite of the lack of cars) and build housing alongside. During construction works, several underground sections of the bunker complex were found. They were quickly resealed. Large quantities of marble from the Chancellery were reused on Soviet war memorials and to redecorate the inside of the local U-Bahn station at Mohrenstrasse.

Benedikt and I go for a stroll. We pass a garish shopping mall and several representative offices of the other German *Länder*. Outside the mission of the state of Hessen are a series of tableaux, reminding passers-by that the land on which it was built was part of both Hitler's bunker system and the death strip during communism. Benedikt takes me round the corner, into Vossstrasse. He wants to show me something. Opposite the entrance to a shopping mall is another car park, a particularly shabby one. We walk to the back, and he invites me to clamber over a rusting metal fence. We are standing on some shrubby, derelict land, right in the very heart of the city. He points to me the very spot where Hitler had his writing desk. There is nothing to see, but we decide to take photos anyway.

BERLIN
MEMORIALS

0 1 2 3 4
KM

TWELVE

Subsidy city

The survival of the island of West Berlin

I still keep a suitcase in Berlin.
MARLENE DIETRICH (1957)

It is 16 July 1945. Hitler has been dead for six weeks. The Soviets have raised their flag over the Reichstag. The Western Allies are scampering to catch up. Harry Truman is being driven into the city in an open-top car. 'We saw old men, old women, young women, children from tots to teens carrying packs, pushing carts, pulling carts, evidently ejected by the conquerors and carrying what they could of their belongings to nowhere in particular.' Hitler's folly, the new US president calls it in his diaries. 'I thought of Carthage, Baalbek, Jerusalem, Rome, Atlantis, Peking, Babylon . . . Genghis Khan, Alexander, Darius the Great – but Hitler only destroyed Stalingrad – and Berlin.' The next day Truman was off to Potsdam to meet Stalin ('He is honest, but smart as hell') and to carve up Europe.

It had taken 2.5 million Soviet soldiers, 6,000 tanks and 7,500 aircraft to overcome Nazi defences. The victory had been completed in barely a fortnight. In all, a quarter of a million people were killed in the Battle of Berlin, among them 80,000 from the

Red Army, 100,000 German soldiers, and the rest civilians. Many Berliners lay buried beneath the rubble, 55 million cubic metres of it, enough to build a wall from one end of the country to the other. Survivors wandered the streets aimlessly, shell-shocked or in the vain search for food. Squalor, a sense of helplessness, pervaded the streets for some time. Between November 1943 and March 1944 more than 800,000 Berliners had been made homeless and 7,400 died in nineteen major air raids.

Photographers and illustrators from Lee Miller to Leonard McCombe sent home images of 'blind mutilated soldiers, homeless boys, grannies, starving verminous mothers and infants'. Berliners started to refer to their city as the *Reichsscheiterhaufen*, the Reich's funeral pyre. The images have been captured for posterity by military reconnaissance flights. The closer they get to the centre, the more skeletal the buildings. As Lucius Clay, the cool-headed American general given charge of administering Germany, put it: 'Wherever we looked we saw desolation. It was like a city of the dead.'

The iconography of unconditional surrender is etched in the minds of Germans. It is described evocatively in many books of that era: the women waiting with pails and jugs at the nearest street pump, wiping the blood from their ration cards if a shell strikes and they manage to survive. A bottle of schnapps in return for a scrap of bread. A torch for a morsel of cheese. The Brandenburg Gate, the great symbol of the city, through which the soldiers of Napoleon, Kaiser Wilhelm II and Hitler had marched, had turned itself into a trading floor: sex for food or cigarettes, Lucky Strike preferably. A certain gallows humour emerged. Districts were renamed. Charlottenburg became 'Klamottenburg', the place where desperate people were flogging off their spare clothes. Steglitz was known as *steht nicht* (no longer standing). Lichterfelde was called 'Trichterfelde' (Fields of Craters). The magnificent Tiergarten became a giant vegetable patch, with people planting cabbages and potatoes. Its trees, hundreds of years old, were cut down for firewood. The bitter winters of 1946 and 1947 killed thousands more, just as the Spanish flu had done three decades earlier.

Then there were the outsiders, the refugees from what had been Germany's eastern lands. In his masterful book *Aftermath*, the historian Harald Jähner sets out the enormous challenge facing the Allies and the nascent city authorities: 'After the war over half the population of Germany were neither where they belonged nor wanted to be, including nine million bombed out people and evacuees, 14 million refugees and exiles, 10 million released forced labourers and prisoners, and countless millions of slowly returning prisoners of war.'

At one of the entrances to Hasenheide, the hunting ground of kings and the scene of Covid-busting raves, is a statue. It depicts a woman, face wan, hair scraped back, sitting on a pile of bricks, hammer in her hands. It was originally named *The Sitting One*. Now it is *The Rubble Woman*. Designed by Katharina Szelinski-Singer, fresh out of art school, it was unveiled by the mayor in the presence of the sculptor, her professor and eighty-eight former *Trümmerfrauen* in 1955. The labour of these women has gone down in folklore, as has the era known as *Stunde Null* (Year Zero), most evocatively rendered in Roberto Rossellini's 1947 film of the same name.

With so many men dead or injured or disturbed, it was the lot of these heroic women to rebuild their city, in east and west, brick by brick. The facts are indisputable; the argument revolves around historiography. How many of the subsequent accounts were part of a desperate attempt by the war generation to use the devastation as a means of absolving themselves of guilt, or at least diverting attention from it? A few months before the unveiling of the statue of the rubble woman, a book was published in the United States describing 'the business of raping'. In the first six months of 1945, more than 100,000 women in Berlin (over 1.5 million in total in Germany) between the ages of ten and eighty were raped by Soviet soldiers, in many cases on a multiple and continuing basis. They did not talk about it. They carried on as best they could.

A *Woman in Berlin* is the anonymous account of a thirty-two-year-old who worked in publishing. She chronicled her quest for survival over the two months immediately after the Battle of Berlin. She had the good fortune to speak Russian. She decided to 'adopt' a better-educated officer, to become his courtesan, hoping that he would protect her from the gang rapes and other acts of violence that were occurring all around her. The book was translated into English and published first in the United States in 1954. When a German publisher was eventually found in 1959, *Eine Frau in Berlin* received a hostile reception. The author was accused of being calculating and cold. Most of all, she had besmirched the dignity of German women. The author refused to have any further editions published in German, moved to Switzerland and didn't write again. Nearly half a century later, in 2003, a literary agent revealed that the author was a journalist originally from the town of Krefeld called Marta Hillers, a well-educated woman who spoke French and some Russian and who moved to Berlin in 1934 as a freelance writer. She died in 2001. The book was immediately reissued and this time it received critical acclaim. There is no monument to Hillers for her bravery, at least not one I have found. She was guilty (in the eyes of some) of not sticking to the script, the easy emotional binary of perpetrators and victims.

Alongside basic survival, and stiff upper lip, Berliners yearned for something uplifting. Within two and a half weeks of capitulation, the first music concert was performed. Lew Ljewitsch 'Leo' Borchard was born in Moscow to German parents. He grew up in St Petersburg, acquiring a solid musical education. In 1920 he emigrated to Berlin, as so many Russians were doing after the

Revolution. The maestro Otto Klemperer engaged him as his assistant at the Kroll Opera and in January 1933, the month of Hitler's victory, Borchard conducted the Berlin Philharmonic for the first time.

Two years later he was banned from performing by the Nazis, but continued teaching at his apartment. During the war he and his partner, a journalist called Ruth Andreas-Friedrich, helped to produce false identity papers and procured food and accommodation for Jews in hiding. They began meeting with like-minded comrades, and, as the war was drawing to a close, they daubed the word '*nein*' on walls and distributed flyers. Incredibly, they evaded arrest, and by the end of May 1945, Borchard was conducting the 'Phil' again. With no concert hall available, they took over the Titania Palast cinema, after musicians had cleared it of rubble. It was not easy to assemble the orchestra: thirty-five of its members were dead or had gone missing; many of their instruments had been destroyed, or confiscated by the Allied forces and given to a Russian military band. They played the Overture to Mendelssohn's *A Midsummer Night's Dream*, Mozart's Violin Concerto in A major and Tchaikovsky's Symphony No. 4 to great acclaim.

A week after the concert, Borchard was appointed musical director, replacing Wilhelm Furtwängler, the renowned conductor whose ambivalent relationship to the Nazis made him an object of controversy for the remainder of his life. Borchard's credentials were never in question. He gave twenty-two concerts as lead conductor, only for his career to be tragically cut short within months. A British colonel invited him for dinner at his villa in Grunewald after a concert on 23 August. Andreas-Friedrich, his girlfriend, later wrote that they drank whisky, talked about Bach, Handel and Brahms and ate 'very white sandwiches and very real meat'. The colonel offered to drive him home, but at the border between the British and US sectors (this was before the Western sectors were unified), the officer misinterpreted an American sentry's hand signal to stop. The soldier opened fire, killing Borchard, though the other two passengers survived. The Brits covered up the incident and it was decided by the occupying forces to replace him discreetly with another conductor. In 1995 the Berlin Philharmonic, under Claudio Abbado, marked the fiftieth anniversary of Borchard's death with performances of Mahler's Sixth.

Within weeks of the end of the war, the first signs of normality emerged. Some roads became usable, underground and train lines started to run, and a basic postal service was functioning. One of the biggest challenges was working out what to do with the debris from all the bombed-out buildings. With their part of the city now surrounded, and access to the countryside denied, West Berlin authorities had to find a place to dump it all. The location they found had historical significance. One of the projects for Speer's Germania was a world-beating (it had to be) science institution. The foundation stone for the *Wehrtechnische Fakultät*, the military-industrial college of the Technical University, was laid by Hitler himself. This was to be the core of a new university city, which would have required the destruction of much of the area around the beautiful lakes and forests of Grunewald. Construction was halted in 1941.

The Nazis had managed to build the shell of a building. In 1945 it was blown up. From then on, for the best part of twenty years, up to 800 trucks a day unloaded so much rubble on top of it that it became West Berlin's highest peak. The Allies saw a second purpose for it. The Devil's Mountain, Teufelsberg (named after the nearby lake Teufelsee), fell in the British sector. But under a deal, the Americans took it over and turned it into their largest listening station into the communist East. In 1963 Operation Field Station began, one of the most important assets of the National Security Agency's global ECHELON intelligence-gathering network. The area was secret, sealed-off and heavily protected.

Some 1,500 American and British military and civilians listened in on phone calls and other communications in the Soviet Zone.

Once there was nothing more to dump on Teufelsberg, trees were planted to make the man-made hill more attractive. A ski slope was built, complete with a ski lift, a ski jump (25 metres long with space for 5,000 spectators either side at the bottom) and a toboggan run. The Americans complained about all the activity and its effects on security, so the mini resort was closed down a few years later, in 1969. The station continued to operate until unification. Then it was handed back to the Berlin authorities, who used it for air traffic control until 1999. The equipment was removed, but the buildings and five large radar domes remained. Nobody knew what to do with it. A group of investors bought the complex with the intention of building hotels and apartments, only to abandon the idea. Film-makers and TV companies used it for location shoots, but they came and went. In 2007, the film director David Lynch tried to buy the land to set up a transcendental 'Vedic Peace University'. Now it is a cultural hang-out for hippies and hipsters.

In the three months before the delayed arrival of the Western Allies from the north, west and south, the Soviets had done considerable damage. Between May 1945 and the autumn, they removed some 80 per cent of Berlin's machine-tool production, 60 per cent of its light industrial capacity and much of its electrical generating capability. Generators from Siemens, Borsig and AEG plants were transported away. Also, vast monetary and artistic resources were taken away by 'trophy teams', including tonnes of gold bullion thought to be in the banks and sacks of foreign currency hidden by Nazi leaders. When the British moved into Spandau barracks, they discovered that the Russians had removed all the furniture they could, along with lightbulbs, plugs, door handles and water taps.

At the end of the war, the Brandenburg Gate was barely

standing. The East Germans were responsible for its restoration but the work was carried out in West Berlin. By the time it was completed, relations between the Russians and the Western Allies had broken down so completely that there was no formal handover. The quadriga was loaded onto the back of a large truck and left in Pariser Platz to be collected by the East Berlin authorities.

With each month, as tensions rose, West Berlin felt ever more isolated, a surrounded island in the most militarized zone in the world. Berlin, as previous centuries attested, was always an acquired taste for many Germans. That process of alienation and isolation would grow rapidly for the duration of the Cold War.

Four years exactly after Hitler's downfall the Basic Law was approved, bringing the Federal Republic of Germany into existence. Bonn, Beethoven's birthplace on the Rhine, was chosen ahead of Frankfurt as the seat of government. Berlin, or West Berlin, had a different status, under the aegis of the Allies. The choice mattered. Bonn was 600 kilometres away from the former seat of Hohenzollern, Prussian and Nazi power. It was as close to Germany's western border as one could find. It was small and unthreatening to the regions under the federal devolved system. The Bonn Republic assumed its own persona in the image of the city. It was just what Germans wanted their 'new' country to be – quiet, prosperous, clean, orderly and peaceful. Everything that Berlin was not. Konrad Adenauer, the first chancellor of post-war West Germany, loathed the place. As mayor of Cologne in the 1920s, he closed the blinds of his train compartment on the rare occasions he had the misfortune to cross the Elbe. He regarded the whole of eastern Germany, and the wide-open flat landscape, as unfathomable, socialist, nationalist and Protestant. He called the landscape around Berlin 'the Asian steppes'.

The contrast between the new chancellor in Bonn and the mayor of West Berlin was stark. Ernst Reuter was one of the city's main advocates, and an unlikely bulwark against East German communism. Drafted in the First World War, he was captured by the Russians in 1917. He converted to the cause, joining the Bolsheviks. Lenin sent him to the town of Saratov to establish an autonomous region for ethnic Germans on the Volga. On his return to Germany in 1918, he joined the KPD and was named the First Secretary of its Berlin section. After a series of ideological battles, he was expelled in 1922 and rejoined the SPD. He became a city administrator, best known for introducing a unified ticket for public transport. Briefly imprisoned by the Nazis, he went into exile in Turkey. After the war, he became mayor of the western part of the city. With the enclave on the verge of collapse, he made a speech that would define Berlin's resistance. On 9 September 1948, in front of the burnt-out Reichstag, Ernst Reuter addressed a crowd of 300,000 people: 'Today the people of Berlin will make their voice heard. People of America, England, France, Italy – look at this city. You cannot abandon this city and its people. You must not abandon it.'

Five years later, Reuter died from a sudden heart attack. His funeral was attended by more than one million people. His name adorns a particularly ugly roundabout in Charlottenburg, one or two other places and a medal for contributions to city administration. Yet it is a mystery to me why he is not regarded as one of the heroes of post-war Germany. Much of the rest of the country appeared willing to turn its back on Berlin. Reuter was not. Nor were the Allies, and one American in particular.

On 24 June 1948, Soviet troops closed all road and rail connections to the Western sectors. The blockade had begun. Within a few days, shipping on the Spree and Havel rivers was halted; electric power, which had been supplied to West Berlin by plants in the Soviet Zone, was cut off; and supplies of fresh food from the surrounding countryside were suddenly unavailable. The Four Power status of Berlin, agreed upon by the Allied victors, had not included any provisions regarding traffic by land to and from Berlin through the Soviet Zone. It had, however, established three air corridors from the Western Zones to the city.

The following day, General Lucius Clay, with the approval of Truman, gave the order to initiate 'Operation Vittles'. The Berlin Airlift, bringing in food and fuel to the people of West Berlin, remains one of the great logistical feats of modern times. It is remembered by the last generation still alive as the moment when the Americans, aided by the British and others, saved the 2.5 million inhabitants of the Western sectors of Berlin. The centre of operations was at Tempelhof, launching pad of Zeppelins and planned gateway for Germania. The French reinforced the operation by building a runway near Lake Tegel (which would become the main commercial airport for six decades). Planes were unloaded, refuelled and pilots fed in record time, before returning to the West. Some 230 US and 150 British planes were deployed; up to ten thousand tonnes of supplies were flown in daily, including coal and other heating fuels for the winter. As the air bridge increased in effectiveness the Soviets did everything they could, short of direct military confrontation, to down the flights, shining searchlights to blind pilots at night or buzzing them with their own fighter jets. Altogether, about 275,000 flights succeeded in keeping West Berliners alive for nearly a year.

On the northwest corner of Tempelhof, close to a U-Bahn station called *Platz der Luftbrücke* (Air Bridge Square), stands a memorial, the first to be built after the war. It is striking, if not aesthetically pleasing – three concrete arcs pointing westwards, symbolizing the three air corridors. Berliners call it the *Hungerkralle* (hunger claw). An inscription on its base records the names and ranks of the seventy-eight service personnel killed during the airlift. Similar monuments stand close to Frankfurt Airport and the Celle Air Base outside Hanover, from where the flights took off.

Around the perimeter of Tempelhof Field, a series of tableaux explains the airfield's complicated history, which dates to a settlement of the Knights Templar 800 years ago. Such is its expanse, it was a parade ground favoured by princes, kings and dictators. The first annual march was held during the reign of the Soldier King in 1722. Local farmers were compensated for the damage, but when the marches became too frequent, and the payments too high, they were bought out. After the founding of the Reich in 1871, the marches became grander and a few decades later the site became a military transport hub. By the 1930s it was the most important airport in the world. On 1 May 1933 it was used for one of the biggest Nazi rallies. And then came war, division, the blockade and the airlift. All these moments, snippets of a wider Berlin history, are marked on signage boards on either side of the tarmac.

The last plane took off from this giant site in 2008. Three years later, developers submitted plans for the usual mix of offices and homes, plus a large public library. The mayor at the time, Klaus Wowereit, insisted that only a quarter of the site could be built on; the rest would be turned over to a recreational park. Even that was too much for the locals. For the past decade it has been home to urban gardeners, yoga enthusiasts, hipsters, dope smokers, barbecuers and rollerbladers.

The history of the Western enclave of Berlin is one of military dependency (on the Allies) and economic dependency (on West Germany). Just about everything had to be brought in. *Soforthilfe* (emergency aid) was granted several times. By the early 1960s, this had been institutionalized. Annual support grants were agreed, including tax breaks for companies in a vain attempt to stop them going elsewhere. Each year the packages were renewed and invariably increased. These included location subsidies, rent-controlled apartments and income tax reductions of 30 per cent.

Some federal agencies were moved to the city, with state employees receiving an even larger 'Berlin supplement'.

The yearning of East Berliners to flee to the Western half of their city is well known. Less is said about the brain drain from the West. The powerhouse of the Wilhelmine era became a production-free zone. The low point may have been in 1971, when the Bonn government granted workers in West Berlin an 8 per cent pay increase. Dubbed by the locals as *Zitterprämie*, the 'jitters premium' was maintained even until a few years after reunification. Surrounded, many Berliners developed their own form of claustrophobia. The suicide rate was twice as high as in the rest of the country.

Berlin became the city of the displaced and distressed, the adventurous and the angry. As it sought to rebuild at speed, it embraced its own aesthetic. Or perhaps it might be more accurate to say that in many cases it jettisoned aesthetics.

Bombsites still peppered the city. Many façades were still riddled with bullet holes. Architects, developers and city planners had faced a series of intense challenges – how to rehouse hundreds of thousands of people, at scale and at speed, and how to rebuild infrastructure. For the more far-sighted, how to create something different from all that had come before, with all its associations of Prussian militarism and the Third Reich?

In the East, the direction seemed clear. As part of the 1951 National Reconstruction Programme, the Ministry of Construction produced sixteen 'principles of urban design', including a new showcase boulevard named after Stalin. Therefore, to outdo East Berlin's ambition (or so it felt at the time), and also to supply affordable housing to a still-devastated West Berlin, the West German Senate announced plans for a global architecture competition called Interbau.

The island city wooed global starchitects, from Le Corbusier to Walter Gropius to Oscar Niemeyer and Hans Scharoun. The biggest project was the building of an entire district, the Hansaviertel. In the 1870s, to the north of the Tiergarten and to the west of the Reichstag, a new residential quarter was built on what had previously been flood plains. Hansa-Viertel became a middle-class area, largely of professionals and intellectuals. It had contained a high number of Jews – until they were forced out; many were sent to their deaths to clear the way for Germania. It was particularly heavily bombed but the decision was made not to rebuild but to start from scratch. Never had there been an architectural exhibition on such a grand scale. The new Hansaviertel was designed on an area of 25 hectares, containing 1,300 residential units, a library, two churches, two schools and a shopping centre – all in the heart of Berlin. More than fifty prominent architects from fourteen countries were involved.

Whenever I walk around the centre of both Berlins, East and West, I am struck by the brutalism of those parts of the city that were bombed and hastily rebuilt. The bleak, grey and inter-minably long winter accentuates the ugliness of so much of the built environment. And then suddenly, with almost no interlude, no warning, when summer arrives the city is transformed. The lakes, riverbanks and canal come to life. People flock to outdoor bars in squares such as Viktoria-Luise-Platz in Schöneberg (named after Kaiser Wilhelm's only daughter, whose star-studded wedding in 1913 marked the final great social outing for Hohenzollerns), Kollwitzplatz in Prenzlauer Berg and Chamissoplatz in Bergmannkiez (where I've spent much of my time). Perhaps it is this juxtaposition and the rarity of classic aesthetics that makes Berlin's most beautiful spots all the more pleasurable.

In 1964 the first tenants moved into the Märkisches Viertel, which was described by one critic as a 'hope for designers in many European countries'. This was the first of West Berlin's giant residential complexes, built on almost empty land in the northern peripheries, separated by the newly built Wall from the East German district of Pankow. It was based on a planning paradigm called *Urbanität durch Dichte* (urbanity through density), imbued with a belief in progress and modernity. All aspects had been 'scientifically' calculated to the needs of the population – shops, schools, playgrounds, football pitches, nursing homes and medical centres. Unlike the hierarchical *Mietskaserne* (rental barracks) of the nineteenth century, the new developments were rigorously egalitarian: no more wealthy in the front and working class towards the back.

Yet it didn't take long for the Märkisches Viertel to be denounced. In 1968, the years of protests, *Der Spiegel* ran a six-page article calling the project 'a grey hell' and 'the bleakest product of concrete architecture'. It quoted inhabitants as saying they were living in a 'barracks' and a 'prison camp'.

The best-known of the developments is Gropiusstadt, closer to the centre of the city, in Neukölln. It was named after and originally conceived by the architect Walter Gropius. His original blueprint called for 16,000 flats in blocks of no more than five storeys high, with wide swathes of green between the buildings. But the plans were changed after the construction of the Wall as housing needs had become more acute. The buildings were to be up to thirty storeys high, making them among the tallest residential buildings in the whole of Germany. Gropius, who by then was living in America, was blindsided. He would not live to see his mini city completed in 1975. Shortly before his death, he remarked: 'Our cities are getting uglier and uglier.'

Gropiusstadt was made famous, for all the wrong reasons, by a young woman also made famous for all the wrong reasons. Christiane Felscherinow was born in Hamburg in 1956. She moved with her parents to West Berlin when she was six. Shortly after, her parents divorced. Her father was an alcoholic. By the time she was thirteen she was a heroin addict and became a sex worker. In 1978, two journalists from the news magazine *Stern* interviewed her. The three became confidants of sorts, and over several months she gave them an insight into the desperate plight of dozens of young people in and around Zoo S-Bahn station. The result was a series of articles, culminating in a book published the following year called *Wir Kinder vom Bahnhof Zoo*, translated as *The Story of Christiane F.* Written in her name, but in reality ghostwritten, the account manages to be both intensely depressing and humane, describing a strong community spirit as well as the squalor, not least of where she lived, in a miserable flat in Gropiusstadt. 'From afar it looks well kept,' she writes. 'But when you go between the high rises it stinks of piss and shit. That was because children couldn't climb fast enough up to their flats because the lifts were most of the time broken.'

The book is one of the most evocative accounts of Cold War West Berlin. Celebrity, of a fashion, awaited Christiane three years later with the release of a film of her life. The biopic instantly achieved cult status thanks in large part to David Bowie, who played a cameo role and was also the main contributor to the soundtrack from the albums he had made while living in Berlin – although footage of him playing a concert is actually spliced from one he had just done in New York. Christiane F. was catapulted from a life of shooting up, and servicing men in West Berlin's public toilets to becoming a 'junkie princess', hanging out with artists and celebrities in LA and doing drugs with them. She tried various ventures, acting in a punk film and appearing on an American talk show hosted by Nina Hagen, the godmother of punk, called *Café Paradise*. None of it really worked out. At the end of the 1980s, shortly before the Wall fell, she moved to Greece for a short time. In 1996 her son was born; she gave him, at the age of twelve, the story of her life to read. She spent some time in Amsterdam, but on her return to Berlin she had her parenting rights briefly withdrawn. In 2013, she wrote her own 'real' book,

My Second Life, which received mixed reviews. Now into her sixties, she complains about intrusion, while admitting that she cannot get clean from drugs.

And what of the place where Christiane F. grew up? The original idea of Berliners of different demographic groups living side by side failed as soon as the Senate decreed that upwardly mobile families would be charged higher rent. Nearly nine-tenths of tenants in Gropiusstadt are in social housing. It has several conflicting problems at play – the dominance of white far right groups and the large clusters of residents with a migrant background, gangs on all sides seeking to carve out territory.

It would be wrong to be too maudlin about the architecture of Cold War West Berlin; after all, its very appeal derives more from grit than from conventional notions of beauty. A building on the outskirts of Marseilles provided the model for one of the more intriguing examples of early post-war Berlin design. Le Corbusier's *Unité d'habitation* in Marseilles, completed in 1952, was instantly hailed as one the most exciting social housing projects anywhere in the world. He was invited to Berlin where, close to the Olympic stadium, a site that was derelict and only a few years earlier vacated by British troops, he produced a similar model. Tucked away behind Heerstrasse, a main road heading west, the multicoloured high-rise Corbusier House remains a remarkable, if hidden, part of Berlin's skyline. Gropius said of it: 'Any architect who does not find this building beautiful, had better lay down his pencil.'

One of the most inspirational contributions of the Cold War era came in the saddest part of town. Potsdamer Platz, once a glamorous central square and then the no man's land of divided Berlin, was a bombed-out husk, a place where wild animals would scamper between the watchtowers. On the Western side, travelling circus companies would use the derelict land as their temporary home. With its swooping and soaring views of a torn city, Wim Wenders's elegiac 1987 film, *Wings of Desire* (I prefer the German title, *Heaven over Berlin*), evokes the discontinuity. In one scene an old man wanders across an expanse of weeds that is part of what was the square, muttering, 'It's got to be here somewhere. I can't find Potsdamer Platz.'

The barren area immediately to the south and west of the Wall was to become the Kulturforum and home to two of the city's most eye-catching buildings. In 1932, the Nazis forced the Bauhaus school to leave its campus in Dessau. Its director, Mies van der Rohe, left for the United States. He returned briefly in the 1960s to design one building, the Neue Nationalgalerie, New National Gallery. Dominated by its giant rectangular ground-floor upper pavilion, it received a mixed review from critics, at the time likened to a large petrol station, now more akin to a modern airport. The original design was not intended for Berlin, but for the headquarters of the Bacardi Rum company in Santiago de Cuba. The 1958 revolution put paid to that idea, so the architect revived the design and put it to a different use. It was given a makeover in recent years by David Chipperfield.

Close by is perhaps the most appreciated of all West Berlin's cultural centres, the Philharmonic. The man behind it was Hans Scharoun, a veteran architect originally tasked by the Allies to come up with a grand plan for the city (until the Soviets stopped all such cooperation). Despite that, he left his mark with this one flamboyant yellow structure, its upward sweep topped with gold sheeting. It opened, defiantly, in 1963. From Herbert von Karajan to Simon Rattle, the Philharmonic has always attracted the world's best. It was one of the few places right next to the Wall that more refined Berliners dared to visit. For the best part of three decades the centre of gravity moved west. Parts of Charlottenburg and Schöneberg were still deemed desirable. Kreuzberg and Neukölln to the south were the preserve of more bohemian Berliners, while Moabit and Wedding to the north retained their working-class roots.

It was to Grunewald, as ever, that the wealthy cleaved, alongside other suburbs in the southwest such as Zehlendorf, where US forces built their HQ, and Dahlem, home to another American gift, the Free University, and the city's prettiest U-Bahn station, which sports a thatched roof, and a city farm. But even tranquil spots like these, as far away from the Cold War tension as it was possible to be, contain dark secrets.

A roughly hewn stumpy granite headstone reads, 'Dr. phil', and gives the dates and places of his birth and death. This is the unlikely location of Rudi Dutschke's grave, in the grounds of St Anne's Church. How on earth did the radical leftist shot on the Ku'damm who died abroad years later end up here in Dahlem, of all places? I have come here with Alan Posener, a one-time Maoist turned columnist for a right-wing newspaper, *Die Welt*, and someone who epitomizes the fraught politics of Berlin. We walk into the church, where the organist – she turns out to be a virologist who volunteers in her free time – plays us 'Ave Maria'.

The trigger for the great wave of protests, for the ascent of the *Achtundsechziger* generation, the 68-ers, came the summer of the year before. On 2 June 1967, the Shah of Iran was attending a performance of *The Magic Flute* at the Deutsche Oper in Charlottenburg. Protesters – German, Iranian and others – gathered outside to heckle him. They were quickly set upon by pro-Shah demonstrators, infiltrated and orchestrated by the Shah's intelligence service. The police, out of their depth and frightened of escalation, made a charge for the leftists. One man, twenty-six-year-old humanities student Benno Ohnesorg, fled into a side street to take refuge. He was tracked by a plain-clothes officer and shot point-blank. Ohnesorg, who had never been on a demo before, bled to death. His wife was about to give birth. The mayor eventually resigned, later to become a figure in the peace movement. The officer who pulled the trigger, Karl-Heinz Kurras, was acquitted – he said he was only doing his job. Forty years later, in 2009, documents revealed that he had been an informant for the Stasi.

As ever in Berlin, the commemoration of these events was complicated. The work, by the Austrian sculptor Alfred Hrdlicka, is a remarkable example of the raw and the artistic coming together. On a tall block of bronze, he depicts violence and confusion, the helmets of policemen, arms, legs, a club, the helpless hands of an invisible person in the background, the face of an onlooker, twisted limbs. It is not immediately clear who is perpetrating, who is collaborating. The work was completed in 1971. Hrdlicka wanted it erected at the exact spot where Ohnesorg was shot down, the courtyard at Krumme Strasse 66. The residents objected. It took two decades for the argument to be resolved. It was placed outside the opera house, in front of the U-Bahn exit, a hundred metres or so away from the scene of the crime – a more prominent spot. Under the relief is an explanation, which states that Ohnesorg's death 'was a signal for the beginning of the student and extra-parliamentary movement that protested against exploitation and oppression especially in the countries of the Third World struggling for radical democratisation in their own countries'. In a classic Berliner case of interminable delay followed by overcompensation, in 2008 a plaque was unveiled on the street near the murder spot (now a residents' car park). At the end of a long description of the events of that day in 1967, it concludes: 'The action taken by the police, the defamatory reports in the gutter press, the one-sided views expressed by leading politicians, and the acquittal of the policeman provided a justification for both the radicalisation and a growing readiness among part of the student opposition, to use violence.'

The touchpaper may have been lit that day, but the anticapitalist, 'anti-imperialist' movement had been developing for several years. Berlin was by no means unique – think 1968, think Paris, think anti-Vietnam protests in America and around the world. Arguably, its legacy had deeper roots in West Germany. One wing of the movement developed into the terrorist organizations of the 1970s, most notoriously Andreas Baader and Ulrike Meinhof's Red Army Faction. The other stayed largely within the mainstream and made its mark on subsequent generations at the top of German politics.

Born in 1940, Dutschke was brought up in the East German system. As a schoolboy he joined the FDJ, the Communist Party youth wing, largely because it was only through the official system that you could play top-level sport. He wanted to be a decathlete. By the early 1960s, he was spending most of his time in the West. He registered as a refugee three days before the Wall went up, and when it did, he and some friends tried to tear down parts of it and, using a rope, threw leaflets over it. It was his first political action. In 1965 he was elected to the political council of the West Berlin SDS, the student socialist organization which had broken away from the Social Democrats. He spent time with similar groups in the US and Latin America, arguing that 'systematic, limited and controlled confrontations with the power structure' would bring out the authoritarian nature of Western powers. He was equally dismissive of communist dictatorship, travelling to Czechoslovakia to support protesters of the Prague Spring.

On his return, Dutschke was leaving the SDS offices on the Ku'damm on the evening of 11 April 1968, wheeling his bicycle to a nearby pharmacy to pick up medicine for his sick son, when he was approached by a man who asked him his name. Calling him a 'dirty Communist pig', the assailant then pumped him with three bullets. A video taken shortly after by a passer-by shows the victim's shoes scattered across the road, encircled by forensic chalk. His bike lies on its side, his briefcase still attached to it. Josef Bachmann, a painter and decorator, an itinerant petty criminal originally from the East, ran off, but was eventually caught. During questioning, he said he had been inspired by the assassination of Martin Luther King. Bachmann was sentenced to (only) seven years in jail, but within a few months he took his own life.

The shock and fury in the protest movement, and more widely across a swathe of German society, was huge. Dutschke and his wife, the activist Gretchen Klotz, regularly ran the gauntlet of insults and death threats. A right-wing member of the Bundestag described him as 'an unwashed, lousy and filthy creature'. Activists blamed the Springer group for encouraging the assassination attempt. *Bild*, the main tabloid, had mounted a campaign against Dutschke, at one point urging readers to 'eliminate the trouble-makers'. In response to the attempt on Dutschke's life, thousands of students marched from the Free University to Springer HQ, next to the still-new Berlin Wall, and tried to ransack the building.

Dutschke survived, but struggled to regain his memory and went on to have regular epileptic seizures. After being refused entry by several countries, he was invited by Cambridge University to recuperate in the UK and to finish his doctoral studies there. Just over a year later, the new Conservative government of Edward Heath expelled him, fearing he would foment trouble. He moved to Denmark and then back to Germany, but he never fully recovered from his injuries and died in 1979, aged thirty-nine.

His widow wanted him returned to his homeland. She asked the pastor at St Anne's, Helmut Gollwitzer, a long-time friend and fellow radical, for help. Gollwitzer told her that there were no free spots left in the cemetery, but that he would get in touch with his predecessor, Martin Niemöller. One of the most important clerical critics of the Nazis, after the war Niemöller had moved to the state of Hesse where he was head of the Protestant church. He told Gollwitzer they could give the burial spot reserved for him in Berlin to Dutschke. The funeral was attended by thousands.

Posener, the journalist I had come to see the grave with, has had a curious political journey. Part British, part German, part Jewish, part Protestant, born in London and raised in Malaysia, he too was a radical activist. A fan of Dutschke, he was deemed such a radical that he was banned by the GDR from entering East Berlin. He took part in the protests against the Springer newspaper group, only many decades later to join it as a commentator. He would now still be seen as a maverick, but more of a conservative one. The week we visited St Anne's Church he wrote about it in his column, describing the music played for us and my surprise at the diffidence of Dutschke's grave. 'For a moment the angel of history seems to float through space and does not, as with Walter Benjamin, see "a single catastrophe" that is constantly piling rubble upon rubble and throwing it at his feet, but rather the path to a country that has actually overcome adolescence.'

In December 1963, *Atlantic* magazine published a three-way conversation involving Günter Grass and two other writers, Walter Höllerer and Walter Hasenclever. They were asked to muse about divided Berlin and its role in contemporary culture. Grass encapsulated what Berliners saw as the essential difference between their encircled island city and everywhere else. West Germany, he said, 'sickened me'. Everything was about business. 'Berliners are not so easily fobbed off with platitudes. This leads me to the point that Berlin is probably the only city in Germany that can boast of an atmosphere which is genuinely metropolitan. The other cities are much more provincial.'

Grass encapsulated the difference; he also inadvertently understated it. Berlin was cut off from the rest of West Germany; still under Allied control, it didn't even technically belong to the Bundesrepublik. Culturally it was far away. The economic miracle from the early 1950s had provided West Germans with the opportunity to start afresh, or at least to forget about what had happened only a few years earlier. The first foreign package holidays, the new car and the neat new home provided the balm, the anaesthetic. West Berlin, for all its woes, perhaps because of all its woes, wanted to start afresh in a different way, to build something new in the mind. It would never be easy; it was often – with the benefit of hindsight – more than a little naive. But at least it was something. The Berlin that Grass referred to was more metropolitan, more risk-taking, more exciting than not just the rest of Germany, but many comparative cities. Gritty Berlin was already challenging post-war norms.

Long before the 'poor but sexy' title was bestowed on Berlin by its mayor, Klaus Wowereit, in 2003, West Berlin sought to present itself as Europe's centre of culture. The first major initiative was the Berlin Film Festival in 1951. It took a while for the image of the city as a cultural refuge to take hold, but when it did, it stuck. The countercultural music scene became one of the biggest draws. *Macht kaputt, was euch kaputt macht* (Destroy what is destroying you) – the lyrics of a 1970s song by the punk band Ton Steine Scherben – became one of many anarchist and squatter anthems.

Although many have tried to embody 1970s Berlin, only some have succeeded, and one artist towers above them all. When David Bowie died in January 2016, the German Foreign Office tweeted: 'You are now among Heroes. Thank you for helping to bring down The Wall.' He spent barely two years living in the city, so why is he regarded as synonymous with it? *Rolling Stone* magazine, which followed him throughout, wrote this a few months after his death: 'Bowie and Berlin were well matched. He absorbed and reflected its darkness and angularity, and, in turn, it rehabilitated his creative drive and artistic hunger.' Bowie had arrived from a drug-fuelled sojourn in LA, 'skeletal and shattered'. Berlin, in its Cold War grunginess, gave him space. He could wander around the clubs and bars, the shops and the sights with a freedom he did not enjoy elsewhere. Many of the most famous venues he frequented still stand: SO36, denoting its Kreuzberg postcode, has from the early 1970s hosted music waves from punk onwards. The Paris Bar in Charlottenburg has hosted the likes of Jack Nicholson and Madonna. Its walls are adorned with works from artists ranging from Sigmar Polke to Julian Schnabel. Martin Kippenberger is said to have given so many paintings on permanent loan that he came and went, eating and drinking, without the need to pay. It might work for some celebrities, but it is too refined, and certainly too expensive, for the next generation of more rebellious artists.

Bowie's apartment building at Hauptstrasse 155 in Schöneberg, now memorialized with a plaque, is as plain now as it was then (it is currently occupied by a dentist's practice). Yet there, with Iggy Pop, Brian Eno and a new set of German friends, and at the Hansa Studios, he created some of his most inspired work – the three albums that make up his Berlin Trilogy: *Low*, *Heroes* and *Lodger*. Bowie would later remark, 'Berlin has the strange ability to make you write only the important things.'

A decade after leaving the city, Bowie returned in 1987 on his Glass Spider global tour. Playing in front of the derelict Reichstag, a quarter of the speakers turned east, he declared, 'The band sends our best wishes to all of our friends who are on the other side of The Wall.' A cheer was clearly audible from the other side. As border guards looked on, the East Berlin crowd chanted, 'The Wall must fall.' The extent of his role in helping to usher in the great events of 1989 is much debated. What probably mattered for him most was that Berlin enabled him to banish his demons – as it has countless others before and since. When the mayor, Michael Müller, unveiled a plaque outside his flat in 2018, he opted not for the grandiloquent but the ironic: 'You have to imagine that David Bowie came to West Berlin in 1976 to get off drugs.'

Weimar decadence, Christiane F., Bowie and Berghain form part of a continuum, a contemporary branding – inadvertent or not – of Berlin exceptionalism, of a city that the world's curious and put-upon cleave to.

In the wonderful gem that is the Märkisches Museum, one of the first items on display is a jukebox dating back to 1962. Visitors are encouraged to select from seventy songs that are associated with Berlin. They can do the same on Spotify, which has digitized the collection. Bowie's 'Heroes' comes in at a surprisingly low number 13, Lou Reed's 'Berlin' at 10 and Marlene Dietrich's 'suitcase' at 3. In top spot is a song entitled 'Pack your swimming costume' sung in 1951 by eight-year-old Cornelia Froboess, child star later turned actress: Berlin cool meets irony, perhaps.

The stereotype of the migrant to West Berlin is the draft dodger, the student, the hippie, the artist and musician, the young person from abroad or elsewhere in West Germany who sought the frisson and freedoms of the island city. The other motivation, of those coming from the East, from just a few kilometres away, was of a more existential kind.

As Germans from West Berlin seeped out of the city, another group did everything they could to get in. Between 1949 and 1961 one in six of the GDR population fled, almost all through what was still a relatively porous border between East and West Berlin. The numbers grew exponentially as the economy deteriorated and as freedoms were eroded. In 1952, some 180,000 fled. The next year the figure had almost doubled to 331,000. And so on. Half of the refugees were under twenty-five years old.

The communist regime did everything it could to stem the tide. Relatives of those who had fled were punished. In the early years, in the tensest period on either side of the Berlin blockade, Stasi and KGB carried out kidnappings in Western districts of the city to spirit people back over to the East. People were bundled into cars or vans, often in broad daylight and initially with little done to prevent it. These were predominantly East Germans who had upped sticks but also some West Berliners and even foreigners who were deemed to be undermining communism. Within two years of the end of the Second World War, the Americans estimated that 2,000 people had gone missing.

In all, between 1949 and 1989 some four million East Germans fled for the West, the majority using West Berlin as the passage out. At the height of the influx there were ninety refugee centres plus numerous emergency shelters. By far the largest number, nearly 1.5 million in total, were processed in one camp.

'THE FREE WORLD WELCOMES YOU', read a huge banner at the entrance.

The Marienfelde Refugee Centre, in the southern fringes of the city, had been established a few years earlier to house German refugees sent out from Poland and the Eastern lands after the Nazi surrender in 1945. Barely had that problem been dealt with than it was being put to a second use – to process people fleeing the GDR. Within days of its reopening in April 1953 by the West German president, Theodor Heuss, it was bursting at the seams. The processes were precise. On arrival, refugees were required to supply a first round of personal information. They received a health certificate and a processing slip noting the next steps. Twelve stages were involved, an orderly progression from station to station inside the one building, each noted by a stamp. New arrivals were told not to speak out of turn. Signs at the entrance of each room warned: 'Attention! Danger of spies! Robbery!' Refugees were told never to reveal details of their escape to anyone in the camp. They were each questioned by intelligence officers from the three Allies, debriefings that took place in secure rooms off site, venues that were assigned code names, at locations that changed frequently. The camp was fenced in and guarded. Visitors were not normally allowed, and photography was strictly forbidden. Everyone was on the lookout for sleepers or informants, and they were not wrong. It transpired, when East German files were accessed after reunification, that the Stasi had rented several flats nearby within camera and listening distance of Marienfelde. It was officially listed by the GDR as 'an enemy object'.

The number of refugees dwindled to a trickle after the building of the Wall. Between 1989 and 1990 the flow was briefly resurrected before unification rendered escape redundant. The camp finally closed in 1990, or rather it was supposed to. In the 2000s it was dusted down to accommodate ethnic Germans leaving Russia. Since 2015 it has provided homes to just under 700 refugees a year, fleeing Syria, Afghanistan and other war zones, who have had small flats built for them at the back. It is always full.

The front part of the building, where East Germans were methodically processed, is now a small museum. 'Nobody thought the centre would last long,' says Axel Klausmeier, who runs the organization that looks after Berlin's memorials to the Wall. 'It was only supposed to be temporary.' It has a quaint, other-worldly feel, telling a familiar story with empathy – the escapes, sometimes dramatic, sometimes not, the dislocation and complicated sense of loss that always followed. Yet it had, at the last count, only 12,000 visitors in a year. On one of my visits, I came across a man who told me that his father had been processed here in 1955. He was then sent to the town of Ludwigshafen. 'None of his relatives could be told he had gone,' he told me. The family was required to spend years pretending he hadn't existed.

The problem throughout the post-war era was that West Berlin did not make or do anything. It was a drain on the rest of the country. By the mid-1980s, more than half the city's budget was covered by West German taxpayers (along with paying for the stationing of Allied troops). West Berlin had the highest percentage of people aged over sixty-five (more than 25 per cent compared to the average of 12 per cent for West Germany), plus an army of students, but very few professionals, and even fewer young families. There were precious few people deemed 'economically productive' and even fewer companies willing to brave the instability and the grunge to employ them. It was far easier to relocate. All the politics was in Bonn. Finance in Frankfurt; insurance in Munich; media in Hamburg; advertising in Düsseldorf. Heavy industry in the Ruhr. Car production in Stuttgart and Munich. Precision engineering, the *Mittelstand*, the powerhouse of the economic miracle, was everywhere but in the island city.

As Berlin's population continued to fall, the city authorities went on another recruitment drive (not dissimilar to the Great Elector in the seventeenth century). The shortage this time was manual labour. West Berlin went from having virtually no foreign workers in 1960 to 10 per cent of the entire workforce by 1975. And then more. The *Gastarbeiter* (guest workers) propped up the city, but they had precious few rights. Their children, dubbed 'suitcase children', were often sent between their home country and Germany as their parents struggled to make ends meet. Alongside the Turks came Yugoslavs (as they were called then, but mainly Croats), Italians, Greeks and Spanish. These workers populated the cheapest and emptiest parts of town, those closest to the Wall – Kreuzberg, Neukölln and Wedding – indeed in some neighbourhoods becoming the largest community. Neukölln still has more welfare recipients than any other district in Germany; it also has a high number of chic hipster restaurants – the urban experience in microcosm.

The recruitment of Turkish workers started in 1961 and formally ended in 1973 due to the first oil crisis and increasing unemployment. Successive attempts were made to reduce the number of migrants when the recruitment agreement formally lapsed, but they all failed. In 1983 Helmut Kohl, pledging to halve the size of the migrant population, offered guest workers repatriation payments. In addition to a one-time payment of 10,500 Deutschmarks for workers (equivalent to £11,100 today) and 1,500 Deutschmarks for each child (around £1,900 today), the initiative stipulated that the money any returnees had paid into the pension fund would be refunded to them (thereby forfeiting their right to a pension in Germany). Very few accepted the incentives to go home; instead, members of their families joined them. This initiative was shelved in 1984 due to lack of interest.

The guest worker scheme changed the face of Germany, and Berlin, forever. Now Germany's Turkish population is estimated at 2.75 million, around 150,000 of whom live in Berlin – although these figures do not take into account the third, fourth, or fifth generation of Turkish-Germans who reside in the city. Turkish people make up by far the largest ethnic minority in the city and the largest community outside of Turkey itself. By the late 1970s, West Berlin had already become the second-largest Turkish city after Istanbul. Yet despite the island city's desire to feel international, it was still overwhelmingly white and Christian. Some, particularly older, Berliners spoke of 'Überfremdung', being overwhelmed by outsiders. Heinrich Lummer, Senator of the Interior for Berlin in the early 1980s, said of Kreuzberg: 'I'm not in my homeland here. That's been stolen from me by the foreigners.' He may have been an arch-conservative, but he spoke for many Germans – particularly non-Berliners, who looked more than ever on the city as something alien.

The Turkish community is now part of Berlin's furniture. Little Istanbul, the neighbourhood between Kottbusser Tor and Oranienstrasse, is the traditional heart of 'Turkish Berlin'. The doner kebab is now a €4-billion industry; it is said that there are more kebab shops in Berlin than in Istanbul. According to official figures, Turks across Germany own 90,000 businesses, employing 500,000 people. They account for eighteen MPs, up from fourteen in 2017. Fatih Akin, born in Hamburg to Turkish parents, has twice won the German Film Award for Best Director. Ugur Sahin and Özlem Türeci, the two scientists responsible for developing the BioNTech vaccine during the pandemic, hailed originally from Turkish families, though they have expressed unease at being held up as immigrant role models. A new hybrid language has emerged. '*Kiezdeutsch*', a term which originated in 2006 to replace the pejorative descriptors '*Türkendeutsch*' and '*Kanak Sprak*' (a slang term which has recently been reappropriated) encompasses both a variety of German and an informal style of speech used in the community.

Migration to the GDR was based on its own version of utility. From the early 1970s until the collapse of the system, up to 200,000 'contract workers' were brought in from Algeria, Cuba, Mozambique, Vietnam, Angola and other 'fraternal' states for purposes of 'socialist economic integration' – otherwise known mainly as cheap labour. They were mostly kept apart from the rest of society, designated to dormitories.

Germany has come a long way in the past half-century, Berlin particularly. The guest workers became a permanent minority in a country with little understanding of itself as a land of immigration. Gerhard Schröder's centre-left government in the late 1990s took the first substantive steps to reform immigration. Moving away from Germany's policy of *jus sanguinis*, blood rights, the government announced that children born in Germany on or after 1 January 2000 to non-German parents could acquire German citizenship at birth if at least one parent had a permanent residence permit.

By 2013 more than 30 per cent of Berlin's population had a

migrant background. Yet it was not until the following year that Turkish-Germans born in the country could retain dual citizenship into adulthood. According to one research organization, barely 30 per cent of Turkish residents in Germany have the right to vote in their country of residence.

The refugee influx of 2015 produced the second big wave. The first-generation *Gastarbeiter* were joined by Syrians, Iraqis, Afghan and Iranians, new groups giving the city another new identity, a new story to tell. Of the one million refugees who arrived in Germany in 2015, 79,000 went to Berlin – almost sixty-five times as many as in the less populated neighbouring state of Mecklenburg-Vorpommern. Some 10,000 arrived in one month, November 2015, alone. The hangars of the disused Tempelhof Airport served as temporary housing to 2,000 people, including 500 children, as their claims for asylum were assessed. Nearly 500 refugees were housed in the former Stasi headquarters in Lichtenberg. Berlin witnessed several campaigns of public solidarity, many initiated by the Turkish communities in Kreuzberg and Neukölln, which gathered donations and sought to provide food, blankets and clothing for the incoming refugees, along with legal counsel and German classes.

At the same time, Berlin's reception of the refugees was marked by administrative chaos. The already precarious housing market buckled under the pressure. The city council battled with local districts to requisition sports halls and other publicly owned buildings. The State Office for Health and Social Affairs in Moabit saw hundreds of refugees queue for eight hours a day, often for weeks, to register; many of them depended on local volunteering organizations for food or shelter in the meantime. Delays in processing became the new normal. More money quickly became available; more employees were hired to deal with the backlog. '*Wir schaffen das*,' said Angela Merkel. We can handle this, and in practical terms Germany did. Yet as with every migration wave over Berlin's eight centuries, this one demonstrated the enduring ambivalence on all sides about who belongs and what it entails to belong. That question is as unresolved now as it ever was. And yet somehow the city muddles along, absorbing people along the way.

THIRTEEN

Erich's lamp shop

The other Berlin, to the East

*Berlin is the testicles of the West. Every time I want to
make the West scream, I squeeze on Berlin.*
NIKITA KHRUSHCHEV (1958)

In 1979 the Politburo of the Socialist Unity Party decided to
build a new housing complex in the northern end of East
Berlin, between Prenzlauer Berg and Pankow. They wanted this to
be a green oasis. In order to make room, entire blocks of flats were
pulled down. A gasworks was decommissioned. At the heart of it
was going to be a statue to a hero of communism.

The man being honoured was Ernst Thälmann. Originally
from Hamburg, he led the KPD for many of the Weimar years. As
Nazi violence increased on the streets, in 1932 he established the
paramilitary group Antifaschistische Aktion. Antifa, as it is
commonly known, has adapted to the times, and now mounts
protests against the Alternative für Deutschland (AfD), and other
groups of the far right. When the Nazis gained power in January
1933, Thälmann tried to persuade the SPD to mount a joint
national strike. As ever, the left could not agree. He was a marked
man. Within days of the Reichstag fire in March, Thälmann was
seized by the Gestapo from a safe house in Charlottenburg. Held

in solitary confinement for eleven years, he was regularly beaten and whipped. He smuggled out various appeals to fellow communists to help. Stalin did not seek his release after the Molotov–Ribbentrop Pact with Germany; he was a better symbol of oppression in incarceration. Thälmann was shot on Hitler's personal orders in Buchenwald in 1944.

Moscow became a refuge, and source of inspiration, for a large group of German communists escaping Hitler. Within a few years, however, Stalin had become increasingly suspicious of the extent of their influence. During the purges, the NKVD, his secret police, launched its Germany Operation, targeting anyone who had German citizenship, spoke the language or was otherwise connected with the country. Some 55,000 people were arrested, of whom nearly 42,000 were murdered, the rest receiving long prison sentences. Only one-quarter of all German exiles in the USSR survived. Of the nine members of the KPD Politburo who had fled there, the only two to emerge unscathed were Walter Ulbricht and Wilhelm Pieck, not for their particular skills but for their unconditional loyalty to Stalin.

Even before Soviet forces had taken the city in the Battle of Berlin, Ulbricht, Pieck and a tiny group of comrades had arrived there. Having failed in 1848 and in 1917, those communists in exile and at home who had survived the purges and the Nazis hoped their time had finally come. However, throughout the early postwar period, as the two parts of the city divided, as the blockade was mounted, as tensions rose, Stalin never trusted the GDR leadership. He and his designates micromanaged the Berlin question. Between 1945 and 1952 he summoned Ulbricht and Pieck seven times to his office in the Kremlin.

Berlin was at the centre of the world, but again for all the wrong reasons. Its two dismembered constituent parts were unable to support themselves and were entirely dependent on others. The dream of the most hardened German ideologues, of a self-standing communist GDR, was less enthusiastically shared in the Kremlin. On several occasions, Stalin and his successor, Nikita Khrushchev, contemplated trading it away. Ironically, the Soviets only fully committed to it when the Wall was put up in 1961. That decision, and that decision alone, bought time for East Berlin and the GDR.

Plans to honour Thälmann began in 1949, the year the GDR came into being – though the story of his betrayal by Stalin, Ulbricht and Pieck was, naturally, not told. One of the original ideas was a monument on Wilhelmstrasse, in the heart of the old government quarter, opposite the site of Hitler's bombed-out chancellery. The regime did not have the money for a project as ambitious as that, and in any case, it was considered too close to the border with the West. It took three decades for the authorities finally to commit to a plan. Apartments, shops and cultural institutions were to be built around a single monument, to mark Thälmann's hundredth birthday. The project was so important that Erich Honecker decided to oversee it himself. He rejected all the designs put forward by East German artists, deeming them not to be sufficiently monumental. He turned instead to Lev Kerbel, the Soviet Union's most decorated sculptor. The massive 14-metre-high bronze bust, weighing more than 50 tons, with a heroic clenched fist, was inaugurated in 1986, marking the centenary of Thälmann's birth. They had left it late. Three years later the GDR was no more.

A year after unification, on 25 December 1991, on the exact evening the USSR was dissolved, I was sitting with Kerbel in his Moscow studio. Over tea and brandy, watching TV coverage of that momentous night on his small flickering screen, Kerbel reminisced about a system in which he and millions of others had been cocooned. Born on the day of the Bolshevik revolution in 1917, Kerbel made his name creating giant monuments to Lenin and Marx from Prague to Pyongyang – and, of course, Berlin, capital of the German Democratic Republic. Then the system, his entire world, collapsed. He did what he could to adapt. He learned about commercial contracts and started producing sculptures for the new generation of oligarchs, either of themselves, their wives or their mistresses. His daughters didn't look back. One started to work for American television.

The statues all came tumbling down. Or at least some of them did. I remember being part of a jubilant crowd watching the statue of Felix Dzerzhinsky being toppled from outside the KGB headquarters in Moscow, the Lubyanka. No sooner had the trend begun than it either stopped (in the case of Russia), or slowed down (in the case of the former GDR). In the former GDR, a commission of experts was established to determine the future of communist monuments and streets. Its job was to decide which figures from the past were involved in repression and which were not: or to be more precise, to assess 'street names from the period from 1945 to 1989 that refer to active opponents of democracy and at the same time to the intellectual-political pioneers and advocates of Stalinist despotism, the GDR regime, and other unjust Communist regimes'.

The commission's remit was riddled with ambiguity. While some changes were uncontested, others were open to interpretation. One group, calling itself the Committee of the Anti-Fascist Resistance Fighters of the GDR, published an open letter accusing the commission of destroying the memory and the 'anti-fascist principles' of communists who had been murdered by the Nazis. Socialist intellectuals Kurt Tucholsky and August Bebel were reprieved. Clara Zetkin had no such luck. A Jew, Social Democrat and feminist, in the 1920s she was a Communist Party member of the Reichstag for thirteen years, before going into exile in the Soviet Union in 1933. The commission declared that streets leading to the Reichstag must not be named after opponents of parliamentary democracy, and so hers was restored to its pre-war name of Dorotheenstrasse. Yet it was not so punctilious when it came to the suburbs, permitting a Clara-Zetkin-Platz to remain in the eastern district of Hellersdorf. Sometimes the objection was not the name that the street was being changed from, but what it was being changed to. The local council in Mitte did not object to the removal of Otto-Grotewohl-Strasse, named after the GDR's first prime minister. But when members voted to give it a new name, Toleranzstrasse, they were overruled by the Senate, which insisted it be returned to Wilhelmstrasse, honouring the not-entirely-tolerant Wilhelm I. In the end, some 160 street names were identified as 'no longer tolerable', yet only a small number were changed. Some that remain continue to raise eyebrows, such as Bersarinplatz, named after the first Soviet city commander of Berlin.

The atmosphere quickly turned sour. Resentment of *Besserwessis* (West Germans who thought they knew better) was strong. The renaming process dragged on for years. Indeed, the legislation is still in force today, overseen by the Department for the Environment, Transport and Climate Protection of the Berlin Senate. In recent years it has been expanded to include streets 'named after pioneers and advocates of colonialism, slavery and racist-imperialist ideologies'. The arguments are just as fractious.

As for Thälmann and his statue, he was initially deemed undesirable, only to be reprieved. For *Ostalgists*, that marked a victory. Indeed, a total of 613 streets and squares are named after Thälmann across Germany. Should they be? He did, for sure, suffer terribly under the Nazis, but he was also ruthless in helping to drive out the Social Democrats (whom he called 'social fascists') during the 1920s, where necessary joining forces with the Nazis in the early years. He saw them as 'merely an extreme form of the doomed bourgeois order'. He still stands on his plinth, but he cuts a forlorn and absurdly outsized figure against the grey backdrop of a drab housing estate on the busy thoroughfare of Greifswalder Strasse. The word *Held* (hero) has recently been graffitied onto the plinth in huge red and white letters. The green oasis was never more than a small park. In the summer groups of young people drink beer or smoke weed on Thälmann's pedestal (made of Ukrainian marble). They skateboard on it or aim at his nose with paintball guns.

The forty-year story of the German Democratic Republic and its capital East Berlin is characterized by idealism (for some, particularly at the outset), relative stability (for many, at different points) and discontent (among an increasing number) – all the time in the knowledge that the state could survive only through surveillance and that an alternative presented itself across the border. For the most committed, their new state was the fulfilment of dreams that had been dashed in 1848 and 1917.

The establishment of the Deutschmark in June 1948 and of the Federal Republic in May 1949 rendered division permanent; the GDR followed suit, in October. Yet it was never able to compete economically. Many in the East were still able to take the U-Bahn or S-Bahn, or to walk or drive or cycle over the border crossing with relative ease. The border was relatively porous; an identity card and a reason for going over, *nach drüben*, was all that was needed. Anyone carrying a suitcase or wads of money immediately aroused suspicion. Guards manned checkpoints. But still, if you wanted to get out, you could. By 1951, the GDR was haemorrhaging its best, around 10,000 people a month leaving for the West. Entire regions were left without enough doctors, nurses, teachers and engineers.

As the economy went into free fall, as foodstuffs disappeared from shelves, the response of the ruling Communist Party, the SED, was to double down. Its 1952 Congress declared the need to 'build socialism at a forced pace'. Production targets were repeatedly raised, as the standard of living dipped ever lower. By November of that year, sporadic food riots and industrial unrest had occurred in several industrial centres, including Leipzig and Dresden. The death of Stalin in March 1953 came as the East German leadership was at its lowest ebb; word had reached them the previous year that the Kremlin had been prepared to trade off the GDR in return for a unified but militarily neutral Germany (something the Western Allies and the West Germans had bluntly rejected). As those around Stalin jockeyed for his succession, his henchman Lavrenti Beria was not alone in arguing that East Germany should be abandoned. 'What does it amount to? It is not even a real state but one that is kept going only with Soviet troops.'

Stalin's death was met with grief among many East Germans, but it also served as a catalyst for discontent. Any remaining enthusiasm about the new state had long gone. Some citizens chose to leave; a small but vocal group decided to demonstrate in favour of change. The uprising of 16–17 June 1953 marked the one and only occasion prior to its eventual downfall that a protest movement challenged the state's hegemony. Unlike the events of 1988–89, the organizers were not environmentalists or civil rights activists gathering in churches, but factory workers. It started, appropriately enough, on Stalinallee. As they marched into the city centre, what began as a few hundred construction workers rapidly grew. Word spread, amplified by Radio in the American Sector (RIAS), the US-sponsored station broadcasting from the West which was widely listened to in the East. The chants gradually changed from economic demands to calls for free elections. At its peak, some 400,000 people took part, in Berlin alone. The Soviet High Command based at the sprawling barracks in Wünsdorf south of the city was alarmed by the scale of the protests and the errors being made by the East German leadership. They saw it as nothing less than an attempted coup, aided and abetted by the West. The next morning Soviet tanks rolled down Leipziger Strasse towards the House of Ministries, where the demonstrators were gathering for a second day. They opened fire. The official register of deaths stands at 267. Some 4,493 citizens were arrested, of whom 200 were executed. Another 1,400 received life sentences.

One of the most evocative accounts of that weekend was a fictionalized one. *Five Days In June*, by Stefan Heym, is an hour-by-hour account of the days up to and including 17 June through the eyes of the protagonist, Comrade Martin Witte, the head of the official trade union at a fictitious engineering enterprise called VEB Merkur. When it was published in 1974 – a full two decades after the uprising – it was immediately banned in the East. Heym based his criticism on the communist leadership's failure to reform, rather than on the system itself. He portrays this moment as a crucially missed opportunity in the East's progression as a socialist state, a more dangerous criticism as it could not be so easily dismissed.

The home of the Federal Finance Ministry, the building on Leipziger Strasse where the June 1953 protesters were gunned down, rivals even the Humboldt Forum as one of Berlin's most contaminated sites. Constructed with extraordinary speed between 1935 and 1936 to house the Nazi Aviation Ministry, it is one of the most intimidating buildings in the city, comprising 2,800 offices, seven kilometres of corridors and seventeen staircases. Despite its strategic location it was strangely spared in the Allied bombardment, transferring from one dictatorship to another with barely a change (though the eagle and swastika were removed from the Hall of Honour). After a brief spell as headquarters for the Soviet military, it was turned into the House of Ministries, accommodating a dozen GDR government departments. The ceremony in 1949 establishing the GDR was held there. After reunification it housed the Treuhand, the state agency created to stress-test and either privatize or shut down state enterprises. It became an object for many in the East, and some in the West, for carrying out its task with excessive zeal. In one of the highest-profile terrorist acts of that era, the Red Army Faction murdered the Treuhand's first chairman, Detlev Rohwedder, in April 1991. The following year the gargantuan edifice was renamed in his honour. After considerable refurbishment, in 1999 the Finance Ministry moved in, but its civil servants have never felt at home. In recent years they were relieved to hear of plans to move them out to a more modern setting, only for those hopes to be dashed by their own minister, fearful of the costs involved. 'Now we're stuck in this Nazi building forever,' one official ruefully told the *Financial Times* in March 2023.

Outside the building two memorials compete for attention. On the entrance wall, behind a colonnade, stands an 18-metre masterpiece of socialist realist art created entirely from hand-painted Meissen porcelain tiles. Joyous men in overalls and women with scarves celebrate life in the GDR. The original version by the artist Max Lingner was more light-hearted. He was ordered to revise it five times, to give it the more determined, disciplined look of citizens building a new land. The final work is more compelling for it, the uniform, rictus smiles on the faces inadvertently depicting the struggles of East Germany. Alongside the mural, which was completed in 1952, is a plaque to the 1953 uprising, and a glass artwork sunken into the ground. The memorial by Wolfgang Rüppel comprises a photographic montage of the protesters under laminated glass. The grey-blue image has been magnified to such a degree that it appears as a collection of dots unless it is looked at from the correct angle.

The uprising and the manner of its suppression destroyed the genuine hopes that many citizens had vested in the GDR. In West Berlin, the main boulevard running alongside the Tiergarten, Charlottenburger Chaussee, was renamed the Street of 17 June.

I recall to a friend how the memory of 9 November 1989 is still fresh in my mind. If you were there, it never really leaves you, I suggest. She gives me a sympathetic, if slightly withering look. 'My memory extends a little further back than yours,' came the

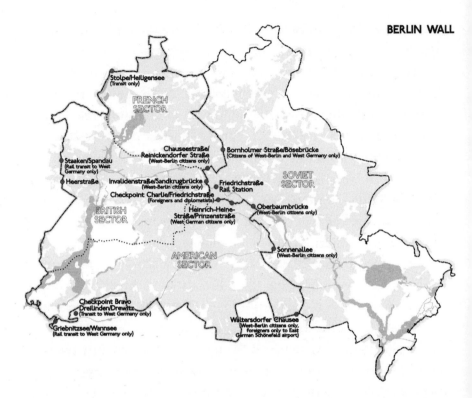

BERLIN WALL

Stolpe/Heiligensee
(Transit only)

FRENCH
SECTOR

Chauseestraße/
Reinickendorfer Straße
(West-Berlin citizens only)

Bornholmer Straße/Bösebrücke
(Citizens of West-Berlin and West Germany only)

Staaken/Spandau
(Rail transit to West
Germany only)

Heerstraße

Invalidenstraße/Sandkrugbrücke
(West-Berlin citizens only)

Checkpoint Charlie/Friedrichstraße
(Foreigners and diplomatists)

Friedrichstraße
Rail Station

SOVIET
SECTOR

BRITISH
SECTOR

Heinrich-Heine-
Straße/Prinzenstraße
(West German citizens only)

Oberbaumbrücke
(West-Berlin citizens only)

AMERICAN
SECTOR

Sonnenallee
(West-Berlin citizens only)

Checkpoint Bravo
Dreilinden/Drewitz
(Transit to West Germany only)

Griebnitzsee/Wannsee
(Rail transit to West Germany only)

Waltersdorfer Chausee
(West-Berlin citizens only,
foreigners only to East
German Schönefeld airport)

dry reply of Annette von Broecker. She saw the Wall go up on 13 August 1961, something far fewer people alive can claim.

The story of this veteran journalist provides a window on post-war Berlin. A war baby, she was four when the Soviets descended on devastated Berlin. The Russians moved east, leaving the area where she lived, Charlottenburg, to the Brits. In 1959, her mother spotted an advertisement in a local paper. It was for an editorial assistant at the Reuters news agency. Neither had a clue what it was, but it sounded interesting. The position required good English and *Abitur* (the equivalent of 'A' level) qualifications. Annette had neither but applied anyway. 'I wanted to be an artist, but I thought that this would be an adventure,' she tells me. She learned to read telex code and acquired the basics. Within two years she found herself witness to one of the great moments of history.

'Berlin Eastern Sector August 13 Reuters – the East West Berlin border was closed early today.'

This 'snap' report was filed by von Broecker's colleague, Adam Kellett-Long, the only Western journalist accredited to East Germany at the time. He had been tipped off that something was afoot. He received a call from a man with a piece of advice: 'Don't go to bed tonight.' Shortly after midnight, the East German news agency, ADN, cranked into action with a report expressing the Warsaw Pact's approval of emergency measures. Kellett-Long jumped in his car and sped to the Brandenburg Gate. He was stopped by a policeman waving a red torch, telling him that he could go no further. 'The border is closed,' he said. That was enough. Kellett-Long rushed home, past a phalanx of military vehicles heading in the opposite direction, to file his urgent report.

Across the now-divided city, at about 1.30 a.m., von Broecker was telephoned at her mum's flat by the news desk in London with Kellett-Long's report. Earlier in the day she had been with him in the East Berlin office. She had taken a taxi back to the West but was stopped by soldiers and told to go through the Brandenburg Gate on foot. 'I still get the jitters when I walk through, thinking there might be a Kalashnikov behind me,' she says. Back at the gate, on the Western side, in the middle of the night, von Broecker watched as soldiers and 'factory military forces' erected barbed wire and the first concrete slabs. One West Berliner reached across to a soldier, offering him a cigarette in the hope of persuading him to down tools. Von Broecker went to other parts of the new frontier to report on East Germans frantically trying to escape, sliding down bedsheets from the side of buildings or looking for river crossings or gaps in the barbed wire.

In the period between the suppression of the June 1953 uprising and August 1961, the flight to the West had accelerated. Some three million people had now gone. Ulbricht persuaded

Khrushchev that something needed to be done. Neither knew quite how the Western powers would react. The spectre of nuclear confrontation dominated international relations. Kennedy had met Khrushchev for a summit in Vienna in June. The US president was startled by the combative tone of the Soviet leader, who, more than a decade after the original blockade, had threatened to cut off Allied access to West Berlin again. When the first barbed wire was put in on that Saturday night in August, Kennedy did not respond, believing the consequences to be too great. Willy Brandt, the mayor of Berlin, rushed back to the city (he had been elsewhere in Germany campaigning) to warn of the 'danger of civil war'. His appeals fell on deaf ears. In Bonn, Adenauer sat tight. Documents released recently showed that he called a meeting with the Soviet ambassador at the Chancellery just three days later, complaining that this 'bothersome and unpleasant' matter had been emphasized 'more than was necessary'. He said he had not asked East Germans to move to the West and would rather that they stayed 'over there'.

The West's passive response emboldened Ulbricht and his junior partner Honecker, who had masterminded the plan, to press forward with the next stage, to upgrade the wire fence into a concrete wall. The 'anti-fascist protection barrier' was being improved well into the mid-1980s, with ever more sophisticated tripwires and automatic weaponry.

The number of people known to have been killed trying to get over the Wall is officially put at ninety-eight, though historians believe the number may be considerably higher due to undocumented deaths. The first person to die was a woman called Ida Siekmann. She threw bedding onto the (West Berlin) pavement below as she jumped out of her third-floor apartment, only to fall badly and die of her injuries. The last-known victim was Winfried Freudenberg who tried to escape by hot air balloon but crashed. That was eight months before the Wall came down.

Günter Litfin was born in 1937. His family had lived in Wedding before moving to Weissensee, which later became part of East Berlin. He dreamed of a career as a costume designer. After completing his apprenticeship in 1957, he worked in an atelier near the Zoo, and was one of the many who commuted between the two sides of the city. On the fateful night, he found himself on the wrong side of the Wall. He quickly lost his job because he couldn't get back over. He and his younger brother cycled along the border looking for possible escape routes. On 24 August, shortly after 4 p.m., he crossed the grounds of the Charité hospital and reached the banks of the Spree between the Friedrichstrasse and Lehrter stations. He jumped in and, after firing a couple of warning shots, border guards fired directly at him. He was hit in the back of the head just metres from the western side. A large crowd had gathered but they were unable to jump in; the water belonged to the East. Litfin's body drifted back to the eastern shore where it was recovered. At his funeral, everyone knew what had happened, but the public presence of Stasi officers ensured that nobody spoke about it.

In 1997, the two officers responsible for his death were put on trial but received sentences of only one year's probation. They argued that they had just been doing their jobs. Only a tiny number of the GDR elite has ever been punished for their crimes. Litfin's brother Jürgen lobbied hard for a memorial to be put up to remember what happened. The river where Liftin was murdered has a new yellow pedestrian bridge named after Golda Meir. (Berlin also has streets named after Yitzhak Rabin, David Ben-Gurion and other famous Israelis.) On the once-deserted western riverbank, an entirely new neighbourhood is being built, a huge upmarket housing complex called Europa City, marketed online to a well-heeled German and international clientele. Along the eastern bank, which was heavily fortified border territory, there is now a pleasant towpath and park. Near to the spot where Litfin jumped in stand chunks of the Wall and a tableau of newspaper cuttings, including a *Neues Deutschland* front page which manages to blame the incident on the security forces in the West and portrays the victim as a deviant, a 'homosexual who was well known in certain circles in West Berlin'.

The yearning to cross the wall wasn't entirely in one direction. Between 1957 and 1988, more than half a million people left West Germany for the GDR. Of this number, half were previous GDR citizens. Most wanted to be reunited with their families, some had fallen in love, some were unemployed and thought they could find work, a few were fleeing criminal prosecution. The main reason was homesickness and an overall difficulty in assimilating in the West. Only a small number moved for political reasons. The numbers reduced sharply after the Wall was built, but even in the final year of the regime in 1989, 1,000 people applied to go to the GDR. It is a remarkable story, seldom told (though an exhibition called *Changing Sides* travelled to several small museums in recent years). I went to the northern edge of Berlin in search of evidence. Just off a main road called Blankenfelder Chaussee is a forest and heathland that used to be a military barracks. In a series of huts, up to 300 migrants from the West were held, some for a month or more, and questioned about why they wanted to come, or come back, to the GDR. This was one of twenty such processing centres scattered around the inner German border. For several years after, all that was left was barbed wire and a watch hut with a slit window. That is all gone now; the area has become a pleasant eco-park and botanical garden.

The Wall worked. The exodus stopped. Many of the city's most famous streets found themselves close to the border zone; for three decades they fell silent, populated only by day-trip foreigners, government functionaries or Stasi. The Brandenburg Gate, through which Napoleon's forces marched, and where the new

Reich was celebrated in 1817, was sealed off. Unter den Linden, the grand imperial boulevard, belonged to the East, but it showed few signs of life. The centre of gravity of East Berlin moved eastwards and northwards.

The new model city was based on a series of principles of socialist architecture meticulously set out by the state. The showcase would be the new Stalinallee, combining socialist realism with the neoclassicist Prussian bombast of Schinkel (not that it was described in that way). In place of the old Grosse Frankfurter Strasse came a boulevard more than 2 kilometres long and 100 metres wide, dubbed 'the first street of socialism'. Bauhaus architects who had stayed in East Germany delighted in its ambition. The ground floor of these gargantuan buildings was for public entertainment. The Kosmos cinema contained ten auditoriums and seats for 3,400 people. The Karl Marx Bookstore was a place to meet (though the contents were tightly controlled). The apartments above them, clad with Meissen ceramics, were considered high quality, with heating, hot water, fitted cupboards, tiled bathrooms, waste chutes, intercom telephones and lifts.

In 1961, the year of the Wall and eight years after his death, the avenue was shorn of its association with Stalin and renamed Karl-Marx-Allee. But as the money gradually dried up, so did the plans. The building materials became ever cheaper. The shelves in the grand shops had little on display. The more embattled it became, the more the regime resorted to regimentation and pomp. May Day and other processions took place on the street. A system built on the mantra of anti-fascism was revolutionary but also borrowed some of the symbols and habits of an imperial past that had been refuted in the West. In 1962, the communist authorities reinstated the *Zapfenstreich* marching ceremony in front of the Neue Wache, the guardhouse for the Royal Palace.

One square that came to epitomize East Berlin more than any other started out in medieval times as a hospital just beyond the city walls, surrounded by farms and windmills. It was also an execution site, earning it the moniker *Teufels Lustgarten* (the Devil's pleasure garden). By the eighteenth century it had developed into a wool and cattle market. It also doubled up as an exercise site for soldiers, earning itself a second name, Parade Square. In October 1805, during a visit to the city, Tsar Alexander I was taken to the parade grounds in front of the old King's Gate. To mark the occasion, Friedrich Wilhelm III ordered it to be renamed Alexanderplatz.

During Berlin's heyday in the late nineteenth century, 'Alex' was one of Berlin's great hubs, dominated by its grand elevated railway station connecting with trams, buses and the new U-Bahn line. The square became one of the places to eat, drink and shop, attracting the top three department stores, Tietz, Wertheim and Hahn. At the end of the Second World War, it was a bombed-out mess, but – as with so many of the old palaces and churches and squares – the instruction was not to preserve but to exorcize the memory and build afresh. Redevelopment began in the early 1960s; dozens of houses were torn down and hundreds of people were rehoused. Buses and tramlines were relocated to accommodate plans that would include a series of monumental buildings. Around the square's periphery arose the House of the Teacher, House of Travel and the House of Statistics. A world clock showed the time in fraternal capitals. The favourite of much of the communist top brass was *Brunnen der Völkerfreundschaft* (the Fountain of Friendship Between Peoples).

In October 1969, on the twentieth anniversary of the founding of the GDR, a building was opened that would become a symbol of the city – it has remained so despite unification. At 368 metres high, with a viewing platform and revolving restaurant, the TV Tower became Berlin's tallest building, a symbol of the 'superiority' of communism and impossible to miss for miles around. Not all went smoothly, however. It transpired that on sunny days, the steel sphere at the top of the tower produced a reflection in the shape of a cross, leading the tower to be nicknamed 'the Pope's Revenge'. A furious Walter Ulbricht demanded an explanation from the architects, and a remedy. One suggestion was to cover the tower in non-reflective material; another was to demolish it. Mercifully, nothing was done. For East Berliners, a trip up the super-fast lift to the observation tower and the revolving restaurant just above was the ultimate treat.

By the time the Palace of the Republic opened in 1976 on the site of the demolished Royal Palace, the centre of the socialist metropolis had come into being. With several distinctive buildings of its own, Berlin, capital of the GDR, finally had its own identity. Or at least, some thought it did.

All the way through, a key task dominated: building a new type of collective accommodation. Even though the population had fallen because of the constant stream of people leaving for the West, East Berlin was still struggling to house its population. In April 1955, inside a sports hall, the first Construction Conference of the GDR took place. Its aim was to restructure the city based on planned production. Just half a century later, the city had been transformed. Think GDR architecture, think *Plattenbau*, large prefabricated concrete slabs. (*Platte*, panel; *Bau*, building.) They were pioneered in the Netherlands straight after the First World War, based on earlier American construction methods. They first came to Berlin, to the Lichtenberg district in the East, in the late 1920s in the form of two- and three-storey apartment houses assembled with locally cast blocks. As East Germany rapidly expanded its building programme in the late 1950s, *Plattenbau* became ubiquitous – a cheap, plain and easy way of dealing with the acute housing shortage.

As the engineering developed, higher blocks were constructed. The P2 series was followed by the WBS 70, the WHH GT 18 and Q3A, the names given to the building models an apt description of the approach to aesthetics. For a few decades at least, the programme worked, on its own terms. Nearly a third of East Berliners were rehoused in three satellite cities: Marzahn, Hohenschönhausen and Hellersdorf.

Most of the area that now constitutes Marzahn was marshland. But not all. Since medieval times there has been a small village here, Alt-Marzahn, consisting of a few cobbled streets built around a village green, an animal sanctuary and a windmill which still works. For decades this kitsch interloper has been overlooked and hemmed in by the concrete jungle all around. The area also has a dark past. On the eve of the 1936 Olympics, the Nazis developed their largest internment camp for Roma and Sinti, to shunt them out of the city and to combat 'the gypsy plague'. Some 600 were taken to *Rastplatz* (rest place) Marzahn, an area chosen because it was close to a cemetery and sewerage. The prisoners were used as forced labour before many were sent to concentration camps.

All of that was erased after the war. Between 1977 and 1990, the area became home to around 100,000 people living in around 62,000 apartments in blocks of mostly ten storeys. Marzahn once represented the GDR dream. This is where aspirational, patriotic young families headed. 'How wonderful to live in our newly constructed apartment in Marzahn,' went the official song. 'In Marzahn! In Marzahn!' After unification, as the stream out of the East resumed in earnest, as people sought a better life in the more bourgeois, leafy streets of Western Germany, many of the flats fell empty. Into the void stepped recently arrived immigrants, from Russia and later Syria, Afghanistan and elsewhere, living tensely alongside often low-skilled or old Berliners.

At the same time as the concrete slabs were being erected all over Berlin, in woodland to the north a 'wildlife research area' was being built. Twenty-three detached houses, each with its own sizeable plot of land, were designed for the families of the elite to live and relax, unencumbered by the travails of ordinary comrades. In the Waldsiedlung (forest settlement) near the village of Wandlitz, they enjoyed their own cinema, health centre, swimming pool, tennis court and shooting range, plus a shop stocked with Western goods denied to the masses. In their own restaurant, waiters served gourmet food (by East German standards) and imported fine wines. They even had their own nuclear bunker with space for 400 people, enough to extend to their wider circle of friends and relatives. A few years later an autobahn was constructed especially for them, so they could be whisked the 30 kilometres to their offices in no time. East Berliners had their own nicknames for the compound. One was 'Volvograd'. Another was 'Bonzengetto' (the word *Bonzen* meant bigwigs). A barracks housed troops from the Felix Dzerzhinsky Guards Regiment, the paramilitary wing of the Stasi, who guarded them from thirty watchtowers that circumvented the 5-metre-tall fence of the complex. This was a wall not to prevent citizens from getting out, but to stop them getting in. Yet the Stasi controlled Wandlitz, just as they did the rest of the country. The bodyguard department directly answerable to Mielke, the head of state security, provided the 'protection'. Each of the twenty-three houses was surveilled and bugged by his agents.

Within weeks of the Berlin Wall coming down I went to Waldsiedlung to interview Egon Krenz, the long-time member of the Politburo who was in charge of the GDR in the six weeks around the fall of the Wall. For a few months he managed to hold on to his home, from where he indulged me with a classic exegesis of grievance and a claim to have been misunderstood. Now the settlement is part rehabilitation clinic, part private residences, part destination for curious tourists. A tableau points out where Erich and Margot Honecker, Krenz, Mielke and the rest of them lived.

A few weeks after I saw Krenz, a building complex in East

Berlin was stormed. A crowd had gathered at Normannenstrasse. The street name did not need further explanation. For decades it had been synonymous with fear: the headquarters of the Stasi. That January night in 1990 a mix of pro-democracy protesters and people with something to hide overcame a perfunctory police line, rushing up the stairs, smashing portraits of Mielke and Honecker in their excitement and fury. They were joined by TV crews and other journalists. The aim of most was not to seize the tens of millions of files, but to secure as many as possible, knowing that for weeks Stasi agents had been shredding them. According to one measurement, the paper files they collected stretched to 44 kilometres. Some 15,000 files were destroyed. But 90 per cent were preserved and have been carefully overseen. They navigate a fine line between a person's right to know, and the use of information for blackmailing or other harmful purposes. On 15 January 2020, the thirtieth anniversary of that day, President Steinmeier called the storming a 'profoundly democratic act'.

In November 2021, I returned to Normannenstrasse with two aims. In one of the buildings, I handed in a form to a casually polite young man. With no little trepidation, I was requesting information about my own file. The friendly man greeting me from behind a desk was probably at nursery school when the Wall came down. Was he an *Ossi* or *Wessi*? Such tags don't work for this generation. He told me that my papers were in order, checked my contact details and informed me of the next steps. Did he wonder why I had waited thirty years? I too am not sure why it took me so long.

I then went across to House Number 1 for the start of a tour. Twice a day the Stasi Museum conducts tours, in German just after lunch, and in English in mid-afternoon. Most of the two dozen Germans I was with were too young to remember life back then. The guide, Sven Behrend, took us to the third-floor conference room, where Mielke would receive briefings from his regional and departmental chiefs. He explained in detail to the enrapt group how, from Mielke's desk and his bank of phones, he had a hotline to the border guard, mobile patrols and prison camps. The complex was a small city. It contained a supermarket (including goods plundered from Western tourists at check-points and from citizens returning from permitted visits to relatives), a hairdresser, a travel office and a medical centre that employees were required to use. The three floors capture the extraordinary scope of the Stasi and the minutiae they were interested in. From these wood-panelled rooms, agents could listen to 150,000 phone calls in West Berlin at any one minute, quite the technological achievement. Behrend, whose father fled the GDR, pointed down the road to what was the Stasi's own prison on Magdalenenstrasse. 'It's the longest street in the GDR. When you enter it, it takes a long time to get out.' At this point, the man to my right, probably in his seventies, visibly twitched before recovering his poise. Was he, I wondered, a victim, a former Stasi agent or one of the hundreds of thousands of informers on which the regime had depended? I know I should have done, but I couldn't bring myself to ask him.

From one factory of terror to another. Twenty minutes further north, down a series of quiet suburban streets, is Hohenschönhausen. By now it was getting dark, and sleet was falling. The tram dropped me off at the corner. The former remand prison now has a visitors' centre where I waited until the allotted time to join another tour party. Every citizen in the GDR knew about Normannenstrasse, but they had no idea what went on in Hohenschönhausen. Officially it didn't exist. It was in a closed military zone and was not on any map. Originally a soup kitchen for the industrial poor, it was taken over by Soviet forces in 1945 and expanded to become Special Camp Number 3, where up to 20,000 people were processed on their way to being shipped eastwards to the gulags. That job done, it was transferred to the Stasi who used it, and expanded it further, as a remand centre mainly for people deemed political prisoners.

The memorial centre is run largely by former prisoners. Most of the tour guides are people who have done time. I was shown around by Monika Schneider. In January 1983, she was arrested in Prague, where she had gone to meet a boyfriend from the West. They had previously discussed how she might flee; Schneider had let slip the idea to a work colleague who immediately betrayed her to the authorities. She was taken to Hohenschönhausen for questioning before being sentenced to two and a half years in jail and sent to a women's 'correctional facility' in Hoheneck, in the far south of the GDR. For all that time she was subjected to psychological torture, not being told the fate of her two young sons. She was regularly given a document that authorised their adoption. She refused to sign it.

On their arrest, prisoners were driven around for hours to disorient them, in unmarked rickety vans that could have been mistaken for a baker's truck. They had no idea where they were. Most thought they were in a remote part of the country, miles from Berlin. They were often kept in isolation; the aim of months of interrogation by trained experts was to break them and extract incriminating statements. Most prisoners were ordinary people who had committed the crime of just wanting to leave.

Schneider showed our small group the tiny cells in the basement, close enough together to hear the cries of other prisoners, with slits in the doors for food to be handed over. She pointed out the 'hospital wing' and the morgue. We walked past one of the vans used for the transportation, and crossed the snowy courtyard to the 'tiger cages', exercise areas surrounded by barbed wire and monitored by armed guards walking above them. Even after all this time, victims like Schneider do not contain their anger, not just at their treatment but also at the refusal of the 'new'

German state to punish the perpetrators. She has given several newspaper interviews drawing attention to the issue, one that has largely faded from view. The injustice, she told one newspaper, 'will haunt me for the rest of my days'. In a TV interview, she pointed out that former state security officials have received substantial pensions, while 'their ex-prisoners are fobbed off with €300 [a month]' – plus a free travel pass. Many of these people, some of whom she recognizes, still live around the corner in Hohenschönhausen. After all, why give up a comfortable rent-controlled flat, even after a regime has changed? 'Where is the respect, the recognition of a difficult path in life, for the courage to stand up in a dictatorship?'

The paradox is that it was only in the final years of the GDR that West Berlin, and the West German state, reconciled themselves to the fact of division. The Basic Treaty, signed in December 1972, had provided the first steps towards normality. East and West had established permanent missions in the other's capital. It did not mark formal recognition, but it came close. In 1987 two major events occurred that appeared to cement this reality. Separate celebrations of Berlin's 750th anniversary were held in both Berlins. Queen Elizabeth II and presidents Reagan and Mitterrand headed the list of dignitaries at the West Berlin celebrations. It is worth remembering that the downfall of the state and the reunification of the city did not feel remotely on the agenda. Indeed, in September of that year, Chancellor Kohl had received Honecker with full honours in Bonn. President Richard von Weizsäcker praised the GDR leader as a 'German among Germans'.

For several years the GDR government had been making its own preparations for Berlin's big anniversary. They realized that their capital needed a makeover. Buildings were spruced up. The churches and concert halls of Gendarmenmarkt were redecorated.

A new hotel, the absurdly opulent Grand, was built, courtesy of Japanese investment. The heart of old Cölln, where it all began, the warren of streets that comprised the Nikolaiviertel, was returned to its historical roots. Except that it wasn't. Beginning in 1981, a team headed by the architect Günter Stahn got to work. The houses were reconstructed according to historical records, giving the illusion that a part of old Berlin had returned. The prefabricated communist high-rises all around make it look like a dolls' village; as ever, Berliners found a nickname for it, 'Honecker's Disneyland'. The result was a gloriously tasteless mix of fake rococo gables, columns and archways superimposed on *Plattenbau*. The German word *spiessig* is hard to translate. The closest term might be 'tacky', or 'petty bourgeois'. Out of their urge to compete with West Berlin, the GDR created an eponymous small town in the heart of Berlin. Sweet and harmless, and a pleasant place to drink a beer, but very un-Berlin. What might be more typically Berlin is the fact that the ancient kitsch sits alongside the socialist realist kitsch. On six concrete panels above a restaurant called Mutter Hoppe stands a mural providing a 'socialist history of Berlin'. Each segment depicts an era, starting with the communist uprising in 1919, then the Nazi dictatorship and ending with the liberation of the city by Red Army troops handing out food to citizens.

That was the East Berlin I arrived in at the start of 1988 as a correspondent for the *Daily Telegraph*. I had no sense then that the country to which I was accredited would shortly not exist. As 1989 progressed, the demonstrations intensified. The focal point for many of the protests that autumn was Leipzig. Yet of all the extraordinary moments of my time in East Berlin, one location sticks out: the Gethsemane church in the heart of Prenzlauer Berg. Whenever I got off the U2 U-Bahn at Schönhauser Allee and walked the short distance to the church, I could hear my footsteps. The area felt even darker than most in East Berlin. On one side, a couple of streets away, was the Wall. On the other, row upon row of brick tenements. Many of these turn-of-the-century blocks had escaped unscathed in the war, but had been neglected subsequently. True communists yearned for new-build high-rise blocks, denoting a fresh start. Those who didn't mind the shortcomings of the old apartments formed a habitat of nonconformists – intellectuals, artists and other contrarians. Many buildings lay empty, with crumbling balconies and staircases, or attracted squatters.

By the time the Wall fell, almost 90 per cent of the housing in Prenzlauer Berg was still heated with coal ovens, around half had no bath, and a quarter still shared a hallway toilet. Within a decade, fewer than 10 per cent of the district's original residents remained. Those that did were the lucky ones who managed to secure controlled rents. Today these same properties, spruced up, are among the most desired and expensive in the city, both to buy and to rent. Prenzlauer Berg is synonymous with smashed avocado on toast and mimosas for weekend brunch. A cliché, yes, but it happens to be true. There is some humour, much resignation and no little anger among the *Hineingeborenen* (those born and brought up in the GDR, or their descendants) towards the gentrifiers from Germany or abroad.

By the middle of 1989, the only outsiders in the area were foreign journalists who were making contacts with dissidents in the eco-church, Zionskirche, at the bottom of Kastanienallee, and those in the Gethsemane. Many pastors in East Germany allowed protesters to hold meetings inside their churches, believing them to be sacrosanct. One weekend in October 1989 marked the turning point. Inside the Gethsemane, people linked arms, sang hymns and said prayers. By Sunday, hundreds were camped inside. The authorities served notice that they would clear the area. Those inside – and by this stage I was one of them – could see the searchlights through the windows and hear the yelping of police dogs. A few weeks earlier, Krenz had praised the Chinese government for cracking down on the student movement in Beijing that June. Krenz's speech was widely disseminated by the East German state media as a warning to protesters back home. The service ended. The priest, an unsung hero by the name of Bernd Albani, invited us to leave in silence. We had no idea whether we would encounter our own version of Tiananmen outside. I counted about fifty army trucks. A loudhailer told us to put our hands on our heads. Hundreds were taken away, chanting 'No violence' as they were hit with truncheons while being bundled into vans. Yet nobody was killed. The communist state was losing its nerve in front of our eyes. Even then, however, nobody thought that within a month the system would collapse so spectacularly – and so peacefully.

I was reminiscing with Axel Klausmeier, the man in charge of preserving the Wall, or rather the tiny segments that are left. Since 2009 he has been head of the Berlin Wall Foundation, a not-for-profit organization established to ensure its twenty-eight-year history is properly preserved and told. The foundation looks after a cluster of sites, including Checkpoint Charlie, the Marienfelde barracks, the East Side Gallery, the memorial to Litfin and an expanse of the Wall called the Parliament of Trees Against War and Violence (so very Berlin). 'The instinct of everyone, particularly people in the East, was to get rid of it as soon as possible – all of it,' Klausmeier tells me. Such was the pain, the disorientation and the desperate need to draw a line that few politicians or experts would be seen defending the Wall's preservation. Plus, there was money to be made in selling chunks of it. Even though there is very little left, and even though it has been down longer than it was up, the 'Wall' is still cited in tourist surveys as the number one attraction. Berlin's history relies on the imagination.

Klausmeier is standing with me on Bernauer Strasse, the most important part of the Wall still standing – 220 metres of it, to be precise. Because of the location of the city's districts, the street was surrounded by walls on three sides. It is now meticulously preserved, with a series of memorials depicting the most famous moments of its history, including the amazing escapes in the first few hours and days, in which residents used blankets, sheets and towels to jump down from their housing blocks in the East to the road below in the West. As Regine Hildebrandt, resident in number 4, famously put it: 'My head was in the West, my arse was in the East.'

The inhabitants of Bernauer Strasse and adjacent streets were forcibly removed. In the neighbouring graveyard, suspended between East and West, some 2,000 graves were exhumed and the remains taken to other cemeteries. One building became a powerful symbol of division. The neo-Gothic Church of Reconciliation, built in the middle of Bernauer Strasse in 1894, was bombed in the war, repaired in the 1950s and brought back into use. In 1961, it found itself in no man's land, its front door belonging to the death strip. The East German authorities wanted to demolish it, but, so locals would have it, they feared divine retribution. Some twenty-four years later they finally summoned the courage to remove the building in order 'to increase the security, order and cleanliness on the state border with West Berlin'. The moment it was blown up in 1985 – just four years before the Wall came down – is still etched on the minds of Berliners. Where the church once was now stands a circular Chapel of Reconciliation. Outside is a moving sculpture of a kneeling couple clinging on to each other for dear life. Copies of it exist in Coventry Cathedral and at the Hiroshima Peace Memorial Museum.

Klausmeier has over the past two decades written several books and articles documenting the Wall – cycling to the remotest parts of the city to jot down details of a mark on the ground or a streetlamp or any other quirk he fears will be lost. Because of its location, Bernauer Strasse became the most fortified part of the Wall. From the Western side, it was high on the itinerary of visiting dignitaries, among them Martin Luther King and Robert Kennedy. They were still reinforcing it the year before the Wall came down. 'This is the place where things always happened,' Klausmeier notes. 'It is important that we remember and that we don't commodify the memory.'

From the mid-1950s to 2006, Amerika Haus on Hardenbergstrasse was the United States' official cultural centre in West Berlin. Situated close to the Zoo station, it housed a library, exhibition space and a cinema. With the Cold War over, it became a private photography museum called C/O. During the pandemic and shortly after, the museum staged one of the most evocative and popular exhibitions about the GDR, earning big visitor numbers and rave reviews. Harald Hauswald is one of the most important figures in contemporary German photography and a major international name. With his grey hair reaching halfway down his back, his long beard and reading glasses perched on the end of his nose, he is hard to miss; his one or two personal tours of the show were a particular hit. The exhibition, entitled *Voll das Leben!* (Full of life!), features pictures of everyday life, from tea dances to snogging punks to women peering inside shops to see if they had anything in stock, to soldiers loitering and smoking, to crowds of young people at the famous 1988 Bruce Springsteen concert at Weissensee. He always shot in black-and-white because colour film was more expensive and of variable quality. The irony and humour of his work were deemed subversive. The authorities were concerned about his lack of optimism and opened a file on him.

The show begins with the Stasi's interest in Hauswald. A wall is plastered with excerpts from his files, which ran to 1,400 pages – obsessive, one might think, but quite normal for a person of interest. He was given a code name, *Radfahrer*, or bike rider, because they thought he had organized a cycle protest (they got the wrong person). At one point he was being watched by up to a hundred agents and from inside their spluttering Wartburgs they were photographing him taking photographs. They would regularly go into his apartment and rifle through his possessions (something I and pretty much anyone of interest, local or foreign, got used to in those days).

As a teenager in a dreary small town called Radebeul, near Dresden, Hauswald worked as a roadie for a popular GDR band, before taking jobs as a painter and scaffolder. In 1978, he made it to Berlin. He took whatever jobs he could to subsidize his passion, photography. In the mid-1980s, working under a pseudonym, he started being published in West German publications such as *Die Zeit*, *Stern* and *taz*. The Stasi struggled to nail his 'crimes' because he insisted on being paid not in cash but in camera equipment and good-quality Kodak film. It was in 1987, when he published – through a Munich-based publishing house – an anthology entitled *East Berlin, The Other Side of a City*, that they finally went after him. He was a single father, and they took his eleven-year-old daughter, Anna, into care.

At his studio on the northern fringes of Prenzlauer Berg, towards Weissensee, I ask Hauswald about life after the GDR. He and some colleagues set up photography agency Ostkreuz almost by accident. Within a couple of months of the fall of the Wall, a group of artists were invited to Paris by the Institut Français. There they hatched the idea of setting up their own company. It started out in a flat on Frankfurter Allee. Five changes of location later they have a hip courtyard office, with twenty-five photographers from across Europe. They now do the usual mix of advertising, press, fashion and corporate. But he keeps coming back to history. We talk about *Vergangenheitsaufarbeitung* – coming to terms with the history of the Third Reich for which Germany is so renowned. We talk about the similar memorialization of the GDR, issues of equivalence and of remembering and forgetting. For years after reunification, he says, personal memories were too raw. 'For the first ten years nobody wanted to know. It was too fresh, too sensitive. As soon as it became history, people felt able to talk about it again.' That moment may now be waning. 'The danger is that as time passes, we forget what the reality was.' I then mention Russia's invasion of Ukraine and Hauswald becomes even more animated: 'You can't convey what it means to strive for freedom.'

To walk down any street in the heart of old Berlin is to see one era overlaid on another. 'I am a witness, just as others were witnesses to Nazi crimes,' Hauswald says. The real work on memorializing GDR history has barely begun.

FOURTEEN

They came and never left

Berlin's curious relationship with Russia

*What is there to say about a city in which people get up at
six in the morning, eat dinner at two in the afternoon and
go to bed long before the chickens?*

IVAN TURGENEV (1847)

'Nowhere have the threads of Russian–German relations
been so dramatically played out as in Berlin. All German
roads to Russia went through Berlin; all Russian roads to Germany
went through Berlin. It was the stage.' Karl Schlögel is a walking
encyclopaedia, and in some ways an embodiment, of the tortured
history of the two countries. Germany's most accomplished
historian of the bilateral relationship, he has been feted and
shunned in turn by the Russian government. When his seminal
work, *Das russische Berlin* (Russian Berlin), was first published in
1998, he was invited by the Russian ambassador to launch it at the
embassy. 'They had to get Daimler-Benz and VW to sponsor
the buffet, as the Russians said they had run out of money.'
Schlögel is sitting with me in the book-laden study of his apartment
just off Prager Platz, the heart of twentieth-century Russian Berlin
in the western district of Wilmersdorf. *Tout Berlin* had been
invited to the party, he recalls. The guest list included the GDR
ex-spymaster Markus Wolf; the president of the Academy of

Sciences; politicians, academics, diplomats. This was the era of *Annäherung*, the grand rapprochement with Russia across the West, and particularly in Germany, the tail-end of the era of Boris Yeltsin. It was just over a year before the ascent to power of Vladimir Putin.

Now, a quarter of a century on, the embassy is sealed off on one side, the police on high alert following Russia's invasion of Ukraine. Schlögel is an outspoken critic of Putin – a position that was not until recently shared by many. In 2014, he turned down the then-prestigious Pushkin Medal, awarded for a significant contribution to promoting the study of Russian culture abroad, in protest at the annexation of Crimea and the first invasion of Ukraine. 'I wouldn't be invited to present my work again,' he muses. 'I've since been attacked as a German nationalist, a NATO spy, a reactionary.' We talk in detail about contemporary politics, about Putin's mission to drive an independent Ukraine off the map, and about Germany's struggles to comprehend the nature of Kremlin power. I tell Schlögel that the stiflingly close relationship between the two countries – a mix of mercantilism, sentimentalism and naivety – has always exercised me. I have berated politicians about it – one of their retorts has merit: Brits have no right to criticize given the role that London has played in laundering Russian money and reputations. I have berated journalists for not investigating the links between the German state and Russian energy, as personified in former chancellor Gerhard Schröder's role as Kremlin cheerleader. The response tended to be that there was 'no story' as he hadn't done anything illegal.

On 24 February 2022, everything changed. Some Berliners talk of the invasion having a greater effect than even the fall of the Wall. It marked the unravelling of so many moral assumptions of the post-war and post-unification era. Before Putin's war, criticism of Russia was regarded in many Berlin circles as gauche. Germany, good Germany, was required to atone for its war crimes on the

Eastern Front. The reconciliation achieved through Willy Brandt's *Ostpolitik* was deemed beyond reproach and irreversible.

Russia's rare interludes of modernization and integration into Europe always had a strong German element. Peter the Great recruited thousands of Germans – military experts, scientists and architects – to develop his dream city, St Petersburg, on the site of a captured Swedish fortress. But the great German wave is associated more with another leader, one whose portrait stood on Angela Merkel's desk at the Chancellery for more than a decade. Sophie Friederike Auguste, Princess of Anhalt-Zerbst, was the daughter of an obscure German prince, Christian August von Anhalt-Zerbst, but she was related through her mother to the grander dukes of Holstein. At age fourteen she was chosen to be the wife of her cousin, Karl Ulrich, Duke of Holstein-Gottorp, grandson of Peter the Great and heir to the Russian throne. She converted from German Lutheranism to Orthodoxy, taking a new name, Yekaterina, or Catherine. The marriage took place in 1745 and, as history relates, was a disaster. When Empress Elizabeth died in 1761, Catherine struck against her husband. With the support of the army and of 'enlightened' elements of society, she had herself proclaimed empress at Kazan Cathedral. Her husband was assassinated eight days later, with or without her say-so.

During the first five years of Catherine's reign, as many as 30,000 people came to Russia, most of them from what is today Germany (all but Jews – she wouldn't countenance them). They were drawn by the promise of their own land, freedom of religion and exemption from military service – a mirror of the incentives and the motivations that had attracted the French Huguenots and the Dutch to Germany. They settled in the St Petersburg area, in southern Russia, on the Black Sea and along the Volga river. In the Volga region alone, a hundred 'colonies' were established. The Germans integrated as farmers, craftsmen and entrepreneurs. The Napoleonic wars led to a second wave of settlers; by the middle of the nineteenth century, the number of Russian-Germans in Russia had risen to more than half a million.

Between the end of the nineteenth and the beginning of the twentieth centuries approximately 35,000 Germans were employed in public and military service. Some 300 Germans held high office as governors. Of the first twelve ministers of finance in the Russian government, five were Germans. By 1914, 28,500 of the 1.5 million people who lived in Moscow were Germans, making them the second largest ethnic group. One in eight merchants were Germans. St Petersburg, the capital, had more than fifty German-language newspapers. Yet as war broke out, Germans were suddenly seen as suspect, as potential enemies within. With the onset of revolution in 1917, the tide turned, and it was to Germany – and Berlin in particular – that the first big wave of Russians headed.

The most pivotal figure of all had already spent some time in the German capital. Lenin had lived in Berlin for a few months in 1895 researching the work of Marx and Engels in the Reading Room of the Royal Library (later the Prussian State Library). 'A few steps from my flat is the Tiergarten (a magnificent park, the most beautiful and largest in Berlin), the Spree in which I bathe daily, and the city railway station,' he wrote in a letter to his mother. He gained a reasonable knowledge of the city and in the subsequent two decades maintained links with leftist activists, although he was somewhat sceptical of their resolve. He was all too aware that Berlin had previously never managed to stage a successful revolution. Indeed, he is said to have joked that German revolutionaries would not storm a railway station without first buying a platform ticket.

From inside the forbidding complex, behind its heavily guarded black iron gates barely 300 metres from the Brandenburg Gate, the embassy has long been a Russian fortress at the heart of the

German capital. It is the centre point for an extraordinary relationship, one that has influenced the city for centuries. From its construction in the eighteenth century, with its thirteen large front windows looking onto Unter den Linden, the baroque Palais Kurland was at the heart of high society. Via a series of aristocratic owners, it ended up in 1805 in the hands of Countess Dorothea von Kurland. She passed it on to her daughter, Dorothea von Sagan, who at the instigation of Tsar Alexander I married a French nobleman, Edmond de Talleyrand-Périgord. Such were the connections between European royalty. In 1837, the younger Dorothea sold the building to Nicholas I. The building was completely revamped, with windowpanes and roof irons, plus 146 carts of soil, all brought from Russia.

Closed during the two world wars, in 1941 it briefly became an internment camp before being occupied by the Reich Ministry for the Occupied Eastern Territories, only to be destroyed by bombing raids in February 1944. For the next seven years, the Soviets moved to Karlshorst, their largest military base inside the city, while the embassy was built afresh. Their new mission was opened on Revolution Day 1952, three times larger than the original palace. Its interior, with gilded pillars, mirrored glass, marble and stucco, manages to combine the imposing, impressive and vulgar. The focal point of the large banqueting hall is a stained-glass window that runs the entire height of the wall and depicts Moscow's Spassky Tower, the main entrance to the Kremlin, under a colourful rainbow. This has never been an ordinary mission. From inside, Soviet diplomats judged how far they could go on breaking the rules. Should they work with the Chancellery and Foreign Ministry around the corner or with the agitators seeking to bring them down? After all, there has never been a single group of Russians in the city with a single allegiance. Many of Russia's internal struggles have been fought out in Berlin.

In the 1920s, the poet Vladislav Khodasevich called Berlin, not entirely flatteringly, 'the stepmother of all Russian cities'. Between 1917 and 1923 there were around 360,000 Russians in Berlin, a melting pot of monarchists, anarchists, revolutionaries, those making money and those trying to make ends meet, by trading currencies on the black market or driving taxis.

The poor stayed East ('twas ever thus in Berlin), much of the street action congregating around the Schlesischer Bahnhof (the Silesia station). Moscow was always within reach, a vast, flat landscape ahead. As he was leaving for his first posting to the Soviet capital in 1931, Hans von Herwarth, a young German diplomat (and later opponent of the Nazis who leaked important information to the Western Allies), wrote of the area around the Schlesischer station: 'One felt that another world began from here. The people on the platforms, the smells, the whole atmosphere was unrecognisably eastern.'

The better-off Russian emigrants ended up in Charlottenburg and Wilmersdorf, where their descendants remain today. It was called, *inter alia*, 'Saint Petersburg at Wittenbergplatz'. Tram drivers of that era called out '*Russland*' as they pulled into Bülowstrasse, one of the main streets leading into the district. Orthodox churches, shops, cinemas and restaurants opened for the diaspora. The Ku'damm was dubbed 'Nöpski Prospekt', a neologism after Lenin's New Economic Policy (NÖP) and St Petersburg's central avenue, Nevsky Prospekt; Charlottenburg became Charlottengrad. Most Russians didn't bother to learn German and made few German friends. Many signs were in Cyrillic, with only the odd one stating, 'German spoken here'. The journalist and diarist Ilya Ehrenburg, who took a room in a boarding house in Prager Platz straight after the First World War, noted that cakes in the Josty Café had been made from frostbitten potatoes and cigars with Havana labels had been made from cabbage leaves steeped in nicotine. 'At every step, you could hear Russian spoken. Dozens of Russian restaurants were opened –

with balalaikas and zurnas, with gypsies, pancakes, shashliks and, naturally, the inevitable heartbreak.'

Many of the great Russian writers and artists of their generation sought sanctuary in Berlin. By the mid-1920s, some 200 Russian-language newspapers, magazines and journals had been established, and an equal number of publishing houses. This was the city of Vladimir Nabokov, Marina Tsvetayeva, Alexei Tolstoy, Boris Pasternak, Vladimir Mayakovsky, Sergei Yesenin and Maxim Gorky. Some stayed for years, others were merely passing through. The radical American dancer, Isadora Duncan, returned to the city where in 1904 she had established her first girls' gymnastics and dance school in Grunewald. By now she had married Yesenin, a poet eighteen years her junior. He spent their sojourn in Berlin on drunken rampages, living the Weimar-era life. In 1922, the film-maker Sergei Eisenstein, in his prime, spent time touring, lecturing and studying some of the techniques being developed at the UFA studios in Babelsberg. In October of the same year, the first Russian Art Exhibition took place at the Galerie van Diemen on Unter den Linden (next to where the Komische Oper now stands). It was one of the great installations of its era, featuring more than 200 works of the avant-garde, among them Chagall, Kandinsky and Malevich. That it was organized by the International Bureau of the Fine Arts section of the Soviet People's Commissariat for Education was not considered out of place.

For some, Berlin became a new home; for others, it was an extraterritorial waiting room, a transit point to more desirable destinations such as Paris or Prague or Vienna. For all, the city was a sanctuary. Some Russians became homesick and returned. As revolution begat civil war, retrenchment and the early years of Stalin, the arguments within Berlin's Russian community, the fears and the conspiracy theories, became ever sharper.

The writer who stayed the longest allowed the fraught politics of his host city and the country of his birth to pass him by. Vladimir Nabokov epitomizes one type of Russian abroad, the one who stays because it is comfortable and yet disdains the ease of life it affords them. This phenomenon of entitlement and ingratitude is just as evident in contemporary Berlin, where Putin-supporting Russians appear little disturbed by events. In 1920, Nabokov's well-to-do family fled Bolshevik Russia for Berlin, where his father set up an émigré newspaper, *Rul* (Rudder). Nabokov joined them two years later, after completing his studies at Cambridge, only for his father to be shot and killed by two monarchists during a conference of the Constitutional Democratic Party (known as the Kadets) at the Philharmonic. Its form of liberal centrist politics was regarded as anathema by the other exiles, both Tsarists and Bolsheviks. His mother and sister fled to Prague, but Nabokov stayed. Indeed, he stayed for the next fifteen years as he couldn't think of anywhere else to go.

He rarely took part in global or German affairs because they didn't concern him. He knew few Germans except for his various landladies, local shopkeepers and immigration officials to whom he had to infrequently report. Instead, he confined himself to the minutiae of life in the city. And like so many Berliners he rarely ventured out of his neighbourhood, which for him was Charlottengrad, plus some sauntering after butterflies in the Grunewald forest. Not for him the gritty working-class districts in the East where the street battles were being fought. 'Nabokov's Berlin', as it came to be known, was circadian street scenes, life on the trams, the funfair of Lunapark and matches at the Sportpalast. He played football, as a goalkeeper, occasionally coached boxing and gave regular tennis lessons at a club just off the Ku'damm, sometimes ten a day, as his main source of income. None of these venues exist now.

His early novels, published while he was in Berlin, used the city as a geographical point of reference while rarely enquiring further. In 1925, the *New Yorker* magazine published his short story 'A Guide to Berlin', a series of vignettes that illustrate the safe bourgeois side of the city – the Russian word *poshly* equating to the German *spiessig*. 'The horse-drawn tram has vanished, and so will the trolley, and some eccentric Berlin writer of the 21st century, wishing to portray our time, will go to a museum of technological history and locate a 100-year-old streetcar, yellow, uncouth, with old-fashioned curved seats, and in a museum of old costumes dig up a black, shiny-buttoned conductor's uniform,' he wrote. His response to the political mayhem around him was to record for posterity everyday trifles. While Nabokov stayed until 1937, seemingly undisturbed by the hegemony of the Nazis, by the end of the 1920s many of the Russian artists had left, some returning to their homeland, others to Paris or New York or safer climes. This first wave was diminishing; the Russian influence on Berlin fell into abeyance, but not for long.

On 11 September 1994, precisely at 19.03, a packed train snaked out of the station at the start of an 1,800-kilometre journey home. This was the last train from the secret town of Wünsdorf to Moscow. Four years after unification, Soviet forces vacated their largest base in East Germany. The event was marked by an afternoon festival, covered live on regional television. 'Could you imagine such coverage now?' bemoans Werner Borchert, a retired local schoolteacher, as he shows me around this vast and largely empty complex, only fifty minutes by train from the centre of Berlin. Throughout the Cold War, Zossen-Wünsdorf was dubbed 'Little Moscow' or 'the forbidden city'. Surrounded by 17 kilometres of concrete walls, with checkpoints on the inside and out, the largest garrison outside the USSR was designated extraterritorial land; it did not appear on any official map. At its peak, 50,000 Soviet personnel were based there, plus another 10,000 family members. The place had everything: its own schools, hospitals, theatres, bus service, supermarkets, bakery, even an ornate concert hall. Some 1,000 heavily vetted GDR citizens provided service support, doing repairs, administration, catering and other non-sensitive tasks. They were closely watched and forbidden from ever talking about their work.

Borchert runs through the history: in 1910, during the reign of Kaiser Wilhelm II, this area was used as a military training ground. As it grew during the First World War, part of it also served as a prisoner-of-war camp. The Kaiser believed that Muslim soldiers serving under the British, French and Russians might be susceptible to encouragement to treason, and to switch sides. As a 'gift' to them, he ordered that a small mosque be built on the site. It came to be known as *Halbmondlager* (Half Moon Camp). Very few of the soldiers ended up defecting and the place of worship was eventually demolished. The Third Reich saw a building boom here; new barracks and hangars for tanks were constructed on the grounds as the 5th Panzer Division established its base. They shared facilities with the Army Sports School and the athletes competing in the 1936 Olympics. From 1937, as Hitler developed his war plans, a series of a dozen bunker buildings, 20 metres in depth and 3 metres thick, were now constructed across the site. They were camouflaged as country houses and connected by a tunnel. The German Supreme Command moved in days before the invasion of Poland. Military strategy was coordinated in Maybach I and II, while the Zeppelin bunker provided communication to the fronts in Stalingrad, France and Africa.

On 15 March 1945, 500 American bomb sorties dropped 7,000 bombs on the site. Much of it was damaged, though many of the bunkers survived. Within days of the Nazi surrender, the Soviets moved in. It took them eight more years, however, to turn Wünsdorf into the headquarters of the High Command of the Group of Soviet Armed Forces in Germany. They had originally chosen Potsdam, but that was deemed to be too close to West Berlin and too close to the Americans.

The Russians have been gone almost as long as they were there, but their ghostly traces are still evident all around Berlin. Near Wünsdorf, Sperenberg airfield lies abandoned, as are airfields at Rangsdorf and Schönwalde. Military camps at places like Jüterbog and Bernau still await a new purpose. As does the disused and still-dangerous bombing practice site at Kyritz-Ruppiner Heath, near the site of the Battle of Wittstock in the Thirty Years War. In the three decades since the Russians' hasty departure, repeated efforts have been made to turn Wünsdorf into something, anything. Most have failed, Borchert points out, as he drives me around the district in the pouring rain.

One idea was to turn the area into a venue for trade fairs. Then it was thought that civil servants coming to Berlin from Bonn in the late 1990s might like to move there. One or two authorities moved in, such as the State Office for Roads and the State Office for Monument Protection, and some new homes were built, but what little early enthusiasm there was quickly ebbed away.

Borchert, who worked for children's television in the GDR and later in the culture section of the regional network, had the idea of turning Wünsdorf into a book town, an equivalent of Hay-on-Wye in the UK. Together with other locals, eight independent antiquarian bookshops were opened in 1998 in buildings that once housed shops for the soldiers. In the early years, the initiative was supported by the region of Brandenburg, as part of the larger attempts to regenerate East German communities. When the subsidies stopped flowing, the shops could not make ends meet. Now only three remain. Borchert shows me around the one he used to run (he's given it up now). Many of the 350,000 old books they acquired, specializing in military history, are in storage; others are gathering dust. 'Very few people come just for the books. People going for walking holidays load

up now with e-books.' Booksellers cross-subsidize their income
by doing tours of the bunkers. The rest of the area is a hotchpotch
of retirement homes, small-scale tourism and film sets. Plus,
one other purpose, like many a derelict site across the former
GDR: from the start of 2016, Wünsdorf's barracks have housed
more than 1,000 asylum seekers from Syria and elsewhere, to
the displeasure of some locals, who have mounted several
arson attacks.

History assaults you at every turn here, but it is often hidden.
Borchert points me to one long block. In January 1919, Friedrich
Ebert made a secret visit to discuss with the generals how to
put down the Spartacist rebellion. At the end of May, Rosa
Luxemburg's beaten and battered body, dug out from the
Landwehr Canal in Berlin, was brought here for a secret autopsy.
In June 1953, Soviet troops made their way from Wünsdorf to
Berlin to put down the workers' uprising. By contrast, in the
autumn of 1989, they remained here in their barracks.

We drive past a couple of nondescript restaurants that have
sprung up over the past decade. In a former aviation museum is a
Chinese restaurant called Peking Gardens ('We're thinking of our
future,' Borchert comments, drolly). Next door, in what was the
Russian *banya* (bathhouse), is a Greek restaurant. Neither is
doing a roaring trade. On the way to the Officers' House, the most
impressive of all Wünsdorf's sites, is a giant weather-beaten statue
of Lenin. Unlike those in Berlin and elsewhere, they didn't bother
to take this one down; it helps the passing tourist trade and has
come in handy for a couple of the film shoots. The Haus der
Offiziere is a remarkable relic of Soviet military grandeur,
comprising five buildings. The pool house has not been used for
thirty years, but its faded turquoise tiles speak to a sense of pomp
and permanence, as does the concert hall, where officers used to
watch choirs, theatre ensembles and visiting troupes from the
Bolshoi. A side building was given over to a huge diorama, 32

metres long and 6 metres high, showing a film of the Battle of Berlin on a loop with the latest Soviet-era lighting and sound special effects. The departing military offered to keep it on as a museum, as long as the state of Brandenburg paid for it. When that offer was declined, the Russians stripped everything from it and piled it onto a train.

On summer weekends ghoulish tourists can pay for a torchlight tour of the bunkers, a rare source of income deriving from the site. Two tiny museums exist, and both give me the jitters. The Garrison Museum, which was opened in 2001, celebrates the role of the military at Wünsdorf. It is an example of a community museum where people collect and exhibit everything they can get their hands on, and it is little more than a paean of praise to the 5th Panzer Division. There are even photographs and displays of the sports school that, if one was being a little ungenerous, could be mistaken for an homage to the Aryan body beautiful. I was taken aback by its lack of perspective. The museum is as far removed from the contemporary sensibilities driving, say, the Humboldt Forum, as it is possible to be. I kept my counsel. In any case, I wonder how many people take the time to visit.

Borchert then takes me, via a connecting passageway, to a former horses' stable, to the Red Star Museum. Using items that were left behind by the departing soldiers, it attempts to recreate the everyday life of the Soviet military in Germany – from Nazi capitulation in 1945 to withdrawal. It succeeds, after a fashion. Visitors are greeted first with a bust of Marshal Georgy Zhukov, who commanded the final assault on Berlin, alongside old telephones, cooking utensils and even a dentist's chair. Marriage certificates and photo albums are interspersed with uniforms and weapons. No attempt is made to contextualize, to suggest that it was anything but virtuous or to debunk the language of pro-paganda. Thus, one picture showing Soviet soldiers guarding East Germans building the Wall is described merely as 'securing the border of the GDR with West Berlin'. Another photograph shows Soviet tanks rolling down the streets of Prague, with a brass band and a crowd welcoming them. It is captioned, without any explanation, 'Operation Danube, 1968'. I find out afterwards that the museum has received money from the Russian energy conglomerate, Gazprom.

Each wave of Russians has left its own imprint. Whereas the 1920s influx contained monarchists, revolutionaries and those simply trying to escape the turbulence, the small trickle of arrivals in the 1970s and 1980s consisted largely of dissidents and Jews permitted to leave the motherland.

The collapse of Soviet communism after 1991 led to the biggest wave of all – the *Spätaussiedler*, or 'late re-settler' ethnic Germans. These Germans' forebears had lived in Russia for two centuries. When Hitler revoked his pact with Stalin and invaded the USSR, the Germans stranded in the country were seen as potential fifth columnists. In August 1941, the Central Committee of the Communist Party decreed the expulsion to Siberia of more than 400,000 Volga Germans, for 'treasonous activity'. They were later joined by a similar number expelled from Ukraine and other Soviet republics. An estimated quarter of a million died in the gulags of starvation and disease. In 1948, Stalin made the banishment permanent, declaring that Russia's Germans were permanently forbidden to return to European Russia; this decree was rescinded after his death in 1953.

The collapse of the Soviet Union meant yet another turning point in Russian-German history and identity. The Federal Office for Migration and Refugees reckons that more than 4.5 million ethnic Germans have arrived in the country from communist Eastern Europe and the USSR since 1950. Half of that total came in the 1990s. According to Article 116 of the Basic Law, on arrival they automatically received German citizenship. Yet they were often seen as foreigners, indeed, felt like foreigners. Their knowledge of the German language was variable (unlike other migrants they didn't need to take a test). Today they are almost nowhere to be seen in West Berlin, confining themselves to the high-rise estates of the East (some 25,000 live in Marzahn, slightly smaller numbers in Hellersdorf and Hohenschönhausen). They have generally low educational attainment, cutting themselves off from much of mainstream German life, leaving themselves susceptible to the twin blandishments of Putin propaganda (courtesy of the Russia Today television station, now rebranded RT) and the far right AfD.

Throughout the 1990s and into the 2000s, an incongruous mix of Russians settled in Berlin – dissidents, artists and nouveaux riches. The Internet is full of the same kinds of services that were afforded to the Russians of the 1920s – an entire infrastructure of restaurants, dentists, discos and clubs, via kindergartens and driving schools to estate agents. The requirements of this more middle-class group have been unspectacular: to find the cheapest, closest and most readily available place to lead a safe Western lifestyle. Berlin is not the city of oligarchs and other assorted super-rich: London has traditionally been their home.

Berlin's younger Russian diaspora is largely artistic; nowhere outside Moscow and St Petersburg has as many Russian painters, musicians and writers, drawn by cheap(er) rents and the scene. Several Russians have made it big: the great Brezhnev–Honecker kiss, accompanied by the words, 'My God, help me to survive this deadly love' of graffiti artist Dmitry Vrubel; the Panda theatre in the old brewery in Prenzlauer Berg holding gigs, poetry slams and open mic nights; or the *Russendisko* of artist, DJ and wannabe mayor of Berlin Vladimir Kaminer in the revived Café Burger on Torstrasse. Vladimir Sorokin, one of Russia's best-known writers, signed his first publishing contract in Berlin in 1988 and has been showered with grants and praise ever since. In

2017, Vrubel put it like this: 'Berlin has become a kind of ideal Moscow; the kind of Moscow we'd all like to live in.'

This community has recently become angrier, part of a wider brain drain of more educated opponents of the Putin regime that was politicized by the protests a decade ago led by Alexei Navalny. When it comes to hypocrisy, London is perhaps the most egregious example, but it does not have a monopoly. Berlin – the same Berlin that curried favour with the Kremlin, made itself dependent on Russian gas and counts among its number many Putin-supporting Russians and one-time Soviet Germans – is the same city that is now one of the chosen homes of dissidents. It is to its Charité hospital that Navalny was flown by the German government after being poisoned on Putin's orders in Siberia.

Nowhere better illustrates this confusion than the Soviet war memorial that overlooks Treptower Park in the southeast of the city. The site, where some 7,000 Red Army soldiers are buried, is dominated by a sparse concrete avenue. On either side are eight granite sarcophagi, each representing a Soviet republic, and each engraved with quotes from Stalin in gold letters. The culmination is a 12-metre-high statue of a soldier: with a sword in one hand, he cradles a child in the other, while trampling on a swastika. He stands atop a pedestal made from marble reclaimed from the ruins of Hitler's Chancellery. A few weeks into Putin's invasion of Ukraine in February 2022, protesters daubed (in English) on the pedestal: 'Ukrainian blood on Russian hands'. The statue of Thälmann in Prenzlauer Berg was similarly defaced.

Germans, and Berliners, are still working through the consequences of this war. In the days and weeks that followed Putin's invasion of Ukraine I went through a series of huge swings. I was stunned and impressed by Olaf Scholz's *Zeitenwende* speech, in which the chancellor surprised even members of his coalition by announcing a huge increase in military spending and promising that Germany would take a far more active role in the defence of Europe. Germans were finally being told that the true interpretation of *Vergangenheitsaufarbeitung* (working through history) was that you have to fight for what you believe in. 'People have been educated out of any form of understanding of war,' the military historian Winfried Heinemann tells me. The 'demilitarisation of history', as he calls it, makes it harder to explain to German audiences what is required to withstand Russian aggression.

Across Berlin, the Ukrainian blue and yellow flag hangs on government buildings, cultural centres, from people's windows. Is this displacement therapy, virtue-signalling or hard-edged political support? A mixture, for sure: I can also see graffiti (you see graffiti on pretty much every building in parts of Berlin) attacking NATO and calling for 'peace'. Whose peace? For most of the year, for day after day, on platform 13 of the central railway station, refugees from Ukraine arrived, were welcomed and housed. Crowds march in defence of Ukraine and a permanent vigil is held outside the forbidding Russian embassy. Yet around the corner, the state-run Russian House of Science and Culture on Friedrichstrasse – the largest such institution in the world – continues impervious to all the noise around. And in many a cafe you still hear people, people who should know better, equivocating about Russia, even defending it. A new term has been coined for them: salon pacifists. I hope their number is waning.

In the twilight, confronting me straight ahead, is a tank. A T-34, with the words *Za Rodinu* (To the motherland) emblazoned alongside it. I'm in the grounds of the German-Russian Museum in Karlshorst, a guest at the 2022 commemoration of the Allied victory over the Nazis. It is taking place in the very hall where, on the evening of 8 May 1945, the Germans signed their unconditional surrender.

In a city with so many great museums, this is another gem,

tucked away in the East. The main chamber has been kept exactly as it was all those years ago – an austere, long, dark brown wooden table, covered in green baize, with the four flags behind, marked left to right for the British, the Soviets, the Americans and the French. The building had been an officers' mess during the Third Reich; after 1945 it became a Soviet military headquarters, a closed city, in the heart of communist East Berlin. In 1967, the building itself was turned into the 'Museum of the Unconditional Surrender of Fascist Germany in the Great Patriotic War', to which East German schoolchildren were taken. When the Russians left in 1994, it was handed to the city of Berlin, and the museum was curated afresh, to be overseen by committees of both the German and Russian governments. It was not an easy juggling act, but the history – the blockades of Stalingrad and Leningrad, the mass killings, the planned starvations – was generally well told.

I had visited the museum several times before, but this time it felt different. The invitation email was convoluted. Yes, the twenty-seven million Soviet war dead would be remembered, it read, but not in the usual way. The museum leadership 'utterly condemns' the Russian invasion of Ukraine, the invitation letter added... and as a result had changed its name and removed the Russian flag. As I arrived, four police vans were waiting down the side street in case of trouble. I took my place early in the hall. Covid rules were still being strictly applied, so only fifty guests had been allowed to attend.

The ceremony was short. Onto the stage came a German vocalist, Ukrainian pianist and Russian cellist. The soloist started singing. 'We share the same biology, regardless of ideology . . . the Russians love their children too.' The lyrics from Sting's 1985 hit, 'Russians'. On this evening of all evenings, they choose such cloying sentimentality. I'm already in a funk by the time they're joined by the museum's director, Jörg Morré. He asks us to stand for a minute's silence to commemorate the victims of Nazi crimes and the victims of the current war, from both sides. Had I heard him right? Instead of something unequivocal, he delivered something close to moral equivalence. I stood, as requested, but was relieved when proceedings closed after barely half an hour. Berlin prides itself on its openness, but in this one case struggles to differentiate between a people and its government. The contortions of Germany's relationship with Russia – the lessons well learned, and the lessons wrongly learned – are being laid bare, more than ever.

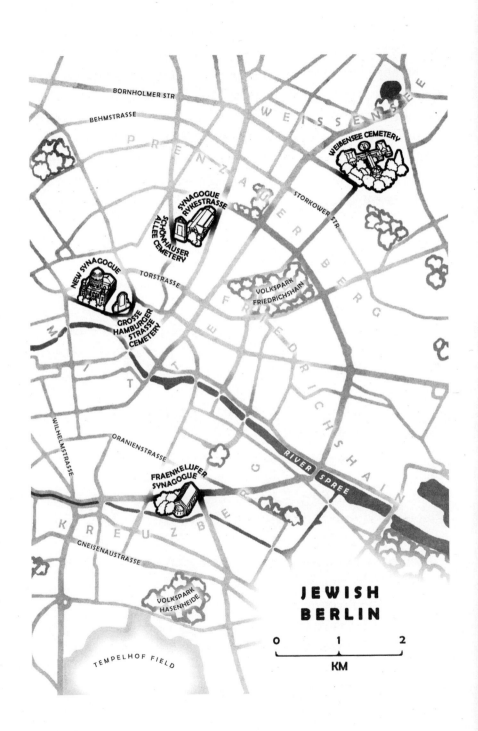

JEWISH BERLIN

0   1   2

KM

FIFTEEN

Back where they belong

The later history of the city's Jews

*Berlin, Berlin, great city of misery! In you there is nothing
to find but anguish and martyrdom.*
HEINRICH HEINE (1822)

This was the guest list every self-respecting Berliner wanted to
be on.

'Its decoration is as rich as it is tasteful and involuntarily
reminiscent of the magic rooms of the Alhambra and the most
beautiful monuments of the Arab world. The ceiling, walls,
columns, arches and windows are adorned with extravagant
splendour. With their gold carvings, they form a wonderful
Arabesque wreath that intertwines to form a harmonious whole,
producing a fairy-like, otherworldly effect.' The *National-Zeitung*,
one of the city's daily papers, had been given a sneak preview of
the New Synagogue on the eve of its consecration. Thousands
flocked to the streets to watch the arrival of the great and the good
in their horse-drawn carts, a suitably grand affair for a building
whose grandeur would not have been out of place in Golden Age
Spain. Some 3,000 worshippers had secured a place that day,
5 September 1866. The official delegation was led by Bismarck
(Minister-President of Prussia at the time), his ministers Friedrich

Albrecht zu Eulenburg (interior), August von der Heydt (commerce and industry) and Heinrich von Mühler (culture); alongside them were Field Marshal Friedrich Graf von Wrangel and other military leaders, the president of police Otto von Bernuth and mayor of Berlin Karl Theodor Seydel. Mere members of parliament had to occupy rows further back. Not all went smoothly; the guests and the crowds were greeted by hailstones and thunderstorms.

Work had begun on the synagogue on Oranienburger Strasse seven years earlier under the guidance of two of Berlin's premier architects of the time, Eduard Knoblauch and Friedrich August Stüler (a student of Schinkel). When the Moorish-style structure was unveiled it was instantly praised as one of the most impressive places of worship, indeed one of the most startling buildings, in all the city. The golden dome of the main temple could be seen for miles around, glistening in the winter snow, gleaming in the summer sun. Its splendour corresponded to the status that Jews, or at least prominent Jews, enjoyed in the city. The late nineteenth century marked a rare moment of Jewish acceptability and respectability, more so even than that of the Enlightenment under Friedrich the Great. Berlin's Jews never numbered more than 5 per cent of the population, but in the late nineteenth century they were influential not just in commerce and finance – dominating the big banks, Deutsche, Dresdner and Darmstadter – but also in politics, culture and science. The most important newspaper groups, Ullstein and Mosse, were owned by Jews. The New Synagogue became a focal point, not just of worship but also of social and cultural life, for more than half a century. In January 1930 Albert Einstein played the violin in a charity concert, one of the hottest tickets of that era.

I am discussing its history with Hermann Simon, one of the most exceptional figures in contemporary Berlin Jewry. He talks me through the grim milestones of the century that followed. In

November 1938, the synagogue was set upon by the Nazis on Kristallnacht. Thugs desecrated the Torah scrolls, smashed furniture, piled up the contents on a pyre and set fire to them. The building was partially saved thanks to the bravery of a police officer from the local precinct, who rushed to the scene and ordered the arsonists to disperse, drawing his pistol and informing them that it was a historic landmark. In November 1943 the building was all but destroyed by Allied bombers. In summer 1958 the East Berlin city council decided to pull down the main nave and other remnants that were still standing. Only the front of the building had been preserved, and it had remained in terrible condition for decades. Exactly half a century after its desecration, the first stone was laid to rebuild the synagogue. This was November 1988; the GDR government was still in existence, but the project was underwritten by the West German government, which donated one million Deutschmarks to get it going.

Simon's life exemplifies the terrible history of Jews in Berlin – and a certain redemption. First his mother: an orphan at the age of nineteen, in 1941 Marie Jalowicz Simon was sent into forced labour at a Siemens factory, going from home to home, all the time hiding, famished, often exploited, and living in unsanitary conditions. She avoided almost certain death one time by telling the postman who was delivering her a summons from the job centre that the woman under that name had disappeared; then in June 1942, dressed only in her petticoat and pretending to be a neighbour, she slipped past the two SS men who had been sent to pick her up. On the rare occasions she needed to venture onto the street, she would not wear the yellow star required of Jews. For a time, she stayed in a villa outside the city with a circus performer before being 'sold' for 15 Reichsmarks (around £70 in today's money) to a syphilitic ardent Nazi. Like Inge Deutschkron and very few others, she had survived the horrors in hiding.

Yet her personal story would not have come to light had it not been for the persistence of her son. After the war, she followed the strictures of the young East German state, which exhorted its people to focus not on the legacy but on constructing a new state. Shortly after the war, she met an old school friend, Heinrich Simon. They married and settled in their hometown, where Marie embarked on an academic career, teaching classics and the history of philosophy at the Humboldt University.

Having been wary of talking about her experiences throughout her adult life, and with the GDR long gone, she agreed to tell all to her son just before her death in 1998. In nine months of conversations, his tape recorder perched on a table in his parents' apartment, Simon produced seventy-seven tapes of her recollections and 900 pages of transcribed notes. That became one of the most remarkable memoirs of its kind. *Untergetaucht* – translated into English as *Gone to Ground* – is the story of the 1,700 Jews who became 'U-boats'. Written in the present tense, it is as raw as it is powerful. His mother recalls one incident during the Battle of Berlin when, like so many Berlin women, she is raped by a Soviet soldier. She describes him as a 'sturdy, friendly character' called Ivan. As for her time underground, she admits that she was living 'illegally', though she points out, 'The Nazis were illegal, not me.' She then tells her son, 'I have emigrated from Hitler's Germany to the Germany of Goethe and Johann Sebastian Bach, and I feel very comfortable there.'

Simon and I are discussing all of this while drinking tea. He has managed to find perhaps the only place in Prenzlauer Berg that is not hipster central; with its dusty chandeliers and embroidered chairs, Café Meyer recalls old Berlin. His mother was determined to give him as tranquil an upbringing as possible in the early days of the GDR. He studied history and oriental studies at the Humboldt, where he received his doctorate in 1975. From 1975 to 1985 he worked as a research assistant of medieval coins at the National Museums in Berlin.

In 1988, Simon was involved in the first exhibition on Jewish life in East Berlin; he needed official approval for the content. Timed to coincide with the fiftieth anniversary of the November pogrom, it was first displayed in the Ephraim Palais in the Nikolaiviertel, before transferring to the Martin Gropius Building in West Berlin (in a rare example of cross-border cultural co-operation). It is a remarkable history, remarkable because of how small the community was. The total number of people officially registered as Jews in communist East Berlin in 1988 was all of 210. Workers were allowed to take Jewish holidays, but rarely did. There were barely enough people to observe collective religious or social festivals. East Berlin had one kosher butcher – which apparently sold better-quality meat than the non-kosher ones. Other Jewish groups existed, even smaller, in cities such as Leipzig, Halle, Dresden, Schwerin and Erfurt. I ask Simon about post-war antisemitism. He suggests that it was 'more or less the same level' in the East as in the West. He points to two issues specific to the GDR: a political line that saw Israel predominantly as an 'imperialist' and 'occupying' power, and the official remembrance of history. The 'anti-fascist' state did not dwell on the role of its citizens in supporting and propagating Nazism. 'The teaching was all about East Germans being victims.'

Adherence to the state afforded protection but required a near-total disavowal of Jews' commitment to their religion, or at least any public manifestation of that commitment. The GDR was merely following a tradition in which Jews had always been told to be 'more German' in order to achieve success, much as Moses Mendelssohn and Walter Rathenau had done. It is worth recalling here an essay Rathenau had written half a century earlier, in 1897, with a stark message to fellow Jews to assimilate:

> In the midst of German life [there is] an isolated, strange human tribe, resplendently and conspicuously adorned, hot-blooded

and animated in its behaviour. The forced cheerfulness of these
people does not betray how much old, unquenched hatred rests
on their shoulders . . . they live in a semi-voluntary, invisible
ghetto, not a living member of the people, but a foreign organism
inside its body.

East Berlin had just one synagogue in operation, just up the road on Rykestrasse, a beautiful brick building that resembles a neo-Romanesque basilica. Consecrated in 1904, it is now the best-preserved and, with its more than 2,000 seats, the second-largest synagogue structure in Europe, after the Great Synagogue in Budapest. It escaped torching because of its proximity to neigh-bouring apartment blocks. Services were still being held here as late as 1940, at which point the building was confiscated and turned into a military warehouse. There was an attempt to rebuild it in 1953, but it was only after unification, with the commitment and resources of the new German state, that in 2005 it was restored to its pre-war grandeur.

In 1988, Simon became the director of the newly founded Centrum Judaicum Foundation whose main task was to bring the New Synagogue back to life. 'One thing we'll have to deal with is the ruin next door that used to be the synagogue on the Oranienburger Strasse,' he said at the time. 'Sooner or later, we'll have to rebuild it – even as a ruin – and the money will have to come from somewhere.' They did, and it did. From the outside it looks as if the whole building has been restored, but it is only the façade and gilded dome. The building was not rededicated as a synagogue, but does contain a small prayer room, alongside a permanent exhibition on Jewish life in Berlin.

Simon made sure that the process, from the first stone to completion, did not extend longer than the seven years of 1859 to 1866. So much of what happened that day in May 1995 resembled the original ceremony. The VIP list was just as impressive, from

President Bill Clinton to Chancellor Helmut Kohl. The speeches were just as long. 'I had to wait for the bigwigs to finish before it was my turn,' Simon recalls. In his address, he talks of 'shouldering the responsibility for the reconstruction of this house where the scars of history are permanently visible through the visual confrontation of what was with what is'. And the rain. Just as a century earlier in front of Bismarck, 'it was biblical. The heavens were crying.'

Throughout this period and up to 2015 when he stepped down, Simon was instrumental in galvanizing politicians and city planners to focus more on Berlin's Jewish heritage. He initiated and curated several exhibitions on Jewish life and the remembrance of victims, a career for which he has received a number of decorations and honorary degrees. Yet he says it was never easy. As in the nineteenth century, as in the late twentieth and into the twenty-first, the Jews of East and West Berlin were influenced by different geographies and different histories, and now different political systems. 'We spoke the same language, but we spoke past each other. The distrust was tough.'

Whatever the tensions, the work has proceeded apace. Berlin's rediscovery of its Jewish heritage is not confined to memorialization. The city is developing a modern Jewish outlook, doing all it can to attract Jews whose forebears had been murdered or forced to leave – and those who had not known the city. The process is often fraught; it is invariably laced with history, but it is also sincere and optimistic. I ask Simon about his identity. Given everything his mother lived through and he lived through, what exactly is he and where does he belong? I give him four choices and ask him to rank them in order. He hesitates momentarily, then offers this:

First Berliner, then a Jew, then German, then European.

I repeat this question to several Jews I meet in the city. Almost always I'm given a different answer.

*

The Wilhelmine era may have been the halcyon period, but Weimar also marked a flourishing, at least among the more established, of the Jewish community. A quarter of all Nobel prizes won by Germans in the first third of the twentieth century were won by German Jews. Plays directed by Max Reinhardt dominated the stage, Arnold Schoenberg and Kurt Weill composed music, Max Liebermann and Lesser Ury created great art (albeit of different styles), and Otto Klemperer and Bruno Walter conducted concerts to huge audiences. And yet throughout this period, antisemitic raids and assassinations increased.

In 1900 there were 92,000 Jews in the city. By 1925 the Jewish population peaked at 173,000, six times larger than the second-biggest community in Germany, in Frankfurt. Some had fled pogroms elsewhere in Europe in the late nineteenth century, others had come more recently. Some of the newly arrived planned to pass through Berlin on their way to the ports of Bremen and Hamburg and eventually to the US. But a lack of funds and visas meant that many ended up staying. These Yiddish-speaking *Ostjuden* (Jews from the East) were looked down upon by wealthier and more assimilated Jews in Charlottenburg and Wilmersdorf.

One of the most moving, and prescient, accounts of this group was produced in 1927. Joseph Roth, a newspaper journalist and author, was born just outside Lviv in what was then Galicia, an eastern province of the Habsburg Empire. *The Wandering Jews* is a short non-fiction book about those who fled or were displaced from Lithuania, Poland and Russia in the aftermath of the Bolshevik Revolution, the First World War and the redrawing of the map of Europe that followed. Many ended up in Vienna and Berlin. The author describes the Scheunenviertel, the barn district that had been a gathering point for poor Jews for centuries, as a 'strange sad ghetto world' filled with 'grotesque Eastern figures' holding 'a thousand years of pain in their eyes'.

Almost all the Jews who got out just in time and began new lives elsewhere washed their hands of Germany and Berlin; that was the most understandable response. What is extraordinary is the small number who didn't. And the number of descendants of that generation who came back to the city, ultimately finding a reconciliation of sorts.

Heinz Berggruen was born months before the outbreak of the First World War. He was brought up in comfortable Wilmersdorf. The son of a businessman, he went to the local Goethe-Gymnasium and then the Humboldt in 1932. The following year, as Hitler took power, his parents sent him to study in Toulouse and Grenoble, from where he submitted freelance newspaper articles to the *Frankfurter Zeitung*, using only the initials HB to get around restrictions on Jewish writers. The family emigrated to the United States in 1936. He began working as an art critic at the *San Francisco Chronicle* and then as a curator in the city's recently opened museum, where he helped stage an exhibition by Diego Rivera, with whose wife, Frida Kahlo, he proceeded to have a brief affair. Towards the end of the war, after taking up US citizenship, he was sent by the signal corps to Munich and Berlin, where his language would come in useful. He was struck by the devastation (his old family home had been reduced to rubble).

After the war Paris became his home, and it was there that he became friends with Pablo Picasso. By the 1980s he had become one of the world's most accomplished collectors. Then, after over sixty years of exile, he returned to his home city in 1996, bringing 113 works with him. The Berlin Senate offered him the Stülerbau, a former officers' barracks located opposite the Charlottenburg Palace, a neoclassical building with a distinctive dome. The Museum Berggruen now contains several hundred works by some of the greatest masters of early modern art, all donated by a Jew who fled the city. Challenged by those who disagreed with his decision to return, he said he wanted to reacquaint the city of his birth with the 'degenerate' art banned by the Nazis: 'I've been in the position where I can show the Germans again what Picasso and Klee are like, and they appreciate it greatly.' In 2000, Berggruen sold the collection to the Prussian Cultural Heritage Foundation for a fifth of its valuation of €750 million. He saw this as a gesture of reconciliation. 'Berlin should shine,' he said, with a moving economy of language. He was frequently to be seen at his own museum, talking to visitors and checking on postcard sales in the shop. Even though it contains some of Picasso's most celebrated works, the museum does not market itself as one of Berlin's top destinations (which it should be). It is as if the city finds such magnanimity a little embarrassing and hard to fathom.

Berggruen died at the American Hospital in Neuilly-sur-Seine, outside Paris, in February 2007. And yet, like Marlene Dietrich, like others, he had stipulated a wish to be buried in Berlin. He lies in Waldfriedhof Dahlem, on the edge of the Grunewald forest, a chosen place of rest for many actors and artists. His funeral was attended by Angela Merkel and President Horst Köhler.

The memorials to the Holocaust tell the story of horror, suffering and depravity. What many of them do not do – it is usually not their remit – is tell the story of Jews' earlier contribution to Berlin life. The cemeteries help to do that.

Weissensee is one of the largest Jewish cemeteries in Europe, home to over 115,000 graves, from the lavish mausoleums of the wealthy on the periphery to the small sunken graves of the more impecunious in the centre. Established in 1880, it had 150 full-time employees by the time the Nazis came to power. During the war, it became a place where desperate Jews went to hide, either clambering inside tombs or concealing themselves in foliage. During the GDR, the site was neglected, leading to graves being damaged by roots of trees, weeds, and lichen, and providing a home for sixty-four species of spiders, thirty-nine species of ground beetles and five kinds of bats. It was not until the 1970s that the East German parliament designated the cemetery a historical memorial. A few years earlier, plans to build an elevated motorway over it were stopped only at the last minute by intensive lobbying from the tiny Jewish community. The cemetery is still wild and unkempt in places; it takes forever to walk around it. Of all its sections, one strikes me in particular: a special memorial area erected in 1927 by the Reichsbund jüdischer Frontsoldaten, the Imperial Association of Jewish Combat Soldiers. With a monumental altar at its heart, the remains of more than 12,000 soldiers who fell in the First World War are simply but beautifully arranged. More than 100,000 Jews fought for the Kaiser, a higher proportion than the rest of the population, and many were volunteers.

The cemetery on Schönhauser Allee was founded earlier, in 1827, on the grounds of an old brewery and dairy farm, and served the Jewish community for half a century. On the now-fashionable Kollwitzplatz, next to a Georgian restaurant, tour groups gather to be shown a tall portico, adorned with two Stars of David. This gate marked the start of the Jew's Path, *Judengang*, also called *Totenpfad*, Path of the Dead, a long alleyway hidden between garden sheds and tenements which Jewish mourners were allowed to use. (It is said that Friedrich Wilhelm III found the sight of 'miserable looking Jewish mourners' on the main highway offensive.) The route now stands in what is called the magic triangle between the high-value properties of Schönhauser Allee, Kollwitzstrasse and Knaackstrasse, shrouded in ivy and populated by maple, linden and chestnut trees.

The most visited grave belongs to Max Liebermann. His death, of natural causes in February 1935, was ignored by the media, even though he had been one of Germany's best-known painters. The Prussian Academy of Arts, of which he had been president for thirteen years – until its decision in 1933 no longer to exhibit

Jewish artists – refused to honour him. At his funeral, only thirty-eight mourners signed the condolence book. In 1943 his wife Martha took an overdose rather than face impending deportation to the Theresienstadt concentration camp. Only in 1960 were her remains transferred from Weissensee and laid to rest next to the grave of her husband. A few months after her suicide, the Nazis looted the family's art collection. The Liebermanns had refused to leave the country, opting instead for a form of internal exile at their home next to the Brandenburg Gate on Pariser Platz, which is now a moving museum to his life and art. Shortly before he died, Max Liebermann told one of his last visitors: 'I no longer look out the window of this room – I do not want to see the new world around me.'

Another Jew who gave his life to Berlin and to art was James Simon. A cotton factory owner and subsequently a banker, he was one of the richest men in Berlin, one of a small group of Jews allowed to join Kaiser Wilhelm II's 'gentlemen's evenings'. Although the term 'Court Jews' of the Friedrich the Great era no longer existed, the notion of assimilated and therefore 'respectable' Jews, as distinct from other Jews, was still very much alive. Simon spent over a quarter of his income on social initiatives and on art. He funded special concerts for workers and their families, a residence for child labourers and established public bathhouses. In 1898, with the Kaiser's blessing, he founded and financed the German Orient Society, bringing back a host of Egyptian and other artistic treasures that would be housed in the various museums of the Museum Island. They, like the Humboldt Forum and others, are in the throes of heated discussions about theft and cultural appropriation.

Simon was a philanthropist extraordinaire. He donated his Renaissance collection of around 500 objects to the newly built Kaiser Friedrich Museum, today named the Bode Museum, after the general director of the Prussian Art Collections, Wilhelm von

Bode. Simon followed this with a further 350 works, primarily made up of German and Dutch wooden sculptures from the late Middle Ages. No other collector in this period came close. Simon died in 1932, the year before Hitler's seizure of power, and was given a proper funeral at Schönhauser. Soon after, the Nazis made sure his name was erased from the collective memory of art in Berlin. The East Germans also didn't want much to do with this member of the super-rich, though the Gemäldegalerie did host a commemoration for him in 1982. Even after reunification it took another decade for the city to rediscover one of its greatest patrons. As part of the reinvention of the Museum Island, a new main entrance building and exhibition space was designed by David Chipperfield; it was named the James Simon Galerie.

One small postscript: in the last days of the war, several German soldiers tried to hide in some of the cemetery's cisterns, just as Jewish civilians had tried to conceal themselves at Weissensee. The deserters were discovered by the Gestapo and hanged on its trees. A memorial plaque recalls the episode: 'They wanted no more killing; and that meant their death.'

Weissensee was built to accommodate the overspill in 1880; Schönhauser Allee had performed the same function in 1827. The first Jewish cemetery in Berlin, on Grosse Hamburger Strasse in Mitte, dates back to the first concerted arrivals in 1671. The cluster of lanes around were outside the city walls, a collection of hovels for the poorest, the *Ostjuden*. I smile whenever I walk around the area now, past the Michelin-starred restaurants, hipster bars and bijoux boutiques. As with so many streets in Berlin, but particularly here, history confronts the new comfortable.

The cemetery's first occupants were Berlin's *Schutzjuden*, the 'protected Jews'. By the time it had filled up and closed in 1827, the *Alter Jüdischer Friedhof* (Old Jewish Cemetery) had squashed more than 2,500 graves together in its small confines. The most famous of them all was Moses Mendelssohn. The cemetery on

Grosse Hamburger Strasse was situated in the heart of Jewish life in Berlin, with shops, cafes and community centres nearby. The New Synagogue would be built just up the road. Alongside the site, the first Jewish old people's home was built in 1844 and a boys' school in 1863. From late 1941 the Gestapo transformed the retirement home into a staging point: some 55,000 Jews were summoned to report there and were taken directly to the various camps. Once the building was emptied of all human life, the home and the cemetery were destroyed. The Nazis then turned the buildings into an air-raid shelter, using tombstones as wall reinforcements, digging trenches through the graveyard and discarding the remains that they encountered. In 1945, the grounds were transformed into a mass burial site for around 2,500 soldiers and civilian victims of Allied air raids. The area remained largely derelict in the early years of the GDR, but eventually some attempts were made to clear it.

In 1985 one of the earliest, simplest and most evocative of all memorials to the Holocaust was placed at the entrance to the cemetery. Thirteen gaunt and barefoot bronze men, women and children dressed in worn clothes, both close together and un-settlingly far apart, stare straight ahead. The work, entitled *Jewish Victims of Fascism*, was originally intended for the women's concentration camp Ravensbrück. The entire site was renovated in 2008, when some of the remaining tombstone fragments were assembled along the wall of the cemetery. A memorial honouring Mendelssohn is the only free-standing tombstone in the burial grounds. This is a place that Berlin gets right. It is impossible, I always think, for people not to stop and reflect. Sadly, that is not the feeling I get whenever I go to the Jewish Museum, on the other side of the Wall, between the Springer building and the start of Kreuzberg. Maybe it is the location. Maybe the building itself is too dramatic. It does too much, thereby stifling what it contains inside.

The Jewish Museum, Europe's largest, is the masterwork of

Daniel Libeskind. In the pantheon of post-war architecture, it is ranked with David Chipperfield's restoration of the bombed-out Neues Museum and with Mies van der Rohe's original 1960s Neue Nationalgalerie. Libeskind's is a remarkable and disconcerting structure. Five zinc-clad voids slice through the vertical axis of the building, interspersed with concrete shafts, in the shape of a lightning bolt or broken Star of David. Libeskind uses the voids to address the physical emptiness that resulted from the annihilation of Jewish life in the Shoah. One void contains an installation called *Shalekhet* (Fallen leaves) by Israeli artist Menashe Kadishman, in which 10,000 faces with open mouths cut from heavy iron plates cover the floor. The most harrowing aspect of the building is the Holocaust Tower, an isolated splinter. When you walk into the cold concrete silo you can hear nothing and you are surrounded by high walls and only a narrow slit of light at the very top.

On 9 September 2001, before an audience of dignitaries that included Chancellor Gerhard Schröder, President Johannes Rau and former US Secretary of State Henry Kissinger, the Jewish Museum was officially inaugurated. It immediately became, and has been since, one of Berlin's most visited historical and cultural venues. The proceedings began with a performance of Gustav Mahler's Seventh Symphony by the Chicago Symphony Orchestra led by Daniel Barenboim. The conductor had played alongside Libeskind when the future architect was a twelve-year-old musical prodigy.

The museum was expanded in 2007 to incorporate an eighteenth-century courthouse next door. The *Kollegienhaus* (Collegiate House) is the last surviving baroque palace of the Friedrichstadt district designed by Philipp Gerlach during the reign of Friedrich Wilhelm I. In the 1960s it was converted into West Berlin's civic museum, to rival the Märkisches Museum in the GDR. After unification, such duplications were deemed redundant. Libeskind reworked the building, adding a glass portal. In the grounds is a Garden of Exile, with forty-nine concrete stelae laid out on slanting ground, olive bushes growing on top, intended to symbolize the disorientating experience of being driven into exile. Forty-eight of them contain soil from Berlin and one from Jerusalem.

Berlin did have a dedicated Jewish museum before this one. It opened in the grounds of the New Synagogue six days before the Nazis took power; it didn't survive long. This contemporary one has already had its fair share of controversy. In 2019, its director, Peter Schaefer, was forced to step down over an exhibition called *Welcome to Jerusalem* which was denounced by some as pro-Palestinian. Israel's prime minister, Benjamin Netanyahu, wrote to Merkel demanding the exhibition's closure. Schaefer, a renowned scholar of religious history, had already been criticized for inviting a Palestinian scholar to give a lecture at the museum and giving a personal tour to the cultural director of the Iranian embassy. Any discussion about Israel, let alone other aspects of Judaism, is especially fraught in Germany.

But there is a different concern about the museum. What exactly is it for? Who is it for? The lower part, dedicated to the Holocaust, is so overwhelming that visitors can often struggle through the far less harrowing content, a multimedia exhibition of *Jewish Life in Germany Past and Present*. The messaging, however, seems confused. Is this about religion or culture? A celebration or a commemoration? Is it for Jews, non-Jews, Berliners or outsiders? My favourite aspect is the one welcome moment of levity. A celebrity Hall of Fame along one of the staircases contains portraits of the many famous Jews who have influenced German life. From Primo Levi to Leonard Bernstein to Walter Benjamin, Marc Chagall, Magnus Hirschfeld and Anne Frank. Also on the wall, close to each other stand Jesus Christ, Karl Marx and Amy Winehouse.

Maybe the confusion has an explanation. The Jewish community in contemporary Berlin bears little resemblance to that which once thrived in the city. Alongside the couple of hundred Jews in the GDR, the number in the West grew slowly during the Cold War years. By 1989 there were barely 30,000 Jews in the whole of Germany, of whom under 10,000 were in West Berlin. But the picture today is quite different. Some estimates put the Jewish population of Berlin as high as 100,000, still well below the figure pre-1933 but a marked increase, nonetheless. The reason? Four in five of Berlin's present-day Jewish population are Russian speakers, migrants from Russia, Ukraine and Belarus who flocked to all parts of the country in the 1990s and received automatic residence and work permits.

Germany's overall Jewish population, almost extinguished during the Shoah, is now Europe's third largest – behind France and Britain. By 2002, for the first time more Jews from the ex-USSR emigrated to Germany (19,000) than to Israel (18,000) or the US (10,000). As for Israelis, nobody quite knows the number and whether they are just staying for a while or plan to settle for good. Until recently they would register with their embassy; now they often don't bother. Quite a few of them have second EU passports in any case.

I discuss the demographics with Gesa Ederberg, a woman of unusual extraction. Born to a Lutheran family in the picturesque university city of Tübingen in Baden-Württemberg, she first visited Israel on holiday at the age of thirteen, fell in love with Judaism and decided to convert. In 2007, she became a rabbi at the New Synagogue in Berlin, to the consternation of some Orthodox in the community, who struggled with a woman and a convertee. Now Germans do not have to go abroad to be trained as rabbis and cantors. In the grounds of the University of Potsdam, the first seminary since the Holocaust was established shortly after unification.

Some of Ederberg's congregation are descendants of survivors of the camps in Poland and further afield. They were on their way to Israel or the US, 'and got stuck in Berlin or married a non-Jewish local and decided to stay', she explains. As for the latest influx of young Israelis, she says many are not religious. They come not to explore history but to imbibe the Berlin artistic and music scene. 'It's often only when they're here do they realise how much Jewish baggage they bring with them.'

Ederberg pushes back against what she calls an 'excessive focus' on the Shoah. 'I keep on saying – there is another Germany.' Yet she is equally adamant that antisemitism has become more, not less, vocal in the past few years. 'Every day Jews make conscious, personal decisions. Do you speak Hebrew loudly on the U-Bahn? Do you wear the kippah? Do you tuck your Star of David under your T-shirt?'

Then she adds: 'Berlin is the only city in Germany I could live in. It's the only city in the world I'd want to live in. It's where I am and who I am.'

The German government strains every sinew, not just to atone, but also to make recently arrived Jews feel welcome. One of the sad by-products of its efforts, however, is security. Every building that has anything to do with Judaism – synagogues, seminaries, schools, shops, cultural centres – has reinforced gates, CCTV or round-the-clock police guard, and usually all of them. The extent of the danger was brought home in October 2019 when a far right gunman tried to force his way into a synagogue in Halle, a couple of hours to the southwest of the capital. After failing to get in, the man fatally shot two people nearby and injured two others. The attack took place on the holy day of Yom Kippur.

I cross the Admiral's Bridge to get to my final destination. With its cobblestone street and old gas lanterns, in the summer the bridge is one of the best places to hang out. Hundreds of people sit on bollards or on the ground, playing music, drinking beer, eating pizza, watching the odd boat or canoe cruise down the Landwehr Canal. It is relaxed, cosmopolitan Berlin at its best. On its north side stands a building with a different history.

Berlin currently has eight working synagogues. In the early twentieth century, the Kreuzberg community decided to correct an imbalance of not having one in the southern part of the city. The Fraenkelufer synagogue that was built in 1916 by the Jewish architect Alexander Beer became the third largest and one of the most impressive. It was torched and looted on Kristallnacht in 1938 and the land was taken over by the Wehrmacht to store military vehicles. By the end of the war only the façade of the main synagogue and a cramped and plain social hall next door remained, a fraction of the original buildings. This period was captured by the American war photographer Robert Capa in a series for *Life* magazine, of people clearing away the rubble and the first service taking place on what remained of the site in September 1945, barely months after the Nazi capitulation. Some of Capa's pictures hang in the hall, on permanent loan; the rest are in New York. At its re-dedication in 1959, the community consisted largely of survivors and returnees, many of whom lived and worked in the immediate vicinity. In the 1980s and 1990s, immigrants from the former Soviet Union joined the community.

'My grandchildren are the sixth generation connected with this place,' Mario Marcus tells me as he shows me around. His grandfather, who had a chemist's shop around the corner, was a member of the original congregation. Marcus himself has been an active member of the synagogue for more than fifty years and is now on the committee overseeing its restoration. His parents fled as children just before the Holocaust but came back in 1951; in spite of everything, they felt more at home in Berlin than in England, America or France, where they had spent time. As he shows me around, I am struck by the yellow of the stained-glass windows. Their beauty is obscured on the outside of the building by a thick sheet of opaque reinforced glass. That, Marcus tells me, was in response to repeated instances of people throwing bricks into the windows. All around are high walls, cameras and a permanent police presence. During services the street outside, on the banks of the canal, is blocked on both sides by police cars. I tell him I find this depressing, to which he responds dryly, 'In Germany, unlike in other countries, at least they organize and pay for all the security.'

Late in 2023, to coincide with the eighty-fifth anniversary of Kristallnacht, they are planning to lay the foundation stone for a new complex that will house a hall, teaching rooms, a community centre and a library – although Marcus is not counting on Berlin's notorious bureaucracy to keep to the deadline. Completion is scheduled for 2026, but again he is not holding his breath. When it does eventually materialize, it is likely to be spectacular. Even though the project itself is not that grand in scale or lucrative (the city is putting up around €25 million) the architectural competition is likely to attract some big global names. This will be the first time a synagogue destroyed by the Nazis on Kristallnacht will be rebuilt in its entirety in Berlin. Few projects will be as emotionally charged, or as prominent, as this. The Fraenkelufer synagogue may well become the symbol of a new Jewish community.

The project is being overseen by the parliamentary leader of the SPD in Berlin's House of Representatives. Nothing untoward there; it is, after all, the governing party in the city. Raed Saleh comes from Sebastia, a small town close to Nablus, in the Israeli-occupied West Bank. His parents fled to Germany for a better life when Saleh was five. His father worked in a bakery in Spandau while his mother looked after their nine children. While in school, Saleh worked in Burger King to help support the family; he also joined the SPD.

The world's traumatized flock to the city that once unleashed trauma, finding common cause with those who suffered at its hands.

SIXTEEN

Fear of normality

Berlin today

Berlin is a city condemned forever to become, never to be.
KARL SCHEFFLER (1910)

As marketing slogans go, you'd be hard pressed to find much worse. 'Feel the pulse of progress', it reads, in English, naturally, at Potsdamer Platz station. This was once the heart of the city; now it is a succession of glass and steel skyscrapers, a memorial to the worst of 1990s globalization.

In October 1990, when the two Germanies became one again, when the two Berlins became one again, all the impetus was towards a fresh start. Throw caution to the wind. Tear down that wall once and for all. Erase history. Put up monuments to 'progress'.

It has been more than three decades since reunification. Has Berlin become a world city again? Could it, finally, be described as normal?

As ever with the city, nothing has come easily. The Bundestag voted to move the capital from sleepy Bonn in June 1991, but only by the narrowest of majorities. This was the rebirth or birth (depending on your view) of the 'Berlin Republic'. Several anxious

MPs pointed out that this would be not just a geographical relocation from one end of the country to the other, from the far west to the far east. It would be psychological too. And so it has proved to be.

The fall of the Wall precipitated another of Berlin's habitual migration waves. Many from the former GDR moved west, not so much to old West Berlin as to the smaller, more orderly small towns of the Federal Republic. Into their place came waves of foreigners and West Germans, snapping up cheap properties and wanting to savour what was left of the 'original' Berlin. The city is now home to 3.5 million people, just over 30 per cent of whom did not live there when the city was brought back together.

In the 1990s, on reunification, the chaos of the physical space gave it an immediate and unique selling point. Roughly a third of the buildings in the East had become vacant. DJs and musicians, the anarchic and entrepreneurial, set up clubs in abandoned warehouses and basements; artists set up studios. Nobody knew how long a venue would last, adding to the frisson of the new discovery.

According to official figures, one-third of foreign tourists now go to Berlin for the music scene. Tomes have been written about the best-known venue, Berghain, its history as a former heating plant, its drugs scene, the sex, the music and the big names who tried, and sometimes failed, to get past the bouncers. I talk about its allure to an Italian friend, Andrea, who moved to Berlin a decade ago 'to seek a second chance' and to revel in its queer scene. He is to be found pretty much every weekend at Berghain. The rest of the time he has a senior job at one of the top e-commerce companies. Everyone he knows at Berghain, foreign and German – and it seems he really does know everyone – goes for its sense of abandon. He says it is more than that. 'Everyone,' he tells me, 'comes to escape from something in their lives. And to walk on the border of freedom and chaos. Berlin and Berghain are magnets for the traumatised, and for revelations.' No other city, he adds, comes close.

The city's pull remains as strong as ever, giving rise to the same questions as have been asked down the centuries. Who is a Berliner? Whose Berlin is it anyway? As with the Huguenots, the Dutch, the Russians and the Jews, each group of new Berliners – German and foreign – challenges those who claim to understand the city best. English is now ubiquitous in the city, with many foreigners seeing no need to learn the native language. As for the hundreds of thousands of German incomers, they are lumped together by Berliners and ritually denounced as 'Swabians', a term that geographically locates them in the southwest state of Baden-Württemberg (from which some but by no means the majority come). More than that, it denotes any of the following: well-to-do, bourgeois, square. In other words, not belonging to Berlin. *Schwabenhass* (hatred of Swabians) has now entered the lexicon, most of all for gentrifying the city, for pushing up prices.

So do these newbies assimilate into new Berlin and become 'proper' Berliners? Or do they change it? The answer, as throughout the city's history, is both.

A city that wants to be global while paying little heed to globalization. That is one of Berlin's particular traits. It is also one of the most unhurried of capitals. It is easy to get out of, and when you do, nature is never far away. But many parts of the city itself, for all its attempts at modernizing, still retain the feel of the village, or rather a collection of villages knitted together. My years of traipsing from one end to the other, finding myself in the obscurest of settings, have left some of my Berlin friends quizzical. Many do not venture beyond their own neighbourhood.

Berlin is quieter, quirkier, less consumerist – and cheaper – than equivalent cities. At least, it used to be. Housing has always been at the heart of political tensions. The rental barracks of the nineteenth century, with so many people living cheek by jowl, helped lead to the development of the socialist movement; in the 1920s and 1930s rent strikes were commonplace as politics lurched to the extremes. West Berlin of the Cold War was synonymous with squats. Since reunification, the city has been growing on average by 40,000 people per year, many upwardly mobile people from other parts of Germany and abroad. As a result, low-income residents have been pushed further out. Yet the city's population is still below the peak before the Second World War. Germany has one of the lowest home-owning rates in Europe and, over the past decade, rent in the capital has more than doubled.

Two radical initiatives have been launched; neither has yet succeeded but neither has disappeared. In 2020 the city tried to impose a rent cap, but the Constitutional Court struck it down, arguing that such powers lie with the federal government. The other initiative was an attempt to expropriate (or nationalize) properties from any corporate landlord that owns more than 3,000 apartments. The total number of apartments at stake was nearly a quarter of a million. The campaigners cite two provisions of the constitution. They argue that Article 14 allows for property to be taken back into public ownership if it is being misused: 'Property entails obligations. Its use shall also serve the public good.' This, they say, is corroborated by the subsequent Article 15, which states: 'Land, natural resources and means of production may for the purpose of socialisation be transferred to public ownership or other forms of public enterprise by a law that determines the nature and extent of compensation.'

So much of what defines Berlin meets at the issue of housing: the city that has long prided itself on its socialism and working-class solidarity (but can never quite get its revolutions to succeed); the city that is suspicious of outside influences only to co-opt them; the city that always seeks to be different. Berlin does not want to be like New York or London. It wants to be at the centre of the world; but it also wants a quiet life.

Historian Benedikt Goebel attributes the problem to something more prosaic: a failure of planning. He has spent his career agitating for a new approach, curating an exhibition a few years ago on *Berlin's Stolen Centre*. Yes, monuments and memorials are put up, particularly to the crimes of the twentieth century; yes, tourists flock to the Brandenburg Gate and the other sights; but, he argues, the historical heart of the city has been denuded of life. Whereas so much of Berlin is buzzing, much of the very centre, the streets behind and between Unter den Linden and Alexanderplatz, remain almost dead, especially at night and at weekends. Restaurants have sprung up, of varying quality. In a bid to inject some street life, a southern section of Friedrichstrasse has been closed to car traffic (to the fury of motorists), but most of the shops have little charm and little custom. Part of this is the legacy of late-GDR architecture; some of it is global and contemporary.

There is another, more inspiring way of looking at the new Berlin. It is the city that continues to think hard about its difficult past, and how that past influences the future.

Walk briskly past the hideous headquarters of Daimler and Sony (courtesy of starchitects Renzo Piano and Helmut Jahn) on Potsdamer Platz and you will find the remnants of a railway terminus. Anhalter Bahnhof, and the area around it, is the Berlin story in microcosm. Of all the stations of the great era of industrialization of the mid-nineteenth century, this was the most evocative. Built in 1841, it started relatively small. As the money rolled in, as Berlin grew in status and power, it was demolished and reopened in 1880, by both Kaiser Wilhelm I and Bismarck. The lavish terminus, the 'gateway to the south', would cater for four classes of ticket holders – with a separate entrance (and hotel) for royal and diplomatic visitors. Its intricate terracotta entrance portico was dominated by a sculpture, *Day and Night*, by Ludwig Brunow. Modelled on Michelangelo, it depicts two figures: Night, a woman, and Day, a man. As she falls asleep, he awakens – the eternal cycle of life. These statues held the great clock which welcomed people from destinations as far away as Naples and Athens. The glamorous square onto which the station faced was named Askanischer Platz, in honour of the House of Ascania, the ruling dynasty of Anhalt since the Middle Ages. At its peak in the 1930s, trains left the six platforms at Anhalter Bahnhof every three to five minutes, carrying an average of 44,000 people a day, around sixteen million a year, making it one of the busiest stations in Europe.

Now only its façade remains, a husk. Like the Kaiser Wilhelm Memorial Church, the chipped tooth at the end of the Ku'damm, it is one of several once-grand nineteenth-century edifices that stand as testament to human folly. Albert Speer had more grandiose plans for a north–south axis, and the station stood in his way. Instead, the Nazis got diverted by the war, and so they used the station (one of three in the city, the others being Grunewald and the Moabit goods depot) to transport Jews to the gas chambers. On 2 June 1942, at 6.07 a.m., a train carrying fifty elderly Jewish men and women left platform 1 for Theresienstadt, the first in a succession of death transports from Anhalter Bahnhof.

On one single night, eighteen months later, on 23 November 1943, a Royal Air Force raid reduced much of Anhalter to rubble, though some of the tracks survived. By late 1945 and over two desperately cold winters, the area around the station became a tent city. Tens of thousands of Germans, forced out from their Eastern lands, arrived at the ruin, disoriented, with nowhere to go. A reverse caravan. Margaret Bourke-White, a *Life* magazine photographer, took a series of images of emaciated women and children filling every space, some clinging to the sides of those trains that managed to leave. 'They began to resemble barnacles,' she wrote. The trains continued to use the roofless building from

1946 to 1952, but as the destinations ended up mostly in the GDR, the authorities there re-routed the tracks to serve the Ostbahnhof station after that. What remained of Anhalter Bahnhof was left derelict until all but the portico was demolished in 1960. A large concert venue, the Tempodrom, was later built on the grounds, alongside a sports field named after Lilli Henoch. Germany's greatest multisports athlete in the 1920s (and a Jew), who set world records in shot, discus and the long jump, she was deported along with her mother and shot by the Nazis in the Riga Ghetto in September 1943.

Over the last few years, whenever I walked past this desolate area, my thoughts turned to Germany's willingness to take in the world's most destitute – the more than a million refugees from Syria, Iraq and Afghanistan and more recently a similar number from Ukraine. The migrant story never stops. In 2022, it was salutary to stand on platform 13 of Hauptbahnhof, Berlin's gleaming new central station, watching thousands of Ukrainians descending, bewildered, from special trains. They were greeted by volunteers wearing brightly coloured bibs, providing them haven. Many Ukrainians will return home; most of those from the Middle East and North Africa will inevitably become the next generation of Berliners, people who come from somewhere to seek solace in this of all cities.

Two museums, one recently opened, the second and larger one planned for 2026, aim to put the refugee story in a German context; both have deliberately been sited at Anhalter Bahnhof. The sports pitch will soon be no more, as the ground will be laid for a new Exile Museum that will tell the human stories of migrants around the world. The station's portico ruins will form its front, with a new structure, a wide arc designed by a Danish architect, Dorte Mandrup, directly behind it.

Across the road, in a far less grand modern building, an exhibition centre opened during the pandemic that marks one of the most important attempts yet to help explain Berlin's confused identity. It is called *Dokumentationszentrum Flucht, Vertreibung, Versöhnung*. Described as 'Germany's new Centre for Learning and Remembrance for Displacement, Expulsion and Forced Migration', it devotes half of its space to addressing an issue that until recently was not part of mainstream political discourse.

More than 12.5 million physically and emotionally scarred people, who had lost their homes in what had been German lands in the East, had to be hurriedly re-settled and absorbed into post-war West and East Germany in just a few years. In some municipalities, expellees came close to constituting a majority. Every fifth person in Germany is from a family of expellees and yet for decades the issue was considered toxic. It scratches at a sore, asking the painful question of whether the Germans, the culprits, can ever be seen as victims. With each generation that has passed, the discussion seems to have become more, not less, agonizing.

Few commemorative projects in Berlin are as controversial as this. The idea of a permanent exhibition for Germany's displaced was first mooted back in 1999. For decades the issue was the exclusive preserve of the right or far right. The Federation of Expellees was formed in 1957 to lobby for Germans driven from their homes. A number of laws were passed, notably the 'Law of Return' which granted citizenship to any 'ethnic' German, no matter where they found themselves. Hence the huge influx from the former USSR in the 1980s and 1990s. The organization was led by a veteran member of parliament from the CDU, who ended up endorsing the AfD.

In recent years, the immediate post-war era has become an object of increased interest among German historians and sociologists. The great achievement of the museum, wrote the columnist Jörg Lau, is to remember German suffering without relativizing that suffering. 'Sudden expulsions; preventative flight, organised deportations, evacuations, expropriations, deprivation of rights, rape, mass murder – everything that is terrible is represented here,' he writes. He describes it as 'a house for the unhoused'.

Around ten million of the displaced made it to West Germany. The more than two million who ended up in the GDR were officially forgotten; these *Umsiedler*, 'new citizens', were never recognized, even though they comprised fully a fifth of the whole population. They could not talk about what happened to them, compounding their sense of disorientation. Reunification in 1990 allowed the descendants of these once-new GDR citizens to finally unearth and understand the history.

The first floor of the exhibition focuses on stories from afar: the refugees from the Sahel, Syria, former Yugoslavia and other war regions and the heroic story of the German boat that in the 1980s helped save more than 10,000 Vietnamese from the high seas. The floor above looks at the more contentious subject of the German displaced. Both sections focus on questions of universal significance: why are people expelled or forced to migrate? What are the paths they have to travel? What does it mean to lose one's homeland? How can those affected make a new start? Each mention of the Second World War is followed by the phrase 'which was initiated by Germany'. I have the feeling that every information board has been pored over by dozens of museum folk in advance; the sensitivities are acute.

Liberally scattered on tables are copies of a special supplement of the newspaper *Die Welt* focusing on the exhibition. Its lead piece is written by Wolfgang Thierse. Speaker of the Bundestag for a decade on either side of the millennium, he too comes from the displaced. Like many, he can call on personal experience. His family was forced to flee Breslau, now Wroclaw. A Social Democrat, Thierse fought hard to give the issue political priority, ensuring that it featured in the coalition agreement of the first Merkel government in 2005. Under the heading 'Loss and suppression can make you ill', Thierse says, 'Painful history must be portrayed and made tangible in a way that does not offset Nazi crimes or suggest moral equivalence, but rather shows their inseparable connection.' He then adds, 'Does the argument never end? Is the story of flight and displacement also a past that does not want to pass?'

Berlin often struggles to get the basics right. The story of its new airport, delayed a dozen years and still malfunctioning, has left a scar. As has the fiasco of the September 2021 general elections. City Hall had seemingly forgotten that the vote was taking place on the same day as the Berlin Marathon, leading to chaos. Shortly before stepping down as mayor that same year, Michael Müller insisted that criticism is as old as the city itself. The solution was to learn from history: 'We have the wit, we have the plans of our forefathers since the middle of the nineteenth century, who within a few years transformed Berlin from a village to a metropolis of millions – and we have the experiences of suffering of the twentieth century – to be successful in the future.'

Given all that it has been through, given the terror of many Berliners of being like others, what exactly does success mean for their city now? If it is about being a *Weltstadt*, that was achieved only once, for that brief period between 1871 and 1914. Is it on course to achieve the accolade of 'world city' again? Does it want it? And what does it mean in a contemporary context?

The city government thinks it knows the answer, or at least the direction of travel. It recently published its 'Strategy for 2030', talking of Berlin as 'the city of freedom'. It draws explicit parallels with the past, 'a place of longing for social change' just as it was 'in the 1920s, 1970s, 1980s and 1990s'. It goes on: 'A place of two dictatorships in the twentieth century, the short age of extremes, today's Berlin stands for new beginnings.' In other words, it is about continuing to question, continuing to learn.

Berlin never stands still. It is never satisfied. It never believes it has the answer. That is what makes this city remarkable, what draws the world to it and what impels me to keep coming back.

For my last morning of research, I do what I have always promised myself I would never do. I decide to go up the TV Tower, communist East Berlin's pride and joy, spruced up and repurposed for the modern era. The furniture is still GDR best, all orange and brown – kitsch seemingly still sells. The vegan breakfast menu offers home-made carrot and pea dip, with lentil salad, sunflower seeds and soy yoghurt with granola. I choose the traditional option of hearty meats and cheeses. For the next two hours I circumnavigate the city three times, hoping that an aerial view will provide further clues about the city's future.

Blessed by a bright blue sky, I gaze down at Unter den Linden and all the landmarks. I notice how small the Brandenburg Gate really is and how tiny it would have been if Albert Speer had got his way. I get a sense of how the Humboldt Forum might, before too long, start to feel integral to the centre of the city. Turning back eastwards again I see the dome of the New Synagogue glistening in the sun. The Volksbühne theatre nearby is far larger and more imposing than I realized. And then come the row upon row of spectacularly ugly concrete blocks in the East, stretching as far as the eye can see. Lenin no longer stands tall; Leninallee is now the blandly named Landsberger Allee. But the Soviet legacy is ever visible, unlike the Nazi legacy, which is thrust back onto the city through memorials. You cannot see so much of Berlin's history, but you can feel it everywhere.

Berlin does not come together, but it somehow hangs together. From on high, as at ground level, it is still a work in progress, as it almost always has been. It is not a city in the conventional sense, but a succession of ruptures, each superimposing itself on what came before. Each era creates a new set of buildings and a new set of inhabitants, each embarking on the never-ending task of reinvention.

Acknowledgements

This book has been a labour of love for me stretching five years, indeed more than three decades if I take into account my earlier incarnations in the divided Berlin of old. I couldn't have completed it – and I certainly wouldn't have had so much fun – without the assistance and company of so many people.

Some I have known for the duration. Others came into my Berlin life while I was researching *Why the Germans Do it Better*; yet others I met for the first time during my latest venture, among them many inspiring historians, city planners, architects and archaeologists.

I apologize in advance if I have omitted anyone.

For their time and insights, I am grateful to Sandra Anusiewicz Baer, Deirdre Berger, Maria Böttche, Annette von Broecker, David Chipperfield, Gesa Edeberg, Felix Escher, Harald Hauswald, Winfried Heinemann, Hans-Albert Hoffmann, Dieter Hoffmann-Axthelm, Harald Jähner, Axel Klausmeier, Kerstin Krupp, Neil MacGregor, Jane Martens, Brendan Nash, Hermann Simon, Florian Schmidt, Karl Schlögel, Julius Schoeps and Philipp Wasserscheidt.

I was privileged to meet a number of museum directors: Hartmut Dorgerloh at the Humboldt Forum, Urte Evert at the

Spandau Citadel, Raphael Gross at the Deutsches Historisches Museum, Matthias Wemhoff at the Museum of Prehistory and Early History. Thanks to them and to other museum colleagues: Werner Borchert at Wünsdorf, Kay-Uwe von Damaros at the Topography of Terror, Alexander Klein at the Museum of Military History in Dresden, Susanne Lehmann at Rixdorf, Mario Marcus at Fraenkelufer, Michael Mathis at the Humboldt Forum and Antje Zeiger at the Thirty Years War Museum in Wittstock.

I'm grateful to my colleagues at Young Königswinter, Thomas Matussek and Mari Mittelhaus, to Paul Smith at the British Council in Berlin and to Katharina von Ruckteschell-Katte at the Goethe Institut in London.

Particular thanks go to the German ambassador to London, Miguel Berger, and to his predecessor, Andreas Michaelis, and to their colleagues for all their support over several years, including Susanne Frane and Clemens Kohnen; to Philip Roessler and others at the Auswärtiges Amt in Berlin. And to the British ambassador to Berlin, Jill Gallard, Deputy Head of Mission Kieran Drake, and their colleagues too.

For their hospitality and friendship, I'm very grateful to Thomas Bagger, Charlie Best and Eliza Mellor, Hélène de Bock and Kai Küstner, David Cannadine and Linda Colley, Corazon Rial y Costas, Uwe Fechner, Andrew Gilmour, Philip Green and Susan Marks, Tanit Koch, Benedetta Lacey and Mark Pallis, Rüdiger Lentz, Oliver Moody, Andrea Ricciarelli, Jess Smee, William Spaulding, Miles Taylor, Daniel Tetlow and to Johannes Vogel and Sarah Darwin.

As readers of the book will attest, this was a journey that involved many people providing me with geographic and historical insights I might not otherwise have gathered. The following did all of that, but they also gave up considerable time to read later manuscripts of the book and to provide comments. I am therefore hugely indebted to the following: Robert and Monika Birnbaum,

Barbara Burckhardt and Hardy Schmitz, Guy Chazan, Benedikt Goebel, Reiner Kneifel-Haverkamp, Tony Joyce, Andreas Kossert, Jörg and Mariam Lau, Damien McGuinness, Claudia Melisch, Alan Posener and Boris Ruge.

It has been a pleasure to work with the team at Atlantic again, with managing director Will Atkinson, publicist Kate Straker and other colleagues; I've immensely enjoyed working with my new editor, Poppy Hampson. In Berlin, I'm grateful to my agent Michaela Röll, and I'm delighted to have Jonny Geller as my global agent and to be part of his fabulous team at Curtis Brown.

This book would not be what it is without my two researchers. Roberta Ahlers enthusiastically got the project going; as for Isabel (Izzy) Blankfield, she is a star in the making, as Columbia University is about to find out.

To my family – my wife Lucy and my daughters Alex and Constance – as ever, for their love and support during this and many journeys past, present and future. I dedicate this book to Lucy's father, Eric Ash, who left Charlottenburg long ago but always kept a suitcase in Berlin.

List of Maps

Maps on pp. viii–ix, p. 72, p. 82, p. 242, p. 324 drawn by Jamie Whyte.

p. 22, Grundriss Der Beyden Churf. Residentz Stätte Berlin Und Cölln an Der Spree, Johann Gregor Memhardt, 1652 (Digitale Landesbibliothek Berlin)

p. 143, *Fighting for the Soul of Germany: The Catholic Struggle for Inclusion After Unification* by Rebecca Ayako Bennette, Cambridge, Mass.: Harvard University Press, Copyright © 2012 by the President and Fellows of Harvard College. Used by permission. All rights reserved.

p. 230, Welthauptstadt Germania (CPA Media Pte Ltd/Alamy Stock Photo)

p. 284, Berlin Wall and the border control checkpoints until 1989 (© A. Darmochwal/User: Sansculotte/Wikimedia Commons, CC-BY-SA-3.0)

Notes

Introduction

3 'a place of longing for those who have found it too cramped elsewhere' – F. Steinmeier, speech on the occasion of award of honorary citizenship of the State of Berlin to the Federal President, Berlin, 4 October 2021.

One: Eight hundred years and one world house

13 'This is the great new problem of mankind' – M. L. King, *Where Do We Go from Here: Chaos or Community?*, Beacon Press, 2010.

15 'meeting point of three ancient glaciers' – see B. White-Spunner, *Berlin: The Story of a City*, Simon & Schuster, 2020, pp. 28–33.

18 'The first two books stipulate the finances and privileges of the city' – *Berlinisches Stadtbuch*, Grunert, 1883.

20 'The population grew slowly' – see A. Richie, *Faust's Metropolis: A History of Berlin*, HarperCollins, Kindle edition, 2013, pp. 110–38.

26 'The Central Council of Jews accused the musicians' – 'Antisemitismus-Beauftragter kritisiert Rammstein-Video', *Süddeutsche Zeitung*, 28 March 2019, https://www. sueddeutsche.de/kultur/rammstein-video-single-deutschland-1.4386620 (accessed 25 January 2023).

Two: *Nobody's palace*

37 'The people rubbed their eyes' – V. Mayer, 'Wilhelm von Boddien. Das Spendeherz', *Tagesspiegel*, 28 November 2008, https://www.tagesspiegel.de/kultur/das-spenderherz-1718989.html (accessed 19 April 2023).

38 'Gregor Gysi' – 'Rettungsaktion für den Palast und Gysi', *nd*, 22 November 1997, https://www.nd-aktuell.de/artikel/687707.rettungsaktion-fuer-den-palast-und-gysi.html (accessed 2 December 2022).

39 'a compromise between Honecker and Hohenzollern'– 'Paßt zum Palazzo eine Preußenkuppel?', *taz*, 21 April 1992, p. 21, https://taz.de/Passt-zum-Palazzo-eine-Preussenkuppel/! 1673365/ (accessed 2 August 2022).

41 'like Chernobyl' – B. Savoy in conversation with J. Häntzschel, 'Das Humboldt-Forum ist wie Tschernobyl', *Süddeutsche Zeitung*, 21 July 2017, p. 9.

Three: *A very modern conflict*

48 'So, now we are destroyed' – A. Gryphius, *Deutscher Gedichte. Erster Theil.* (*Sonnette, Das Erste Buch*), Lischke, 1657, pp. 14–15.

50 'cowardly weakling' – see B. Simms, *Europe: The Struggle for Supremacy, 1453 to the Present*, Penguin, 2013.

54 'A new war threatens' – B. Brecht, *Gesammelte Werke*, Bd. 17, p. 1149.

55 'much more than a distant piece of history' – R. Pfister, 'Apokalypse Merkel', *Spiegel*, 1 June 2018, https://www.spiegel.de/politik/angela-merkel-und-der-blick-auf-die-geschichte-apokalypse-merkel-a-00000000-0002-0001-0000-000157647567?context=issue (accessed 2 December 2022).

55 'recurring pattern' – F. Haupt, B. Kohler, 'Es ist richtig, dass das jetzt ein anderer übernimmt', *Frankfurter Allgemeine*

Zeitung, 30 October 2021, https://www.faz.net/aktuell/politik/inland/merkel-im-interview-ueber-fluechtlinge-die-csu-den-zustand-der-welt-und-ihr-blick-aufs-aelterwerden-17609086.html (accessed 19 April 2023).

Four: Les nouveaux Prussiens

64 'Admission of Fifty Families of Protected Jews; But They Are Not to Have Synagogues' – see C. A. Macartney (ed.), *The Habsburg and Hohenzollern Dynasties in the Seventeenth and Eighteenth Centuries, in Documentary History of Western Civilization*, Harper & Row, 1970, pp. 259–63.

69 'A day in a beautiful city combined with dark history' – 'Oranienburg & Sachsenhausen: Day trip from Berlin', Tours By Locals, https://www.toursbylocals.com/Oranienburg-Sachsenhausen-VIP-all-inclusive-private-tour-full-day-Berlin (accessed 19 April 2023).

70 'Brandenburger Gold Coast' – see F. Brahm and E. Rosenhaft (eds.), *Slavery Hinterland: Transatlantic Slavery and Continental Europe, 1680–1850*, Boydell & Brewer, 2016, pp. 26–30.

71 'luxuries at the royal court' – see R. L. Gawthrop, *Pietism and the Making of Eighteenth-Century Prussia*, Cambridge University Press, 1993, p. 57.

71 'King *in* Prussia' – see H. Holborn, *A History of Modern Germany: 1648–1840*, Princeton University Press, 1982, p. 104.

71 'Friedrich had himself crowned in an elaborate ceremony' – see C. Clark, 'When culture meets power: the Prussian coronation of 1701,' in H. Scott and B. Simms (eds.), *Cultures of Power in Europe during the Long Eighteenth Century*, Cambridge University Press, 2007, pp. 14–35.

74 'court of the muses' – see E. Exner, 'The Sophies of Hanover and Royal Prussian Music', *Kulturgeschichte Preußens, Colloquien 6*, 2018.

Five: The torments of hell

77 'hus to wusterhausen' – see 'Stadtjubiläum', *kw-im-internet.de*, November 2019, https://www.kw-im-internet.de/Artikel/ Stadtjubilaeum/5644 (accessed 25 January 2023).

78 'he dismantled every facet of his father's court' – see P. Baumgart, 'Friedrich Wilhelm I. (1713–1740)', in F. Kroll (ed.), *Preußens Herrscher. Von den ersten Hohenzollern bis Wilhelm II*, C. H. Beck, 2000, pp. 134–159. Here p. 141.

79 'the king was known to walk the streets' – see S. Fischer-Fabian, *Preußens Gloria: Der Aufstieg eines Staates*, Bastei Lübbe, 2007, p. 86.

80 'Akzisemauer' – S. Schmettau, *Plan De La Ville De Berlin*, Neaulm Libraire, 1757.

85 'All that remains' – B. Seewald, 'So muss "der Tiefpunkt höfischer Malerei" wirklich gedeutet werden', *Die Welt*, 5 May 2022. https://www.welt.de/geschichte/article206621383/ Das-zeigt-das-beruehmte-Tabakskollegium-wirklich.html (accessed 2 December 2022).

87 'a monument to commemorate his 50,000th kill' – R. Waite, *Kaiser and Führer: A Comparative Study of Personality and Politics*, University of Toronto Press, 1998, pp. 3–67.

89 'to stir up passions that were just about to settle down' – 'Picture Plays and People', *New York Times*, 28 May 1922.

90 'the most destructive role of all the German territorial states' – H. Kathe, *Der "Soldatenkönig": Friedrich Wilhelm I. 1688– 1740*, Akademie Verlag, 1978.

90 'the first protector and promoter of human rights in the 18th century' – W. Venohr, *Der Soldatenkönig. Revolutionar auf dem Thron*, Ullstein Verlag, 1988, p. 350.

Six: Sparta and Athens

93 'that evil man' – see H. Holborn, *A History of Modern Germany 1684–1840*, Princeton University Press, 1982.

96 'a state of homosexual debauchery' – Voltaire, *Mémoires de M. de Voltaire*, Chez Robinson, 1784.

96 'Grecian taste in love' – J. G. Zimmermann, M. Neuman (trans.), 'On Frederick's Supposed Grecian Taste in Love', *Select Views of the Life, Reign, and Character of Frederick the Great, King of Prussia*, Hookham and Carpenter, 1792, pp. 45–6.

106 'The two best-known hostesses' – see U. Im Hof, *Enlightenment: An Introduction (The Making of Europe)*, John Wiley and Sons, 1994, p. 116.

110 'the Mendelssohn family' – see J. Schoeps, *Das Erbe der Mendelssohns: Biographie einer Familie*, Fischer Taschenbuch Verlag, 2011.

112 'The cover depicts' – W. Freiherr von Müffling, *Wegbereiter und Vorkämpfer für das neue Deutschland*, J. F. Lehmanns Verlag, 1933.

113 'Erich Honecker granted an audience to Robert Maxwell' – 'Verleger Robert Maxwell von Erich Honecker empfangen', *nd*, 26 August 1980, https://www.nd-archiv.de/artikel/234408. verleger-robert-maxwell-von-erich-honecker-empfangen.html (accessed 25 January 2023).

115 'It meticulously avoided taking any definite standpoint whatsoever' – C. Lattek, 'Preussen: Versuch Einer Bilanz, the Prussia Exhibition, Berlin, August to November 1981', *History Workshop*, 13, 1982, 174–180, JSTOR, http://www.jstor.org/stable/4288414 (accessed 15 February 2023).

115 'a cunning attempt "to rehabilitate the Prussian militarism that unleashed two world wars"' – E. Lentz, 'Prussia Rediscovered in West German Display', *New York Times*, 24 August 1981, https://www.nytimes.com/1981/08/24/arts/prussia-rediscovered-in-west-german-display.html (accessed 15 February 2023).

115 'Berlin succumbed to Friedrich-mania' – M. Chambers, 'Germans bury Prussia taboo to fete Frederick', Reuters, 27 January 2012, https://www.reuters.com/article/uk-germany-

frederick-idUSLNE80Q00W20120127 (accessed 15 February 2023).

Seven: Reformers and radicals

119 'This evening the entire town was illuminated' – *Le Moniteur*, 4 November 1806.

120 'horse thief of Berlin' – see S. Magill, 'When Napoléon conquered Berlin', *Exberliner*, 11 March 2022, https://www. exberliner.com/berlin/when-napoleon-conquered-berlin/ (accessed 15 February 2023).

122 'soul of national virtue' – see T. Fisher, G. Fremont-Barnes, B. Cornwell, *The Napoleonic Wars: The Rise and Fall of an Empire*, Osprey Publishing, 2004, p. 254.

125 'German Romanticism emerged' – see H. Kohn, 'Romanticism and the Rise of German Nationalism', *The Review of Politics*, vol. 12, no. 4, 1950, pp. 443–72, JSTOR, http://www.jstor.org/ stable/1404884 (accessed 7 October 2022).

127 'complete human being' – see M. Wertz, 'Education and Character: The Classical Curriculum of Wilhelm von Humboldt', *Fidelio*, vol. 5, no. 2, Summer 1996.

130 'the only institution' – see C. Clark, *Time and Power: Visions of History in German Politics, from the Thirty Years' War to the Third Reich*, Princeton University Press, 2021, p. 164.

132 'Berlin's first popular uprising' – see M. Gailus, 'Food Riots in Germany in the Late 1840s', *Past & Present*, no. 145, 1994, pp. 157–93, JSTOR, http://www.jstor.org/stable/651248 (accessed 13 January 2023).

135 'Germany is in ferment within' – Friedrich Wilhelm IV, 'To My People and to the German Nation', declaration issued 21 March 1848.

135 'There are no revolutions in Germany' – A. de Tocqueville, *Oeuvres complètes. L'ancien régime et la Révolution*, vol. 2, Paris, 1952, p. 69.

136 'I used to visit the cemetery' – K. Kollwitz, *Das neue Kollwitz Werk*, Reissner, 1933.

Eight: Finally, very rich

141 'the parvenu capital' – see S. Hastings, *Sybille Bedford: A Life*, Knopf Doubleday, 2021.

141 'Theodor Fontane had written' – E. Schnurr, 'Berlin's Turn of the Century Growing Pains', *Spiegel*, 22 November 2012, https://www.spiegel.de/international/germany/the-late-19th-century-saw-the-birth-of-modern-berlin-a-866321.html (accessed 14 April 2023).

144 'at the Palace of Versailles' – see H. F. Nöhbauer, *Ludwig II of Bavaria, Louis II de Bavière*, Taschen, 1998.

144 'On 16 June, on a brilliantly clear Sunday' – see A. Bartetzky, 'Feier des Reiches aus Eisen und Blut', *Frankfurter Allgemeine Zeitung*, 16 June 2021, https://www.faz.net/aktuell/feuilleton/debatten/berliner-siegesfeier-am-16-juni-1871-17390445.html?printPagedArticle=true#pageIndex_2 (accessed 15 February 2023).

145 'feared that they would be overshadowed' – see D. Clay Large, *Berlin*, Basic Books, 2001, p. xxi.

149 'The economic boom' – see F. Escher, *Berlin Wird Metropole: Eine Geschichte der Region*, Elsengold Verlag, 2020.

155 'For when the German has once learned' – Kaiser Wilhelm II, speech to the North German Regatta Association, 18 June 1901.

156 'The most beautiful city in the world' – W. Rathenau, *Die schönste Stadt der Welt*, CEP Europäische Verlagsanstalt, 2015 [1899].

156 'three quarters of its buildings' – *Baedeker's Berlin and its Environs*, Baedeker, 1903.

158 'trying to be cultured' – K. Scheffler, *Berlin – ein Stadtschicksal*, Suhrkamp Verlag, 2015 [1910].

Nine: Sleeping in shifts

159 'The streets were laid out in parallel lines' – see A. Cripps, 'Mietskasernes: Working Class Berlin, 1871–1922', 19 March 2014, https://aaroncrippsblog.wordpress.com/2014/03/19/mietskasernes-working-class-berlin-1871-1922/ (accessed 14 April 2023).

162 'Engels saw the *Zimmer* as' – 'Schrank, Esstisch, Anrichte: Das steckt hinter dem legendären "Berliner Zimmer"', *Berliner Zeitung*, 18 April 2017, https://www.berliner-zeitung.de/mensch-metropole/schrank-esstisch-anrichte-das-steckt-hinter-dem-legendaeren-berliner-zimmer-li.10821 (accessed 15 February 2023).

162 'In the poorest parts of the city' – see A. Lange, *Das wilhelminische Berlin*, Dietz, 1984, p. 42.

163 'flat, barren plains' – E. Dronke, *Berlin*, Die Andere Bibliothek, 2019 [1846].

163 'Yet another building has collapsed' – D. Kalisch, R. Bial, *Haussegen oder Berlin wird Weltstadt*, EOD Network, 2013 [1866].

166 'The sociologist George Steinmetz' – G. Steinmetz, 'Workers and the Welfare State in Imperial Germany', *International Labor and Working-Class History*, 40, 1991, pp. 18–46. JSTOR, http://www.jstor.org/stable/27671962 (accessed 15 February 2023).

167 'By 1900, more than 60 per cent of Berliners' – W. Ribbe (ed.), *Geschichte Berlins. Vol. II. Von der Märzrevolution bis zur Gegenwart*, C. H. Beck, 1987, pp. 692–7.

170 'repugnant, ugly and mean' – see P. Paret, *The Berlin Secession: Modernism and Its Enemies in Imperial Germany*, Harvard University Press, 1980.

171 'All middle-class life' – see T. Fecht, *Käthe Kollwitz: Works in Color*, Random House, 1988, p. 6.

172 'The souls of countless workers' – see I. Berndt, I. Flemming,

Käthe Kollwitz in Berlin: Ein Stadtrundgang, Lukas Verlag, 2015, p. 55.

175 'It has now become something of a pietà' – Kollwitz K., *The Diary and Letters of Kaethe Kollwitz*, Northwestern University Press, 1988.

Ten: At the edge of my days

177 'Born in Leipzig' – see L. Fischer, *Anita Berber, ein getanztes Leben. Eine Biographie*, Hendrik Bäßler Verlag, 2014.
181 'People have said' – K. Tucholsky, 'White Spots', *Berlin! Berlin! Dispatches From the Weimar Republic*, Berlinica, 2013, pp. 66–8.
183 'The cauldron was growing hotter' – G. Grosz, *A Small Yes and a Big No*, Allison & Busby, 1982.
190 'Some of the most enduring representations of the era' – F. Hessel, *Walking in Berlin*, Scribe, 2016.
193 'My drawings expressed my despair' – G. Grosz, op. cit.
196 'One of the first public pioneers of gay life' – see R. Beachy, *Gay Berlin: Birthplace of a Modern Identity*, Vintage, 2015.
199 'smashed buildings' – C. Isherwood, *Christopher and His Kind*, Random House, 2012 [1976], p. 135.
205 'I grew up in this big, sober, austere Berlin' – A. Döblin, '[Mein Standort]' (1930), *Schriften zu Leben und Werk*, Fischer Klassik, 1986, pp. 193–4.

Eleven: The city that cannot stop remembering

209 'In total, more than 2,800 prisoners' – 'Die Blutnächte von Plötzensee', Gedenkstätte Plötzensee, https://www. gedenkstaette-ploetzensee.de/die-blutnaechte-von-ploetzensee (accessed 15 February 2023).
217 'Berlin had 160,000 registered Jews' – 'German Jews During

The Holocaust, 1939–1945', United States Holocaust Memorial
Museum, https://encyclopedia.ushmm.org/content/en/article/
german-jews-during-the-holocaust (accessed 19 April 2023).

218 'As Deutsche Bahn' – 'Gemeinsame Erklärung gegen
Antisemitismus und Rassismus von DB, BVB, Daimler,
Deutsche Bank und VW', Deutsche Bahn Konzern, YouTube,
26 January 2021, https://www.youtube.com/watch?v=
BnZBtRrF6i0&ab_channel=DeutscheBahnKonzern (accessed
15 February 2023).

224 'Operation Valkyrie' – see W. Heinemann, *Operation
'Valkyrie': A Military History of the 20 July 1944 Plot*, De
Gruyter Oldenbourg, 2022.

226 'Goebbels was said to have called Berlin' – Klußmann, 'Labor
der Diktatur', *Spiegel Geschichte*, 24 September 2012,
https://www.spiegel.de/geschichte/labor-der-diktatur-a-
22ed87ad-0002-0001-0000-000088536783?context=issue
(accessed 15 February 2023).

226 'In the November 1932 general election' – see R. Lemmons,
'Goebbels and Der Angriff', *European History*, 9, 1994, p. 41.

228 'Hitler's dream was to raze swathes of Berlin' – K. Connolly,
'Story of cities #22: how Hitler's plans for Germania would
have torn Berlin apart', the *Guardian*, 14 April 2016.

235 'discovered a marble bull' – C. Bauer, S. Kollmann, '"Weißer
Stier vom Humboldthain" in Berlin wieder aufgetaucht',
Berlin Morgenpost, 13 April 2022, https://www.morgenpost.de/
berlin/article235065573/Verschwundener-Stier-von-Hitler-
Bildhauer-wiedergefunden.html (accessed 14 April 2023).

Twelve: Subsidy city

243 '16 July 1945' – see H. Jähner, *Aftermath: Life in the Fallout of
the Third Reich*, W. H. Allen, 2022.

245 'After the war over half the population' – Jähner, op.cit., p. i.

250 'Ernst Reuter was one of the city's main advocates' – see
W. Brandt, R. Löwenthal, *Ernst Reuter. Ein Leben für die
Freiheit* (*Eine politische Biographie*), Kindler Verlag, 1957.

264 '*Atlantic* magazine' – 'Writers in Berlin: A Three-Way
Discussion', *The Atlantic*, December 1963, https://www.
theatlantic.com/magazine/archive/1963/12/writers-in-berlin-a-
three-way-discussion/657554/ (accessed 19 April 2023).

265 'poor but sexy' – K. Wowereit, interview with *Focus Money*,
November 2003.

265 '*Rolling Stone* magazine' – M. Charlton, 'Bowie's Berlin: the
locations behind the lyrics', *Rolling Stone*, https://www.
rollingstone.co.uk/music/bowies-berlin-the-locations-behind-
the-lyrics-10413/ (accessed 15 February 2023).

271 'Helmut Kohl, pledging to halve the size of the migrant
population' – C. Hecking, 'Kohl Wanted Half of Turks Out
of Germany', *Spiegel*, 1 August 2013, https://www.spiegel.de/
international/germany/secret-minutes-chancellor-kohl-
wanted-half-of-turks-out-of-germany-a-914376.html (accessed
15 February 2023).

271 'Germany's Turkish population is estimated at 2.75 million'
– *Einwohnerinnen und Einwohner im Land Berlin am 31.
Dezember 2019.* https://download.statistik-berlin-brandenburg.
de/3d9a920b098obdof/01f3c6a853b2/SB_A01-05-00_2019h02_
BE.pdf (accessed 2 December 2022).

272 'more kebab shops in Berlin than in Istanbul' – S. Khalil,
'Germany's favourite fast food', *BBC Travel*, 9 February 2017,
https://www.bbc.com/travel/article/20170203-germanys-
favourite-fast-food (accessed 15 February 2023).

273 '79,000 went to Berlin' – B. Katz, L, Noring, N. Garrelts, 'Cities
and Refugees: The German Experience', Centennial Scholar
Initiative at Brookings City Solution, 4, 2016, p. 18,
https://www.brookings.edu/wp-content/uploads/2016/09/
cs_20160920_citiesrefugees_germanexperience.pdf (accessed
15 February 2023).

273 'campaigns of public solidarity' – B. Togral Koca, 2019, 'Urban citizenship and the spatial encounter between Turkish migrants and Syrian refugees in Berlin', Raumforschung und *Raumordnung/Spatial Research and Planning*, Sciendo, Warsaw, vol. 77, iss. 6, 2019, pp. 567–581, https://www.econstor. eu/bitstream/10419/222201/1/rara-2019-0023.pdf (accessed 15 February 2023).

273 'administrative chaos' – M. Eddy and K. Johannsen, 'Migrants Arriving in Germany Face a Chaotic Reception in Berlin', *New York Times*, 26 November 2015, https://www.nytimes. com/2015/11/27/world/europe/germany-berlin-migrants-refugees.html (accessed 15 February 2023).

Thirteen: Erich's lamp shop

278 'The commission's remit' – T. Harmsen, 'Überlebt Wilhelm die Straßen-Schlacht?', *Berliner Zeitung*, 18 September 1991, p. 22.

279 'In recent years it has been expanded' – 'Ausführungsvor-schriften zu § 5 des Berliner Straßengesetzes (AV Benennung)', Berlin, Senatsverwaltung für Umwelt, Verkehr und Klimaschutz, 2020, p. 3.

286 'The number of people known to have been killed' – H. Hertle, M. Nooke, 'The Victims at the Berlin Wall, 1961–1989', *Special CWIHP Research Report*, August 2011.

291 'the Pope's Revenge' – U. Dibelius, *Die Namen des Berliner Fernsehturms*, Zentral- und Landesbibliothek Berlin, 2007.

297 'The injustice, she told one newspaper' – M. Riepl, 'Das Unrecht verfolgt mich – bis an mein Lebensende', *Berliner Morgenpost*, 10 March 2012, https://www.morgenpost.de/ printarchiv/familie/article106060332/Das-Unrecht-verfolgt-mich-bis-an-mein-Lebensende.html (accessed 19 April 2023).

Fourteen: They came and never left

307 'Russia's rare interludes of modernization' – see K. Schlögel, *Das Russische Berlin*, Suhrkamp, 2019.

308 'A few steps from my flat' – 'Lenin in Moabit', *Das war Moabit. Informationsschrift anlässlich des 100. Jahrestages der Eingemeindung Moabits in die Stadt Berlin*. SED – Kreis Tiergarten, Berlin, 1961, https://moabitonline.de/46 (accessed 15 February 2023).

310 'the stepmother of all Russian cities' – V. Khodasevich, 'Всё каменное. В каменный пролет', I. P. Andreeva et al. (eds.), *Sobranie sochinenii v chetyrekh tomakh*, Moscow: Soglasie, 1996, p. 266.

310 'Saint Petersburg at Wittenbergplatz' – see Schlögel, op. cit.

315 'Sperenberg airfield lies abandoned' – C. Fahey, 'The Forbidden City: inside the abandoned Soviet camp of Wünsdorf', the *Guardian*, 11 January 2017, https://www.theguardian.com/cities/2017/jan/11/forbidden-city-inside-abandoned-soviet-camp-wunsdorf-east-germany (accessed 15 February 2023).

319 'Berlin's younger Russian diaspora' – see G. Chazan, 'Auf wiedersehen, Putin: Berlin's new Russian émigrés', *Financial Times*, 24 March 2017, https://www.ft.com/content/4bc00646-0e83-11e7-b030-768954394623 (accessed 15 February 2023).

Fifteen: Back where they belong

325 'Some 3,000 worshippers had secured a place' – 'Die Eröffnung der neuen Berliner Synagoge in der Oranienburger Straße und Louis Lewandowski' in S. Han, A. Middelbeck-Varwick, M. Thurau (eds.), *Bibel – Israel – Kirche. Studien zur jüdisch-christlichen Begegnung. Festschrift für Rainer Kampling*, Aschendorff, 2018, pp. 505–11.

328 'one of the most remarkable memoirs of its kind' – M. Jalowicz Simon, *Gone to Ground*, Profile Books, 2014.

331 'shouldering the responsibility for the reconstruction' –
H. Simon, 'Eröffnung der Neuen Synagoge als Centrum
Judaicum', speech at the Stiftung Neue Synagoge Berlin-
Centrum Judaicum, 7 May 1995.

344 'The project is being overseen' – 'Synagoge am Fraenkelufer in
Berlin-Kreuzberg: Raed Saleh schlägt Wiederaufbau vor',
Berliner Zeitung, 9 November 2017, https://www.berliner-
zeitung.de/mensch-metropole/synagoge-am-fraenkelufer-in-
berlin-kreuzberg-raed-saleh-schlaegt-wiederaufbau-vor-li.12255
(accessed 19 April 2023).

Sixteen: Fear of normality

349 'Historian Benedikt Goebel attributes the problem to
something more prosaic' – B. Goebel, 'Banalitätsmonster an
historischem Standort: Tiefpunkt der Berliner Architektur',
Berliner Zeitung, 19 October 2022, https://www.berliner-
zeitung.de/mensch-metropole/banalitaetsmonster-an-
historischem-standort-tiefpunkt-der-berliner-architektur-
li.278173 (accessed 15 February 2023).

350 'Margaret Bourke-White' – M. Bourke-White, *'Dear
Fatherland, Rest Quietly': A Report on the Collapse of Hitler's
'Thousand Years'*, Pickle Partners Publishing, 2018.

353 'Around ten million of the displaced' – see A. Kossert, *Flucht:
Eine Menschheitsgeschichte*, Siedler, 2020.

Bibliography

Baumgart, P., 'Friedrich Wilhelm I (1713–1740)', in F. Kroll (ed.), *Preußens Herrscher. Von den ersten Hohenzollern bis Wilhelm II*, C. H. Beck, 2000, p. 134–59.

Beachy, R., *Gay Berlin: Birthplace of a Modern Identity*, Vintage, 2015.

Beevor, A., *Berlin: The Downfall 1945*, Viking, 2002.

Bisky, J., *Berlin: Biographie einer großen Stadt*, Rowohlt e-Book, Kindle edition, 2019.

Bluhm, D. and Nitsche, R., *Berlin ist das Allerletzte: Absagen in höchsten Tönen*, Transit Buchverlag, 1993.

Boegel, N., *Berlin – Hauptstadt des Verbrechens: Die dunkle Seite der Goldenen Zwanziger*, Penguin, 2018.

Bourke-White, M., *"Dear Fatherland, Rest Quietly": A Report on the Collapse of Hitler's "Thousand Years"*, Pickle Partners Publishing, 2018.

Brahm, F. and Rosenhaft, E. (eds.), *Slavery Hinterland: Transatlantic Slavery and Continental Europe, 1680–1850*, Boydell & Brewer, 2016.

Clark, C., *Iron Kingdom: The Rise and Downfall of Prussia 1600–1947*, Allen Lane, 2006.

— *Revolutionary Spring: Fighting for a New World 1848–1849*, Allen Lane, 2023.

— 'When culture meets power: the Prussian coronation of 1701,' in Scott, H. and Simms, B. (eds.), *Cultures of Power in Europe during the Long Eighteenth Century*, Cambridge University Press, 2007, pp. 14–35.

Clay Large, D., *Berlin*, Basic Books, 2001.

Craig, G., *Germany: 1866–1945*, Oxford University Press, 1978.

Cramer, K., *The Thirty Years' War & German Memory in the Nineteenth Century*, University of Nebraska Press, 2007.

Döblin, A., '[Mein Standort]' (1930), *Schriften zu Leben und Werk*, Fischer Klassik, 1986, pp. 193–4.

Dronke, E., *Berlin*, Die Andere Bibliothek, 2019.

Escher, F., *Berlin Wird Metropole: Eine Geschichte der Region*, Elsengold Verlag, 2020.

Fischer-Fabian, S., *Preußens Gloria: Der Aufstieg eines Staates*, Bastei Lübbe, 2007.

Fontane, T., *Die Poggenpuhls*, Aufbau Taschenbuch, 2013.

Gawthrop, R. L., *Pietism and the Making of Eighteenth-Century Prussia*, Cambridge University Press, 1993.

Grosz, G., *A Small Yes and a Big No*, Allison & Busby, 1982.

Hegemann, W., *Das steinerne Berlin. Geschichte der grössten Mietskasernenstadt der Welt*, Vieweg, 1976.

Heinemann, W., *Operation 'Valkyrie': A Military History of the 20 July 1944 Plot*, De Gruyter Oldenbourg, 2022.

Hessel, F., *Walking in Berlin*, Scribe, 2016.

Heym, S., *Five Days in June*, Prometheus Books, 1978.

Hilmes, O., *Berlin 1936: Sixteen Days in August*, The Bodley Head, 2018.

Hoffmann-Axthelm, D., *Preußen am Schlesischen Tor: Die Geschichte der Köpenicker Straße 1589–1989*, Berlin Story Verlag GmbH; 1. Aufl. edition, 2015.

Holborn, H., *A History of Modern Germany: 1648–1840*, Princeton University Press, 1982.

Hubatsch, W., *Frederick the Great of Prussia: Absolutism and Administration*, Thames and Hudson, 1975.

Im Hof, U., *Enlightenment: An Introduction* (*The Making of Europe*), John Wiley & Sons, 1994.

Jähner, H., *Aftermath: Life in the Fallout of the Third Reich*, W. H. Allen, 2021.

Jalowicz Simon, M., *Gone to Ground*, Profile Books, 2014.

Kalisch, D. and Bial, R., *Haussegen oder Berlin wird Weltstadt*, EOD Network, 2013.

Kathe, H., *Der "Soldatenkönig": Friedrich Wilhelm I. 1688–1740*, Akademie Verlag, 1978.

Katz, B., Noring, L. and Garrelts, N., 'Cities and Refugees: The German Experience', Centennial Scholar Initiative at Brookings City Solution, 4, 2016.

Kohn, H., 'Romanticism and the Rise of German Nationalism', *The Review of Politics*, vol. 12, no. 4, 1950, pp. 443–72.

Kossert, A., *Flucht: Eine Menschheitsgeschichte*, Siedler, 2020.

Kugler, F. T. and Moriarty, E. A. (trans.), *History of Frederick the Great: Comprehending a Complete History of the Silesian Campaigns and the Seven Years' War*, Henry G. Bohn, 1845.

Ladd, B., *The Ghosts of Berlin: Confronting German History in the Urban Landscape*, University of Chicago Press, 1998.

Lange, A., *Das wilhelminische Berlin*, Dietz, 1984.

Lanz, A., *Berlin aufgemischt: abendländisch, multikulturell, kosmopolitisch? Die politische Konstruktion einer Einwanderungsstadt*, transcript Verlag, 2015.

Macartney, C. A. (ed.), *The Habsburg and Hohenzollern Dynasties in the Seventeenth and Eighteenth Centuries*, in *Documentary History of Western Civilization*, Harper & Row, 1970.

MacGregor, N., *Germany: Memories of a Nation*, Allen Lane, 2014.

McKay, S., *Berlin: Life and Loss in the City That Shaped the Century*, Viking, 2022.

Müffling, W. von, *Wegbereiter und Vorkämpfer für das neue Deutschland*, J. F. Lehmanns Verlag, 1933.

Ribbe, W. (ed.), *Geschichte Berlins. Vol. II. Von der Märzrevolution bis zur Gegenwart*, C. H. Beck, 1987.

Richie, A., *Faust's Metropolis: A History of Berlin*, HarperCollins, Kindle edition, 2013.

Schendel, D., *Architectural Guide Berlin*, Dom Publishers, 2019.

Schlögel, K., *Das Russische Berlin*, Suhrkamp, 2019.

Schneider, P., *Berlin Now: The City after the Wall*, Farrar, Straus and Giroux, 2014.

Schoeps, J., *Das Erbe der Mendelssohns: Biographie einer Familie*, Fischer Taschenbuch Verlag, 2011.

Shirer, W., *The Rise and Fall of the Third Reich*, Arrow Books, 1960.

Steinmetz, G., 'Workers and the Welfare State in Imperial Germany', *International Labor and Working-Class History*, 40, 1991, pp. 18–46.

Sullivan, P. and Krueger, M., *Berlin: A Literary Guide for Travellers*, I.B. Tauris, 2016.

Togral Koca, B., 'Urban citizenship and the spatial encounter between Turkish migrants and Syrian refugees in Berlin', *Raumforschung und Raumordnung/Spatial Research and Planning*, Sciendo, Warsaw, vol. 77, 6, 2019, pp. 567–81.

Vassiltchikov, M., *The Berlin Diaries: 1940–1945*, Pimlico, 1999.

Venohr, W., *Der Soldatenkönig. Revolutionar auf dem Thron*, Ullstein Verlag, 1988.

Verein für die Geschichte Berlins (ed.): *Chronik der Cöllner Stadtschreiber von 1542–1605*, Vereins für die Geschichte Berlins, 1865.

Voltaire, Mémoires de M. de Voltaire, Chez Robinson, 1784.

Waite, R., *Kaiser and Führer: A Comparative Study of Personality and Politics*, University of Toronto Press, 1998.

White-Spunner, B., *Berlin: The Story of a City*, Simon & Schuster, 2020.

Index